TITLE 19 DOMESTIC RELATIONS

Table of Contents

CHAPTER 1. GENERAL PROVISIONS 2
CHAPTER 2. DOMICILE 2
CHAPTER 3. MARRIAGE GENERALLY 3
    ARTICLE 1. GENERAL PROVISIONS 3
    ARTICLE 2. LICENSE AND CEREMONY 5
    ARTICLE 3. ANTENUPTIAL AGREEMENTS, MARRIAGE CONTRACTS, AND POSTNUPTIAL SETTLEMENTS 10
CHAPTER 4. ANNULMENT OF MARRIAGE 11
CHAPTER 5. DIVORCE 12
CHAPTER 6. ALIMONY AND CHILD SUPPORT 15
    ARTICLE 1. GENERAL PROVISIONS 15
    ARTICLE 2. GEORGIA CHILD SUPPORT COMMISSION 52
CHAPTER 7. PARENT AND CHILD RELATIONSHIP GENERALLY 53
    ARTICLE 1. GENERAL PROVISIONS 53
    ARTICLE 2. LEGITIMACY 60
    ARTICLE 3. DETERMINATION OF PATERNITY 62
CHAPTER 8. ADOPTION 68
    ARTICLE 1. GENERAL PROVISIONS (EFFECTIVE UNTIL SEPTEMBER 1, 2018) 68
CHAPTER 8. ADOPTION 89
    ARTICLE 1. GENERAL PROVISIONS (EFFECTIVE UNTIL SEPTEMBER 1, 2018) 89
    ARTICLE 1. GENERAL PROVISIONS (EFFECTIVE SEPTEMBER 1, 2018) 90
    ARTICLE 2. EMBRYO TRANSFERS 140
CHAPTER 9. CHILD CUSTODY PROCEEDINGS 141
    ARTICLE 1. GENERAL PROVISIONS 141
    ARTICLE 2. CHILD CUSTODY INTRASTATE JURISDICTION ACT 148
    ARTICLE 3. UNIFORM CHILD CUSTODY JURISDICTION AND ENFORCEMENT ACT 149
    ARTICLE 4. POWER OF ATTORNEY FOR THE CARE OF A MINOR CHILD 160
CHAPTER 10. ABANDONMENT OF CHILD OR SPOUSE 174

CHAPTER 1. GENERAL PROVISIONS

§ 19-1-1. Injunctions and restraining orders authorized in domestic relations actions
§ 19-1-1. Injunctions and restraining orders authorized in domestic relations actions

(a) As used in this Code section, the term "domestic relations action" shall include any action for divorce, alimony, equitable division of assets and liabilities, child custody, child support, legitimation, annulment, determination of paternity, termination of parental rights in connection with an adoption proceeding filed in a superior court, any contempt proceeding relating to enforcement of a decree or order, a petition in respect to modification of a decree or order, an action on a foreign judgment based on alimony or child support, and adoption. The term "domestic relations action" shall also include any direct or collateral attack on a judgment or order entered in any such action.
(b) Upon the filing of any domestic relations action, the court may issue a standing order in such action which:
  (1) Upon notice, binds the parties in such action, their agents, servants, and employees, and all other persons acting in concert with such parties;
  (2) Enjoins and restrains the parties from unilaterally causing or permitting the minor child or children of the parties to be removed from the jurisdiction of the court without the permission of the court, except in an emergency which has been created by the other party to the action;
  (3) Enjoins and restrains each party from doing or attempting to do or threatening to do any act which injures, maltreats, vilifies, molests, or harasses or which may, upon judicial determination, constitute threats, harassment, or stalking the adverse party or the child or children of the parties or any act which constitutes a violation of other civil or criminal laws of this state; and
  (4) Enjoins and restrains each party from selling, encumbering, trading, contracting to sell, or otherwise disposing of or removing from the jurisdiction of the court, without the permission of the court, any of the property belonging to the parties except in the ordinary course of business or except in an emergency which has been created by the other party to the action.
(c) Upon written motion of a party, the standing order provided for in this Code section shall be reviewed by the court at any rule nisi hearing.

§§ 19-1-2 through 19-1-6

Reserved. Repealed by Ga. L. 1991, p. 94, § 19, effective March 14, 1991.

CHAPTER 2. DOMICILE

§ 19-2-1. Place of domicile; how domicile changed, generally

(a) The domicile of every person who is of full age and is laboring under no disability is the place where the family of the person permanently resides, if in this state. If a person has no family or if his family does not reside in this state, the place where the person generally lodges shall be considered his domicile.
(b) The domicile of a person sui juris may be changed by an actual change of residence with the avowed intention of remaining at the new residence. Declaration of an intention to change one's domicile is ineffectual for that purpose until some act is done in execution of the intention.

§ 19-2-2. Election between two or more domiciles; domicile of transients

(a) If a person resides indifferently at two or more places in this state, the person shall have the privilege of electing which of such places shall be his domicile. If the election is made known generally among those with whom the person transacts business in this state, the place chosen shall be the person's domicile. If no such election is made or if an election is made but is not generally known among those with whom the person transacts business in this state, third persons may treat any one of the places in which the person resides as his domicile and it shall be so held; and in all such cases a person who habitually resides a portion of the year in one county and another portion of the year in another shall be deemed a resident of both, so far as to subject him to actions in either for contracts made or torts committed in such county.
(b) Transient persons whose business or pleasure causes a frequent change of residence and who have no family permanently residing at one place in this state shall be deemed, as to third persons, to be domiciled at such place as they at the time temporarily occupy.

§ 19-2-3. Domicile of married person

The domicile of a married person shall not be presumed to be the domicile of that person's spouse.

§ 19-2-4. Domicile of minor

(a) If a minor child's parents are domiciled in the same county, the domicile of that child shall be that of the parents. If a minor child's parents are divorced, separated, or widowed, or if one parent is not domiciled in the same county as the other parent, the child's domicile shall be that of the custodial parent. The domicile of a minor child born out of wedlock shall be that of the child's mother.
(b) Where a child's parents have voluntarily relinquished custody of the child to a third person or have been deprived of custody by court order, the child's domicile shall be that of the person having legal custody of the child. If there is no legal custodian, the child's domicile shall be that of his guardian if the guardian is domiciled in this state. If there is neither a legal custodian nor a guardian, the domicile of the child shall be determined as if he were an adult.

§ 19-2-5. Domicile of person under guardianship

Persons of full age who for any cause are placed under the power of a guardian have the same domicile as the guardian.

§ 19-2-6. Change of domicile which is dependent on that of another; change of ward's domicile affecting inheritance

(a) A person whose domicile for any reason is dependent upon that of another cannot effect a change of his own domicile.
(b) A guardian cannot change the domicile of his ward by a change of his own domicile or in any other fashion so as to interfere with the rules of inheritance or succession or otherwise to affect the rights of inheritance of third persons.

CHAPTER 3. MARRIAGE GENERALLY
ARTICLE 1. GENERAL PROVISIONS
§ 19-3-1. Prerequisites to valid marriage

To constitute a valid marriage in this state there must be:
(1) Parties able to contract;
(2) An actual contract; and
(3) Consummation according to law.

§ 19-3-1.1. Common-law marriage; effectiveness

No common-law marriage shall be entered into in this state on or after January 1, 1997. Otherwise valid common-law marriages entered into prior to January 1, 1997, shall not be affected by this Code section and shall continue to be recognized in this state.

§ 19-3-2. Who may contract marriage; parental consent

(a) To be able to contract marriage, a person must:
(1) Be of sound mind;
(2) Except as provided in subsection (b) of this Code section, be at least 18 years of age;
(3) Have no living spouse of a previous undissolved marriage. The dissolution of a previous marriage in divorce proceedings must be affirmatively established and will not be presumed. Nothing in this paragraph shall be construed to affect the legitimacy of children; and
(4) Not be related to the prospective spouse by blood or marriage within the prohibited degrees.
(b) If either applicant for marriage is 16 or 17 years of age, parental consent as provided in Code Section 19-3-37 shall be required.

§ 19-3-3. Degrees of relationship within which intermarriage prohibited; penalty; effect of prohibited marriage

(a) Any person who marries a person to whom he knows he is related, either by blood or by marriage, as follows:
 (1) Father and daughter or stepdaughter;
 (2) Mother and son or stepson;
 (3) Brother and sister of the whole blood or the half blood;
 (4) Grandparent and grandchild;
 (5) Aunt and nephew; or
 (6) Uncle and niece
shall be punished by imprisonment for not less than one nor more than three years.
(b) Marriages declared to be unlawful under subsection (a) of this Code section shall be void from their inception.

§ 19-3-3.1. Marriages between persons of same sex prohibited; marriages not recognized

(a) It is declared to be the public policy of this state to recognize the union only of man and woman. Marriages between persons of the same sex are prohibited in this state.
(b) No marriage between persons of the same sex shall be recognized as entitled to the benefits of marriage. Any marriage entered into by persons of the same sex pursuant to a marriage license issued by another state or foreign jurisdiction or otherwise shall be void in this state. Any contractual rights granted by virtue of such license shall be unenforceable in the courts of this state and the courts of this state shall have no jurisdiction whatsoever under any circumstances to grant a divorce or separate maintenance with respect to such marriage or otherwise to consider or rule on any of the parties' respective rights arising as a result of or in connection with such marriage.

§ 19-3-4. Nature of consent required

To constitute an actual contract of marriage, the parties must consent thereto voluntarily without any fraud practiced upon either. Drunkenness at the time of marriage, brought about by art or contrivance to induce consent shall be held as fraud.

§ 19-3-5. What marriages void; legitimacy of issue; effect of later ratification

(a) Marriages of persons unable to contract, unwilling to contract, or fraudulently induced to contract shall be void. However, the issue of such a marriage born before the marriage is annulled and declared void by a competent court shall be legitimate.
(b) In the case of persons unwilling to contract or fraudulently induced to do so, a subsequent consent and ratification of the marriage, freely and voluntarily made, accompanied by cohabitation as husband and wife shall render the marriage valid. In the case of a marriage void on one of the grounds specified in paragraphs (1) through (3) of Code Section 19-3-2, after removal of the impediment to marriage, a subsequent free and voluntary consent and ratification of the marriage accompanied by cohabitation as husband and wife shall likewise render the marriage valid.

§ 19-3-6. Effect of restraints on marriage; when valid

Marriage is encouraged by the law. Every effort to restrain or discourage marriage by contract, condition, limitation, or otherwise shall be invalid and void, provided that prohibitions against marriage to a particular person or persons or before a certain reasonable age or other prudential provisions looking only to the interest of the person to be benefited and not in general restraint of marriage will be allowed and held valid.

§ 19-3-7. Contracts attempting to force marriage void

The policy of the law being opposed equally to restrictions on marriage and to marriages not the result of free choice, all contracts or bonds made to hinder or to force marriage are deemed fraudulent and void.

§ 19-3-8. Interspousal tort immunity continued

Interspousal tort immunity, as it existed immediately prior to July 1, 1983, shall continue to exist on and after July 1, 1983.

§ 19-3-9. Each spouse's property separate

The separate property of each spouse shall remain the separate property of that spouse, except as provided in Chapters 5 and 6 of this title and except as otherwise provided by law.

§ 19-3-10. Right of married persons to contract; presumptions

A married person may make contracts with other persons; but, when a transaction between a husband and wife is attacked for fraud by the creditors of either, the onus shall be on the husband and wife to show that the transaction was fair. If a husband or a wife has a separate estate and purchases property from persons other than his or her spouse, the onus shall be upon a creditor levying on such property as the property of the other spouse to show fraud or to show that the husband or wife did not have the means with which to purchase the property.

§ 19-3-11. Gift from spouse allowed, but not presumed

Repealed by Ga. L. 1981, p. 704, § 1, effective July 1, 1981.

ARTICLE 2. LICENSE AND CEREMONY
§ 19-3-30. Issuance, return, and recording of license

(a) Marriage licenses shall be issued only by the judge of the probate court or his clerk at the county courthouse between the hours of 8:00 A.M. and 6:00 P.M., Monday through Saturday.
(b) (1) No marriage license shall be issued to persons of the same sex.
(2) If one of the persons to be married is a resident of this state, the license may be issued in any county of this state. If neither the male nor the female to be married is a resident of this state, the license shall be issued in the county in which the ceremony is to be performed.
(c) The license shall be directed to the Governor or any former Governor of this state, any judge, including judges of state and federal courts of record in this state, city recorder, magistrate, minister, or other person of any religious society or sect authorized by the rules of such society to perform the marriage ceremony; such license shall authorize the marriage of the persons therein named and require the Governor or any former Governor of this state, judge, city recorder, magistrate, minister, or other authorized person to return the license to the judge of the probate court with the certificate thereon as to the fact and date of marriage within 30 days after the date of the marriage. The license with the return thereon shall be recorded by the judge in a book kept by such judge for that purpose.
(d) The fact of issue of any unrecorded marriage license may be established by affidavit of either party to a ceremonial marriage, which affidavit shall set forth the date, the place, and the name and title of the official issuing the license.
(e) In the event that any marriage license is not returned for recording, as provided in subsection (c) of this Code section, either party to a ceremonial marriage may establish the marriage by submitting to the judge of the probate court the affidavits of two witnesses to the marriage ceremony setting forth the date, the place, and the name of the official or minister performing the ceremony. The judge shall thereupon reissue the marriage license and enter thereon the certificate of marriage and all dates and names in accordance with the evidence submitted and shall record and cross-index same in the proper chronological order in the book kept for that purpose.
(f) Any other provisions of this Code section or any other law to the contrary notwithstanding, the judge of the probate court of any county which has within its boundaries a municipality that has a population according to the United States decennial census of 1950 or any future such census greater than that of the county seat of the county is authorized to appoint a clerk for the purpose of granting marriage licenses in the municipality at an office designated by the judge. The licenses shall be issued only between the hours prescribed in subsection (a) of this Code section.

§ 19-3-30.1. Premarital education

(a) In applying for a marriage license, a man and woman who certify on the application for a marriage license that they have successfully completed a qualifying premarital education program shall not be charged a fee for a marriage license. The premarital education shall include at least six hours of instruction involving marital issues, which may include but not be limited to conflict management, communication skills, financial responsibilities, child and parenting responsibilities, and extended family roles. The premarital education shall be completed within 12 months prior to the application for a marriage license and the couple shall undergo the premarital education together. The premarital education shall be performed by:
  (1) A professional counselor, social worker, or marriage and family therapist who is licensed pursuant to Chapter 10A of Title 43;
  (2) A psychiatrist who is licensed as a physician pursuant to Chapter 34 of Title 43;
  (3) A psychologist who is licensed pursuant to Chapter 39 of Title 43; or
  (4) An active member of the clergy when in the course of his or her service as clergy or his or her designee, including retired clergy, provided that a designee is trained and skilled in premarital education.
(b) Each premarital education provider shall furnish each participant who completes the premarital education required by this Code section a certificate of completion.

§ 19-3-31. Issuance of licenses at satellite courthouses in certain counties

Notwithstanding any other law, in all counties having a population in excess of 400,000 according to the United States decennial census of 1990 or any future such census or in counties where the county site is located in an unincorporated portion of the county, the judge of the probate court or his or her clerk shall be authorized to issue the marriage licenses provided for by Code Section 19-3-30 and to take and perform any and all other actions prescribed in Code Section 19-3-30 either at the courthouse located at the county site or at any permanent satellite courthouse within the county which has been established and constructed by the governing authority of the county and has been designated by the governing authority of the county as a courthouse annex or by similar designation has been established as an additional courthouse to the courthouse located at the county site.

§ 19-3-32. Penalty for improper issuance of license

If any judge of the probate court or clerk issues a marriage license in violation of subsection (a) of Code Section 19-3-30, the judge or clerk, as the case may be, shall be guilty of a misdemeanor.

§ 19-3-33. Application for marriage license; contents; supplement marriage report

(a) A marriage license shall be issued on written application therefor, made by the persons seeking the license, verified by oath of the applicants. The application shall state that there is no legal impediment to the marriage and shall give the full present name of the proposed husband and the full present name of the proposed wife with their dates of birth, their present addresses, and the names of the father and mother of each, if known. If the names of the father or mother of either are unknown, the application shall so state. The application shall state that the persons seeking the license have or have not completed premarital education pursuant to Code Section 19-3-30.1. If the application states that the applicants seeking issuance of the license have completed premarital education, then the applicants shall submit a signed and dated certificate of completion issued by the premarital education provider.
(b) An application supplement-marriage report shall be prepared in connection with each marriage license. Except for the information in paragraph (3) of this subsection, the application supplement-marriage report shall be completed as a part of each application for a marriage license. The application supplement-marriage report shall state, at a minimum, the following:
  (1) The full name, date of birth, and social security number for each applicant;
  (2) The number this marriage would be for each applicant; and
  (3) After the ceremonial marriage has been performed, the date of the marriage ceremony and the county where the marriage ceremony occurred.

§ 19-3-33.1. Use of surname in application for marriage license

(a) The form for application for marriage licenses shall be designed and printed in such a manner that applicants therefor shall designate the surnames which will be used as their legal surnames after the marriage is consummated. The legal surnames shall be designated as provided in subsection (b) of this Code section.

(b) A spouse may use as a legal surname his or her:
 (1) Given surname or, in the event the given surname has been changed as provided in Chapter 12 of this title, the surname so changed;
 (2) Surname from a previous marriage;
 (3) Spouse's surname; or
 (4) Surname as provided in paragraph (1) or (2) of this subsection in conjunction with the surname of the other spouse.

§ 19-3-34. Marriage application to be filed; use as evidence; transmission to the state registrar

(a) Except as provided in subsection (b) of this Code section, the application for a marriage license shall be filed in the office of the judge of the probate court before a marriage license shall be issued and shall remain in the permanent files in the office of the judge. It may be used as evidence in any court of law under the rules of evidence made and provided in similar cases.
(b) The application supplement-marriage report form provided for in Code Section 19-3-33 shall be transmitted to the state registrar pursuant to Code Section 31-10-21. No original or duplicate application supplement-marriage report form need be retained by any official or employee of the probate court beyond the time required for transmission to the state registrar of vital records and confirmation of such transmission and receipt. While in the temporary custody of the probate court, application supplement-marriage report forms shall not be available for public inspection or copying or admissible in any court of law.

§ 19-3-35. Issuance of license to applicants otherwise eligible

When both applicants for a marriage license are eligible to receive that license pursuant to the other provisions of this chapter and that license is otherwise authorized to be issued pursuant to the other provisions of this chapter, that license may be issued immediately and without any waiting period.

§ 19-3-35.1. AIDS brochures; listing of HIV test sites; acknowledgment of receipt

(a) Any term used in this Code section and defined in Code Section 31-22-9.1 shall have the meaning provided for such term in Code Section 31-22-9.1.
(b) The Department of Public Health shall prepare a brochure describing AIDS, HIV, and the dangers, populations at risk, risk behaviors, and prevention measures relating thereto. That department shall also prepare a listing of sites at which confidential and anonymous HIV tests are provided without charge. That department shall further prepare a form for acknowledging that the brochures and listings have been received, as required by subsection (c) of this Code section. The brochures, listings, and forms prepared by the Department of Public Health (formerly known as the Department of Human Resources for these purposes) under this subsection shall be prepared and furnished to the office of each judge of the probate court no later than October 1, 1988.
(c) On and after October 1, 1988, each person who makes application for a marriage license shall receive from the office of the probate judge at the time of the application the AIDS brochure and listing of HIV test sites prepared and furnished pursuant to subsection (b) of this Code section. On and after October 1, 1988, no marriage license shall be issued unless both the proposed husband and the proposed wife sign a form acknowledging that both have received the brochure and listing.

§ 19-3-36. Proof of age of applicants

The judge of the probate court to whom the application for a marriage license is made shall satisfy himself or herself that the provisions set forth in Code Section 19-3-2 regarding age limitations are met. If the judge does not know of his or her own knowledge the age of a party for whom a marriage license is sought, the judge shall require the applicant to furnish the court with documentary evidence of proof of age in the form of a birth certificate, driver's license, baptismal certificate, certificate of birth registration, selective service card, court record, passport, immigration papers, alien papers, citizenship papers, armed forces discharge papers, armed forces identification card, or hospital admission card containing the full name and date of birth. In the event an applicant does not possess any of the above but appears to the judge to be at least 25 years of age, the applicant, in lieu of furnishing the judge with one of the above, may give an affidavit to the judge stating the applicant's age. Applicants who have satisfactorily proved that they have reached the age of majority may be issued a marriage license immediately.

§ 19-3-37. Parental consent to marriage of underage applicants; when necessary; how obtained

(a) Definitions. As used in this Code section, the term:
(1) "Guardian" shall be held to include the same relationships between spouses as the relationships described in paragraph (2) of this subsection between parents and means:
   (A) Any person at least five years older than the applicant standing in loco parentis to the applicant for at least two years;
   (B) Any person at least five years older than the applicant with whom the applicant has lived for at least two years and who has or would be allowed to claim the applicant as a dependent for the purposes of a federal dependent income tax deduction;
   (C) Any relative by blood or marriage at least five years older than the applicant and with whom the applicant has lived at least two years, when the whereabouts of the applicant's parents are unknown; or
   (D) A court appointed guardian.
(2) "Parent" means:
   (A) Both parents if the parents are living together;
   (B) The individual who has sole custody if the parents are divorced, separated, or widowed; or
   (C) Either parent if the parents are living together but one parent is unavailable because of illness or infirmity or because he is not within the boundaries of this state or because physical presence is impossible.
(b) When parental consent required; how obtained. In cases where the parties applying for a license are 16 or 17 years of age, their ages to be proved to the judge of the probate court as provided in Code Section 19-3-36, the parents or guardians of each underage applicant shall appear in person before the judge and consent to the proposed marriage, provided that if physical presence because of illness or infirmity is impossible, an affidavit by the incapacitated parent or guardian along with an affidavit signed by a licensed attending physician stating that the parent or guardian is physically incapable of being present shall suffice. The licensed attending physician shall include only those physicians licensed under Chapter 34 of Title 43 or under corresponding requirements pertaining to licensed attending physicians in sister states.
(c) Alternative methods for obtaining parental consent.
(1) When the parents or guardians of any underage applicants requiring parental consent reside within the state but in a county other than the county where the marriage license is to be issued, it shall not be necessary for the parents or guardians to appear in person before the judge of the probate court of the latter county and consent to the proposed marriage, if the parents or guardians appear in person and consent to the proposed marriage before the judge of the county in which they reside.
(2) Where the parents or guardians of any underage applicants requiring parental consent reside outside the state, it shall not be necessary for the parents or guardians to appear in person before the judge of the probate court and consent to the proposed marriage, if the parents or guardians appear in person before the judicial authority of their county who is authorized to issue marriage licenses and consent to the proposed marriage before the judicial authority. If the parents or guardians are physically incapable of being present because of illness or infirmity, the illness or infirmity may be attested to by an attending physician licensed in such state, as is provided for in subsection (a) of this Code section.
(3) Where the alternate provisions for parental consent are utilized under paragraph (1) or (2) of this subsection, the parents or guardians shall obtain a certificate from the judge of the probate court or the proper judicial officer before whom they have appeared with the seal and title of the official appearing thereon, the certificate containing information to the effect that the parents or guardians appeared before the judge or judicial officer and consented to the proposed marriage.

§ 19-3-38. Notification of parents of underage applicants; additional fee

Reserved. Repealed by Ga. L. 2006, p. 141, § 6D/HB 847, effective July 1, 2006.

§ 19-3-39. Certification and recordation of marriage after publication of banns

If the Governor or any former Governor of this state, any judge, city recorder, magistrate, minister, or other authorized person joins in marriage persons whose banns have been published, the person shall certify the fact to the judge of the probate court of the county where the banns were published, who shall record the same in the same book in which marriage licenses are recorded.

§ 19-3-40. Blood test for sickle cell disease; information to be provided

(a) As used in this Code section, the term "blood test for sickle cell disease" means a blood test for sickle cell anemia, sickle cell trait, and other detectable abnormal hemoglobin.

(b) The Department of Public Health shall prepare information for public dissemination on the department's website describing the importance of obtaining a blood test for sickle cell disease and explaining the causes and effects of such disease. Such information shall recommend that each applicant applying for a marriage license obtain a blood test for sickle cell disease prior to obtaining a marriage license. Such information may also be provided as a brochure or other document. The department shall make such information available in electronic format to the probate courts of this state which shall disseminate such information to all persons applying for marriage licenses.

§ 19-3-41. Department of Public Health marriage manual; distribution; rules and regulations

(a) The Department of Public Health shall prepare a marriage manual for distribution by the judge of the probate court or his clerk to all applicants for a marriage license. The manual shall include, but shall not be limited to, material on family planning.
(b) The manual provided for in subsection (a) of this Code section shall be issued by the judge of the probate court or his clerk to applicants for a marriage license at the same time the marriage license is issued.
(c) The Department of Public Health shall promulgate rules and regulations to implement this Code section.
(d) In order to be nonsectarian, the manual will include resource referral information for those who might have questions regarding religious beliefs in the areas covered by the marriage manual.

§ 19-3-42. Effect on marriage due to the lack of authority in person officiating

A marriage which is valid in other respects and supposed by the parties to be valid shall not be affected by want of authority in the minister, Governor or any former Governor of this state, judge, city recorder, magistrate, or other person to solemnize the same; nor shall such objection be heard from one party who has fraudulently induced the other to believe that the marriage was legal.

§ 19-3-43. Marriage in another state; effect in this state

All marriages solemnized in another state by parties intending at the time to reside in this state shall have the same legal consequences and effect as if solemnized in this state. Parties residing in this state may not evade any of the laws of this state as to marriage by going into another state for the solemnization of the marriage ceremony.

§ 19-3-44. Return of license to parties

(a) The judge of the probate court of each county shall return to the parties to a marriage the license and the return thereon after the same have been recorded as provided by law. This subsection shall be applicable to all marriage licenses and the returns thereon recorded after March 25, 1958.
(b) Upon request of either of the parties, the judge of the probate court of each county is authorized, as to marriage licenses with the returns thereon recorded prior to March 25, 1958, to return the license:
(1) To the parties to the marriage if the marriage is not dissolved and the parties are not living in a state of separation;
(2) To the surviving party to the marriage if one of the parties is deceased; or
(3) To the party first requesting the license if the parties are divorced.

§ 19-3-45. Actions for improper issuance of marriage license; attorney's fee and court costs; disposition of balance of recovery

Any judge of the probate court who by himself or his clerk knowingly grants a license without the required consent or without proper precaution in inquiring into the question of minority shall forfeit the sum of $500.00 for every such act, to be recovered at the action of the father or mother, if living, and, if not, at the action of the guardian or legal representative of either of such contracting parties, provided that under no circumstances shall more than one action be maintained by the father or mother, guardian, or legal representative of either of such contracting parties in connection with any one marriage; and provided, further, that no such action shall be brought prior to the expiration of 60 days from the date that the marriage becomes public and that no action under this Code section shall be maintained after the expiration of 12 months from the date the marriage becomes public. A recovery shall be had against the offending judge and his bondsmen. From the recovery a reasonable attorney's fee, to be fixed by the presiding judge trying the case, shall be paid to the attorney representing the person bringing the action and, after the payment of court costs, one-third of the remainder of the recovery shall be paid to the person bringing the action; and the remaining two-thirds shall be paid to the county educational fund of the county of the judge's residence. A judge who in good faith destroys physician's certificates of pregnancy and all records of the certificates under his control in accordance with the provisions of law shall not be prosecuted under this Code section for failure to require such a certificate from the applicants for a marriage license, if a birth certificate is issued for a child born to the applicants within the period of gestation after the marriage license was issued.

§ 19-3-46. Forfeiture for officiating at marriage without license or banns

The Governor or any former Governor of this state, any judge, city recorder, magistrate, minister, or other person authorized to perform the marriage ceremony who joins in marriage any couple without a license or the publication of banns shall forfeit the sum of $500.00, to be recovered and appropriated as set forth in Code Section 19-3-45.

§ 19-3-47. Penalty for filing false information in application for license

Any person who willfully furnishes false information in connection with the application and issuance of any marriage license, either in the application for the license, in furnishing proof of age, or in the physician's certificate as to pregnancy, shall be guilty of a misdemeanor.

§ 19-3-48. Penalty for officiating at illegal marriage ceremony

If the Governor or any former Governor of this state, any judge, city recorder, magistrate, minister, or other person authorized to perform the marriage ceremony joins together in matrimony any man and woman without a license or the publication of banns or if the person performing the marriage ceremony knows of any disability of either of the parties which would render a contract of marriage improper and illegal, that person shall be guilty of a misdemeanor.

§ 19-3-49. Acceptance by judges of tips, consideration, or gratuities

In addition to any compensation otherwise provided by law, any judge who performs a marriage ceremony at any time, except normal office hours, may receive and retain as personal income any tip, consideration, or gratuity voluntarily given to such judge for performing such marriage ceremony.

ARTICLE 3. ANTENUPTIAL AGREEMENTS, MARRIAGE CONTRACTS, AND POSTNUPTIAL SETTLEMENTS

§ 19-3-60. Definition; marriage as valuable consideration

(a) As used in this article, the term "antenuptial agreement" means a contract entered into prior to a marriage that determines property rights or contemplates a future settlement to one spouse as to a future resolution of issues, including, but not limited to, year's support, spousal support, and equitable division of property.
(b) Marriage is a valuable consideration; and a spouse stands, as to property of the other spouse settled upon a spouse by marriage contract, as do other purchasers for value, provided that by the contract a spouse shall not incapacitate himself or herself from paying his or her existing just debts.

§ 19-3-61. Effect of minority of party

The minority of either party to an antenuptial agreement or to a marriage contract shall not invalidate it, so long as the party is of lawful age to contract marriage.

§ 19-3-62. Requirements and construction of antenuptial agreements

An antenuptial agreement shall be in writing, signed by both parties who agree to be bound, and attested by at least two witnesses, one of whom shall be a notary public. Antenuptial agreements shall be liberally construed to carry into effect the intention of the parties, and no want of form or technical expression shall invalidate such agreements.

§ 19-3-63. Construction of marriage contract; attestation

Every marriage contract in writing, made in contemplation of marriage, shall be liberally construed to carry into effect the intention of the parties, and no want of form or technical expression shall invalidate the same. Such marriage contract shall be in writing, signed by both parties who agree to be bound, and attested by at least two witnesses, one of whom shall be a notary public.

§ 19-3-64. Voluntary execution of antenuptial agreement; conveyance of property during marriage

A person may voluntarily execute an antenuptial agreement, or he or she may at any time during the marriage, either indirectly through trustees or directly to his or her spouse, convey any property to which he or she has title, subject to the rights of prior purchasers or creditors without notice.

§ 19-3-65. Powers of superior court judge in appointing and removing trustees and protecting trust estate

The judge of the superior court of the county of a spouse's domicile may at any time, upon petition, exercise equitable powers in appointing, removing, or substituting trustees or in granting any order for the protection of the trust estate, exercising a wise discretion as to the terms on which the appointment shall be made or on which the order shall be granted.

§ 19-3-66. Enforcement of marriage contracts, postnuptial settlements, and antenuptial agreements

(a) Marriage contracts and postnuptial settlements shall be enforced at the instance of all persons in whose favor there are limitations of the estate.
(b) Antenuptial agreements may be enforced by a court of equity at the instance of:
 (1) The parties to the marriage; or
 (2) The offspring of the marriage and their heirs at any time after the death of a spouse; provided, however, that when enforced at the instance of such offspring and their heirs, the court may enforce in favor of other persons.

§ 19-3-67. Recordation of marriage contracts and voluntary settlements; effect of failure to record

Repealed by Ga. L. 2018, p. 155, § 1-1/HB 190, effective July 1, 2018.

§ 19-3-68. Application for order compelling recordation; effect of application; liability of trustee refusing to record

Repealed by Ga. L. 2018, p. 155, § 1-1/HB 190, effective July 1, 2018.

CHAPTER 4. ANNULMENT OF MARRIAGE
§ 19-4-1. When annulments may be granted

Annulments of marriages declared void by law may be granted by the superior court, except that annulments may not be granted in instances where children are born or are to be born as a result of the marriage.

§ 19-4-2. Right to file for annulment or divorce

Parties who enter into a marriage which is declared void by law shall have the right to file:
(1) A petition for annulment; or
(2) A petition for divorce, if grounds for divorce exist.

§ 19-4-3. Petition by next friend

A petition for annulment may be filed by next friend for minors or persons of unsound mind.

§ 19-4-4. Procedure

All matters of service, jurisdiction, procedure, residence, pleading, and practice for obtaining an annulment of marriage shall be the same as those provided by law for obtaining a divorce, with the exception that a decree of annulment may be ordered at any time, in open court or in chambers, when personal service is had at least 30 days beforehand and no contest or answer is filed.

§ 19-4-5. Effect of annulment

A decree of annulment, when rendered, shall have the effect of a total divorce between the parties of a void marriage and shall return the parties thereto to their original status before marriage. However, a decree of annulment shall not operate to relieve the parties to a marriage of criminal charges or responsibilities occasioned by the marriage.

CHAPTER 5. DIVORCE
§ 19-5-1. Total divorces authorized; trial; referral for alternative dispute resolution

(a) Total divorces may be granted in proper cases by the superior court. Unless an issuable defense is filed as provided by law and a jury trial is demanded in writing by either party on or before the call of the case for trial, in all petitions for divorce and permanent alimony the judge shall hear and determine all issues of law and of fact and any other issues raised in the pleadings.
(b) In any county in which there has been established an alternative dispute resolution program pursuant to Chapter 23 of Title 15, known as the "Georgia Court-annexed Alternative Dispute Resolution Act," the judge may, prior to trial, refer all contested petitions for divorce or permanent alimony to the appropriate alternative dispute resolution method. In counties in which an alternative dispute resolution program has not been established, a judge may nonetheless refer any disputed divorce case to an appropriate alternative dispute resolution method if a method is reasonably available without additional cost to the parties.

§ 19-5-2. Residence requirements; venue

No court shall grant a divorce to any person who has not been a bona fide resident of this state for six months before the filing of the petition for divorce, provided that any person who has been a resident of any United States army post or military reservation within this state for one year next preceding the filing of the petition may bring an action for divorce in any county adjacent to the United States army post or military reservation; and provided, further, that a nonresident of this state may file a petition for divorce, in the county of residence of the respondent, against any person who has been a resident of this state and of the county in which the action is brought for a period of six months prior to the filing of the petition.

§ 19-5-3. Grounds for total divorce

The following grounds shall be sufficient to authorize the granting of a total divorce:
(1) Intermarriage by persons within the prohibited degrees of consanguinity or affinity;
(2) Mental incapacity at the time of the marriage;
(3) Impotency at the time of the marriage;
(4) Force, menace, duress, or fraud in obtaining the marriage;
(5) Pregnancy of the wife by a man other than the husband, at the time of the marriage, unknown to the husband;
(6) Adultery in either of the parties after marriage;
(7) Willful and continued desertion by either of the parties for the term of one year;
(8) The conviction of either party for an offense involving moral turpitude, under which he is sentenced to imprisonment in a penal institution for a term of two years or longer;
(9) Habitual intoxication;
(10) Cruel treatment, which shall consist of the willful infliction of pain, bodily or mental, upon the complaining party, such as reasonably justifies apprehension of danger to life, limb, or health;

(11) Incurable mental illness. No divorce shall be granted upon this ground unless the mentally ill party has been adjudged mentally ill by a court of competent jurisdiction or has been certified to be mentally ill by two physicians who have personally examined the party; and he has been confined in an institution for the mentally ill or has been under continuous treatment for mental illness for a period of at least two years immediately preceding the commencement of the action; and the superintendent or other chief executive officer of the institution and one competent physician appointed by the court, after a thorough examination, make a certified statement under oath that it is their opinion that the party evidences such a want of reason, memory, and intelligence as to prevent the party from comprehending the nature, duties, and consequences of the marriage relationship and that, in the light of present day medical knowledge, recovery of the party's mental health cannot be expected at any time during his life. Notice of the action must be served upon the guardian of the person of the mentally ill person and upon the superintendent or other chief executive officer of the institution in which the person is confined. In the event that there is no guardian of the person, then notice of the action shall be served upon a guardian ad litem, who shall be appointed by the court in which the divorce action is filed, and upon the superintendent or chief executive officer of the institution in which the person is confined. The guardian and superintendent shall be entitled to appear and be heard upon the issues. The status of the parties as to the support and maintenance of the mentally ill person shall not be altered in any way by the granting of the divorce;
(12) Habitual drug addiction, which shall consist of addiction to any controlled substance as defined in Article 2 of Chapter 13 of Title 16; or
(13) The marriage is irretrievably broken. Under no circumstances shall the court grant a divorce on this ground until not less than 30 days from the date of service on the respondent.

§ 19-5-4. Effect of collusion, consent, guilt of like conduct, or condonation

(a) No divorce shall be granted under the following circumstances:
(1) The adultery, desertion, cruel treatment, or intoxication complained of was occasioned by the collusion of the parties, with the intention of causing a divorce;
(2) The party complaining of the adultery, desertion, cruel treatment, or intoxication of the other party was consenting thereto;
(3) Both parties are guilty of like conduct; or
(4) There has been a voluntary condonation and cohabitation subsequent to the acts complained of, with notice thereof.
(b) In all such cases, the respondent may plead in defense the conduct of the party bringing the action and the jury may, on examination of the whole case, refuse a divorce.

§ 19-5-5. Petition; contents and verification; demand for detailed statement

(a) The action for divorce shall be brought by written petition and process, the petition being verified by the petitioner.
(b) The petition shall show:
(1) The residence or last known address of the respondent;
(2) That the applicant meets the residence requirements for bringing an action for divorce or that the applicant is bringing a counterclaim and is not required to meet the residence requirements;
(3) The date of the marriage and the date of the separation;
(4) Whether or not there are any minor children of the parties and the name and age of each minor child;
(5) The statutory ground upon which a divorce is sought; and
(6) Where alimony or support or division of property is involved, the property and earnings of the parties, if such is known.
(c) The respondent, at any time before trial, may file with the court a written demand for a detailed statement of the facts on which the grounds in the petition are predicated. The respondent shall cause a copy of the demand to be served upon the petitioner or upon the petitioner's counsel of record and the facts demanded shall be added to the petition in the form of an amendment thereto.

§ 19-5-6. Grant of divorce to respondent without necessity of counterclaim

When a petition for divorce is filed, the respondent may recriminate in his answer and ask a divorce in his favor. If, at the trial, the court or jury believes that the respondent rather than the petitioner is entitled to a divorce, they may so find upon legal proof.

§ 19-5-7. Transfer of property after filing of petition; lis pendens notice

After a petition for divorce has been filed, no transfer of property by either party, except a bona fide transfer in payment of preexisting debts, shall pass title so as to avoid the vesting thereof according to the final verdict of the jury in the case; provided, however, that the title to real property shall not be affected by the filing of an action for divorce unless a notice of lis pendens, as provided for by Code Section 44-14-610, is filed in the office of the clerk of the superior court of the county in which the real property is situated and is recorded by the clerk in a book kept by him for that purpose.

§ 19-5-8. Pleading and practice

The same rules of pleading and practice applicable to ordinary civil actions shall apply to actions for divorce, alimony, and custody of minor children, except as otherwise specifically provided in this chapter. No verdict or judgment by default shall be taken in any such case but the allegations of the pleadings shall be established to the satisfaction of the court by the verified pleadings, by affidavit, by evidentiary hearing, or otherwise, as provided in Code Section 19-5-10.

§ 19-5-9. Incompetency to serve as juror

A juror who has conscientious scruples as to the granting of divorces shall be incompetent to serve in divorce cases. At the request of either party, the court may question the panel concerning such scruples.

§ 19-5-10. Duty of judge in undefended divorce cases; appointment of attorney; evidentiary hearings; evidentiary attacks on prior judgments

(a) In divorce cases which are not defended by the responding party, the judge shall determine that the asserted grounds for divorce are legal and sustained by proof or shall appoint an attorney of the court to discharge that duty for him. An evidentiary hearing for the determination of the existence of the grounds for divorce and for the determination of issues of alimony, child support, and child custody and other issues is authorized but not required. If no evidentiary hearing is held, the determination of such matters may be made upon the verified pleadings of either party, one or more affidavits, or such other basis or procedure as the court may deem proper in its discretion.
(b) The provisions of subsection (a) of this Code section shall apply to proceedings pending on July 1, 1987, as well as to proceedings filed on or after that date.
(c) Any motion to set aside or other proceeding to attack a judgment which attacks a judgment entered in a divorce case prior to July 1, 1987, and which is based upon an alleged failure to properly establish evidence supporting the judgment must be commenced prior to July 1, 1988, or thereafter be totally barred. The bar established by this subsection is in addition to and not in lieu of any other statute or rule of law which would operate as a bar to such a motion or other proceeding; and this subsection shall not operate to revive any otherwise barred right to prosecute any such motion or other proceeding.

§ 19-5-11. Use of confession as evidence; corroboration

The confessions of a party to acts of adultery or cruel treatment shall be received with great caution; if unsupported by corroborating circumstances and if made with a view to be evidence in the case, such confessions shall not be deemed sufficient to grant a divorce.

§ 19-5-12. Form of judgment and decree

(a) A final judgment of divorce shall be prepared so as to conform to the pleadings and the evidence and may restore a maiden or prior name, if requested. It shall be prepared in form substantially as follows:

"FINAL JUDGMENT AND DECREE

Upon consideration of this case, upon evidence submitted as provided by law, it is the judgment of the court that a total divorce be granted, that is to say, a divorce a vinculo matrimonii, between the parties to the above stated case upon legal principles.

It is considered, ordered, and decreed by the court that the marriage contract heretofore entered into between the parties to this case, from and after this date, be and is set aside and dissolved as fully and effectually as if no such contract had ever been made or entered into.

Petitioner and Respondent in the future shall be held and considered as separate and distinct individuals altogether unconnected by any nuptial union or civil contract whatsoever and both shall have the right to remarry.

Decree and order entered this   day of   ,   .

Judge, Superior Court"

(b) When applicable, any one or more of the following clauses shall be included in the form of the judgment:

The court restores to (Petitioner/Respondent) his/her prior or maiden name, to wit:

The court awards custody of the children of the parties as follows:

The court fixes alimony as follows:

(c) In any case which involves the determination of child support, the form of the judgment shall also include all of the information set forth in paragraph (2) of subsection (c) of Code Section 19-6-15. The final judgment shall have attached to it the child support worksheet containing the calculation of the final award of child support and any schedule that was prepared for the purpose of calculating the amount of child support. The final judgment shall specify a sum certain amount of child support to be paid.

(d) When applicable, the court shall also include in the final judgment the ability to use income deduction orders as set forth in Code Sections 19-6-30 and 19-6-32.

§ 19-5-13. Disposition of property in accordance with verdict

The verdict of the jury disposing of the property in a divorce case shall be carried into effect by the court by entering such judgment or decree or taking such other steps as are usual in the exercise of the court's equitable powers to execute effectually and fully the jury's verdict.

§ 19-5-14. New trial

New trials may be granted in actions for divorce as in other cases.

§ 19-5-15. Effect of divorce

A total divorce annuls a marriage from the time of the rendition of the decree, unless the divorce is granted for a cause rendering the marriage void originally, in which case the divorce serves to annul the marriage from its inception. However, the issue of the marriage shall not be rendered born out of wedlock by a divorce, except in cases of pregnancy of the wife by a man other than the husband at the time of the marriage, unknown to the husband.

§ 19-5-16. Restoration of maiden or prior name

In all divorce actions, a party may pray in his pleadings for the restoration of a maiden or prior name. If a divorce is granted, the judgment or decree shall specify and restore to the party the name so prayed for in the pleadings.

§ 19-5-17. Determination of parties' rights; preventing remarriage forbidden

When a divorce is granted, the jury or the judge, as the case may be, shall determine the rights of the parties. No person shall be placed under a disability that would prevent remarriage.

CHAPTER 6. ALIMONY AND CHILD SUPPORT

ARTICLE 1. GENERAL PROVISIONS

§ 19-6-1. Alimony defined; when authorized; how determined; lien on estate of party dying prior to order; certain changes in parties' assets prohibited

(a) Alimony is an allowance out of one party's estate, made for the support of the other party when living separately. It is either temporary or permanent.
(b) A party shall not be entitled to alimony if it is established by a preponderance of the evidence that the separation between the parties was caused by that party's adultery or desertion. In all cases in which alimony is sought, the court shall receive evidence of the factual cause of the separation even though one or both of the parties may also seek a divorce, regardless of the grounds upon which a divorce is sought or granted by the court.
(c) In all other cases in which alimony is sought, alimony is authorized, but is not required, to be awarded to either party in accordance with the needs of the party and the ability of the other party to pay. In determining whether or not to grant alimony, the court shall consider evidence of the conduct of each party toward the other.
(d) Should either party die prior to the court's order on the issue of alimony, any rights of the other party to alimony shall survive and be a lien upon the estate of the deceased party.
(e) Pending final determination by the court of the right of either party to alimony, neither party shall make any substantial change in the assets of the party's estate except in the course of ordinary business affairs and except for bona fide transfers for value.

§ 19-6-2. Attorney's fees; when and how granted; enforcement

(a) The grant of attorney's fees as a part of the expenses of litigation, made at any time during the pendency of the litigation, whether the action is for alimony, divorce and alimony, or contempt of court arising out of either an alimony case or a divorce and alimony case, including but not limited to contempt of court orders involving property division, child custody, and child visitation rights, shall be:
(1) Within the sound discretion of the court, except that the court shall consider the financial circumstances of both parties as a part of its determination of the amount of attorney's fees, if any, to be allowed against either party; and
(2) A final judgment as to the amount granted, whether the grant is in full or on account, which may be enforced by attachment for contempt of court or by writ of fieri facias, whether the parties subsequently reconcile or not.
(b) Nothing contained in this Code section shall be construed to mean that attorney's fees shall not be awarded at both the temporary hearing and the final hearing.
(c) An attorney may bring an action in his own name to enforce a grant of attorney's fees made to him pursuant to this Code section.

§ 19-6-3. Temporary alimony; petition and hearing; factors considered; discretion of judge; revision and enforcement of order; effect of failure to comply

(a) Whenever an action for divorce or for permanent alimony is pending, either party may apply at any time to the presiding judge of the court in which the same is pending, by petition, for an order granting the party temporary alimony pending the issuance of a final judgment in the case. After hearing both parties and the evidence as to all the circumstances of the parties and as to the fact of marriage, the court shall grant an order allowing such temporary alimony, including expenses of litigation, as the condition of the parties and the facts of the case may justify.
(b) In arriving at a decision, the judge shall consider the peculiar necessities created for each party by the pending litigation and any evidence of a separate estate owned by either party. If the separate estate of the party seeking alimony is ample as compared with that of the other party, temporary alimony may be refused.
(c) At a hearing on the application for temporary alimony, the merits of the case are not in issue; however, the judge, in fixing the amount of alimony, may inquire into the cause and circumstances of the separation rendering the alimony necessary and in his discretion may refuse it altogether.
(d) On application, an order allowing temporary alimony shall be subject to revision by the court at any time and may be enforced either by writ of fieri facias or by attachment for contempt.
(e) A failure to comply with the order allowing temporary alimony shall not deprive a party of the right either to prosecute or to defend the case.

§ 19-6-4. When permanent alimony authorized; how enforced

(a) Permanent alimony may be granted in the following cases:
(1) In cases of divorce;
(2) In cases of voluntary separation; or

(3) Where one spouse, against the will of that spouse, is abandoned or driven off by the other spouse.
(b) A grant of permanent alimony may be enforced either by writ of fieri facias or by attachment for contempt.

§ 19-6-5. Factors in determining amount of alimony; effect of remarriage on obligations for alimony

(a) The finder of fact may grant permanent alimony to either party, either from the corpus of the estate or otherwise. The following shall be considered in determining the amount of alimony, if any, to be awarded:
(1) The standard of living established during the marriage;
(2) The duration of the marriage;
(3) The age and the physical and emotional condition of both parties;
(4) The financial resources of each party;
(5) Where applicable, the time necessary for either party to acquire sufficient education or training to enable him to find appropriate employment;
(6) The contribution of each party to the marriage, including, but not limited to, services rendered in homemaking, child care, education, and career building of the other party;
(7) The condition of the parties, including the separate estate, earning capacity, and fixed liabilities of the parties; and
(8) Such other relevant factors as the court deems equitable and proper.
(b) All obligations for permanent alimony, however created, the time for performance of which has not arrived, shall terminate upon remarriage of the party to whom the obligations are owed unless otherwise provided.

§ 19-6-6. Liability after grant of alimony

(a) When permanent alimony is granted, the party liable for alimony shall cease to be liable for any debt or contract of the former spouse of the liable party.
(b) Upon the grant of permanent alimony, the property of the liable party set apart for the support of the former spouse shall not be subject to the liable party's debts or contracts as long as the former spouse of the liable party shall live.

§ 19-6-7. Interest in deceased party's estate after grant of permanent alimony

After permanent alimony is granted, upon the death of the party liable for the alimony the other party shall not be entitled to any further interest in the estate of the deceased party by virtue of the marriage contract between the parties; however, such permanent provision shall be continued to the other party or a portion of the deceased party's estate equivalent to the permanent provision shall be set apart to the other party.

§ 19-6-8. Voluntary separation, abandonment, or driving off of spouse -- Agreement for support as bar to alimony

In cases of voluntary separation or in cases where one spouse, against the will of that spouse, is abandoned or driven off by the other spouse, a party voluntarily, by contract or other written agreement made with his spouse, may make an adequate provision for the support and maintenance of such spouse, consistent with the means of the party and the former circumstances of the spouse. Such an agreement shall be a bar to the right of the spouse to permanent alimony.

§ 19-6-9. Voluntary separation, abandonment, or driving off of spouse -- Equity may compel support

Absent the making of a voluntary contract or other agreement, as provided in Code Section 19-6-8, and on the application of a party, the court, exercising its equitable powers, may compel the spouse of the party to make provision for the support of the party and such minor children as may be in the custody of the party.

§ 19-6-10. Voluntary separation, abandonment, or driving off of spouse -- Petition for alimony or child support when no divorce pending -- Order and enforcement; equitable remedies; effect of filing for divorce

When spouses are living separately or in a bona fide state of separation and there is no action for divorce pending, either party, on the party's own behalf or on the behalf of the minor children in the party's custody, if any, may institute a proceeding by petition, setting forth fully the party's case. Upon three days' notice to the other party, the judge may hear the same and may grant such order as he might grant were it based on a pending petition for divorce, to be enforced in the same manner, together with any other remedy applicable in equity, such as appointing a receiver and the like. Should the petition proceed to a hearing before a jury, the jury may render a verdict which shall provide the factual basis for equitable relief as in Code Section 19-6-9. However, such proceeding shall be held in abeyance when a petition for divorce is filed bona fide by either party and the judge presiding has made his order on the motion for alimony. When so made, the order shall be a substitute for the aforesaid decree in equity as long as the petition is pending and is not finally disposed of on the merits.

§ 19-6-11. Voluntary separation, abandonment, or driving off of spouse -- Petition for alimony or child support when no divorce pending -- Appeals

A judgment of the superior court in a case brought under Code Section 19-6-10 shall be appealable on the same terms as are prescribed in divorce cases.

§ 19-6-12. Voluntary separation, abandonment, or driving off of spouse -- Effect of subsequent cohabitation between spouses on permanent alimony

The subsequent voluntary cohabitation of spouses, where there has been no total divorce between them, shall annul and set aside all provision made either by deed or decree for permanent alimony; provided, however, that the rights of children under any deed of separation or voluntary provision or decree for alimony shall not be affected by such subsequent voluntary cohabitation of the spouses.

§ 19-6-13. Liability of parents for necessaries furnished to children pending voluntary provision or court order

Until otherwise provided voluntarily or by decree or order of a court, each party shall be liable to third persons for the board and support and for all necessaries furnished to or for the benefit of the parties' children.

§ 19-6-14. Child support and custody pending final divorce; liability to third persons for necessaries

Pending a final judgment in an action for divorce, the judge presiding may grant as temporary child support a sum sufficient for the support of the children of the parties in accordance with Code Section 19-6-15. The judge may also hear and determine who shall be entitled to the care and custody of the children until the final judgment in the case. If a sum is awarded for the support of the children, the party who is required to pay the support shall not be liable to third persons for necessaries furnished to the children.

§ 19-6-15. Child support; guidelines for determining amount of award; continuation of duty of support; duration of support

(a) Definitions. As used in this Code section, the term:
(1) Reserved.
(2) "Adjusted income" means the determination of a parent's monthly income, calculated by deducting from that parent's monthly gross income one-half of the amount of any applicable self-employment taxes being paid by the parent, any preexisting order for current child support which is being paid by the parent, and any theoretical child support order for other qualified children, if allowed by the court. For further reference see paragraph (5) of subsection (f) of this Code section.
(3) "Basic child support obligation" means the monthly amount of support displayed on the child support obligation table which corresponds to the combined adjusted income and the number of children for whom child support is being determined.
(4) "Child" means child or children.
(5) Reserved.
(6) "Child support obligation table" means the chart in subsection (o) of this Code section.
(6.1) "Child support services" means the entity within the Department of Human Services and its contractors that are authorized to enforce a duty of support.
(7) "Combined adjusted income" means the amount of adjusted income of the custodial parent added to the amount of adjusted income of the noncustodial parent.

(8) "Court" means a judge of any court of record or an administrative law judge of the Office of State Administrative Hearings.

(9) "Custodial parent" means the parent with whom the child resides more than 50 percent of the time. Where a custodial parent has not been designated or where a child resides with both parents an equal amount of time, the court shall designate the custodial parent as the parent with the lesser support obligation and the other parent as the noncustodial parent. Where the child resides equally with both parents and neither parent can be determined as owing a greater amount than the other, the court shall determine which parent to designate as the custodial parent for the purpose of this Code section.

(10) "Deviation" means an increase or decrease from the presumptive amount of child support if the presumed order is rebutted by evidence and the required findings of fact are made by the court pursuant to subsection (i) of this Code section.

(11) "Final child support amount" means the presumptive amount of child support adjusted by any deviations.

(12) "Gross income" means all income to be included in the calculation of child support as set forth in subsection (f) of this Code section.

(13) "Health insurance" means any general health or medical policy. For further reference see paragraph (2) of subsection (h) of this Code section.

(14) "Noncustodial parent" means the parent with whom the child resides less than 50 percent of the time or the parent who has the greater payment obligation for child support. Where the child resides equally with both parents and neither parent can be determined as owing a lesser amount than the other, the court shall determine which parent to designate as the noncustodial parent for the purpose of this Code section.

(15) "Nonparent custodian" means an individual who has been granted legal custody of a child, or an individual who has a legal right to seek, modify, or enforce a child support order.

(16) "Parent" means a person who owes a child a duty of support pursuant to Code Section 19-7-2.

(17) "Parenting time deviation" means a deviation allowed for the noncustodial parent based upon the noncustodial parent's court ordered visitation with the child. For further reference see subsections (g) and (i) of this Code section.

(18) "Preexisting order" means:

(A) An order in another case that requires a parent to make child support payments for another child, which child support the parent is actually paying, as evidenced by documentation as provided in division (f)(5)(B)(iii) of this Code section; and

(B) That the date and time of filing with the clerk of court of the initial order for each such other case is earlier than the date and time of filing with the clerk of court of the initial order in the case immediately before the court, regardless of the age of any child in any of the cases.

(19) "Presumptive amount of child support" means the basic child support obligation including health insurance and work related child care costs.

(20) "Qualified child" or "qualified children" means any child:

(A) For whom the parent is legally responsible and in whose home the child resides;

(B) That the parent is actually supporting;

(C) Who is not subject to a preexisting order; and

(D) Who is not before the court to set, modify, or enforce support in the case immediately under consideration.

Qualified children shall not include stepchildren or other minors in the home that the parent has no legal obligation to support.

(21) "Split parenting" can occur in a child support case only if there are two or more children of the same parents, where one parent is the custodial parent for at least one child of the parents, and the other parent is the custodial parent for at least one other child of the parents. In a split parenting case, each parent is the custodial parent of any child spending more than 50 percent of the time with that parent and is the noncustodial parent of any child spending more than 50 percent of the time with the other parent. A split parenting situation shall have two custodial parents and two noncustodial parents, but no child shall have more than one custodial parent or noncustodial parent.

(22) "Theoretical child support order" means a hypothetical child support order for qualified children calculated as set forth in subparagraph (f)(5)(C) of this Code section which allows the court to determine the amount of child support as if a child support order existed.

(23) "Uninsured health care expenses" means a child's uninsured medical expenses including, but not limited to, health insurance copayments, deductibles, and such other costs as are reasonably necessary for orthodontia, dental treatment, asthma treatments, physical therapy, vision care, and any acute or chronic medical or health problem or mental health illness, including counseling and other medical or mental health expenses, that are not covered by insurance. For further reference see paragraph (3) of subsection (h) of this Code section.

(24) "Work related child care costs" means expenses for the care of the child for whom support is being determined which are due to employment of either parent. In an appropriate case, the court may consider the child care costs associated with a parent's job search or the training or education of a parent necessary to obtain a job or enhance earning potential, not to exceed a reasonable time as determined by the court, if the

parent proves by a preponderance of the evidence that the job search, job training, or education will benefit the child being supported. The term shall be projected for the next consecutive 12 months and averaged to obtain a monthly amount. For further reference see paragraph (1) of subsection (h) of this Code section.

(25) "Worksheet" or "child support worksheet" means the document used to record information necessary to determine and calculate monthly child support. For further reference see subsection (m) of this Code section.

(b) Process of calculating child support. Pursuant to this Code section, the determination of monthly child support shall be calculated as follows:

(1) Determine the monthly gross income of both the custodial parent and the noncustodial parent. Gross income may include imputed income, if applicable. The determination of monthly gross income shall be entered on the Child Support Schedule A -- Gross Income;

(2) Adjust each parent's monthly gross income by deducting the following from the parents' monthly gross income and entering it on the Child Support Schedule B -- Adjusted Income if any of the following apply:

   (A) One-half of the amount of self-employment taxes;
   (B) Preexisting orders; and
   (C) Theoretical child support order for qualified children, if allowed by the court;

(3) Add each parent's adjusted income together;

(4) Locate the basic child support obligation by referring to the child support obligation table. Using the figure closest to the amount of the combined adjusted income, locate the amount of the basic child support obligation. If the combined adjusted income falls between the amounts shown in the table, then the basic child support obligation shall be based on the income bracket most closely matched to the combined adjusted income. The basic child support obligation amount stated in subsection (o) of this Code section shall be rebuttably presumed to be the appropriate amount of child support to be provided by the custodial parent and the noncustodial parent prior to consideration of health insurance, work related child care costs, and deviations;

(5) Calculate the pro rata share of the basic child support obligation for the custodial parent and the noncustodial parent by dividing the combined adjusted income into each parent's adjusted income to arrive at each parent's pro rata percentage of the basic child support obligation;

(6) Find the adjusted child support obligation amount by adding the additional expenses of the costs of health insurance and work related child care costs, prorating such expenses in accordance with each parent's pro rata share of the obligation and adding such expenses to the pro rata share of the basic child support obligation. The monthly cost of health insurance premiums and work related child care costs shall be entered on the Child Support Schedule D -- Additional Expenses. The pro rata share of the monthly basic child support obligation and the pro rata share of the combined additional expenses shall be added together to create the monthly adjusted child support obligation;

(7) Determine the amount of child support for the custodial parent and the noncustodial parent resulting in a monthly sum certain payment due to the custodial parent by assigning or deducting credit for actual payments for health insurance and work related child care costs from the basic child support obligation;

(8) In accordance with subsection (i) of this Code section, deviations subtracted from or added to the presumptive amount of child support shall be applied, if applicable, and if supported by the required findings of fact and application of the best interest of the child standard. The proposed deviations shall be entered on the Child Support Schedule E -- Deviations. In the court's or the jury's discretion, deviations may include, but shall not be limited to, the following:

   (A) High income;
   (B) Low income;
   (C) Other health related insurance;
   (D) Life insurance;
   (E) Child and dependent care tax credit;
   (F) Travel expenses;
   (G) Alimony;
   (H) Mortgage;
   (I) Permanency plan or foster care plan;
   (J) Extraordinary expenses;
   (K) Parenting time; and
   (L) Nonspecific deviations;

(9) Any benefits which the child receives under Title II of the federal Social Security Act shall be applied against the final child support amount. The final child support amount for each parent shall be entered on the child support worksheet, together with the information from each of the utilized schedules;

(10) The parents shall allocate the uninsured health care expenses which shall be based on the pro rata responsibility of the parents or as otherwise ordered by the court. Each parent's pro rata responsibility for uninsured health care expenses shall be entered on the child support worksheet;

(11) In a split parenting case, there shall be a separate calculation and final order for each parent; and

(12) When there is more than one child for whom support is being determined, the court shall establish the amount of support and the duration of such support in accordance with subsection (e) of this Code section.

When, within two years of a final order being entered, there is a likelihood that a child will become ineligible to receive support, the court may allow for the use of separate worksheets. Separate worksheets shall show the final child support amount to be paid for all such children and the adjusted amount of support to be paid as each child becomes ineligible to receive support during such two-year period. Such worksheets shall be attached to the final order. Such order shall contain findings as required by law. A final order entered pursuant to this paragraph shall not preclude a petition for modification.

(c) Applicability and required findings.

(1) The child support guidelines contained in this Code section are a minimum basis for determining the amount of child support and shall apply as a rebuttable presumption in all legal proceedings involving the child support responsibility of a parent. This Code section shall be used when the court enters a temporary or permanent child support order in a contested or noncontested hearing or order in a civil action filed pursuant to Code Section 19-13-4. The rebuttable presumptive amount of child support provided by this Code section may be increased or decreased according to the best interest of the child for whom support is being considered, the circumstances of the parties, the grounds for deviation set forth in subsection (i) of this Code section, and to achieve the state policy of affording to children of unmarried parents, to the extent possible, the same economic standard of living enjoyed by children living in intact families consisting of parents with similar financial means.

(2) The provisions of this Code section shall not apply with respect to any divorce case in which there are no minor children, except to the limited extent authorized by subsection (e) of this Code section. In the final judgment or decree in a divorce case in which there are minor children, or in other cases which are governed by the provisions of this Code section, the court shall:

(A) Specify in what sum certain amount, the duration of such support, and from which parent the child is entitled to permanent support as determined by use of the worksheet or multiple worksheets when there is more than one minor child;

(B) Specify in what manner, how often, to whom, and until when the support shall be paid;

(C) Include a written finding of each parent's gross income as determined by the court or the jury;

(D) Determine whether health insurance for the child involved is reasonably available at a reasonable cost to either parent. If the health insurance is reasonably available at a reasonable cost to the parent, then the court shall order that the child be covered under such health insurance;

(E) Include written findings of fact as to whether one or more of the deviations allowed under this Code section are applicable, and if one or more such deviations are applicable as determined by the court or the jury, the written findings of fact shall further set forth:

(i) The reasons the court or the jury deviated from the presumptive amount of child support;

(ii) The amount of child support that would have been required under this Code section if the presumptive amount of child support had not been rebutted; and

(iii) A finding that states how the court's or the jury's application of the child support guidelines would be unjust or inappropriate considering the relative ability of each parent to provide support and how the best interest of the child who is subject to the child support determination is served by deviation from the presumptive amount of child support;

(F) Specify the amount of the noncustodial parent's parenting time as set forth in the order of visitation;

(G) Include a written finding regarding the use of benefits received under Title II of the federal Social Security Act in the calculation of the amount of child support; and

(H) Specify the percentage of uninsured health care expenses for which each parent shall be responsible.

(3) When child support is ordered, the party who is required to pay the child support shall not be liable to third persons for necessaries furnished to the child embraced in the judgment or decree.

(4) In all cases, the parties shall submit to the court their worksheets and schedules and the presence or absence of other factors to be considered by the court pursuant to the provisions of this Code section.

(5) In any case in which the gross income of the custodial parent and the noncustodial parent is determined by a jury, the court shall charge the provisions of this Code section applicable to the determination of gross income. The jury shall be required to return a special interrogatory determining gross income. The court shall determine adjusted income, health insurance costs, and work related child care costs. Based upon the jury's verdict as to gross income, the court shall determine the presumptive amount of child support in accordance with the provisions of this Code section. The court shall inform the jury of the presumptive amount of child support and the identity of the custodial and noncustodial parents. In the final instructions to the jury, the court shall charge the provisions of this Code section applicable to the determination of deviations and the jury shall be required to return a special interrogatory as to deviations and the final award of child support. The court shall include its findings and the jury's verdict on the child support worksheet in accordance with this Code section and Code Section 19-5-12.

(6) Nothing contained within this Code section shall prevent the parties from entering into an enforceable agreement contrary to the presumptive amount of child support which may be made the order of the court pursuant to review by the court of the adequacy of the child support amounts negotiated by the parties, including the provision for medical expenses and health insurance; provided, however, that if the agreement negotiated by the parties does not comply with the provisions contained in this Code section and does not contain findings of fact as required to support a deviation, the court shall reject such agreement.

(7) In any case filed pursuant to Chapter 11 of this title, relating to the "Child Support Recovery Act," the "Uniform Reciprocal Enforcement of Support Act," or the "Uniform Interstate Family Support Act," the court shall make all determinations of fact, including gross income and deviations, and a jury shall not hear any issue related to such cases.

(d) Nature of guidelines; court's discretion. In the event of a hearing or trial on the issue of child support, the guidelines enumerated in this Code section are intended by the General Assembly to be guidelines only and any court so applying these guidelines shall not abrogate its responsibility in making the final determination of child support based on the evidence presented to it at the time of the hearing or trial. A court's final determination of child support shall take into account the obligor's earnings, income, and other evidence of the obligor's ability to pay. The court shall also consider the basic subsistence needs of the parents and the child for whom support is to be provided.

(e) Duration of child support responsibility. The duty to provide support for a minor child shall continue until the child reaches the age of majority, dies, marries, or becomes emancipated, whichever first occurs; provided, however, that, in any temporary, final, or modified order for child support with respect to any proceeding for divorce, separate maintenance, legitimacy, or paternity entered on or after July 1, 1992, the court, in the exercise of sound discretion, may direct either or both parents to provide financial assistance to a child who has not previously married or become emancipated, who is enrolled in and attending a secondary school, and who has attained the age of majority before completing his or her secondary school education, provided that such financial assistance shall not be required after a child attains 20 years of age. The provisions for child support provided in this subsection may be enforced by either parent, by any nonparent custodian, by a guardian appointed to receive child support for the child for whose benefit the child support is ordered, or by the child for whose benefit the child support is ordered.

(f) Gross income.

(1) Inclusion to gross income.

(A) Attributable income. Gross income of each parent shall be determined in the process of setting the presumptive amount of child support and shall include all income from any source, before deductions for taxes and other deductions such as preexisting orders for child support and credits for other qualified children, whether earned or unearned, and includes, but is not limited to, the following:

(i) Salaries;
(ii) Commissions, fees, and tips;
(iii) Income from self-employment;
(iv) Bonuses;
(v) Overtime payments;
(vi) Severance pay;
(vii) Recurring income from pensions or retirement plans including, but not limited to, United States Department of Veterans Affairs, Railroad Retirement Board, Keoghs, and individual retirement accounts;
(viii) Interest income;
(ix) Dividend income;
(x) Trust income;
(xi) Income from annuities;
(xii) Capital gains;
(xiii) Disability or retirement benefits that are received from the Social Security Administration pursuant to Title II of the federal Social Security Act;
(xiv) Disability benefits that are received pursuant to the federal Veterans' Benefits Act of 2010, 38 U.S.C. Section 101, et seq.;
(xv) Workers' compensation benefits, whether temporary or permanent;
(xvi) Unemployment insurance benefits;
(xvii) Judgments recovered for personal injuries and awards from other civil actions;
(xviii) Gifts that consist of cash or other liquid instruments, or which can be converted to cash;
(xix) Prizes;
(xx) Lottery winnings;
(xxi) Alimony or maintenance received from persons other than parties to the proceeding before the court;
(xxii) Assets which are used for the support of the family; and
(xxiii) Other income.

(B) Self-employment income. Income from self-employment includes income from, but not limited to, business operations, work as an independent contractor or consultant, sales of goods or services, and rental properties, less ordinary and reasonable expenses necessary to produce such income. Income from self-employment, rent, royalties, proprietorship of a business, or joint ownership of a partnership, limited liability company, or closely held corporation is defined as gross receipts minus ordinary and reasonable expenses required for self-employment or business operations. Ordinary and reasonable expenses of self-employment or business operations necessary to produce income do not include:

(i) Excessive promotional, travel, vehicle, or personal living expenses, depreciation on equipment, or costs of operation of home offices; or

(ii) Amounts allowable by the Internal Revenue Service for the accelerated component of depreciation expenses, investment tax credits, or any other business expenses determined by the court or the jury to be inappropriate for determining gross income.

In general, income and expenses from self-employment or operation of a business should be carefully reviewed by the court or the jury to determine an appropriate level of gross income available to the parent to satisfy a child support obligation. Generally, this amount will differ from a determination of business income for tax purposes.

(C) Fringe benefits. Fringe benefits for inclusion as income or "in kind" remuneration received by a parent in the course of employment, or operation of a trade or business, shall be counted as income if the benefits significantly reduce personal living expenses. Such fringe benefits might include, but are not limited to, use of a company car, housing, or room and board. Fringe benefits shall not include employee benefits that are typically added to the salary, wage, or other compensation that a parent may receive as a standard added benefit, including, but not limited to, employer paid portions of health insurance premiums or employer contributions to a retirement or pension plan.

(D) Variable income. Variable income such as commissions, bonuses, overtime pay, military bonuses, and dividends shall be averaged by the court or the jury over a reasonable period of time consistent with the circumstances of the case and added to a parent's fixed salary or wages to determine gross income. When income is received on an irregular, nonrecurring, or one-time basis, the court or the jury may, but is not required to, average or prorate the income over a reasonable specified period of time or require the parent to pay as a one-time support amount a percentage of his or her nonrecurring income, taking into consideration the percentage of recurring income of that parent.

(E) Military compensation and allowances. Income for a parent who is an active duty member of the regular or reserve component of the United States armed forces, the United States Coast Guard, the merchant marine of the United States, the commissioned corps of the Public Health Service or the National Oceanic and Atmospheric Administration, the National Guard, or the Air National Guard shall include:

(i) Base pay;

(ii) Drill pay;

(iii) Basic allowance for subsistence, whether paid directly to the parent or received in-kind; and

(iv) Basic allowance for housing, whether paid directly to the parent or received in-kind, determined at the parent's pay grade at the without dependent rate, but shall include only so much of the allowance that is not attributable to area variable housing costs.

Except as determined by the court or jury, special pay or incentive pay, allowances for clothing or family separation, and reimbursed expenses related to the parent's assignment to a high cost of living location shall not be considered income for the purpose of determining gross income.

(2) Exclusions from gross income. Excluded from gross income are the following:

(A) Child support payments received by either parent for the benefit of a child of another relationship;

(B) Benefits received from means-tested public assistance programs such as, but not limited to:

(i) PeachCare for Kids Program, Temporary Assistance for Needy Families Program, or similar programs in other states or territories under Title IV-A of the federal Social Security Act;

(ii) Food stamps or the value of food assistance provided by way of electronic benefits transfer procedures by the Department of Human Services;

(iii) Supplemental security income received under Title XVI of the federal Social Security Act;

(iv) Benefits received under Section 402(d) of the federal Social Security Act for disabled adult children of deceased disabled workers; and

(v) Low-income heating and energy assistance program payments;

(C) Foster care payments paid by the Department of Human Services or a licensed child placing agency for providing foster care to a foster child in the custody of the Department of Human Services; and

(D) A nonparent custodian's gross income.

(3) Social Security benefits.

(A) Benefits received under Title II of the federal Social Security Act by a child on the obligor's account shall be counted as child support payments and shall be applied against the final child support amount to be paid by the obligor for the child.

(B) After calculating the obligor's monthly gross income, including the countable social security benefits as specified in division (1)(A)(xiii) of this subsection, and after calculating the amount of child support, if the presumptive amount of child support, as increased or decreased by deviations, is greater than the social security benefits paid on behalf of the child on the obligor's account, the obligor shall be required to pay the amount exceeding the social security benefit as part of the final order in the case.

(C) After calculating the obligor's monthly gross income, including the countable social security benefits as specified in division (1)(A)(xiii) of this subsection, and after calculating the amount of child support, if the presumptive amount of child support, as increased or decreased by deviations, is equal to or less than the social security benefits paid to the nonparent custodian or custodial parent on behalf of the child on the obligor's account, the child support responsibility of that parent shall have been met and no further child support shall be paid.

(D) Any benefit amounts under Title II of the federal Social Security Act as determined by the Social Security Administration sent to the nonparent custodian or custodial parent by the Social Security Administration for the child's benefit which are greater than the final child support amount shall be retained by the nonparent custodian or custodial parent for the child's benefit and shall not be used as a reason for decreasing the final child support amount or reducing arrearages.

(4) Reliable evidence of income.

(A) Imputed income. When establishing the amount of child support, if a parent fails to produce reliable evidence of income, such as tax returns for prior years, check stubs, or other information for determining current ability to pay child support or ability to pay child support in prior years, and the court or the jury has no other reliable evidence of the parent's income or income potential, gross income for the current year may be imputed. When imputing income, the court shall take into account the specific circumstances of the parent to the extent known, including such factors as the parent's assets, residence, employment and earnings history, job skills, educational attainment, literacy, age, health, criminal record and other employment barriers, and record of seeking work, as well as the local job market, the availability of employers willing to hire the parent, prevailing earnings level in the local community, and other relevant background factors in the case. If a parent is incarcerated, the court shall not assume an ability for earning capacity based upon pre-incarceration wages or other employment related income, but income may be imputed based upon the actual income and assets available to such incarcerated parent.

(B) Modification. When cases with established orders are reviewed for modification and a parent fails to produce reliable evidence of income, such as tax returns for prior years, check stubs, or other information for determining current ability to pay child support or ability to pay child support in prior years, and the court or jury has no other reliable evidence of such parent's income or income potential, the court or jury may impute income as set forth in subparagraph (A) of this paragraph, or may increase the child support of the parent failing or refusing to produce evidence of income by an increment of at least 10 percent per year of such parent's gross income for each year since the final order was entered or last modified and shall calculate the basic child support obligation using the increased amount as such parent's gross income.

(C) Rehearing. If income is imputed pursuant to subparagraph (A) of this paragraph, the party believing the income of the other party is higher than the amount imputed may provide within 90 days, upon motion to the court, evidence necessary to determine the appropriate amount of child support based upon reliable evidence. A hearing shall be scheduled after the motion is filed. The court may increase, decrease, or leave unchanged the amount of current child support from the date of filing of either parent's initial filing or motion for reconsideration. While the motion for reconsideration is pending, the obligor shall be responsible for the amount of child support originally ordered. Arrearages entered in the original child support order based upon imputed income shall not be forgiven. When there is reliable evidence to support a motion for reconsideration of the amount of income imputed, the party seeking reconsideration shall not be required to prove the existence of grounds for modification of an order pursuant to subsection (k) of this Code section.

(D) Willful or voluntary unemployment or underemployment. In determining whether a parent is willfully or voluntarily unemployed or underemployed, the court or the jury shall ascertain the reasons for the parent's occupational choices and assess the reasonableness of these choices in light of the parent's responsibility to support his or her child and whether such choices benefit the child. A determination of willful or voluntary unemployment or underemployment shall not be limited to occupational choices motivated only by an intent to avoid or reduce the payment of child support but can be based on any intentional choice or act that affects a parent's income. A determination of willful or voluntary unemployment or underemployment shall not be made when an individual's incarceration prevents employment. In determining willful or voluntary unemployment or underemployment, the court may examine whether there is a substantial likelihood that the parent could, with reasonable effort, apply his or her education, skills, or training to produce income. Specific factors for the court to consider when determining willful or voluntary unemployment or underemployment include, but are not limited to:

(i) The parent's past and present employment;

(ii) The parent's education and training;

(iii) Whether unemployment or underemployment for the purpose of pursuing additional training or education is reasonable in light of the parent's responsibility to support his or her child and, to this end, whether the training or education may ultimately benefit the child in the case immediately under consideration by increasing the parent's level of support for that child in the future;

(iv) A parent's ownership of valuable assets and resources, such as an expensive home or automobile, that appear inappropriate or unreasonable for the income claimed by the parent;

(v) The parent's own health and ability to work outside the home; and

(vi) The parent's role as caretaker of a child of that parent, a disabled or seriously ill child of that parent, or a disabled or seriously ill adult child of that parent, or any other disabled or seriously ill relative for whom that parent has assumed the role of caretaker, which eliminates or substantially reduces the parent's ability to work outside the home, and the need of that parent to continue in the role of caretaker in the future. When considering the income potential of a parent whose work experience is limited due to the caretaker role of that parent, the court shall consider the following factors:

(I) Whether the parent acted in the role of full-time caretaker immediately prior to separation by the married parties or prior to the divorce or annulment of the marriage or dissolution of another relationship in which the parent was a full-time caretaker;

(II) The length of time the parent staying at home has remained out of the work force for this purpose;

(III) The parent's education, training, and ability to work; and

(IV) Whether the parent is caring for a child who is four years of age or younger. If the court or the jury determines that a parent is willfully or voluntarily unemployed or underemployed, child support shall be calculated based on a determination of earning capacity, as evidenced by educational level or previous work experience. In the absence of any other reliable evidence, income may be imputed to the parent pursuant to a determination that gross income for the current year is based on a 40 hour workweek at minimum wage. A determination of willful and voluntary unemployment or underemployment shall not be made when an individual is activated from the National Guard or other armed forces unit or enlists or is drafted for full-time service in the armed forces of the United States.

(5) Adjustments to gross income.

(A) Self-employment. One-half of the self-employment and Medicare taxes shall be calculated as follows:

(i) Six and two-tenths percent of self-employment income up to the maximum amount to which federal old age, survivors, and disability insurance (OASDI) applies; plus

(ii) One and forty-five one-hundredths of a percent of self-employment income for Medicare

and this amount shall be deducted from a self-employed parent's monthly gross income.

(B) Preexisting orders. An adjustment to the parent's monthly gross income shall be made on the Child Support Schedule B -- Adjusted Income for current preexisting orders for a period of not less than 12 months immediately prior to the date of the hearing or such period that an order has been in effect if less than 12 months prior to the date of the hearing before the court to set, modify, or enforce child support.

(i) In calculating the adjustment for preexisting orders, the court shall include only those preexisting orders meeting the criteria set forth in subparagraph (a)(18)(B);

(ii) The priority for preexisting orders shall be determined by the date and time of filing with the clerk of court of the initial order in each case. Subsequent modifications of the initial support order shall not affect the priority position established by the date and time of the initial order. In any modification proceeding, the court rendering the decision shall make a specific finding of the date, and time if known, of the initial order of the case;

(iii) Adjustments shall be allowed for current preexisting support only to the extent that the payments are actually being paid as evidenced by documentation including, but not limited to, payment history from a court clerk, the child support services' computer data base, the child support payment history, or canceled checks or other written proof of payments paid directly to the other parent. The maximum credit allowed for a preexisting order is an average of the amount of current support actually paid under the preexisting order over the past 12 months prior to the hearing date;

(iv) All preexisting orders shall be entered on the Child Support Schedule B -- Adjusted Income for the purpose of calculating the total amount of the credit to be included on the child support worksheet; and

(v) Payments being made by a parent on any arrearages shall not be considered payments on preexisting orders or subsequent orders and shall not be used as a basis for reducing gross income.

(C) Theoretical child support orders. In addition to the adjustments to monthly gross income for self-employment taxes provided in subparagraph (A) of this paragraph and for preexisting orders provided in subparagraph (B) of this paragraph, credits for either parent's other qualified child living in the parent's home for whom the parent owes a legal duty of support may be considered by the court for the purpose of reducing the parent's gross income. To consider a parent's other qualified children for determining the theoretical child support order, a parent shall present documentary evidence of the parent-child relationship to the court. Adjustments to income pursuant to this subparagraph may be considered in such circumstances in which the failure to consider a qualified child would cause substantial hardship to the parent; provided, however, that such consideration of an adjustment shall be based upon the best interest of the child for whom child support is being awarded. If the court, in its discretion, decides to apply the qualified child adjustment, the basic child support obligation of the parent for the number of other qualified children living with such parent shall be determined based upon that parent's monthly gross income. Except for self-employment taxes paid, no other amounts shall be subtracted from the parent's monthly gross income when calculating a theoretical child support order under this subparagraph. The basic child support obligation for such parent shall be multiplied by 75 percent and the resulting amount shall be subtracted from such parent's monthly gross income and entered on the Child Support Schedule B -- Adjusted Income.

(D) Multiple family situations. In multiple family situations, the priority of adjustments to a parent's monthly gross income shall be calculated in the following order:

(i) Preexisting orders according to the date and time of the initial order as set forth in subparagraph (B) of this paragraph; and

(ii) Application of any credit for a parent's other qualified children using the procedure set forth in subparagraph (C) of this paragraph.

(g) Parenting time deviation. The court or the jury may deviate from the presumptive amount of child support as set forth in subparagraph (i)(2)(K) of this Code section.

(h) Adjusted support obligation. The child support obligation table does not include the cost of the parent's work related child care costs, health insurance premiums, or uninsured health care expenses. The additional expenses for the child's health insurance premiums and work related child care costs shall be included in the calculations to determine child support. A nonparent custodian's expenses for work related child care costs and health insurance premiums shall be taken into account when establishing a final order.

(1) Work related child care costs.

(A) Work related child care costs necessary for the parent's employment, education, or vocational training that are determined by the court to be appropriate, and that are appropriate to the parents' financial abilities and to the lifestyle of the child if the parents and child were living together, shall be averaged for a monthly amount and entered on the child support worksheet in the column of the parent initially paying the expense. Work related child care costs of a nonparent custodian shall be considered when determining the amount of this expense.

(B) If a child care subsidy is being provided pursuant to a means-tested public assistance program, only the amount of the child care expense actually paid by either parent or a nonparent custodian shall be included in the calculation.

(C) If either parent is the provider of child care services to the child for whom support is being determined, the value of those services shall not be an adjustment to the basic child support obligation when calculating the support award.

(D) If child care is provided without charge to the parent, the value of these services shall not be an adjustment to the basic child support obligation. If child care is or will be provided by a person who is paid for his or her services, proof of actual cost or payment shall be shown to the court before the court includes such payment in its consideration.

(E) The amount of work related child care costs shall be determined and added as an adjustment to the basic child support obligation as "additional expenses" whether paid directly by the parent or through a payroll deduction.

(F) (i) The total amount of work related child care costs shall be divided between the parents pro rata to determine the presumptive amount of child support and shall be included in the worksheet and the final order.

(ii) In situations in which work related child care costs may be variable, the court or jury may, in its discretion, remove work related child care costs from the calculation of support, and divide the work related child care costs pro rata, to be paid within a time specified in the final order. If a parent or nonparent custodian fails to comply with the final order:

(I) The other parent or nonparent custodian may enforce payment of the work related child care costs by any means permitted by law; or

(II) Child support services shall pursue enforcement when such unpaid costs have been reduced to a judgment in a sum certain.

(2) Cost of health insurance premiums.

(A) (i) The amount that is, or will be, paid by a parent for health insurance for the child for whom support is being determined shall be an adjustment to the basic child support obligation and prorated between the parents based upon their respective incomes. Payments made by a parent's employer for health insurance and not deducted from the parent's wages shall not be included. When a child for whom support is being determined is covered by a family policy, only the health insurance premium actually attributable to that child shall be added.

(ii) The amount of the cost for the child's health insurance premium shall be determined and added as an adjustment to the basic child support obligation as "additional expenses" whether paid directly by the parent or through a payroll deduction.

(iii) The total amount of the cost for the child's health insurance premium shall be divided between the parents pro rata to determine the total presumptive amount of child support and shall be included in the Child Support Schedule D -- Additional Expenses and written order of the court together with the amount of the basic child support obligation.

(B) (i) If either parent has health insurance reasonably available at reasonable cost that provides for the health care needs of the child, then an amount to cover the cost of the premium shall be added as an adjustment to the basic child support obligation. A health insurance premium paid by a nonparent custodian shall be included when determining the amount of health insurance expense. In determining the amount to be added to the order for the health insurance cost, only the amount of the health insurance cost attributable to the child who is the subject of the order shall be included.

(ii) If coverage is applicable to other persons and the amount of the health insurance premium attributable to the child who is the subject of the current action for support is not verifiable, the total cost to the parent paying the premium shall be prorated by the number of persons covered so that only the cost attributable to the child who is the subject of the order under consideration is included. The amount of health insurance premium shall be determined by dividing the total amount of the insurance premium by the number of persons covered by the insurance policy and multiplying the resulting amount by the number of children covered by the insurance policy. The monthly cost of health insurance premium shall be entered on the Child Support Schedule D -- Additional Expenses in the column of the parent paying the premium.

(iii) Eligibility for or enrollment of the child in Medicaid, the PeachCare for Kids Program, or other public health care program shall satisfy the requirement that the final order provide for the child's health care needs. Health coverage through Medicaid, the PeachCare for Kids Program, or other public health care program shall not prevent a court from also ordering either or both parents to obtain other health insurance for the child.

(3) Uninsured health care expenses.

(A) The child's uninsured health care expenses shall be the financial responsibility of both parents. The final order shall include provisions for payment of uninsured health care expenses; provided, however, that uninsured health care expenses shall not be used for the purpose of calculating the amount of child support. The parents shall divide uninsured health care expenses pro rata, unless otherwise specifically ordered by the court.

(B) If a parent fails to pay his or her pro rata share of the child's uninsured health care expenses, as specified in the final order, within a reasonable time after receipt of evidence documenting the uninsured portion of the expense:

(i) The other parent or the nonparent custodian may enforce payment of the expense by any means permitted by law; or

(ii) Child support services shall pursue enforcement of payment of such unpaid expenses only if the unpaid expenses have been reduced to a judgment in a sum certain amount.

(i) Grounds for deviation.

(1) General principles.

(A) The amount of child support established by this Code section and the presumptive amount of child support are rebuttable and the court or the jury may deviate from the presumptive amount of child support in compliance with this subsection. In deviating from the presumptive amount of child support, consideration shall be given to the best interest of the child for whom support under this Code section is being determined. A nonparent custodian's expenses may be the basis for a deviation as well as a noncustodial parent's ability or inability to pay the presumptive amount of child support.

(B) When ordering a deviation from the presumptive amount of child support, the court or the jury shall consider all available income of the parents and shall make written findings or special interrogatory findings that an amount of child support other than the amount calculated is reasonably necessary to provide for the needs of the child for whom child support is being determined and the order or special interrogatory shall state:

(i) The reasons for the deviation from the presumptive amount of child support;

(ii) The amount of child support that would have been required under this Code section if the presumptive amount of child support had not been rebutted; and

(iii) How, in its determination:

(I) Application of the presumptive amount of child support would be unjust or inappropriate; and

(II) The best interest of the child for whom support is being determined will be served by deviation from the presumptive amount of child support.

(C) No deviation in the presumptive amount of child support shall be made which seriously impairs the ability of the custodial parent to maintain minimally adequate housing, food, and clothing for the child being supported by the order and to provide other basic necessities, as determined by the court or the jury.

(D) If the circumstances which supported the deviation cease to exist, the final order may be modified as set forth in subsection (k) of this Code section to eliminate the deviation.

(2) Specific deviations.

(A) High income. For purposes of this subparagraph, parents are considered to be high-income parents if their combined adjusted income exceeds $30,000.00 per month. For high-income parents, the court shall set the basic child support obligation at the highest amount allowed by the child support obligation table but the court or the jury may consider upward deviation to attain an appropriate award of child support for high-income parents which is consistent with the best interest of the child.

(B) Low income.

(i) If the noncustodial parent can provide evidence sufficient to demonstrate no earning capacity or that his or her pro rata share of the presumptive amount of child support would create an extreme economic hardship for such parent, the court may consider a low-income deviation.

(ii) A noncustodial parent whose sole source of income is supplemental security income received under Title XVI of the federal Social Security Act shall be considered to have no earning capacity.

(iii) The court or the jury shall examine all attributable and excluded sources of income, assets, and benefits available to the noncustodial parent and may consider the noncustodial parent's basic subsistence needs and all of his or her reasonable expenses, ensuring that such expenses are actually paid by the noncustodial parent and are clearly justified expenses.

(iv) In considering a request for a low-income deviation, the court or the jury shall then weigh the income and all attributable and excluded sources of income, assets, and benefits and all reasonable expenses of each parent, the relative hardship that a reduction in the amount of child support paid to the custodial parent would have on the custodial parent's household, the needs of each parent, the needs of the child for whom child support is being determined, and the ability of the noncustodial parent to pay child support.

(v) Following a review of the noncustodial parent's gross income and expenses, and taking into account each parent's basic child support obligation adjusted by health insurance and work related child care costs and the relative hardships on the parents and the child, the court or the jury, upon request by either party or upon the court's initiative, may consider a downward deviation to attain an appropriate award of child support which is consistent with the best interest of the child.

(vi) For the purpose of calculating a low-income deviation, the noncustodial parent's minimum child support for one child shall be not less than $100.00 per month, and such amount shall be increased by at least $50.00 for each additional child for the same case for which child support is being ordered.

(vii) A low-income deviation granted pursuant to this subparagraph shall apply only to the current child support amount and shall not prohibit an additional amount being ordered to reduce a noncustodial parent's arrears.

(viii) If a low-income deviation is granted pursuant to this subparagraph, such deviation shall not prohibit the court or jury from granting an increase or decrease to the presumptive amount of child support by the use of any other specific or nonspecific deviation.

(C) Other health related insurance. If the court or the jury finds that either parent has vision or dental insurance available at a reasonable cost for the child, the court may deviate from the presumptive amount of child support for the cost of such insurance.

(D) Life insurance. In accordance with Code Section 19-6-34, if the court or the jury finds that either parent has purchased life insurance on the life of either parent or the lives of both parents for the benefit of the child, the court may deviate from the presumptive amount of child support for the cost of such insurance by either adding or subtracting the amount of the premium.

(E) Child and dependent care tax credit. If the court or the jury finds that one of the parents is entitled to the Child and Dependent Care Tax Credit, the court or the jury may deviate from the presumptive amount of child support in consideration of such credit.

(F) Travel expenses. If court ordered visitation related travel expenses are substantial due to the distance between the parents, the court may order the allocation of such costs or the jury may by a finding in its special interrogatory allocate such costs by deviation from the presumptive amount of child support, taking into consideration the circumstances of the respective parents as well as which parent moved and the reason for such move.

(G) Alimony. Actual payments of alimony shall not be considered as a deduction from gross income but may be considered as a deviation from the presumptive amount of child support. If the court or the jury considers the actual payment of alimony, the court shall make a written finding of such consideration or the jury, in its special interrogatory, shall make a written finding of such consideration as a basis for deviation from the presumptive amount of child support.

(H) Mortgage. If the noncustodial parent is providing shelter, such as paying the mortgage of the home, or has provided a home at no cost to the custodial parent in which the child resides, the court or the jury may allocate such costs or an amount equivalent to such costs by deviation from the presumptive amount of child support, taking into consideration the circumstances of the respective parents and the best interest of the child.

(I) Permanency plan or foster care plan. In cases where the child is in the legal custody of the Department of Human Services, the child protection or foster care agency of another state or territory, or any other child-caring entity, public or private, the court or the jury may consider a deviation from the presumptive amount of child support if the deviation will assist in accomplishing a permanency plan or foster care plan for the child that has a goal of returning the child to the parent or parents and the parent's need to establish an adequate household or to otherwise adequately prepare herself or himself for the return of the child clearly justifies a deviation for this purpose.

(J) Extraordinary expenses. The child support obligation table includes average child rearing expenditures for families given the parents' combined adjusted income and number of children. Extraordinary expenses are in excess of average amounts estimated in the child support obligation table and are highly variable among families. Extraordinary expenses shall be considered on a case-by-case basis in the calculation of support and may form the basis for deviation from the presumptive amount of child support so that the actual amount of such expense is considered in the final order for only those families actually incurring the expense. Extraordinary expenses shall be prorated between the parents by assigning or deducting credit for actual payments for extraordinary expenses.

(i) Extraordinary educational expenses. Extraordinary educational expenses may be a basis for deviation from the presumptive amount of child support. Extraordinary educational expenses include, but are not limited to, tuition, room and board, lab fees, books, fees, and other reasonable and necessary expenses associated with special needs education or private elementary and secondary schooling that are appropriate to the parent's financial abilities and to the lifestyle of the child if the parents and the child were living together.

(I) In determining the amount of deviation for extraordinary educational expenses, scholarships, grants, stipends, and other cost-reducing programs received by or on behalf of the child shall be considered; and

(II) If a deviation is allowed for extraordinary educational expenses, a monthly average of the extraordinary educational expenses shall be based on evidence of prior or anticipated expenses and entered on the Child Support Schedule E -- Deviations.

(ii) Special expenses incurred for child rearing. Special expenses incurred for child rearing, including, but not limited to, quantifiable expense variations related to the food, clothing, and hygiene costs of children at different age levels, may be a basis for a deviation from the presumptive amount of child support. Such expenses include, but are not limited to, summer camp; music or art lessons; travel; school sponsored extracurricular activities, such as band, clubs, and athletics; and other activities intended to enhance the athletic, social, or cultural development of a child but not otherwise required to be used in calculating the presumptive amount of child support as are health insurance premiums and work related child care costs. A portion of the basic child support obligation is intended to cover average amounts of special expenses incurred in the rearing of a child. In order to determine if a deviation for special expenses is warranted, the court or the jury shall consider the full amount of the special expenses as described in this division; and when these special expenses exceed 7 percent of the basic child support obligation, then the additional amount of special expenses shall be considered as a deviation to cover the full amount of the special expenses.

(iii) Extraordinary medical expenses. In instances of extreme economic hardship involving extraordinary medical expenses not covered by insurance, the court or the jury may consider a deviation from the presumptive amount of child support for extraordinary medical expenses. Such expenses may include, but are not limited to, extraordinary medical expenses of the child or a parent of the child; provided, however, that any such deviation:

(I) Shall not act to leave a child unsupported; and

(II) May be ordered for a specific period of time measured in months.

When extraordinary medical expenses are claimed, the court or the jury shall consider the resources available for meeting such needs, including sources available from agencies and other adults.

(K) Parenting time.

(i) The child support obligation table is based upon expenditures for a child in intact households. The court may order or the jury may find by special interrogatory a deviation from the presumptive amount of child support when special circumstances make the presumptive amount of child support excessive or inadequate due to extended parenting time as set forth in the order of visitation, the child residing with both parents equally, or visitation rights not being utilized.

(ii) If the court or the jury determines that a parenting time deviation is applicable, then such deviation shall be included with all other deviations.

(iii) In accordance with subsection (d) of Code Section 19-11-8, if any action or claim for parenting time or a parenting time deviation is brought under this subparagraph, it shall be an action or claim solely between the custodial parent and the noncustodial parent, and not any third parties, including child support services.

(3) Nonspecific deviations. Deviations from the presumptive amount of child support may be appropriate for reasons in addition to those established under this subsection when the court or the jury finds it is in the best interest of the child.

(j) Involuntary loss of income.

(1) In the event a parent suffers an involuntary termination of employment, has an extended involuntary loss of average weekly hours, is involved in an organized strike, incurs a loss of health, becomes incarcerated, or similar involuntary adversity resulting in a loss of income of 25 percent or more, then the portion of child support attributable to lost income shall not accrue from the date of the service of the petition for modification, provided that service is made on the other parent. It shall not be considered an involuntary termination of employment if the parent has left the employer without good cause in connection with the parent's most recent work.

(2) In the event a modification action is filed pursuant to this subsection, the court shall make every effort to expedite hearing such action.

(3) The court may, at its discretion, phase in the new child support award over a period of up to one year with the phasing in being largely evenly distributed with at least an initial immediate adjustment of not less than 25 percent of the difference and at least one intermediate adjustment prior to the final adjustment at the end of the phase-in period.

(k) Modification.

(1) Except as provided in paragraph (2) of this subsection, a parent shall not have the right to petition for modification of the child support award regardless of the length of time since the establishment of the child support award unless there is a substantial change in either parent's income and financial status or the needs of the child.

(2) No petition to modify child support may be filed by either parent within a period of two years from the date of the final order on a previous petition to modify by the same parent except where:

(A) A noncustodial parent has failed to exercise the court ordered visitation;

(B) A noncustodial parent has exercised a greater amount of visitation than was provided in the court order; or

(C) The motion to modify is based upon an involuntary loss of income as set forth in subsection (j) of this Code section.

(3) (A) If there is a difference of at least 15 percent but less than 30 percent between a new award and a Georgia child support order entered prior to January 1, 2007, the court may, at its discretion, phase in the new child support award over a period of up to one year with the phasing in being largely evenly distributed with at least an initial immediate adjustment of not less than 25 percent of the difference and at least one intermediate adjustment prior to the final adjustment at the end of the phase-in period.

(B) If there is a difference of 30 percent or more between a new award and a Georgia child support order entered prior to January 1, 2007, the court may, at its discretion, phase in the new child support award over a period of up to two years with the phasing in being largely evenly distributed with at least an initial immediate adjustment of not less than 25 percent of the difference and at least one intermediate adjustment prior to the final adjustment at the end of the phase-in period.

(C) All child support service's case reviews and modifications shall proceed and be governed by Code Section 19-11-12. Subsequent changes to the child support obligation table shall be a reason to request a review for modification from child support services to the extent that such changes are consistent with the requirements of Code Section 19-11-12.

(4) A petition for modification shall be filed under the same rules of procedure applicable to divorce proceedings. The court may allow, upon motion, the temporary modification of a child support order pending the final trial on the petition. An order granting temporary modification shall be subject to revision by the court at any time before the final trial. A jury may be demanded on a petition for modification but the jury shall only be responsible for determining a parent's gross income and any deviations. In the hearing upon a petition for modification, testimony may be given and evidence introduced relative to the change of circumstances, income and financial status of either parent, or in the needs of the child. After hearing both parties and the evidence, the court may modify and revise the previous judgment, in accordance with the changed circumstances, income and financial status of either parent, or in the needs of the child, if such change or changes are satisfactorily proven so as to warrant the modification and revision and such modification and revisions are in the child's best interest. The court shall enter a written order specifying the basis for the modification, if any, and shall include all of the information set forth in paragraph (2) of subsection (c) of this Code section.

(5) In proceedings for the modification of a child support award pursuant to the provisions of this Code section, the court may award attorney's fees, costs, and expenses of litigation to the prevailing party as the interests of justice may require. Where a custodial parent prevails in an upward modification of child support based upon the noncustodial parent's failure to be available and willing to exercise court ordered visitation, reasonable and necessary attorney's fees and expenses of litigation shall be awarded to the custodial parent.

(l) Split parenting. In cases of split parenting, a worksheet shall be prepared separately by each custodial parent for each child for whom such parent is the custodial parent, and that worksheet shall be filed with the clerk of court. For each split parenting custodial situation, the court shall determine:

(1) Which parent is the obligor;
(2) The presumptive amount of child support;
(3) The actual award of child support, if different from the presumptive amount of child support;
(4) How and when the sum certain amount of child support owed shall be paid; and
(5) Any other child support responsibilities for each parent.

(m) Worksheets.

(1) Schedules and worksheets shall be prepared by the parties for purposes of calculating the amount of child support. In child support services cases in which neither parent prepared a worksheet, the court may rely on the worksheet prepared by child support services as a basis for its order. Information from the schedules shall be entered on the child support worksheet. The child support worksheets and any schedule that was prepared for the purpose of calculating the amount of child support shall be attached to the final court order or judgment; provided, however, that any order entered pursuant to Code Section 19-13-4 shall not be required to have such worksheets and schedules attached thereto.

(2) The child support worksheet and schedules shall be promulgated by the Georgia Child Support Commission.

(n) Child support obligation table. The child support obligation table shall be proposed by the Georgia Child Support Commission and shall be as codified in subsection (o) of this Code section.

(o) Georgia Schedule of Basic Child Support Obligations.

Georgia Schedule of Basic Child Support Obligations

Combined Adjusted Income	One Child	Two Children	Three Children	Four Children	Five Children	Six Children
$ 800.00	$ 197.00	$ 283.00	$ 330.00	$ 367.00	$ 404.00	$ 440.00
850.00	208.00	298.00	347.00	387.00	425.00	463.00
900.00	218.00	313.00	364.00	406.00	447.00	486.00
950.00	229.00	328.00	381.00	425.00	468.00	509.00

1,000.00	239.00	343.00	398.00	444.00	489.00	532.00
1,050.00	250.00	357.00	415.00	463.00	510.00	554.00
1,100.00	260.00	372.00	432.00	482.00	530.00	577.00
1,150.00	270.00	387.00	449.00	501.00	551.00	600.00
1,200.00	280.00	401.00	466.00	520.00	572.00	622.00
1,250.00	291.00	416.00	483.00	539.00	593.00	645.00
1,300.00	301.00	431.00	500.00	558.00	614.00	668.00
1,350.00	311.00	445.00	517.00	577.00	634.00	690.00
1,400.00	321.00	459.00	533.00	594.00	654.00	711.00
1,450.00	331.00	473.00	549.00	612.00	673.00	733.00
1,500.00	340.00	487.00	565.00	630.00	693.00	754.00
1,550.00	350.00	500.00	581.00	647.00	712.00	775.00
1,600.00	360.00	514.00	597.00	665.00	732.00	796.00
1,650.00	369.00	528.00	612.00	683.00	751.00	817.00
1,700.00	379.00	542.00	628.00	701.00	771.00	838.00
1,750.00	389.00	555.00	644.00	718.00	790.00	860.00
1,800.00	398.00	569.00	660.00	736.00	809.00	881.00
1,850.00	408.00	583.00	676.00	754.00	829.00	902.00
1,900.00	418.00	596.00	692.00	771.00	848.00	923.00
1,950.00	427.00	610.00	708.00	789.00	868.00	944.00
2,000.00	437.00	624.00	723.00	807.00	887.00	965.00
2,050.00	446.00	637.00	739.00	824.00	906.00	986.00
2,100.00	455.00	650.00	754.00	840.00	924.00	1,006.00
2,150.00	465.00	663.00	769.00	857.00	943.00	1,026.00
2,200.00	474.00	676.00	783.00	873.00	961.00	1,045.00
2,250.00	483.00	688.00	798.00	890.00	979.00	1,065.00
2,300.00	492.00	701.00	813.00	907.00	997.00	1,085.00
2,350.00	501.00	714.00	828.00	923.00	1,016.00	1,105.00
2,400.00	510.00	727.00	843.00	940.00	1,034.00	1,125.00
2,450.00	519.00	740.00	858.00	956.00	1,052.00	1,145.00
2,500.00	528.00	752.00	873.00	973.00	1,070.00	1,165.00
2,550.00	537.00	765.00	888.00	990.00	1,089.00	1,184.00
2,600.00	547.00	778.00	902.00	1,006.00	1,107.00	1,204.00
2,650.00	556.00	791.00	917.00	1,023.00	1,125.00	1,224.00
2,700.00	565.00	804.00	932.00	1,039.00	1,143.00	1,244.00
2,750.00	574.00	816.00	947.00	1,056.00	1,162.00	1,264.00
2,800.00	583.00	829.00	962.00	1,073.00	1,180.00	1,284.00
2,850.00	592.00	842.00	977.00	1,089.00	1,198.00	1,303.00
2,900.00	601.00	855.00	992.00	1,106.00	1,216.00	1,323.00
2,950.00	611.00	868.00	1,006.00	1,122.00	1,234.00	1,343.00
3,000.00	620.00	881.00	1,021.00	1,139.00	1,253.00	1,363.00
3,050.00	629.00	893.00	1,036.00	1,155.00	1,271.00	1,383.00
3,100.00	638.00	906.00	1,051.00	1,172.00	1,289.00	1,402.00
3,150.00	647.00	919.00	1,066.00	1,188.00	1,307.00	1,422.00
3,200.00	655.00	930.00	1,079.00	1,203.00	1,323.00	1,440.00
3,250.00	663.00	941.00	1,092.00	1,217.00	1,339.00	1,457.00
3,300.00	671.00	952.00	1,104.00	1,231.00	1,355.00	1,474.00
3,350.00	679.00	963.00	1,117.00	1,246.00	1,370.00	1,491.00
3,400.00	687.00	974.00	1,130.00	1,260.00	1,386.00	1,508.00
3,450.00	694.00	985.00	1,143.00	1,274.00	1,402.00	1,525.00
3,500.00	702.00	996.00	1,155.00	1,288.00	1,417.00	1,542.00
3,550.00	710.00	1,008.00	1,168.00	1,303.00	1,433.00	1,559.00
3,600.00	718.00	1,019.00	1,181.00	1,317.00	1,448.00	1,576.00
3,650.00	726.00	1,030.00	1,194.00	1,331.00	1,464.00	1,593.00
3,700.00	734.00	1,041.00	1,207.00	1,345.00	1,480.00	1,610.00
3,750.00	741.00	1,051.00	1,219.00	1,359.00	1,495.00	1,627.00
3,800.00	749.00	1,062.00	1,231.00	1,373.00	1,510.00	1,643.00
3,850.00	756.00	1,072.00	1,243.00	1,386.00	1,525.00	1,659.00
3,900.00	764.00	1,083.00	1,255.00	1,400.00	1,540.00	1,675.00
3,950.00	771.00	1,093.00	1,267.00	1,413.00	1,555.00	1,691.00
4,000.00	779.00	1,104.00	1,280.00	1,427.00	1,569.00	1,707.00
4,050.00	786.00	1,114.00	1,292.00	1,440.00	1,584.00	1,724.00
4,100.00	794.00	1,125.00	1,304.00	1,454.00	1,599.00	1,740.00
4,150.00	801.00	1,135.00	1,316.00	1,467.00	1,614.00	1,756.00

4,200.00	809.00	1,146.00	1,328.00	1,481.00	1,629.00	1,772.00
4,250.00	816.00	1,156.00	1,340.00	1,494.00	1,643.00	1,788.00
4,300.00	824.00	1,167.00	1,352.00	1,508.00	1,658.00	1,804.00
4,350.00	831.00	1,177.00	1,364.00	1,521.00	1,673.00	1,820.00
4,400.00	839.00	1,188.00	1,376.00	1,534.00	1,688.00	1,836.00
4,450.00	846.00	1,198.00	1,388.00	1,548.00	1,703.00	1,853.00
4,500.00	853.00	1,209.00	1,400.00	1,561.00	1,718.00	1,869.00
4,550.00	861.00	1,219.00	1,412.00	1,575.00	1,732.00	1,885.00
4,600.00	868.00	1,230.00	1,425.00	1,588.00	1,747.00	1,901.00
4,650.00	876.00	1,240.00	1,437.00	1,602.00	1,762.00	1,917.00
4,700.00	883.00	1,251.00	1,449.00	1,615.00	1,777.00	1,933.00
4,750.00	891.00	1,261.00	1,461.00	1,629.00	1,792.00	1,949.00
4,800.00	898.00	1,271.00	1,473.00	1,642.00	1,807.00	1,966.00
4,850.00	906.00	1,282.00	1,485.00	1,656.00	1,821.00	1,982.00
4,900.00	911.00	1,289.00	1,493.00	1,664.00	1,831.00	1,992.00
4,950.00	914.00	1,293.00	1,496.00	1,668.00	1,835.00	1,997.00
5,000.00	917.00	1,297.00	1,500.00	1,672.00	1,839.00	2,001.00
5,050.00	921.00	1,300.00	1,503.00	1,676.00	1,844.00	2,006.00
5,100.00	924.00	1,304.00	1,507.00	1,680.00	1,848.00	2,011.00
5,150.00	927.00	1,308.00	1,510.00	1,684.00	1,852.00	2,015.00
5,200.00	930.00	1,312.00	1,514.00	1,688.00	1,857.00	2,020.00
5,250.00	934.00	1,316.00	1,517.00	1,692.00	1,861.00	2,025.00
5,300.00	937.00	1,320.00	1,521.00	1,696.00	1,865.00	2,029.00
5,350.00	940.00	1,323.00	1,524.00	1,700.00	1,870.00	2,034.00
5,400.00	943.00	1,327.00	1,528.00	1,704.00	1,874.00	2,039.00
5,450.00	947.00	1,331.00	1,531.00	1,708.00	1,878.00	2,044.00
5,500.00	950.00	1,335.00	1,535.00	1,711.00	1,883.00	2,048.00
5,550.00	953.00	1,339.00	1,538.00	1,715.00	1,887.00	2,053.00
5,600.00	956.00	1,342.00	1,542.00	1,719.00	1,891.00	2,058.00
5,650.00	960.00	1,347.00	1,546.00	1,724.00	1,896.00	2,063.00
5,700.00	964.00	1,352.00	1,552.00	1,731.00	1,904.00	2,071.00
5,750.00	968.00	1,357.00	1,558.00	1,737.00	1,911.00	2,079.00
5,800.00	971.00	1,363.00	1,564.00	1,744.00	1,918.00	2,087.00
5,850.00	975.00	1,368.00	1,570.00	1,750.00	1,925.00	2,094.00
5,900.00	979.00	1,373.00	1,575.00	1,757.00	1,932.00	2,102.00
5,950.00	983.00	1,379.00	1,581.00	1,763.00	1,939.00	2,110.00
6,000.00	987.00	1,384.00	1,587.00	1,770.00	1,947.00	2,118.00
6,050.00	991.00	1,389.00	1,593.00	1,776.00	1,954.00	2,126.00
6,100.00	995.00	1,394.00	1,599.00	1,783.00	1,961.00	2,133.00
6,150.00	999.00	1,400.00	1,605.00	1,789.00	1,968.00	2,141.00
6,200.00	1,003.00	1,405.00	1,610.00	1,796.00	1,975.00	2,149.00
6,250.00	1,007.00	1,410.00	1,616.00	1,802.00	1,982.00	2,157.00
6,300.00	1,011.00	1,416.00	1,622.00	1,809.00	1,989.00	2,164.00
6,350.00	1,015.00	1,421.00	1,628.00	1,815.00	1,996.00	2,172.00
6,400.00	1,018.00	1,426.00	1,633.00	1,821.00	2,003.00	2,180.00
6,450.00	1,023.00	1,432.00	1,639.00	1,828.00	2,011.00	2,188.00
6,500.00	1,027.00	1,437.00	1,646.00	1,835.00	2,018.00	2,196.00
6,550.00	1,031.00	1,442.00	1,652.00	1,841.00	2,026.00	2,204.00
6,600.00	1,035.00	1,448.00	1,658.00	1,848.00	2,033.00	2,212.00
6,650.00	1,039.00	1,453.00	1,664.00	1,855.00	2,040.00	2,220.00
6,700.00	1,043.00	1,459.00	1,670.00	1,862.00	2,048.00	2,228.00
6,750.00	1,047.00	1,464.00	1,676.00	1,869.00	2,055.00	2,236.00
6,800.00	1,051.00	1,470.00	1,682.00	1,875.00	2,063.00	2,244.00
6,850.00	1,055.00	1,475.00	1,688.00	1,882.00	2,070.00	2,252.00
6,900.00	1,059.00	1,480.00	1,694.00	1,889.00	2,078.00	2,260.00
6,950.00	1,063.00	1,486.00	1,700.00	1,896.00	2,085.00	2,269.00
7,000.00	1,067.00	1,491.00	1,706.00	1,902.00	2,092.00	2,277.00
7,050.00	1,071.00	1,497.00	1,712.00	1,909.00	2,100.00	2,285.00
7,100.00	1,075.00	1,502.00	1,718.00	1,916.00	2,107.00	2,293.00
7,150.00	1,079.00	1,508.00	1,724.00	1,923.00	2,115.00	2,301.00
7,200.00	1,083.00	1,513.00	1,730.00	1,929.00	2,122.00	2,309.00
7,250.00	1,087.00	1,518.00	1,736.00	1,936.00	2,130.00	2,317.00
7,300.00	1,092.00	1,524.00	1,742.00	1,943.00	2,137.00	2,325.00
7,350.00	1,096.00	1,529.00	1,748.00	1,950.00	2,144.00	2,333.00

7,400.00	1,100.00	1,535.00	1,755.00	1,956.00	2,152.00	2,341.00
7,450.00	1,104.00	1,540.00	1,761.00	1,963.00	2,159.00	2,349.00
7,500.00	1,108.00	1,546.00	1,767.00	1,970.00	2,167.00	2,357.00
7,550.00	1,112.00	1,552.00	1,773.00	1,977.00	2,175.00	2,366.00
7,600.00	1,116.00	1,556.00	1,778.00	1,983.00	2,181.00	2,373.00
7,650.00	1,117.00	1,557.00	1,779.00	1,984.00	2,182.00	2,375.00
7,700.00	1,118.00	1,559.00	1,781.00	1,986.00	2,184.00	2,376.00
7,750.00	1,119.00	1,560.00	1,782.00	1,987.00	2,186.00	2,378.00
7,800.00	1,120.00	1,562.00	1,784.00	1,989.00	2,188.00	2,380.00
7,850.00	1,122.00	1,563.00	1,785.00	1,990.00	2,189.00	2,382.00
7,900.00	1,123.00	1,565.00	1,786.00	1,992.00	2,191.00	2,384.00
7,950.00	1,124.00	1,566.00	1,788.00	1,993.00	2,193.00	2,386.00
8,000.00	1,125.00	1,567.00	1,789.00	1,995.00	2,194.00	2,387.00
8,050.00	1,127.00	1,569.00	1,790.00	1,996.00	2,196.00	2,389.00
8,100.00	1,128.00	1,570.00	1,792.00	1,998.00	2,198.00	2,391.00
8,150.00	1,129.00	1,572.00	1,793.00	1,999.00	2,199.00	2,393.00
8,200.00	1,130.00	1,573.00	1,795.00	2,001.00	2,201.00	2,395.00
8,250.00	1,131.00	1,575.00	1,796.00	2,003.00	2,203.00	2,397.00
8,300.00	1,133.00	1,576.00	1,797.00	2,004.00	2,204.00	2,398.00
8,350.00	1,134.00	1,578.00	1,799.00	2,006.00	2,206.00	2,400.00
8,400.00	1,135.00	1,579.00	1,800.00	2,007.00	2,208.00	2,402.00
8,450.00	1,136.00	1,580.00	1,802.00	2,009.00	2,210.00	2,404.00
8,500.00	1,138.00	1,582.00	1,803.00	2,010.00	2,211.00	2,406.00
8,550.00	1,139.00	1,583.00	1,804.00	2,012.00	2,213.00	2,408.00
8,600.00	1,140.00	1,585.00	1,806.00	2,013.00	2,215.00	2,410.00
8,650.00	1,141.00	1,586.00	1,807.00	2,015.00	2,216.00	2,411.00
8,700.00	1,142.00	1,588.00	1,808.00	2,016.00	2,218.00	2,413.00
8,750.00	1,144.00	1,589.00	1,810.00	2,018.00	2,220.00	2,415.00
8,800.00	1,145.00	1,591.00	1,811.00	2,019.00	2,221.00	2,417.00
8,850.00	1,146.00	1,592.00	1,813.00	2,021.00	2,223.00	2,419.00
8,900.00	1,147.00	1,593.00	1,814.00	2,023.00	2,225.00	2,421.00
8,950.00	1,149.00	1,595.00	1,815.00	2,024.00	2,226.00	2,422.00
9,000.00	1,150.00	1,596.00	1,817.00	2,026.00	2,228.00	2,424.00
9,050.00	1,153.00	1,601.00	1,822.00	2,032.00	2,235.00	2,431.00
9,100.00	1,159.00	1,609.00	1,831.00	2,042.00	2,246.00	2,443.00
9,150.00	1,164.00	1,617.00	1,840.00	2,052.00	2,257.00	2,455.00
9,200.00	1,170.00	1,624.00	1,849.00	2,062.00	2,268.00	2,467.00
9,250.00	1,175.00	1,632.00	1,858.00	2,071.00	2,279.00	2,479.00
9,300.00	1,181.00	1,640.00	1,867.00	2,081.00	2,290.00	2,491.00
9,350.00	1,187.00	1,648.00	1,876.00	2,091.00	2,301.00	2,503.00
9,400.00	1,192.00	1,656.00	1,885.00	2,101.00	2,311.00	2,515.00
9,450.00	1,198.00	1,663.00	1,894.00	2,111.00	2,322.00	2,527.00
9,500.00	1,203.00	1,671.00	1,902.00	2,121.00	2,333.00	2,539.00
9,550.00	1,209.00	1,679.00	1,911.00	2,131.00	2,344.00	2,551.00
9,600.00	1,214.00	1,687.00	1,920.00	2,141.00	2,355.00	2,563.00
9,650.00	1,220.00	1,694.00	1,929.00	2,151.00	2,366.00	2,574.00
9,700.00	1,226.00	1,702.00	1,938.00	2,161.00	2,377.00	2,586.00
9,750.00	1,231.00	1,710.00	1,947.00	2,171.00	2,388.00	2,598.00
9,800.00	1,237.00	1,718.00	1,956.00	2,181.00	2,399.00	2,610.00
9,850.00	1,242.00	1,725.00	1,965.00	2,191.00	2,410.00	2,622.00
9,900.00	1,248.00	1,733.00	1,974.00	2,201.00	2,421.00	2,634.00
9,950.00	1,253.00	1,741.00	1,983.00	2,211.00	2,432.00	2,646.00
10,000.00	1,259.00	1,749.00	1,992.00	2,221.00	2,443.00	2,658.00
10,050.00	1,264.00	1,757.00	2,001.00	2,231.00	2,454.00	2,670.00
10,100.00	1,270.00	1,764.00	2,010.00	2,241.00	2,465.00	2,682.00
10,150.00	1,276.00	1,772.00	2,019.00	2,251.00	2,476.00	2,694.00
10,200.00	1,281.00	1,780.00	2,028.00	2,261.00	2,487.00	2,706.00
10,250.00	1,287.00	1,788.00	2,036.00	2,271.00	2,498.00	2,718.00
10,300.00	1,292.00	1,795.00	2,045.00	2,281.00	2,509.00	2,729.00
10,350.00	1,298.00	1,803.00	2,054.00	2,291.00	2,520.00	2,741.00
10,400.00	1,303.00	1,811.00	2,063.00	2,301.00	2,531.00	2,753.00
10,450.00	1,309.00	1,819.00	2,072.00	2,311.00	2,542.00	2,765.00
10,500.00	1,313.00	1,825.00	2,079.00	2,318.00	2,550.00	2,774.00
10,550.00	1,317.00	1,830.00	2,085.00	2,325.00	2,557.00	2,782.00

10,600.00	1,321.00	1,835.00	2,091.00	2,331.00	2,564.00	2,790.00
10,650.00	1,325.00	1,841.00	2,096.00	2,338.00	2,571.00	2,798.00
10,700.00	1,329.00	1,846.00	2,102.00	2,344.00	2,578.00	2,805.00
10,750.00	1,332.00	1,851.00	2,108.00	2,351.00	2,586.00	2,813.00
10,800.00	1,336.00	1,856.00	2,114.00	2,357.00	2,593.00	2,821.00
10,850.00	1,340.00	1,862.00	2,120.00	2,364.00	2,600.00	2,829.00
10,900.00	1,344.00	1,867.00	2,126.00	2,370.00	2,607.00	2,836.00
10,950.00	1,348.00	1,872.00	2,131.00	2,377.00	2,614.00	2,844.00
11,000.00	1,351.00	1,877.00	2,137.00	2,383.00	2,621.00	2,852.00
11,050.00	1,355.00	1,883.00	2,143.00	2,390.00	2,628.00	2,860.00
11,100.00	1,359.00	1,888.00	2,149.00	2,396.00	2,636.00	2,868.00
11,150.00	1,363.00	1,893.00	2,155.00	2,403.00	2,643.00	2,875.00
11,200.00	1,367.00	1,898.00	2,161.00	2,409.00	2,650.00	2,883.00
11,250.00	1,371.00	1,904.00	2,166.00	2,415.00	2,657.00	2,891.00
11,300.00	1,374.00	1,909.00	2,172.00	2,422.00	2,664.00	2,899.00
11,350.00	1,378.00	1,914.00	2,178.00	2,428.00	2,671.00	2,906.00
11,400.00	1,382.00	1,919.00	2,184.00	2,435.00	2,678.00	2,914.00
11,450.00	1,386.00	1,925.00	2,190.00	2,441.00	2,686.00	2,922.00
11,500.00	1,390.00	1,930.00	2,195.00	2,448.00	2,693.00	2,930.00
11,550.00	1,394.00	1,935.00	2,201.00	2,454.00	2,700.00	2,938.00
11,600.00	1,397.00	1,940.00	2,207.00	2,461.00	2,707.00	2,945.00
11,650.00	1,401.00	1,946.00	2,213.00	2,467.00	2,714.00	2,953.00
11,700.00	1,405.00	1,951.00	2,219.00	2,474.00	2,721.00	2,961.00
11,750.00	1,409.00	1,956.00	2,225.00	2,480.00	2,728.00	2,969.00
11,800.00	1,413.00	1,961.00	2,230.00	2,487.00	2,736.00	2,976.00
11,850.00	1,417.00	1,967.00	2,236.00	2,493.00	2,743.00	2,984.00
11,900.00	1,420.00	1,972.00	2,242.00	2,500.00	2,750.00	2,992.00
11,950.00	1,424.00	1,977.00	2,248.00	2,506.00	2,757.00	3,000.00
12,000.00	1,428.00	1,982.00	2,254.00	2,513.00	2,764.00	3,007.00
12,050.00	1,432.00	1,988.00	2,260.00	2,519.00	2,771.00	3,015.00
12,100.00	1,436.00	1,993.00	2,265.00	2,526.00	2,779.00	3,023.00
12,150.00	1,439.00	1,998.00	2,271.00	2,532.00	2,786.00	3,031.00
12,200.00	1,443.00	2,003.00	2,277.00	2,539.00	2,793.00	3,039.00
12,250.00	1,447.00	2,009.00	2,283.00	2,545.00	2,800.00	3,046.00
12,300.00	1,451.00	2,014.00	2,289.00	2,552.00	2,807.00	3,054.00
12,350.00	1,455.00	2,019.00	2,295.00	2,558.00	2,814.00	3,062.00
12,400.00	1,459.00	2,024.00	2,300.00	2,565.00	2,821.00	3,070.00
12,450.00	1,462.00	2,030.00	2,306.00	2,571.00	2,829.00	3,077.00
12,500.00	1,466.00	2,035.00	2,312.00	2,578.00	2,836.00	3,085.00
12,550.00	1,470.00	2,040.00	2,318.00	2,584.00	2,843.00	3,093.00
12,600.00	1,474.00	2,045.00	2,324.00	2,591.00	2,850.00	3,101.00
12,650.00	1,477.00	2,050.00	2,329.00	2,597.00	2,857.00	3,108.00
12,700.00	1,481.00	2,055.00	2,335.00	2,603.00	2,863.00	3,115.00
12,750.00	1,484.00	2,060.00	2,340.00	2,609.00	2,870.00	3,123.00
12,800.00	1,487.00	2,064.00	2,345.00	2,615.00	2,877.00	3,130.00
12,850.00	1,491.00	2,069.00	2,351.00	2,621.00	2,883.00	3,137.00
12,900.00	1,494.00	2,074.00	2,356.00	2,627.00	2,890.00	3,144.00
12,950.00	1,497.00	2,078.00	2,361.00	2,633.00	2,896.00	3,151.00
13,000.00	1,501.00	2,083.00	2,367.00	2,639.00	2,903.00	3,158.00
13,050.00	1,504.00	2,087.00	2,372.00	2,645.00	2,909.00	3,165.00
13,100.00	1,507.00	2,092.00	2,377.00	2,651.00	2,916.00	3,172.00
13,150.00	1,510.00	2,097.00	2,383.00	2,657.00	2,922.00	3,180.00
13,200.00	1,514.00	2,101.00	2,388.00	2,663.00	2,929.00	3,187.00
13,250.00	1,517.00	2,106.00	2,393.00	2,668.00	2,935.00	3,193.00
13,300.00	1,520.00	2,110.00	2,398.00	2,674.00	2,941.00	3,200.00
13,350.00	1,523.00	2,114.00	2,403.00	2,679.00	2,947.00	3,206.00
13,400.00	1,526.00	2,118.00	2,408.00	2,685.00	2,953.00	3,213.00
13,450.00	1,529.00	2,123.00	2,413.00	2,690.00	2,959.00	3,220.00
13,500.00	1,532.00	2,127.00	2,418.00	2,696.00	2,965.00	3,226.00
13,550.00	1,535.00	2,131.00	2,423.00	2,701.00	2,971.00	3,233.00
13,600.00	1,538.00	2,136.00	2,428.00	2,707.00	2,977.00	3,239.00
13,650.00	1,541.00	2,140.00	2,432.00	2,712.00	2,983.00	3,246.00
13,700.00	1,544.00	2,144.00	2,437.00	2,718.00	2,989.00	3,253.00
13,750.00	1,547.00	2,148.00	2,442.00	2,723.00	2,996.00	3,259.00

13,800.00	1,550.00	2,153.00	2,447.00	2,729.00	3,002.00	3,266.00
13,850.00	1,553.00	2,157.00	2,452.00	2,734.00	3,008.00	3,272.00
13,900.00	1,556.00	2,161.00	2,457.00	2,740.00	3,014.00	3,279.00
13,950.00	1,559.00	2,166.00	2,462.00	2,745.00	3,020.00	3,285.00
14,000.00	1,562.00	2,170.00	2,467.00	2,751.00	3,026.00	3,292.00
14,050.00	1,565.00	2,174.00	2,472.00	2,756.00	3,032.00	3,299.00
14,100.00	1,568.00	2,178.00	2,477.00	2,762.00	3,038.00	3,305.00
14,150.00	1,571.00	2,183.00	2,482.00	2,767.00	3,044.00	3,312.00
14,200.00	1,574.00	2,187.00	2,487.00	2,773.00	3,050.00	3,318.00
14,250.00	1,577.00	2,191.00	2,492.00	2,778.00	3,056.00	3,325.00
14,300.00	1,581.00	2,195.00	2,497.00	2,784.00	3,062.00	3,332.00
14,350.00	1,584.00	2,200.00	2,502.00	2,789.00	3,068.00	3,338.00
14,400.00	1,587.00	2,204.00	2,506.00	2,795.00	3,074.00	3,345.00
14,450.00	1,590.00	2,208.00	2,511.00	2,800.00	3,080.00	3,351.00
14,500.00	1,593.00	2,213.00	2,516.00	2,806.00	3,086.00	3,358.00
14,550.00	1,596.00	2,217.00	2,521.00	2,811.00	3,092.00	3,365.00
14,600.00	1,599.00	2,221.00	2,526.00	2,817.00	3,098.00	3,371.00
14,650.00	1,602.00	2,225.00	2,531.00	2,822.00	3,104.00	3,378.00
14,700.00	1,605.00	2,230.00	2,536.00	2,828.00	3,111.00	3,384.00
14,750.00	1,608.00	2,234.00	2,541.00	2,833.00	3,117.00	3,391.00
14,800.00	1,611.00	2,238.00	2,546.00	2,839.00	3,123.00	3,397.00
14,850.00	1,614.00	2,243.00	2,551.00	2,844.00	3,129.00	3,404.00
14,900.00	1,617.00	2,247.00	2,556.00	2,850.00	3,135.00	3,411.00
14,950.00	1,620.00	2,251.00	2,561.00	2,855.00	3,141.00	3,417.00
15,000.00	1,623.00	2,255.00	2,566.00	2,861.00	3,147.00	3,424.00
15,050.00	1,626.00	2,260.00	2,571.00	2,866.00	3,153.00	3,430.00
15,100.00	1,629.00	2,264.00	2,576.00	2,872.00	3,159.00	3,437.00
15,150.00	1,632.00	2,268.00	2,581.00	2,877.00	3,165.00	3,444.00
15,200.00	1,635.00	2,272.00	2,585.00	2,883.00	3,171.00	3,450.00
15,250.00	1,638.00	2,277.00	2,590.00	2,888.00	3,177.00	3,457.00
15,300.00	1,641.00	2,281.00	2,595.00	2,894.00	3,183.00	3,463.00
15,350.00	1,644.00	2,285.00	2,600.00	2,899.00	3,189.00	3,470.00
15,400.00	1,647.00	2,290.00	2,605.00	2,905.00	3,195.00	3,476.00
15,450.00	1,650.00	2,294.00	2,610.00	2,910.00	3,201.00	3,483.00
15,500.00	1,653.00	2,298.00	2,615.00	2,916.00	3,207.00	3,490.00
15,550.00	1,656.00	2,302.00	2,620.00	2,921.00	3,213.00	3,496.00
15,600.00	1,659.00	2,307.00	2,625.00	2,927.00	3,219.00	3,503.00
15,650.00	1,663.00	2,311.00	2,630.00	2,932.00	3,226.00	3,509.00
15,700.00	1,666.00	2,315.00	2,635.00	2,938.00	3,232.00	3,516.00
15,750.00	1,669.00	2,320.00	2,640.00	2,943.00	3,238.00	3,523.00
15,800.00	1,672.00	2,324.00	2,645.00	2,949.00	3,244.00	3,529.00
15,850.00	1,675.00	2,328.00	2,650.00	2,954.00	3,250.00	3,536.00
15,900.00	1,678.00	2,332.00	2,655.00	2,960.00	3,256.00	3,542.00
15,950.00	1,681.00	2,337.00	2,659.00	2,965.00	3,262.00	3,549.00
16,000.00	1,684.00	2,341.00	2,664.00	2,971.00	3,268.00	3,555.00
16,050.00	1,687.00	2,345.00	2,669.00	2,976.00	3,274.00	3,562.00
16,100.00	1,690.00	2,349.00	2,674.00	2,982.00	3,280.00	3,569.00
16,150.00	1,692.00	2,353.00	2,678.00	2,986.00	3,285.00	3,574.00
16,200.00	1,695.00	2,356.00	2,682.00	2,990.00	3,289.00	3,579.00
16,250.00	1,698.00	2,360.00	2,686.00	2,994.00	3,294.00	3,584.00
16,300.00	1,700.00	2,363.00	2,689.00	2,999.00	3,299.00	3,589.00
16,350.00	1,703.00	2,367.00	2,693.00	3,003.00	3,303.00	3,594.00
16,400.00	1,706.00	2,370.00	2,697.00	3,007.00	3,308.00	3,599.00
16,450.00	1,708.00	2,374.00	2,701.00	3,011.00	3,313.00	3,604.00
16,500.00	1,711.00	2,377.00	2,705.00	3,016.00	3,317.00	3,609.00
16,550.00	1,714.00	2,381.00	2,708.00	3,020.00	3,322.00	3,614.00
16,600.00	1,716.00	2,384.00	2,712.00	3,024.00	3,327.00	3,619.00
16,650.00	1,719.00	2,388.00	2,716.00	3,028.00	3,331.00	3,624.00
16,700.00	1,722.00	2,391.00	2,720.00	3,033.00	3,336.00	3,630.00
16,750.00	1,724.00	2,395.00	2,724.00	3,037.00	3,341.00	3,635.00
16,800.00	1,727.00	2,398.00	2,728.00	3,041.00	3,345.00	3,640.00
16,850.00	1,730.00	2,402.00	2,731.00	3,045.00	3,350.00	3,645.00
16,900.00	1,732.00	2,405.00	2,735.00	3,050.00	3,355.00	3,650.00
16,950.00	1,735.00	2,409.00	2,739.00	3,054.00	3,359.00	3,655.00

17,000.00	1,737.00	2,412.00	2,743.00	3,058.00	3,364.00	3,660.00
17,050.00	1,740.00	2,416.00	2,747.00	3,062.00	3,369.00	3,665.00
17,100.00	1,743.00	2,419.00	2,750.00	3,067.00	3,373.00	3,670.00
17,150.00	1,745.00	2,423.00	2,754.00	3,071.00	3,378.00	3,675.00
17,200.00	1,748.00	2,426.00	2,758.00	3,075.00	3,383.00	3,680.00
17,250.00	1,751.00	2,430.00	2,762.00	3,079.00	3,387.00	3,685.00
17,300.00	1,753.00	2,433.00	2,766.00	3,084.00	3,392.00	3,691.00
17,350.00	1,756.00	2,437.00	2,769.00	3,088.00	3,397.00	3,696.00
17,400.00	1,759.00	2,440.00	2,773.00	3,092.00	3,401.00	3,701.00
17,450.00	1,761.00	2,444.00	2,777.00	3,096.00	3,406.00	3,706.00
17,500.00	1,764.00	2,447.00	2,781.00	3,101.00	3,411.00	3,711.00
17,550.00	1,767.00	2,451.00	2,785.00	3,105.00	3,415.00	3,716.00
17,600.00	1,769.00	2,454.00	2,788.00	3,109.00	3,420.00	3,721.00
17,650.00	1,772.00	2,458.00	2,792.00	3,113.00	3,425.00	3,726.00
17,700.00	1,774.00	2,461.00	2,796.00	3,118.00	3,429.00	3,731.00
17,750.00	1,777.00	2,465.00	2,800.00	3,122.00	3,434.00	3,736.00
17,800.00	1,780.00	2,468.00	2,804.00	3,126.00	3,439.00	3,741.00
17,850.00	1,782.00	2,472.00	2,808.00	3,130.00	3,443.00	3,746.00
17,900.00	1,785.00	2,475.00	2,811.00	3,135.00	3,448.00	3,752.00
17,950.00	1,788.00	2,478.00	2,815.00	3,139.00	3,453.00	3,757.00
18,000.00	1,790.00	2,482.00	2,819.00	3,143.00	3,457.00	3,762.00
18,050.00	1,793.00	2,485.00	2,823.00	3,147.00	3,462.00	3,767.00
18,100.00	1,796.00	2,489.00	2,827.00	3,152.00	3,467.00	3,772.00
18,150.00	1,798.00	2,492.00	2,830.00	3,156.00	3,471.00	3,777.00
18,200.00	1,801.00	2,496.00	2,834.00	3,160.00	3,476.00	3,782.00
18,250.00	1,804.00	2,499.00	2,838.00	3,164.00	3,481.00	3,787.00
18,300.00	1,806.00	2,503.00	2,842.00	3,169.00	3,485.00	3,792.00
18,350.00	1,809.00	2,506.00	2,846.00	3,173.00	3,490.00	3,797.00
18,400.00	1,812.00	2,510.00	2,849.00	3,177.00	3,495.00	3,802.00
18,450.00	1,814.00	2,513.00	2,853.00	3,181.00	3,499.00	3,807.00
18,500.00	1,817.00	2,517.00	2,857.00	3,186.00	3,504.00	3,813.00
18,550.00	1,819.00	2,520.00	2,861.00	3,190.00	3,509.00	3,818.00
18,600.00	1,822.00	2,524.00	2,865.00	3,194.00	3,513.00	3,823.00
18,650.00	1,825.00	2,527.00	2,868.00	3,198.00	3,518.00	3,828.00
18,700.00	1,827.00	2,531.00	2,872.00	3,203.00	3,523.00	3,833.00
18,750.00	1,830.00	2,534.00	2,876.00	3,207.00	3,528.00	3,838.00
18,800.00	1,833.00	2,538.00	2,880.00	3,211.00	3,532.00	3,843.00
18,850.00	1,835.00	2,541.00	2,884.00	3,215.00	3,537.00	3,848.00
18,900.00	1,838.00	2,545.00	2,888.00	3,220.00	3,542.00	3,853.00
18,950.00	1,841.00	2,548.00	2,891.00	3,224.00	3,546.00	3,858.00
19,000.00	1,843.00	2,552.00	2,895.00	3,228.00	3,551.00	3,863.00
19,050.00	1,846.00	2,555.00	2,899.00	3,232.00	3,556.00	3,868.00
19,100.00	1,849.00	2,559.00	2,903.00	3,237.00	3,560.00	3,874.00
19,150.00	1,851.00	2,562.00	2,907.00	3,241.00	3,565.00	3,879.00
19,200.00	1,854.00	2,566.00	2,910.00	3,245.00	3,570.00	3,884.00
19,250.00	1,856.00	2,569.00	2,914.00	3,249.00	3,574.00	3,889.00
19,300.00	1,859.00	2,573.00	2,918.00	3,254.00	3,579.00	3,894.00
19,350.00	1,862.00	2,576.00	2,922.00	3,258.00	3,584.00	3,899.00
19,400.00	1,864.00	2,580.00	2,926.00	3,262.00	3,588.00	3,904.00
19,450.00	1,867.00	2,583.00	2,929.00	3,266.00	3,593.00	3,909.00
19,500.00	1,870.00	2,587.00	2,933.00	3,271.00	3,598.00	3,914.00
19,550.00	1,872.00	2,590.00	2,937.00	3,275.00	3,602.00	3,919.00
19,600.00	1,875.00	2,594.00	2,941.00	3,279.00	3,607.00	3,924.00
19,650.00	1,878.00	2,597.00	2,945.00	3,283.00	3,612.00	3,929.00
19,700.00	1,880.00	2,601.00	2,948.00	3,288.00	3,616.00	3,935.00
19,750.00	1,883.00	2,604.00	2,952.00	3,292.00	3,621.00	3,940.00
19,800.00	1,886.00	2,608.00	2,956.00	3,296.00	3,626.00	3,945.00
19,850.00	1,888.00	2,611.00	2,960.00	3,300.00	3,630.00	3,950.00
19,900.00	1,891.00	2,615.00	2,964.00	3,305.00	3,635.00	3,955.00
19,950.00	1,893.00	2,618.00	2,967.00	3,309.00	3,640.00	3,960.00
20,000.00	1,896.00	2,622.00	2,971.00	3,313.00	3,644.00	3,965.00
20,050.00	1,899.00	2,625.00	2,975.00	3,317.00	3,649.00	3,970.00
20,100.00	1,901.00	2,628.00	2,979.00	3,321.00	3,654.00	3,975.00
20,150.00	1,904.00	2,632.00	2,983.00	3,326.00	3,658.00	3,980.00

20,200.00	1,907.00	2,635.00	2,987.00	3,330.00	3,663.00	3,985.00
20,250.00	1,909.00	2,639.00	2,990.00	3,334.00	3,668.00	3,990.00
20,300.00	1,912.00	2,642.00	2,994.00	3,338.00	3,672.00	3,996.00
20,350.00	1,915.00	2,646.00	2,998.00	3,343.00	3,677.00	4,001.00
20,400.00	1,917.00	2,649.00	3,002.00	3,347.00	3,682.00	4,006.00
20,450.00	1,920.00	2,653.00	3,006.00	3,351.00	3,686.00	4,011.00
20,500.00	1,923.00	2,656.00	3,009.00	3,355.00	3,691.00	4,016.00
20,550.00	1,925.00	2,660.00	3,013.00	3,360.00	3,696.00	4,021.00
20,600.00	1,928.00	2,663.00	3,017.00	3,364.00	3,700.00	4,026.00
20,650.00	1,931.00	2,667.00	3,021.00	3,368.00	3,705.00	4,031.00
20,700.00	1,933.00	2,670.00	3,025.00	3,372.00	3,710.00	4,036.00
20,750.00	1,936.00	2,674.00	3,028.00	3,377.00	3,714.00	4,041.00
20,800.00	1,938.00	2,677.00	3,032.00	3,381.00	3,719.00	4,046.00
20,850.00	1,941.00	2,681.00	3,036.00	3,385.00	3,724.00	4,051.00
20,900.00	1,944.00	2,684.00	3,040.00	3,389.00	3,728.00	4,056.00
20,950.00	1,946.00	2,688.00	3,044.00	3,394.00	3,733.00	4,062.00
21,000.00	1,949.00	2,691.00	3,047.00	3,398.00	3,738.00	4,067.00
21,050.00	1,952.00	2,695.00	3,051.00	3,402.00	3,742.00	4,072.00
21,100.00	1,954.00	2,698.00	3,055.00	3,406.00	3,747.00	4,077.00
21,150.00	1,957.00	2,702.00	3,059.00	3,411.00	3,752.00	4,082.00
21,200.00	1,960.00	2,705.00	3,063.00	3,415.00	3,756.00	4,087.00
21,250.00	1,962.00	2,709.00	3,067.00	3,419.00	3,761.00	4,092.00
21,300.00	1,965.00	2,712.00	3,070.00	3,423.00	3,766.00	4,097.00
21,350.00	1,968.00	2,716.00	3,074.00	3,428.00	3,770.00	4,102.00
21,400.00	1,970.00	2,719.00	3,078.00	3,432.00	3,775.00	4,107.00
21,450.00	1,973.00	2,723.00	3,082.00	3,436.00	3,780.00	4,112.00
21,500.00	1,975.00	2,726.00	3,086.00	3,440.00	3,784.00	4,117.00
21,550.00	1,978.00	2,730.00	3,089.00	3,445.00	3,789.00	4,123.00
21,600.00	1,981.00	2,733.00	3,093.00	3,449.00	3,794.00	4,128.00
21,650.00	1,983.00	2,737.00	3,097.00	3,453.00	3,798.00	4,133.00
21,700.00	1,986.00	2,740.00	3,101.00	3,457.00	3,803.00	4,138.00
21,750.00	1,989.00	2,744.00	3,105.00	3,462.00	3,808.00	4,143.00
21,800.00	1,991.00	2,747.00	3,108.00	3,466.00	3,812.00	4,148.00
21,850.00	1,994.00	2,751.00	3,112.00	3,470.00	3,817.00	4,153.00
21,900.00	1,997.00	2,754.00	3,116.00	3,474.00	3,822.00	4,158.00
21,950.00	1,999.00	2,758.00	3,120.00	3,479.00	3,827.00	4,163.00
22,000.00	2,002.00	2,761.00	3,124.00	3,483.00	3,831.00	4,168.00
22,050.00	2,005.00	2,765.00	3,127.00	3,487.00	3,836.00	4,173.00
22,100.00	2,007.00	2,768.00	3,131.00	3,491.00	3,841.00	4,178.00
22,150.00	2,010.00	2,772.00	3,135.00	3,496.00	3,845.00	4,184.00
22,200.00	2,012.00	2,775.00	3,139.00	3,500.00	3,850.00	4,189.00
22,250.00	2,015.00	2,779.00	3,143.00	3,504.00	3,855.00	4,194.00
22,300.00	2,018.00	2,782.00	3,147.00	3,508.00	3,859.00	4,199.00
22,350.00	2,020.00	2,785.00	3,150.00	3,513.00	3,864.00	4,204.00
22,400.00	2,022.00	2,788.00	3,153.00	3,515.00	3,867.00	4,207.00
22,450.00	2,024.00	2,790.00	3,155.00	3,517.00	3,869.00	4,210.00
22,500.00	2,025.00	2,792.00	3,157.00	3,520.00	3,872.00	4,212.00
22,550.00	2,027.00	2,793.00	3,158.00	3,522.00	3,874.00	4,215.00
22,600.00	2,028.00	2,795.00	3,160.00	3,524.00	3,876.00	4,217.00
22,650.00	2,029.00	2,797.00	3,162.00	3,526.00	3,878.00	4,220.00
22,700.00	2,031.00	2,799.00	3,164.00	3,528.00	3,881.00	4,222.00
22,750.00	2,032.00	2,801.00	3,166.00	3,530.00	3,883.00	4,225.00
22,800.00	2,034.00	2,803.00	3,168.00	3,532.00	3,885.00	4,227.00
22,850.00	2,035.00	2,804.00	3,169.00	3,534.00	3,888.00	4,230.00
22,900.00	2,036.00	2,806.00	3,171.00	3,536.00	3,890.00	4,232.00
22,950.00	2,038.00	2,808.00	3,173.00	3,538.00	3,892.00	4,235.00
23,000.00	2,039.00	2,810.00	3,175.00	3,540.00	3,894.00	4,237.00
23,050.00	2,041.00	2,812.00	3,177.00	3,542.00	3,897.00	4,240.00
23,100.00	2,042.00	2,814.00	3,179.00	3,544.00	3,899.00	4,242.00
23,150.00	2,044.00	2,816.00	3,181.00	3,546.00	3,901.00	4,245.00
23,200.00	2,045.00	2,817.00	3,182.00	3,548.00	3,904.00	4,247.00
23,250.00	2,046.00	2,819.00	3,184.00	3,550.00	3,906.00	4,250.00
23,300.00	2,048.00	2,821.00	3,186.00	3,552.00	3,908.00	4,252.00
23,350.00	2,049.00	2,823.00	3,188.00	3,555.00	3,910.00	4,254.00

23,400.00	2,051.00	2,825.00	3,190.00	3,557.00	3,913.00	4,257.00
23,450.00	2,052.00	2,827.00	3,192.00	3,559.00	3,915.00	4,259.00
23,500.00	2,053.00	2,828.00	3,193.00	3,561.00	3,917.00	4,262.00
23,550.00	2,055.00	2,830.00	3,195.00	3,563.00	3,919.00	4,264.00
23,600.00	2,056.00	2,832.00	3,197.00	3,565.00	3,922.00	4,267.00
23,650.00	2,058.00	2,834.00	3,199.00	3,567.00	3,924.00	4,269.00
23,700.00	2,059.00	2,836.00	3,201.00	3,569.00	3,926.00	4,272.00
23,750.00	2,061.00	2838.00	3,203.00	3,571.00	3,929.00	4,274.00
23,800.00	2,062.00	2,840.00	3,204.00	3,573.00	3,931.00	4,277.00
23,850.00	2,063.00	2,841.00	3,206.00	3,575.00	3,933.00	4,279.00
23,900.00	2,065.00	2,843.00	3,208.00	3,577.00	3,935.00	4,282.00
23,950.00	2,066.00	2,845.00	3,210.00	3,579.00	3,938.00	4,284.00
24,000.00	2,068.00	2,847.00	3,212.00	3,581.00	3,940.00	4,287.00
24,050.00	2,069.00	2,849.00	3,214.00	3,583.00	3,942.00	4,289.00
24,100.00	2,070.00	2,851.00	3,216.00	3,585.00	3,945.00	4,292.00
24,150.00	2,072.00	2,852.00	3,217.00	3,587.00	3,947.00	4,294.00
24,200.00	2,073.00	2,854.00	3,219.00	3,589.00	3,949.00	4,297.00
24,250.00	2,075.00	2,856.00	3,221.00	3,592.00	3,951.00	4,299.00
24,300.00	2,076.00	2,858.00	3,223.00	3,594.00	3,954.00	4,302.00
24,350.00	2,077.00	2,860.00	3,225.00	3,596.00	3,956.00	4,304.00
24,400.00	2,079.00	2,862.00	3,227.00	3,598.00	3,958.00	4,307.00
24,450.00	2,080.00	2,864.00	3,228.00	3,600.00	3,961.00	4,309.00
24,500.00	2,082.00	2,865.00	3,230.00	3,602.00	3,963.00	4,312.00
24,550.00	2,083.00	2,867.00	3,232.00	3,604.00	3,965.00	4,314.00
24,600.00	2,085.00	2,869.00	3,234.00	3,606.00	3,967.00	4,317.00
24,650.00	2,086.00	2,871.00	3,236.00	3,608.00	3,970.00	4,319.00
24,700.00	2,087.00	2,873.00	3,238.00	3,610.00	3,972.00	4,322.00
24,750.00	2,089.00	2,875.00	3,240.00	3,612.00	3,974.00	4,324.00
24,800.00	2,090.00	2,876.00	3,241.00	3,614.00	3,977.00	4,326.00
24,850.00	2,092.00	2,878.00	3,243.00	3,616.00	3,979.00	4,329.00
24,900.00	2,093.00	2,880.00	3,245.00	3,618.00	3,981.00	4,331.00
24,950.00	2,094.00	2,882.00	3,247.00	3,620.00	3,983.00	4,334.00
25,000.00	2,096.00	2,884.00	3,249.00	3,622.00	3,986.00	4,336.00
25,050.00	2,097.00	2,886.00	3,251.00	3,624.00	3,988.00	4,339.00
25,100.00	2,099.00	2,887.00	3,252.00	3,626.00	3,990.00	4,341.00
25,150.00	2,100.00	2,889.00	3,254.00	3,629.00	3,993.00	4,344.00
25,200.00	2,102.00	2,891.00	3,256.00	3,631.00	3,995.00	4,346.00
25,250.00	2,103.00	2,893.00	3,258.00	3,633.00	3,997.00	4,349.00
25,300.00	2,104.00	2,895.00	3,260.00	3,635.00	3,999.00	4,351.00
25,350.00	2,106.00	2,897.00	3,262.00	3,637.00	4,002.00	4,354.00
25,400.00	2,107.00	2,899.00	3,264.00	3,639.00	4,004.00	4,356.00
25,450.00	2,109.00	2,900.00	3,265.00	3,641.00	4,006.00	4,359.00
25,500.00	2,110.00	2,902.00	3,267.00	3,643.00	4,009.00	4,361.00
25,550.00	2,111.00	2,904.00	3,269.00	3,645.00	4,011.00	4,364.00
25,600.00	2,113.00	2,906.00	3,271.00	3,647.00	4,013.00	4,366.00
25,650.00	2,114.00	2,908.00	3,273.00	3,649.00	4,015.00	4,369.00
25,700.00	2,116.00	2,910.00	3,275.00	3,651.00	4,018.00	4,371.00
25,750.00	2,117.00	2,911.00	3,276.00	3,653.00	4,020.00	4,374.00
25,800.00	2,119.00	2,913.00	3,278.00	3,655.00	4,022.00	4,376.00
25,850.00	2,120.00	2,915.00	3,280.00	3,657.00	4,024.00	4,379.00
25,900.00	2,121.00	2,917.00	3,282.00	3,659.00	4,027.00	4,381.00
25,950.00	2,123.00	2,919.00	3,284.00	3,661.00	4,029.00	4,384.00
26,000.00	2,124.00	2,921.00	3,286.00	3,663.00	4,031.00	4,386.00
26,050.00	2,126.00	2,923.00	3,287.00	3,666.00	4,034.00	4,389.00
26,100.00	2,127.00	2,924.00	3,289.00	3,668.00	4,036.00	4,391.00
26,150.00	2,128.00	2,926.00	3,291.00	3,670.00	4,038.00	4,394.00
26,200.00	2,130.00	2,928.00	3,293.00	3,672.00	4,040.00	4,396.00
26,250.00	2,131.00	2,930.00	3,295.00	3,674.00	4,043.00	4,399.00
26,300.00	2,133.00	2,932.00	3,297.00	3,676.00	4,045.00	4,401.00
26,350.00	2,134.00	2,934.00	3,299.00	3,678.00	4,047.00	4,403.00
26,400.00	2,136.00	2,935.00	3,300.00	3,680.00	4,050.00	4,406.00
26,450.00	2,137.00	2,937.00	3,302.00	3,682.00	4,052.00	4,408.00
26,500.00	2,138.00	2,939.00	3,304.00	3,684.00	4,054.00	4,411.00
26,550.00	2,140.00	2,941.00	3,306.00	3,686.00	4,056.00	4,413.00

26,600.00	2,141.00	2,943.00	3,308.00	3,688.00	4,059.00	4,416.00
26,650.00	2,143.00	2,945.00	3,310.00	3,690.00	4,061.00	4,418.00
26,700.00	2,144.00	2,947.00	3,311.00	3,692.00	4,063.00	4,421.00
26,750.00	2,145.00	2,948.00	3,313.00	3,694.00	4,066.00	4,423.00
26,800.00	2,147.00	2,950.00	3,315.00	3,696.00	4,068.00	4,426.00
26,850.00	2,148.00	2,952.00	3,317.00	3,698.00	4,070.00	4,428.00
26,900.00	2,150.00	2,954.00	3,319.00	3,701.00	4,072.00	4,431.00
26,950.00	2,151.00	2,956.00	3,321.00	3,703.00	4,075.00	4,433.00
27,000.00	2,153.00	2,958.00	3,323.00	3,705.00	4,077.00	4,436.00
27,050.00	2,154.00	2,959.00	3,324.00	3,707.00	4,079.00	4,438.00
27,100.00	2,155.00	2,961.00	3,326.00	3,709.00	4,082.00	4,441.00
27,150.00	2,157.00	2,963.00	3,328.00	3,711.00	4,084.00	4,443.00
27,200.00	2,158.00	2,965.00	3,330.00	3,713.00	4,086.00	4,446.00
27,250.00	2,160.00	2,967.00	3,332.00	3,715.00	4,088.00	4,448.00
27,300.00	2,161.00	2,969.00	3,334.00	3,717.00	4,091.00	4,451.00
27,350.00	2,162.00	2,970.00	3,335.00	3,719.00	4,093.00	4,453.00
27,400.00	2,164.00	2,972.00	3,337.00	3,721.00	4,095.00	4,456.00
27,450.00	2,165.00	2,974.00	3,339.00	3,723.00	4,098.00	4,458.00
27,500.00	2,167.00	2,976.00	3,341.00	3,725.00	4,100.00	4,461.00
27,550.00	2,168.00	2,978.00	3,343.00	3,727.00	4,102.00	4,463.00
27,600.00	2,170.00	2,980.00	3,345.00	3,729.00	4,104.00	4,466.00
27,650.00	2,171.00	2,982.00	3,347.00	3,731.00	4,107.00	4,468.00
27,700.00	2172.00	2,983.00	3,348.00	3,733.00	4,109.00	4,471.00
27,750.00	2,174.00	2,985.00	3,350.00	3,735.00	4,111.00	4,473.00
27,800.00	2,175.00	2,987.00	3,352.00	3,738.00	4,114.00	4,475.00
27,850.00	2,177.00	2,989.00	3,354.00	3,740.00	4,116.00	4,478.00
27,900.00	2,178.00	2,991.00	3,356.00	3,742.00	4,118.00	4,480.00
27,950.00	2,179.00	2,993.00	3,357.00	3,744.00	4,120.00	4,483.00
28,000.00	2,181.00	2,994.00	3,359.00	3,746.00	4,122.00	4,485.00
28,050.00	2,182.00	2,996.00	3,361.00	3,748.00	4,125.00	4,488.00
28,100.00	2,184.00	2,998.00	3,363.00	3,750.00	4,127.00	4,490.00
28,150.00	2,185.00	3,000.00	3,365.00	3,752.00	4,129.00	4,492.00
28,200.00	2,186.00	3,001.00	3,366.00	3,754.00	4,131.00	4,495.00
28,250.00	2,188.00	3,003.00	3,368.00	3,756.00	4,133.00	4,497.00
28,300.00	2,189.00	3,005.00	3,370.00	3,758.00	4,136.00	4,500.00
28,350.00	2,190.00	3,007.00	3,372.00	3,759.00	4,138.00	4,502.00
28,400.00	2,192.00	3,009.00	3,374.00	3,761.00	4,140.00	4,504.00
28,450.00	2,193.00	3,010.00	3,375.00	3,763.00	4,142.00	4,507.00
28,500.00	2,194.00	3,012.00	3,377.00	3,765.00	4,145.00	4,509.00
28,550.00	2,196.00	3,014.00	3,379.00	3,767.00	4,147.00	4,512.00
28,600.00	2,197.00	3,016.00	3,381.00	3,769.00	4,149.00	4,514.00
28,650.00	2,199.00	3,017.00	3,382.00	3,771.00	4,151.00	4,516.00
28,700.00	2,200.00	3,019.00	3,384.00	3,773.00	4,153.00	4,519.00
28,750.00	2,201.00	3,021.00	3,386.00	3,775.00	4,156.00	4,521.00
28,800.00	2,203.00	3,023.00	3,388.00	3,777.00	4,158.00	4,524.00
28,850.00	2,204.00	3,025.00	3,390.00	3,779.00	4,160.00	4,526.00
28,900.00	2,205.00	3,026.00	3,391.00	3,781.00	4,162.00	4,528.00
28,950.00	2,207.00	3,028.00	3,393.00	3,783.00	4,164.00	4,531.00
29,000.00	2,208.00	3,030.00	3,395.00	3,785.00	4,167.00	4,533.00
29,050.00	2,210.00	3,032.00	3,397.00	3,787.00	4,169.00	4,536.00
29,100.00	2,211.00	3,034.00	3,398.00	3,789.00	4,171.00	4,538.00
29,150.00	2,212.00	3,035.00	3,400.00	3,791.00	4,173.00	4,540.00
29,200.00	2,214.00	3,037.00	3,402.00	3,793.00	4,175.00	4,543.00
29,250.00	2,215.00	3,039.00	3,404.00	3,795.00	4,178.00	4,545.00
29,300.00	2,216.00	3,041.00	3,406.00	3,797.00	4,180.00	4,548.00
29,350.00	2,218.00	3,042.00	3,407.00	3,799.00	4,182.00	4,550.00
29,400.00	2,219.00	3,044.00	3,409.00	3,801.00	4,184.00	4,552.00
29,450.00	2,220.00	3,046.00	3,411.00	3,803.00	4,186.00	4,555.00
29,500.00	2,222.00	3,048.00	3,413.00	3,805.00	4,189.00	4,557.00
29,550.00	2,223.00	3,050.00	3,415.00	3,807.00	4,191.00	4,560.00
29,600.00	2,225.00	3,051.00	3,416.00	3,809.00	4,193.00	4,562.00
29,650.00	2,226.00	3,053.00	3,418.00	3,811.00	4,195.00	4,564.00
29,700.00	2,227.00	3,055.00	3,420.00	3,813.00	4,197.00	4,567.00
29,750.00	2,229.00	3,057.00	3,422.00	3,815.00	4,200.00	4,569.00

29,800.00	2,230.00	3,058.00	3,423.00	3,817.00	4,202.00	4,572.00
29,850.00	2,231.00	3,060.00	3,425.00	3,819.00	4,204.00	4,574.00
29,900.00	2,233.00	3,062.00	3,427.00	3,821.00	4,206.00	4,576.00
29,950.00	2,234.00	3,064.00	3,429.00	3,823.00	4,208.00	4,579.00
30,000.00	2,236.00	3,066.00	3,431.00	3,825.00	4,211.00	4,581.00

[[

§ 19-6-16. Enforcement of child support orders, decrees, or verdicts

Orders, decrees, or verdicts, permanent or temporary, in favor of the children may be enforced as those in favor of a party.

§ 19-6-17. Application for child support when custody awarded to nonparent or noncustodial parent was not subject to divorce court's jurisdiction; procedure; enforcement; judgment

(a) Whenever the custody of a minor child has been lawfully awarded by any court having jurisdiction thereof to:
(1) Any individual other than a parent of such child at any time subsequent to the rendition of a final divorce decree between the parents of such child; or
(2) A parent as part of the final divorce decree when the court awarding the decree was unable to obtain jurisdiction over the parent without custody for purposes of a determination as to whether the parent should be bound for support of such child and the court's decree contains no specific provisions binding the parent without custody for the support of such child,
the parent or other individual to whom the custody of such child is awarded may apply by petition to the superior court in the county where the parent without custody of such child resides for an order and judgment fixing the amount of support money that the parent without custody shall provide in order to fulfill the parent's natural duty to supply the necessaries of life for such child.
(b) The procedure provided for in this Code section shall be available in cases in which the parent with custody of such child is the petitioner, notwithstanding the fact that the divorce decree and judgment may have been rendered in favor of the parent without custody.
(c) The petition shall be served upon the respondent. The petition shall be heard by the court unless a jury trial is demanded by either party to the case. The judgment shall be reviewable as in other cases. The order or judgment shall likewise be subject to modification in the event of changed circumstances, under the same terms and conditions as are provided for in other cases of child support granted in connection with the rendition of a final decree in divorce cases.
(d) The order and judgment of the court shall remain in effect, except as limited by its own restrictions and subsection (c) of this Code section, so long as the petitioner remains in lawful custody of such child and until such child becomes 18 years of age. Execution may be granted to the petitioner for any sums past due under the order and judgment, in accordance with procedures in other cases of judgments for alimony.
(e) Any payment or installment of support under any child support order is, on and after the date due:
(1) A judgment by operation of law, with the full force and effect and attributes of a judgment of this state, including the ability to be enforced;
(2) Entitled as a judgment to full faith and credit; and
(3) Not subject to retroactive modification.

§ 19-6-18. Revision of judgment for permanent alimony and child support rendered prior to July 1, 1977; petition and hearing; expenses of litigation

(a) The judgment of a court providing permanent alimony for the support of a wife or child or children, or both, rendered prior to July 1, 1977, shall be subject to revision upon petition filed by either the husband or the wife showing a change in the income and financial status of the husband. The petition shall be filed and returnable under the same rules of procedure applicable to divorce proceedings. The petition shall be filed in the proper venue provided by law in civil cases. No petition may be filed by the wife under this Code section within a period of two years from the date of the filing of a previous petition by the wife under this Code section. No petition may be filed by the husband under this Code section within a period of two years from the date of the filing of a previous petition by the husband under this Code section. After hearing both parties and the evidence, the jury, or the judge where a jury is not demanded, may modify and revise the previous judgment so as to provide for the wife or child or children, or both, in accordance with the changed income and financial status of the husband, if such a change in the income and financial status of the husband is satisfactorily proved so as to warrant the modification and revision. In the hearing upon a petition filed as provided in this Code section, testimony may be given and evidence introduced relative to the income and financial status of the wife.

(b) Upon an application as authorized in subsection (a) of this Code section, the merits of whether the wife, or child or children, or both, are entitled to alimony and support are not in issue, but only whether there has been such a substantial change in the income and financial status of the husband as to warrant either a downward or upward revision and modification of the permanent alimony judgment.

(c) An application authorized in subsection (a) of this Code section can be filed only where the husband has been ordered by the final judgment in an alimony or divorce and alimony action to pay permanent alimony in weekly, monthly, annual, or similar periodic payments, and not where the wife, or child or children, or both, have been given an award from the corpus of the husband's estate in lieu of such periodic payment.

(d) Where an application authorized in subsection (a) of this Code section is filed by the husband, the court may require the husband to pay reasonable expenses of litigation as may be incurred by the wife, either for herself or the child or children, or both, in defense thereof.

§ 19-6-19. Revision of judgment for permanent alimony generally -- Petition and hearing; cohabitation with third party as ground for revision; attorney's fees; temporary modification

(a) The judgment of a court providing permanent alimony for the support of a spouse rendered on or after July 1, 1977, shall be subject to revision upon petition filed by either former spouse showing a change in the income and financial status of either former spouse. A petition shall be filed and returnable under the same rules of procedure applicable to divorce proceedings. No petition may be filed by either former spouse under this subsection within a period of two years from the date of the final order on a previous petition by the same former spouse. After hearing both parties and the evidence, the jury, or the judge where a jury is not demanded by either party, may modify and revise the previous judgment, in accordance with the changed income and financial status of either former spouse in the case of permanent alimony for the support of a former spouse, or in accordance with the changed income and financial status of either former spouse if such a change in the income and financial status is satisfactorily proved so as to warrant the modification and revision. In the hearing upon a petition filed as provided in this subsection, testimony may be given and evidence introduced relative to the income and financial status of either former spouse.

(b) Subsequent to a final judgment of divorce awarding periodic payment of alimony for the support of a spouse, the voluntary cohabitation of such former spouse with a third party in a meretricious relationship shall also be grounds to modify provisions made for periodic payments of permanent alimony for the support of the former spouse. As used in this subsection, the word "cohabitation" means dwelling together continuously and openly in a meretricious relationship with another person, regardless of the sex of the other person. In the event the petitioner does not prevail in the petition for modification on the ground set forth in this subsection, the petitioner shall be liable for reasonable attorney's fees incurred by the respondent for the defense of the action.

(c) When an action for revision of a judgment for permanent alimony under this Code section is pending, the court in its discretion may allow, upon motion, the temporary modification of such a judgment, pending the final trial on the petition. In considering an application for temporary modification under this subsection, the court shall consider evidence of any changed circumstances of the parties and the reasonable probability of the petitioner obtaining revision upon final trial. The order granting temporary modification shall be subject to revision by the court at any time before final trial.

(d) In proceedings for the modification of alimony for the support of a spouse pursuant to the provisions of this Code section, the court may award attorneys' fees, costs, and expenses of litigation to the prevailing party as the interests of justice may require.

§ 19-6-20. Revision of judgment for permanent alimony, generally -- Issues for court to consider

In the trial on a petition authorized in subsection (a) of Code Section 19-6-19, the merits of whether a party is entitled to alimony are not an issue. The only issue is whether there has been such a substantial change in the income and financial status of either former spouse, in cases of permanent alimony for the support of a former spouse, as to warrant either a downward or upward revision or modification of the permanent alimony judgment.

§ 19-6-21. Revision of judgment for permanent alimony -- Not available in case of lump sum award

A petition authorized in subsection (a) of Code Section 19-6-19 can be filed only where a party has been ordered by the final judgment in an alimony or divorce and alimony action to pay permanent alimony in weekly, monthly, annual, or similar periodic payments and not where the former spouse of such party has been given an award from the corpus of the party's estate in lieu of such periodic payment.

§ 19-6-22. Revision of judgment for permanent alimony -- Expenses of litigation

Where a petition authorized by subsection (a) of Code Section 19-6-19 is filed by a party obligated to pay alimony, the court may require the party to pay the reasonable expenses of litigation as may be incurred by the party's former spouse on behalf of the former spouse in defense thereof.

§ 19-6-23. Applicability of Code Section 19-6-18 or Code Sections 19-6-19 through 19-6-22 to judgments on or after March 9, 1955

Code Section 19-6-18 or Code Sections 19-6-19 through 19-6-22, as applicable, shall be effective and shall apply to any judgment of a court providing permanent alimony for support, unless rendered prior to March 9, 1955, in which case Code Section 19-6-24 shall apply.

§ 19-6-24. Applicability of Code Section 19-6-18 or Code Sections 19-6-19 through 19-6-22 to judgments prior to March 9, 1955

Code Section 19-6-18 or Code Sections 19-6-19 through 19-6-22, as applicable, shall apply to all judgments for permanent alimony for the support of a wife rendered prior to March 9, 1955, where all the following conditions are met:
(1) Both parties to the case in which the judgment for permanent alimony was rendered consent in writing to the revision, amendment, alteration, settlement, satisfaction, or release thereof;
(2) There are no minor children involved or, if there were minor children at the time the original judgment was rendered, the children are all of age at the time the application is filed;
(3) The judge of the court wherein the original judgment for permanent alimony was rendered approves the revision, amendment, alteration, settlement, satisfaction, or release; and
(4) The consent of the parties, together with the court's approval, is filed with the clerk of the court wherein the original judgment for permanent alimony was rendered.

§ 19-6-25. Revision of judgments for permanent alimony entered prior to March 9, 1955

When any judgment for permanent alimony rendered prior to March 9, 1955, is revised, amended, altered, settled, satisfied, or released, the same shall not thereafter be subject to revision, except upon the conditions specified in Code Section 19-6-24.

§ 19-6-26. Jurisdiction

(a) As used in this Code section, the term:
(1) "Child support order" means a judgment, decree, or order of a court or authorized administrative agency requiring the payment of child support in periodic amounts or in a lump sum and includes (A) a permanent or temporary order and (B) an initial order or a modification of an order.
(2) "Continuing, exclusive jurisdiction" means the authority and jurisdiction of a court to enter or modify a judgment, decree, or order for the payment of child support, as defined in the Full Faith and Credit for Child Support Orders Act, 28 U.S.C. Section 1738B, as amended.
(3) "Foreign child support order" means a judgment, decree, or order of a court or authorized administrative agency of another state requiring the payment of child support in periodic amounts or in a lump sum and includes (A) a permanent or temporary order and (B) an initial order or a modification of an order.
(4) "Modification" means a change in a child support order that affects the amount, scope, or duration of the order and modifies, replaces, supersedes, or otherwise is made subsequent to a child support order or foreign child support order.
(5) "Moving party" means the party initiating an action for the modification of a child support order or foreign child support order.
(6) "Nonmoving party" means the party not initiating an action for the modification of a child support order or foreign child support order.
(7) "State" means a state of the United States, the District of Columbia, the Commonwealth of Puerto Rico, the territories and possessions of the United States, and Indian Country as defined in 18 U.S.C. Section 1151.
(b) A court of this state may exercise continuing, exclusive jurisdiction for purposes of entering a child support order if the court has subject matter and personal jurisdiction to make such a child support order,

and no previous support order has been entered by a court of competent jurisdiction with respect to the child or children named in the support order.

(c) A court of this state may exercise continuing, exclusive jurisdiction for purposes of entering a modification of a child support order issued by a court of this state if the child or children named in the child support order or any party to the action resides in this state.

(d) A court of this state may exercise continuing, exclusive jurisdiction for purposes of entering a modification of a foreign child support order if:

(1) The court has subject matter and personal jurisdiction over the nonmoving party; and

(2) The court of the state issuing the order sought to be modified no longer has continuing, exclusive jurisdiction to modify said order as defined in the Full Faith and Credit for Child Support Orders Act, 28 U.S.C. Section 1738B, as amended.

(3) The parties file a written consent allowing the court to assume continuing, exclusive jurisdiction. This Code section shall be interpreted to effectuate the provisions of Article 3 of Chapter 11 of this title.

(e) Jurisdiction within this state to enforce, by a contempt proceeding or otherwise, a child support order entered by or registered with a court of this state shall be vested concurrently in the court issuing such order, in the court in the county where the person owing the duty of support may be found or is employed, and for in rem proceedings only, in the court in the county where property may be found which is subject to seizure, sale, foreclosure, or other process for application toward the support obligation.

§ 19-6-27. Application for permanent alimony or child support after grant of foreign divorce decree; venue; hearing; review; modification

(a) Whenever, in any foreign country or any other state of the United States, any person obtains a divorce from such person's spouse, which spouse at the time of the filing of the divorce action was a resident of this state, and in the divorce action the spouse was not personally served with petition and process but was served constructively and did not appear, plead, or otherwise waive jurisdiction of the foreign court, the spouse, at any time subsequent to the granting of the foreign divorce decree, may apply to the superior court for an order and judgment for permanent alimony for the support of such spouse and the child or children of the parties, if any. The permanent alimony action shall be filed, pleaded, and tried as if no divorce decree had been entered, even though the foreign decree may be entitled to full faith and credit in dissolving the marriage. If the person who obtained the divorce has become a resident of this state, the action for alimony shall be brought in the county of the person's residence; otherwise, the action shall be brought in the county in which the spouse applying for alimony resides.

(b) The procedure provided for in subsection (a) of this Code section shall not be available for the support of any child or children whose custody and support was legally adjudicated in the foreign court unless custody of the child or children is subsequently changed by a court having jurisdiction of the parties.

(c) A petition brought under this Code section shall be served upon the person who obtained the divorce, as in actions for permanent alimony, and shall be heard by the judge unless a jury trial is demanded by either party to the case. The judgment shall be reviewable as in other cases. The order or judgment shall be subject to modification upon a change of condition, in the same manner that other orders or judgments for permanent alimony are subject to modification.

§ 19-6-28. Enforcement of orders; contempt; service of rule nisi by mail; rule nisi form

(a) In addition to other powers specified in this chapter, the court shall have the power to subject the respondent to such terms and conditions as the court may deem proper to assure compliance with its orders and, in particular, shall have the power to punish the respondent who violates any order of the court to the same extent as is provided by law for contempt of the court in any other action or proceeding cognizable by the court. Any proceeding for compliance pursuant to this authority shall be a part of the underlying action, and a motion for such enforcement shall not constitute the filing of a new action or require the payment of a new filing fee.

(b) In any proceeding to enforce a temporary or permanent grant of alimony or child support by attachment for contempt, the petitioner may serve the motion and rule nisi by mailing a copy of the motion and rule nisi by first-class mail, postage prepaid, to the respondent at the respondent's last known address together with two copies of a notice and acknowledgment conforming substantially to the form specified in subsection (c) of this Code section and a return envelope, postage prepaid, addressed to the sender. If service is perfected by acknowledgment of service in this manner, the petitioner shall file with the court the acknowledgment of the respondent; and such filing shall constitute a return of service. If no acknowledgment of service under this subsection is received by the petitioner within ten days after the date of such mailing, the petitioner shall notify the clerk of court and deposit the costs of service and service of such summons shall be made as provided in Code Section 9-11-4. The costs of such service shall be charged by the clerk of court to the respondent unless the respondent after motion and hearing establishes to the court that there is good reason why such person should not be so charged. A child support contempt motion shall be served upon a respondent with a notice that contains a date certain for hearing which shall be no later than 30 days from the date of service of the motion, unless good cause for a later date is found by the court, in which event the time for a hearing may be extended for up to 30 days.

(c) The form for notice and acknowledgment under subsection (b) of this Code section shall be substantially as follows:

IN THE SUPERIOR COURT OF   COUNTY
STATE OF GEORGIA

	)	
Plaintiff	)	
	)	
v.	)	Civil action
	)	File no.
	)	
	)	
Defendant	)	

RULE NISI NOTICE AND
ACKNOWLEDGMENT

To: (insert the name and address of the person to be served)

The enclosed motion and rule nisi are served pursuant to Official Code of Georgia Annotated Section 19-6-28.

You must complete the acknowledgment part of this form and mail one copy of the completed form to the sender within ten days of the date of mailing to you, which date is set out below.

You must sign and date the acknowledgment. If you are served on behalf of another person and you are authorized to receive process, you must indicate under your signature your authority.

If you do not complete and return this form to the sender within ten days, you or the party on whose behalf you are being served will be required to pay any expenses incurred in serving a summons and complaint in any other manner permitted by law unless good and sufficient cause is shown to the contrary.

If you do complete and mail this form, you or the party on whose behalf you are being served must appear and show cause why you should not be attached for contempt at the time required by the enclosed rule nisi.

I declare, under penalty of perjury, that this Notice and Acknowledgment of Receipt will have been mailed on the date set out below.

Signature

Date of mailing

ACKNOWLEDGMENT OF RECEIPT
OF SUMMONS AND COMPLAINT

I declare, under penalty of perjury, that I received a copy of the motion and of the rule nisi in the above-captioned manner at (insert address).

Signature

Printed name of signer

Authority to receive
service of process

Date of mailing

(d) Service in accordance with subsections (b) and (c) of this Code section is in addition to any other method of service provided by law.

§ 19-6-28.1. Suspension of, or denial of application or renewal of, license for noncompliance with child support order

(a) As used in this Code section, the term:
(1) "License" means a certificate, permit, registration, or any other authorization issued by the Department of Public Safety or any other licensing entity that allows a person to operate a motor vehicle, to engage in a profession, business, or occupation, or to hunt or fish.
(2) "Licensing entity" means any state agency, department, or board of this state which issues or renews any license, certificate, permit, or registration to authorize a person to drive a motor vehicle, to hunt or fish, or to engage in a profession, business, or occupation including those under Article 3 of Chapter 7 of Title 2, the "Georgia Pesticide Use and Application Act of 1976"; Article 13 of Chapter 1 of Title 7, relating to mortgage lenders and mortgage brokers; Chapter 5 of Title 10, the "Georgia Uniform Securities Act of 2008," relating to securities salespersons and investment adviser representatives; Part 2 of Article 1 of Chapter 6 of Title 12, relating to foresters; Chapter 4 of Title 26, relating to pharmacists; Chapter 23 of Title 33, relating to insurance agents, counselors, and other personnel; Chapter 1 of Title 43, relating to professions and businesses; Chapter 39A of Title 43, relating to real estate appraisers; or Chapter 40 of Title 43, relating to real estate brokers and salespersons.
(b) In any proceeding for enforcement of a judgment or order to pay child support, if the court is satisfied by competent proof that the respondent has accumulated support arrears equivalent to or greater than the current support due for 60 days and that the respondent is licensed to conduct a trade, business, profession, or occupation, licensed to hunt or fish, licensed to drive a motor vehicle, owns a motor vehicle which is registered in this state in his or her name, or is applying for the renewal or issuance of any such license or registration, the court may order the appropriate licensing or registering entity to suspend the license or registration or deny the application for such license and to inform the court of the actions it has taken pursuant to such proceedings. Evidence relating to the ability and willingness of the respondent to comply with an order of child support shall be considered by the court prior to the entry of any order under this Code section.
(c) The court shall inform the respondent that competent proof for purposes of proving to a licensing or registering entity that the respondent is in compliance with the order for child support shall be written proof of payment by cash or a certified check, notice issued by the court, or notice from a child support receiver, if such receiver has been appointed.

§ 19-6-29. Inclusion of accident and sickness insurance coverage in order for child support; payroll deductions

(a) In any case before the court involving child support, the court may inquire into the availability of accident and sickness insurance coverage to any person obligated to support and, if such coverage is reasonably available, may include in the order of support provision for such coverage.
(b) Any order of support of a child entered or modified on or after July 1, 1992, which includes provision for accident and sickness insurance may include a provision for payroll deduction of an amount which is sufficient to provide for the payment of premiums of such accident and sickness insurance.
(c) An order for payroll deduction entered pursuant to subsection (b) of this Code section shall be consistent with the provisions of Code Sections 19-6-30 through 19-6-33.1.

§ 19-6-30. Collection of child support by continuing garnishment; child support subject to income deduction

(a) Any order of support of a child entered or modified on or after July 1, 1985, shall contain the following provision:
"Whenever, in violation of the terms of this order there shall have been a failure to make the support payments due hereunder so that the amount unpaid is equal to or greater than the amount payable for one month, the payments required to be made may be collected by the process of continuing garnishment for support."
(b) All cases involving orders of support of a child or spouse being enforced by the entity within the Department of Human Services and its contractors that are authorized to enforce support orders shall be subject to income deduction orders as set forth in Code Sections 19-6-32 through 19-6-33.1.

§ 19-6-31. Definitions

Reserved. Repealed by Ga. L. 2017, p. 646, § 1-12/SB 137, effective July 1, 2017.

§ 19-6-32. Entering income deduction order or medical support notice for award of child support; when order or notice effective; hearing on order

(a) As used in this Code section, the term:
(1) "Child support enforcement agency" means the entity within the Department of Human Services and its contractors that are authorized to enforce a duty of support.
(2) "Court" means judge of any court of record or an administrative law judge of the Office of State Administrative Hearings.
(3) "Earnings" means any form of payment due to an individual, regardless of source, including without limitation wages, salary, commission, bonus, workers' compensation, disability, payments pursuant to a pension or retirement program, and interest.
(4) "IV-D" means Title IV-D of the federal Social Security Act.
(5) "National Medical Support Notice" means a notice as prescribed under 42 U.S.C. Section 666(a)(19) or a substantially similar notice.
(6) "Obligee" means the individual to whom the payment of a support obligation is owed.
(7) "Obligor" means the individual owing a duty of support.
(8) "Payor" means the person that provides earnings to an obligor.
(b) (1) Except as provided for in paragraph (1) of subsection (c) of this Code section, upon the entry of a judgment or order establishing, enforcing, or modifying a child support obligation or spousal support obligation through a court, a separate income deduction order, if one has not been previously entered, shall be entered. If the obligee is an applicant for child support services under IV-D, the obligee shall furnish copies of the support order and the income deduction order to the child support enforcement agency.
(2) For all child support orders, and spousal support orders enforced pursuant to subsection (d) of Code Section 19-11-6, the child support enforcement agency shall be authorized to issue an income deduction order without need for any amendment to the order involved or any further action by a court that issued it, provided that an opportunity for a hearing before a court is afforded. The child support enforcement agency shall also be authorized to issue a National Medical Support Notice to enforce the medical support provisions of such orders, provided that an opportunity for a hearing pursuant to Code Section 19-11-27 is afforded. Such orders or notices may be issued electronically by the child support enforcement agency. The child support enforcement agency shall issue an income deduction order or, when appropriate, a National Medical Support Notice within two business days after the information regarding a newly hired employee is entered into the centralized employee registry pursuant to Code Section 19-11-9.2 and matched with an obligor in a case being enforced by the child support enforcement agency.
(c) (1) (A) All child support orders which are initially issued in this state on or after January 1, 1994, and are not at the time of issuance being enforced by the child support enforcement agency shall provide for the

immediate withholding of such support from the earnings of the individual required by that order to furnish support unless:

(i) A court issuing the order finds there is good cause not to require such immediate withholding; or

(ii) A written agreement is reached between both parties which provides for an alternative arrangement.

(B) For purposes of this subsection, any finding that there is good cause not to require withholding from earnings shall be based on at least a written determination that implementing such withholding would not be in the best interest of the child and proof of timely payment of previously ordered support in cases involving modification of support orders.

(2) All child support orders which are not described in subsection (b) of this Code section or in paragraph (1) of this subsection shall, upon petition of either party to revise such order under Code Section 19-6-19 or to enforce such order under Code Section 19-6-28, be revised to include provisions for withholding such support from the earnings of the individual required by the order to furnish such support if arrearages equal to one month's support accrue but without the necessity of filing application for services under Code Section 19-11-6.

(3) Copies of income deduction orders issued under this subsection shall be provided by the obligee to the obligor, payor, and the family support registry established pursuant to Code Section 19-6-33.1.

(d) An income deduction order shall:

(1) Direct a payor to deduct from all earnings due and payable to an obligor the amount required by the support order to meet the obligor's support obligation;

(2) State the amount of arrearage accrued, if any, under the support order and direct a payor to withhold an additional amount until the arrearage is paid in full;

(3) Direct a payor not to deduct in excess of the amounts allowed under Section 303(b) of the federal Consumer Credit Protection Act, 15 U.S.C. Section 1673(b); and

(4) Direct the payor to send income deduction order payments, including administrative fees authorized by law, to the family support registry established pursuant to Code Section 19-6-33.1.

(e) Income deduction orders shall be effective immediately unless a court upon good cause shown finds that the income deduction order shall be effective upon a delinquency in an amount equal to one month's support or a written agreement is reached between both parties which provides for an alternative arrangement.

(f) An income deduction order shall be effective so long as the order of support upon which it is based is effective or until further order of a court.

(g) When an income deduction order shall be effective immediately, the obligee or child support enforcement agency, as applicable, shall furnish to the obligor a statement of his or her rights, remedies, and duties in regard to the income deduction order. The statement shall state:

(1) All fees or interest which shall be imposed;

(2) The total amount of earnings to be deducted for each pay period until the arrearage, if any, is paid in full and the total amount of earnings to be deducted for each pay period thereafter. The amounts deducted shall not be in excess of that allowed under Section 303(b) of the federal Consumer Credit Protection Act, 15 U.S.C. Section 1673(b);

(3) When the withholding will commence;

(4) That the income deduction order shall apply to current and subsequent payors and periods of employment;

(5) That a copy of the income deduction order shall be provided to the payors;

(6) That the enforcement of the income deduction order may only be contested on the ground of mistake of fact regarding the amount of support owed pursuant to a support order, the arrearages, or the identity of the obligor;

(7) How to contest the withholding; and

(8) That the obligor is required to notify the obligee and, when the obligee is receiving IV-D services, the child support enforcement agency, within seven days of changes in the obligor's address and payors and the addresses of his or her payors.

(h) When an income deduction order is effective upon a delinquency in an amount equal to one month's support, or when an order for spousal or child support was in effect prior to July 1, 1989, the obligee or child support enforcement agency, as applicable, may enforce the income deduction order by providing a notice of delinquency to the obligor. A notice of delinquency shall state:

(1) The terms of the support order;

(2) The period of delinquency and the total amount of the delinquency as of the date the notice is mailed;

(3) All fees or interest which may be imposed;

(4) The total amount of earnings to be deducted for each pay period until the arrearage and all applicable fees and interest are paid in full and the total amount of earnings to be deducted for each pay period thereafter. The amounts deducted shall not be in excess of that allowed under Section 303(b) of the federal Consumer Credit Protection Act, 15 U.S.C. Section 1673(b);

(5) That a copy of the notice of delinquency shall be provided to the payors, together with a copy of the income deduction order. The obligor may apply to a court to contest enforcement of the order once the

notice of delinquency has been received. The application shall not affect the enforcement of the income deduction order until a court enters an order granting relief to the obligor;

  (6) That the enforcement of the income deduction order may only be contested on the ground of mistake of fact regarding the amount of support owed pursuant to a support order, the arrearages, or the identity of the obligor; and

  (7) That the obligor is required to notify the obligee of the obligor's current address and current payors and the address of current payors. All changes shall be reported by the obligor within seven days of the change occurring. If the child support enforcement agency is enforcing such order, the obligor shall make these notifications to the child support enforcement agency instead of to the obligee.

(i) The failure of the obligor to receive the notice of delinquency provided for in subsection (h) of this Code section shall not preclude the income deduction order being subsequently provided to the payor. A notice of delinquency which fails to state an arrearage shall not mean that an arrearage is not owed.

(j) At any time, any party, including the child support enforcement agency, may apply to a court to:

   (1) Modify, suspend, or terminate the income deduction order because of a modification, suspension, or termination of the underlying order for support; or

   (2) Modify the amount of earnings being withheld when the arrearage has been paid.

§ 19-6-33. Notice and service of income deduction order; hearing on enforcement of order; discharge of obligor; penalties

  (a) As used in this Code section, the term:

  (1) "Child support enforcement agency" means the entity within the Department of Human Services and its contractors that are authorized to enforce a duty of support.

  (2) "Court" means judge of any court of record or an administrative law judge of the Office of State Administrative Hearings.

  (3) "Earnings" means any form of payment due to an individual, regardless of source, including without limitation wages, salary, commission, bonus, workers' compensation, disability, payments pursuant to a pension or retirement program, and interest.

  (4) "IV-D" means Title IV-D of the federal Social Security Act.

  (5) "Obligee" means the individual to whom the payment of a support obligation is owed.

  (6) "Obligor" means the individual owing a duty of support.

  (7) "Payor" means the person that provides earnings to an obligor.

(b) The obligee shall provide an income deduction order and in the case of a delinquency, a notice of delinquency, to the payor. The obligee or child support enforcement agency, as applicable, shall provide the notice to payor as set forth in subsection (f) of this Code section.

(c) Service of the initial income deduction order by or upon any person who is a party to a proceeding under this Code section shall be by personal service, by certified mail, return receipt requested, by statutory overnight delivery, or by first-class mail; such order may be served electronically if permitted under Code Section 9-11-5. Service upon a payor or successor payor under this Code section shall be by first-class mail, or such order may be served electronically if permitted under Code Section 9-11-5.

(d) (1) When an income deduction order is effective upon a delinquency in an amount equal to one month's support, the obligor may apply to a court to contest the enforcement of the income deduction order on the ground of mistake of fact regarding the amount of support owed pursuant to a support order, the amount of arrearage of support, or the identity of the obligor. The obligor shall send a copy of his or her pleading to the obligee and, if the obligee is receiving IV-D services, to the child support enforcement agency. The filing of such pleading shall not affect the enforcement of an income deduction order unless a court enters an order granting relief to the obligor. The payment of delinquent support by an obligor upon entry of an income deduction order shall not preclude the income deduction order being provided to the payor.

  (2) When an obligor requests a hearing to contest enforcement of an income deduction order, a court, after due notice to all parties and the child support enforcement agency, if the obligee is receiving IV-D services, shall hear the matter within 30 days after the application is filed and shall not extend the time for hearing unless good cause for a later date is found by a court, in which event the time for a hearing may be extended for up to 30 days. A court shall enter an order resolving the matter within ten days after the hearing and provide such order to the parties and the child support enforcement agency, if the obligee is receiving IV-D services.

(e) When a court determines that an income deduction order is proper pursuant to subsection (d) of this Code section, the obligee shall cause a copy of the income deduction order and in the case of a delinquency, a notice of delinquency, to be provided to the payor. The obligee or child support enforcement agency, as applicable, shall provide the notice to payor as set forth in subsection (f) of this Code section. A copy of the notice to payor, and in the case of a delinquency, a notice of delinquency, shall also be provided to the obligor by the obligee or child support enforcement agency, as applicable.

(f) A notice to payor shall contain only information necessary for the payor to comply with the income deduction order. The payor shall have the duties, penalties, and rights specified in such notice. The notice to payor shall:

(1) Require the payor to deduct from the obligor's earnings the amount specified in the income deduction order, and in the case of a delinquency the amount specified in the notice of delinquency, and to pay such amount to the family support registry established pursuant to Code Section 19-6-33.1. The amount actually deducted plus all administrative charges shall not be in excess of the amount allowed under Section 303(b) of the federal Consumer Credit Protection Act, 15 U.S.C. Section 1673(b);

(2) Instruct the payor to implement the income deduction order no later than the first pay period that occurs after 14 days following the date the notice was mailed;

(3) Instruct the payor to forward, within two business days after each payment date, to the family support registry the amount deducted from the obligor's earnings and a statement as to whether such amount totally or partially satisfies the periodic amount specified in the income deduction order;

(4) Specify that if a payor willfully fails to deduct the proper amount from the obligor's earnings, the payor shall be liable for the amount the payor should have deducted, plus costs, interest, and reasonable attorney's fees;

(5) Provide that the payor may collect up to $25.00 against the obligor's earnings to reimburse the payor for administrative costs for the first payment of an income deduction order and up to $3.00 for each subsequent payment. The payor shall not deduct a fee for complying with any order or notice for enrollment in a health benefit plan;

(6) State that the income deduction order and the notice to payor, and in the case of a delinquency, the notice of delinquency, are binding on the payor until:

  (A) Further notice by the obligee, child support agency, or court; or
  (B) The payor no longer provides earnings to the obligor;

(7) Instruct the payor that, when the payor no longer provides earnings to the obligor, the payor shall notify the obligee and shall also provide the obligor's last known address and the name and address of the obligor's new payor, if known, and that, if the payor willfully violates this paragraph, the payor shall be subject to a civil penalty not to exceed $250.00 for the first violation and $500.00 for any subsequent violation. If the child support enforcement agency is enforcing the income deduction order, the payor shall make such notifications to the child support enforcement agency instead of to the obligee. Penalties shall be paid to the obligee or the child support enforcement agency, whichever is enforcing the income deduction order;

(8) State that no payor may discharge an obligor by reason of the fact that earnings have been subjected to an income deduction order under Code Section 19-6-32 and that a violation of this paragraph shall subject the payor to a civil penalty not to exceed $250.00 for the first violation and $500.00 for any subsequent violation. Penalties shall be paid to the obligee or the child support enforcement agency, whichever is enforcing the income deduction order, if any support is owing. If no support is owing, the penalty shall be paid to the obligor;

(9) Inform the payor that the income deduction order has priority over all other legal processes under state law pertaining to the same earnings and that payment, as required by the income deduction order, is a complete defense by the payor against any claims of the obligor or his or her creditors as to the sum paid;

(10) Inform the payor that if the payor receives income deduction orders requiring that the earnings of two or more obligors be deducted and sent to the same depository, the payor may combine the amounts paid to the depository in a single payment so long as the payor identifies that portion of the payment attributable to each obligor; and

(11) Inform the payor that the payor may receive more than one income deduction order against the same obligor and shall give priority to current child support obligations up to the limits imposed under Section 303(b) of the federal Consumer Credit Protection Act, 15 U.S.C. Section 1673(b).

(g) At any time an income deduction order is being enforced, the obligor may apply to a court for a hearing to contest the continued enforcement of the income deduction order on the same grounds set out in subsection (d) of this Code section, and provide a copy of the pleading requesting such hearing to the obligee and, in IV-D cases, to the child support enforcement agency. Such application shall not affect the continued enforcement of the income deduction order until a court enters an order granting relief to the obligor. The obligee may be liable for improper receipt of moneys pursuant to an income deduction order.

(h) An obligee, or an obligee's agent, shall enforce income deduction orders against an obligor's successor payor who is located in this state in the same manner prescribed in this Code section for the enforcement of an income deduction order against a payor.

(i) The provisions of Article 3 of Chapter 11 of this title, the "Uniform Interstate Family Support Act," shall apply to:

  (1) All income deduction orders originating in this state and directed to another state; and
  (2) All income-withholding orders originating in another state and directed to this state.

(j) Certified copies of payment records maintained by a child support receiver or the child support enforcement agency shall, without further proof, be admitted into evidence in any legal proceeding in this state.

(k) No payor shall discharge an obligor by reason of the fact that his or her earnings have been subjected to an income deduction order under Code Section 19-6-32. A payor who violates this subsection shall be subject to a civil penalty not to exceed $250.00 for the first violation and $500.00 for any subsequent violation. Penalties shall be paid to the obligee or the child support enforcement agency, whichever is enforcing the income deduction order, if any support is owing. If no support is owing, the penalty shall be paid to the obligor.

(l) If a payor is not providing earnings to an obligor or when a payor no longer provides earnings to an obligor, the payor shall notify the obligee and, if the support order is being enforced by the child support enforcement agency, the child support enforcement agency shall provide the obligor's last known address and the name and address of the obligor's new payor, if known. A payor who willfully violates this subsection shall be subject to a civil penalty not to exceed $250.00 for the first violation and $500.00 for any subsequent violation. Penalties shall be paid to the obligee or the child support enforcement agency, whichever is enforcing the income deduction order.

§ 19-6-33.1. Family support registry

(a) As used in this Code section, the term:
(1) "Child support enforcement agency" means the entity within the Department of Human Services and its contractors that are authorized to enforce a duty of support.
(2) "Earnings" means any form of payment due to an individual, regardless of source, including without limitation wages, salary, commission, bonus, workers' compensation, disability, payments pursuant to a pension or retirement program, and interest.
(3) "Income deduction order" means an order which is made pursuant to Code Section 19-6-32 and which becomes effective upon a delinquency which occurred on or after January 1, 1994, or which became effective immediately without a delinquency on or after January 1, 1994.
(4) "IV-D" means Title IV-D of the federal Social Security Act.
(5) "Obligee" means the individual to whom the payment of a support obligation is owed.
(6) "Obligor" means the individual owing a duty of support.
(7) "Payor" means the person that provides earnings to an obligor.
(b) There shall be established and operated a family support registry pursuant to IV-D regulations, and authority and funding shall be provided to the child support enforcement agency for the operation of such registry. The child support enforcement agency shall be authorized to establish and maintain or contract for the establishment and maintenance of the family support registry. The family support registry shall be used for the collection and processing of payments for support orders in all cases which are enforced by the child support enforcement agency and for all other support orders not being enforced by the child support enforcement agency which are subject to an income deduction order.
(c) The child support enforcement agency shall, as required by federal law, redirect payments for support orders in all cases being enforced by the child support enforcement agency and for all other support orders not being enforced by the child support enforcement agency which are subject to an income deduction order. Such payments for support orders being paid to a court, child support receiver, or private party by a payor shall be redirected to the family support registry.
(d) In implementing the family support registry, the child support enforcement agency shall be authorized to:
(1) Receive, process, and disburse payments for child support, child support when combined with spousal support, child support arrears, or child support debt for any court or administrative order;
(2) Maintain records of any payments collected, processed, and disbursed through the family support registry;
(3) Establish and maintain a separate record for payments made through the family support registry as a result of a judgment remedy;
(4) Answer inquiries from any parent concerning payments processed through the family support registry; and
(5) Collect a fee for the processing of insufficient funds checks and issue a notice to the originator of any insufficient funds check that no further checks shall be accepted from such person and that future payments shall be required to be paid by cash or certified funds.
(e) The following procedures shall be followed:
(1) All administrative orders and all court orders entered or modified which provide for income deduction orders for support payments for child support, child support when combined with spousal support, child support arrears, or child support debt shall require that such payments be made through the family support registry; and
(2) The child support enforcement agency shall send or cause to be sent a notice by first-class mail directing that all income deduction order payments shall be made to the family support registry. Orders subject to this redirection include all support orders being enforced by the child support enforcement agency and all other orders not being enforced by the child support enforcement agency which are subject to an income deduction order. The notice shall be sent to the following persons:

(A) Any obligor who is obligated to make payments for support, child support when combined with spousal support, child support arrears or child support debt under court order or administrative order in a IV-D case when the order does not already specify paying through the family support registry; and

(B) Any payor that has been deducting income under Code Section 19-6-32.

(f) Any obligor or payor that receives a notice to redirect payments as specified in subsection (e) of this Code section that fails to make the payments to the family support registry and continues to make payments to the court or to the obligee shall be sent a second notice to redirect payments. The second notice shall be sent by certified mail, return receipt requested or by statutory overnight delivery. Such notice shall contain all the information required to be included in the first notice to redirect payments and shall further state that the obligor or payor has failed to make the payments to the child support enforcement agency and that the obligor or payor shall redirect the payments to the family support registry at the address indicated in the notice. Failure to make payments to the family support registry after a second notice shall be grounds for contempt.

(g) (1) Any payment required to be made to the family support registry which is received by the court, child support receiver, obligee, or child support enforcement agency shall be forwarded to the family support registry within two business days after receipt. All income deduction order payments from payors or such payments forwarded by the court, child support receiver, obligee, or child support enforcement agency shall be identified with the information specified by the family support registry, including but not limited to the court case number, social security number of the obligor, county where the case originated, and name of the obligor.

(2) Except as provided by federal law, the family support registry shall distribute all support amounts payable within two business days after receipt from the payor.

(h) The Department of Human Services shall coordinate the operation of the family support registry with the state case registry created under Code Section 19-11-39 so as to reduce if not eliminate the need for duplicate reporting and information recording. The Department of Human Services shall be authorized to establish and collect an administrative fee from the individual owing a duty of support through the family support registry. Such administrative fee shall be the lesser of:

(1) Two dollars per payment;
(2) Five percent of the amount of each payment; or
(3) The actual cost of processing and distributing the child support from the source to the obligee.

(i) Nothing in this Code section shall allow or require any reduction of child support payments owed to any parent or guardian of a child.

§ 19-6-34. Inclusion of life insurance in order of support

(a) In any case before the court involving child support, the court may include in the order of support provision for life insurance on the life of either parent or the lives of both parents for the benefit of the minor children. The court may order either parent or both parents to obtain and maintain the life insurance.

(b) The amount of the premium for such life insurance may be considered as a deviation to the presumptive amount of child support pursuant to the provisions of Code Section 19-6-15, provided that the court shall review the amount of the premium for reasonableness under the circumstances of the case and the best interest of the child.

(c) Except as provided in subsection (d) of this Code section, an order for child support shall not require maintenance of life insurance for a child's benefit after the child reaches the age of majority and shall not require that the proceeds of life insurance be available for the benefit of a child after the child reaches the age of majority.

(d) The trier of fact, in the exercise of sound discretion, may direct either or both parents to maintain life insurance for the benefit of a child who has not previously married or become emancipated, who is enrolled in and attending a secondary school, and who has attained the age of majority before completing his or her secondary school education, provided that maintenance of such life insurance for the benefit of the child shall not be required after a child attains 20 years of age.

(e) Nothing in this Code section shall prevent parents from entering into an agreement for the provision of life insurance that differs from or exceeds the terms of this Code section.

§ 19-6-35. Child support obligee regarded as creditor for attacking certain judgments and transactions

(a) As used in this Code section, the term:

(1) "Child support obligee" means an individual to whom the payment of a child support obligation is owed and includes a custodial parent or caretaker of a child to whom such support obligation is to be paid or a governmental agency entitled by law to enforce a child support obligation on behalf of such parent, caretaker, or child.

(2) "Child support obligor" means an individual owing a duty of support to a child or children, whether or not such duty is evinced by a judgment, order, or decree.

(b) A child support obligee shall be regarded as a creditor, and a child support obligor shall be regarded as a debtor, as defined in Code Section 18-2-1, for the purposes of attacking as fraudulent a judgment, conveyance, transaction, or other arrangement interfering with the creditor's rights, either at law or in equity.

ARTICLE 2. GEORGIA CHILD SUPPORT COMMISSION

§ 19-6-50. Creation; responsibilities

There is created the Georgia Child Support Commission for the purpose of studying and collecting information and data relating to awards of child support and to create and revise the child support obligation table. The commission shall be responsible for conducting a comprehensive review of the child support guidelines, economic conditions, and all matters relevant to maintaining effective and efficient child support guidelines and modifying child support orders that will serve the best interest of Georgia's children and take into account the changing dynamics of family life. Further, the commission shall determine whether adjustments are needed to the child support obligation table taking into consideration the guidelines set forth in Code Section 19-6-53. Nothing contained in the commission's report shall be considered to authorize or require a change in the child support obligation table without action by the General Assembly.

§ 19-6-51. Members; terms; chairperson, other officers, and committees; staffing and funding

(a) The Georgia Child Support Commission shall be composed of 15 members. The Governor shall appoint all of the members as follows:
  (1) Three members who shall be judges in a superior court;
  (2) One member who shall be a Justice of the Supreme Court of Georgia or a Judge of the Georgia Court of Appeals or the Justice's or Judge's designee;
  (3) Two members of the House of Representatives and two members of the Senate; and
  (4) Seven other members.

Each member of the commission shall be appointed to serve for a term of four years or until his or her successor is duly appointed except the members of the General Assembly, who shall serve until completion of their current terms of office. The initial members of the commission appointed pursuant to paragraph (1) of this subsection shall serve for terms of three years. The initial member of the commission appointed pursuant to paragraph (2) of this subsection shall serve for a term of four years. The initial members of the commission appointed pursuant to paragraph (4) of this subsection shall serve for terms of two years. The initial members of the commission shall be appointed not later than May 22, 2005, and shall serve until their terms expire. The succeeding members of the commission shall begin their terms of office on July 1 of the year in which appointed. A member may be appointed to succeed himself or herself on the commission. If a member of the commission is an elected official, he or she shall be removed from the commission if he or she no longer serves as an elected official.

(b) The Governor shall designate the chairperson of the commission. The commission may elect other officers as deemed necessary. The chairperson of the commission may designate and appoint committees from among the membership of the commission as well as appoint other persons to perform such functions as he or she may determine to be necessary as relevant to and consistent with this article. The chairperson shall only vote to break a tie.

(c) The commission shall be attached for administrative purposes only to the Department of Human Services. The Department of Human Services shall provide staff support for the commission. The Department of Human Services shall use any funds specifically appropriated to it to support the work of the commission.

§ 19-6-52. Meetings; members' expenses

(a) The commission shall hold meetings at the call of the chairperson or as called by the Governor. Meetings shall be open to the public.

(b) A quorum for transacting business shall be a majority of the members of the commission.

(c) Any legislative members of the commission shall receive the allowances provided for in Code Section 28-1-8. Citizen members shall receive a daily expense allowance in the amount specified in subsection (b) of Code Section 45-7-21 as well as the mileage or transportation allowance authorized for state employees. Members of the commission who are state officials, other than legislative members, or state employees shall receive no compensation for their services on the commission, but they shall be reimbursed for expenses incurred by them in the performance of their duties as members of the commission in the same manner as they are reimbursed for expenses in their capacities as state officials or state employees. The funds necessary for the reimbursement of the expenses of state officials, other than legislative members, and state employees shall come from funds appropriated to or otherwise available to their respective departments. All other funds necessary to carry out the provisions of this article shall come from funds appropriated to the House of Representatives and the Senate.

§ 19-6-53. Duties; powers; authorization to retain professional services

(a) The commission shall have the following duties:
(1) To study and evaluate the effectiveness and efficiency of Georgia's child support guidelines;
(2) To evaluate and consider the experiences and results in other states which utilize child support guidelines;
(3) To create and recommend to the General Assembly a child support obligation table consistent with Code Section 19-6-15;
(4) To determine periodically, and at least every four years, if the child support obligation table results in appropriate presumptive awards;
(5) To identify and recommend whether and when the child support obligation table or child support guidelines should be modified;
(6) To develop, publish in print or electronically, and update the child support obligation table and worksheets and schedules associated with the use of such table;
(7) To develop or cause to be developed software and a calculator associated with the use of the child support obligation table and child support guidelines and adjust the formula for the calculations of self-employed persons' income pursuant to applicable federal law, if the commission determines that the calculation affects persons paying or receiving child support in this state;
(8) To develop training manuals and information to educate judges, attorneys, and litigants on the use of the child support obligation table and child support guidelines;
(9) To collaborate with the Institute for Continuing Judicial Education, the Institute of Continuing Legal Education, and other agencies for the purpose of training persons who will be utilizing the child support obligation table and child support guidelines;
(10) To make recommendations for proposed legislation;
(11) To study the appellate courts' acceptance of discretionary appeals in domestic relations cases and the formulation of case law in the area of domestic relations;
(12) To study alternative programs, such as mediation, collaborative practice, and pro se assistance programs, in order to reduce litigation in child support and child custody cases; and
(13) To study the impact of having parenting time serve as a deviation to the presumptive amount of child support and make recommendations concerning the utilization of the parenting time adjustment.
(b) The commission shall have the following powers:
(1) To evaluate the child support guidelines in Georgia and any other program or matter relative to child support in Georgia;
(2) To request and receive data from and review the records of appropriate agencies to the greatest extent allowed by state and federal law;
(3) To accept public or private grants, devises, and bequests;
(4) To enter into all contracts or agreements necessary or incidental to the performance of its duties;
(5) To establish rules and procedures for conducting the business of the commission; and
(6) To conduct studies, hold public meetings, collect data, or take any other action the commission deems necessary to fulfill its responsibilities.
(c) The commission shall be authorized to retain the services of auditors, attorneys, financial consultants, child care experts, economists, and other individuals or firms as determined appropriate by the commission.

CHAPTER 7. PARENT AND CHILD RELATIONSHIP GENERALLY
ARTICLE 1. GENERAL PROVISIONS

§ 19-7-1. In whom parental power lies; how such power lost; recovery for homicide of child

(a) Until a child reaches the age of 18 or becomes emancipated, the child shall remain under the control of his or her parents, who are entitled to the child's services and the proceeds of the child's labor. In the event that a court has awarded custody of the child to one parent, only the parent who has custody of the child is entitled to the child's services and the proceeds of the child's labor.
(b) Parental power shall be lost by:
(1) Voluntary contract releasing the right to a third person;
(2) Consent to the adoption of the child by a third person;

(3) Failure to provide necessaries for the child or abandonment of the child;

(4) Consent to the child's receiving the proceeds of his own labor, which consent shall be revocable at any time;

(5) Consent to the marriage of the child, who thus assumes inconsistent responsibilities;

(6) Cruel treatment of the child;

(7) A superior court order terminating parental rights in an adoption proceeding in accordance with Chapter 8 of this title; or

(8) A superior court order terminating parental rights of the legal father or the biological father who is not the legal father of the child in a petition for legitimation, a petition to establish paternity, a divorce proceeding, or a custody proceeding pursuant to this chapter or Chapter 5, 8, or 9 of this title, provided that such termination is in the best interest of such child; and provided, further, that this paragraph shall not apply to such termination when a child has been adopted or is conceived by artificial insemination as set forth in Code Section 19-7-21 or when an embryo is adopted as set forth in Article 2 of Chapter 8 of this title.

(b.1) Notwithstanding subsections (a) and (b) of this Code section or any other law to the contrary, in any action involving the custody of a child between the parents or either parent and a third party limited to grandparent, great-grandparent, aunt, uncle, great aunt, great uncle, sibling, or adoptive parent, parental power may be lost by the parent, parents, or any other person if the court hearing the issue of custody, in the exercise of its sound discretion and taking into consideration all the circumstances of the case, determines that an award of custody to such third party is for the best interest of the child or children and will best promote their welfare and happiness. There shall be a rebuttable presumption that it is in the best interest of the child or children for custody to be awarded to the parent or parents of such child or children, but this presumption may be overcome by a showing that an award of custody to such third party is in the best interest of the child or children. The sole issue for determination in any such case shall be what is in the best interest of the child or children.

(c) (1) In every case of the homicide of a child, minor or sui juris, there shall be some party entitled to recover the full value of the life of the child, either as provided in this Code section or as provided in Chapter 4 of Title 51.

(2) If the deceased child does not leave a spouse or child, the right of recovery shall be in the parent or parents, if any, given such a right by this paragraph as follows:

(A) If the parents are living together and not divorced, the right shall be in the parents jointly;

(B) If either parent is deceased, the right shall be in the surviving parent; or

(C) If both parents are living but are divorced, separated, or living apart, the right shall be in both parents. However, if the parents are divorced, separated, or living apart and one parent refuses to proceed or cannot be located to proceed to recover for the wrongful death of a child, the other parent shall have the right to contract for representation on behalf of both parents, thereby binding both parents, and the right to proceed on behalf of both parents to recover for the homicide of the child with any ultimate recovery to be shared by the parents as provided in this subsection. Unless a motion is filed as provided in paragraph (6) of this subsection, such a judgment shall be divided equally between the parents by the judgment; and the share of an absent parent shall be held for such time, on such terms, and with such direction for payment if the absent parent is not found as the judgment directs. Payment of a judgment awarded to the parent or parents having the cause of action under this subparagraph or the execution of a release by a parent or parents having a cause of action under this subparagraph shall constitute a full and complete discharge of the judgment debtor or releasee. If, after two years from the date of any recovery, the share of an absent parent has not been paid to the absent parent, the other parent can petition the court for the funds, and the recovery, under appropriate court order, shall be paid over to the parent who initiated the recovery.

(3) The intent of this subsection is to provide a right of recovery in every case of the homicide of a child who does not leave a spouse or child. If, in any case, there is no right of action in a parent or parents under the above rules, the right of recovery shall be determined by Code Section 51-4-5.

(4) In this subsection the terms "homicide" and "full value of the life" shall have the meaning given them in Chapter 4 of Title 51.

(5) In actions for recovery, the fact that the child was born out of wedlock shall be no bar to recovery.

(6) For cases in which the parents of a deceased child are divorced, separated, or living apart, a motion may be filed by either parent prior to trial requesting the judge to apportion fairly any judgment amounts awarded in the case. Where such a motion is filed, a judgment shall not be automatically divided. A postjudgment hearing shall be conducted by the judge at which each parent shall have the opportunity to be heard and to produce evidence regarding that parent's relationship with the deceased child. The judge shall fairly determine the percentage of the judgment to be awarded to each parent. In making such a determination, the judge shall consider each parent's relationship with the deceased child, including permanent custody, control, and support, as well as any other factors found to be pertinent. The judge's decision shall not be disturbed absent an abuse of discretion.

§ 19-7-2. Parents' obligations to child

It is the joint and several duty of each parent to provide for the maintenance, protection, and education of his or her child until the child reaches the age of majority, dies, marries, or becomes emancipated, whichever first occurs, except as otherwise authorized and ordered pursuant to subsection (e) of Code Section 19-6-15 and except to the extent that the duty of the parents is otherwise or further defined by court order.

§ 19-7-3. Actions by grandparents or other family members for visitation rights or intervention; revocation or amendment of visitation rights; appointment of guardian ad litem; mediation; hearing; notification to family members of child's participation in events

(a) As used in this Code section, the term:
(1) "Family member" means a grandparent, great-grandparent, or sibling.
(2) "Grandparent" means the parent of a parent of a minor child, the parent of a minor child's parent who has died, and the parent of a minor child's parent whose parental rights have been terminated.
(3) "Great-grandparent" means the parent of the parent of a parent of a minor child, the parent of the parent of a minor child's parent who has died, and the parent of the parent of a minor child's parent whose parental rights have been terminated.
(4) "Sibling" means the brother or sister of a parent of a minor child, the brother or sister of a minor child's parent who has died, and the brother or sister of a minor child's parent whose parental rights have been terminated.
(b) (1) Except as otherwise provided in paragraph (2) of this subsection:
 (A) Any grandparent shall have the right to file an original action for visitation rights to a minor child; and
 (B) Any family member shall have the right to intervene in and seek to obtain visitation rights in any action in which any court in this state shall have before it any question concerning the custody of a minor child, a divorce of the parents or a parent of such minor child, a termination of the parental rights of either parent of such minor child, or visitation rights concerning such minor child or whenever there has been an adoption in which the adopted child has been adopted by the child's blood relative or by a stepparent, notwithstanding the provisions of Code Section 19-8-19.
(2) This subsection shall not authorize an original action when the parents of the minor child are not separated and the child is living with both parents.
(c) (1) Upon the filing of an original action or upon intervention in an existing proceeding under subsection (b) of this Code section, the court may grant any family member of the child reasonable visitation rights if the court finds by clear and convincing evidence that the health or welfare of the child would be harmed unless such visitation is granted and if the best interests of the child would be served by such visitation. The mere absence of an opportunity for a child to develop a relationship with a family member shall not be considered as harming the health or welfare of the child when there is no substantial preexisting relationship between the child and such family member. In considering whether the health or welfare of the child would be harmed without such visitation, the court shall consider and may find that harm to the child is reasonably likely to result when, prior to the original action or intervention:
 (A) The minor child resided with the family member for six months or more;
 (B) The family member provided financial support for the basic needs of the child for at least one year;
 (C) There was an established pattern of regular visitation or child care by the family member with the child; or
 (D) Any other circumstance exists indicating that emotional or physical harm would be reasonably likely to result if such visitation is not granted.
The court shall make specific written findings of fact in support of its rulings.
(2) An original action requesting visitation rights shall not be filed by any grandparent more than once during any two-year period and shall not be filed during any year in which another custody action has been filed concerning the child. After visitation rights have been granted to any grandparent, the legal custodian, guardian of the person, or parent of the child may petition the court for revocation or amendment of such visitation rights, for good cause shown, which the court, in its discretion, may grant or deny; but such a petition shall not be filed more than once in any two-year period.
(3) While a parent's decision regarding family member visitation shall be given deference by the court, the parent's decision shall not be conclusive when failure to provide family member contact would result in emotional harm to the child. A court may presume that a child who is denied any contact with his or her family member or who is not provided some minimal opportunity for contact with his or her family member when there is a preexisting relationship between the child and such family member may suffer emotional injury that is harmful to such child's health. Such presumption shall be a rebuttable presumption.
(4) In no case shall the granting of visitation rights to a family member interfere with a child's school or regularly scheduled extracurricular activities.
(5) Visitation time awarded to a family member shall not be less than 24 hours in any one-month period; provided, however, that when more than one individual seeks visitation under this Code section, the court shall determine the amount of time to award to each petitioner which shall not be less than 24 hours in any one-month period in the aggregate.

(d) Notwithstanding the provisions of subsections (b) and (c) of this Code section, if one of the parents of a minor child dies, is incapacitated, or is incarcerated, the court may award the parent of the deceased, incapacitated, or incarcerated parent of such minor child reasonable visitation to such child during his or her minority if the court in its discretion finds that such visitation would be in the best interests of the child. The custodial parent's judgment as to the best interests of the child regarding visitation shall be given deference by the court but shall not be conclusive.
(e) If the court finds that the family member can bear the cost without unreasonable financial hardship, the court, at the sole expense of the petitioning family member, may:
  (1) Appoint a guardian ad litem for the minor child; and
  (2) Assign the issue of visitation rights of a family member for mediation.
(f) In the event that the court does not order mediation or upon failure of the parties to reach an agreement through mediation, the court shall fix a time for the hearing of the issue of visitation rights of the family member.
(g) Whether or not visitation is awarded to a family member, the court may direct a custodial parent, by court order, to notify such family member of every performance of the minor child to which the public is admitted, including, but not limited to, musical concerts, graduations, recitals, and sporting events or games.
(h) When more than one family member files an action pursuant to this Code section, the court shall determine the priority of such actions.

§ 19-7-4. Criteria for loss of parental custody

If a child is found under circumstances of destitution and suffering, abandonment, or exposure or if the child has been begging or if it is found that the child is being reared under immoral, obscene, or indecent influences which are likely to degrade his moral character and devote him to a vicious life and it appears to the appropriate court by competent evidence, including such examination of the child as may be practicable, that by reason of the neglect, habitual drunkenness, lewd or other vicious habits, or other behavior of the parents or guardians of the child, it is necessary for the welfare of the child to protect the child from such conditions, the court may order that the parents or guardians be deprived of custody of the child and that appropriate measures as provided by law be taken for the welfare of the child.

§ 19-7-5. Reporting of child abuse; when mandated or authorized; content of report; to whom made; immunity from liability; report based upon privileged communication; penalty for failure to report

(a) The purpose of this Code section is to provide for the protection of children. It is intended that mandatory reporting will cause the protective services of the state to be brought to bear on the situation in an effort to prevent abuses, to protect and enhance the welfare of children, and to preserve family life wherever possible. This Code section shall be liberally construed so as to carry out the purposes thereof.
(b) As used in this Code section, the term:
  (1) "Abortion" shall have the same meaning as set forth in Code Section 15-11-681.
  (2) "Abused" means subjected to child abuse.
  (3) "Child" means any person under 18 years of age.
  (4) "Child abuse" means:
    (A) Physical injury or death inflicted upon a child by a parent or caretaker thereof by other than accidental means; provided, however, that physical forms of discipline may be used as long as there is no physical injury to the child;
    (B) Neglect or exploitation of a child by a parent or caretaker thereof;
    (C) Endangering a child;
    (D) Sexual abuse of a child; or
    (E) Sexual exploitation of a child.
However, no child who in good faith is being treated solely by spiritual means through prayer in accordance with the tenets and practices of a recognized church or religious denomination by a duly accredited practitioner thereof shall, for that reason alone, be considered to be an abused child.
  (5) "Child service organization personnel" means persons employed by or volunteering at a business or an organization, whether public, private, for profit, not for profit, or voluntary, that provides care, treatment, education, training, supervision, coaching, counseling, recreational programs, or shelter to children.
  (6) "Clergy" means ministers, priests, rabbis, imams, or similar functionaries, by whatever name called, of a bona fide religious organization.
  (6.1) "Endangering a child" means:
    (A) Any act described by subsection (d) of Code Section 16-5-70;
    (B) Any act described by Code Section 16-5-73;
    (C) Any act described by subsection (l) of Code Section 40-6-391; or
    (D) Prenatal abuse, as such term is defined in Code Section 15-11-2.

(7) "Pregnancy resource center" means an organization or facility that:
　(A) Provides pregnancy counseling or information as its primary purpose, either for a fee or as a free service;
　(B) Does not provide or refer for abortions;
　(C) Does not provide or refer for FDA approved contraceptive drugs or devices; and
　(D) Is not licensed or certified by the state or federal government to provide medical or health care services and is not otherwise bound to follow the federal Health Insurance Portability and Accountability Act of 1996, P.L. 104-191, or other state or federal laws relating to patient confidentiality.
(8) "Reproductive health care facility" means any office, clinic, or any other physical location that provides abortions, abortion counseling, abortion referrals, or gynecological care and services.
(9) "School" means any public or private pre-kindergarten, elementary school, secondary school, technical school, vocational school, college, university, or institution of postsecondary education.
(10) "Sexual abuse" means a person's employing, using, persuading, inducing, enticing, or coercing any minor who is not such person's spouse to engage in any act which involves:
　(A) Sexual intercourse, including genital-genital, oral-genital, anal-genital, or oral-anal, whether between persons of the same or opposite sex;
　(B) Bestiality;
　(C) Masturbation;
　(D) Lewd exhibition of the genitals or pubic area of any person;
　(E) Flagellation or torture by or upon a person who is nude;
　(F) Condition of being fettered, bound, or otherwise physically restrained on the part of a person who is nude;
　(G) Physical contact in an act of apparent sexual stimulation or gratification with any person's clothed or unclothed genitals, pubic area, or buttocks or with a female's clothed or unclothed breasts;
　(H) Defecation or urination for the purpose of sexual stimulation;
　(I) Penetration of the vagina or rectum by any object except when done as part of a recognized medical procedure; or
　(J) Any act described by subsection (c) of Code Section 16-5-46.
Sexual abuse shall include consensual sex acts when the sex acts are between minors if any individual is less than 14 years of age; provided, however, that it shall not include consensual sex acts when the sex acts are between a minor and an adult who is not more than four years older than the minor. This provision shall not be deemed or construed to repeal any law concerning the age or capacity to consent.
(11) "Sexual exploitation" means conduct by any person who allows, permits, encourages, or requires a child to engage in:
　(A) Prostitution, as defined in Code Section 16-6-9; or
　(B) Sexually explicit conduct for the purpose of producing any visual or print medium depicting such conduct, as defined in Code Section 16-12-100.
(c) (1) The following persons having reasonable cause to believe that suspected child abuse has occurred shall report or cause reports of such abuse to be made as provided in this Code section:
　(A) Physicians licensed to practice medicine, physician assistants, interns, or residents;
　(B) Hospital or medical personnel;
　(C) Dentists;
　(D) Licensed psychologists and persons participating in internships to obtain licensing pursuant to Chapter 39 of Title 43;
　(E) Podiatrists;
　(F) Registered professional nurses or licensed practical nurses licensed pursuant to Chapter 26 of Title 43 or nurse's aides;
　(G) Professional counselors, social workers, or marriage and family therapists licensed pursuant to Chapter 10A of Title 43;
　(H) School teachers;
　(I) School administrators;
　(J) School counselors, visiting teachers, school social workers, or school psychologists certified pursuant to Chapter 2 of Title 20;
　(K) Child welfare agency personnel, as such agency is defined in Code Section 49-5-12;
　(L) Child-counseling personnel;
　(M) Child service organization personnel;
　(N) Law enforcement personnel; or
　(O) Reproductive health care facility or pregnancy resource center personnel and volunteers.
(2) If a person is required to report child abuse pursuant to this subsection because such person attends to a child pursuant to such person's duties as an employee of or volunteer at a hospital, school, social agency, or similar facility, such person shall notify the person in charge of such hospital, school, agency, or facility, or the designated delegate thereof, and the person so notified shall report or cause a report to be made in accordance with this Code section. An employee or volunteer who makes a report to the person designated pursuant to this paragraph shall be deemed to have fully complied with this subsection. Under no

circumstances shall any person in charge of such hospital, school, agency, or facility, or the designated delegate thereof, to whom such notification has been made exercise any control, restraint, or modification or make any other change to the information provided by the reporter, although each of the aforementioned persons may be consulted prior to the making of a report and may provide any additional, relevant, and necessary information when making the report.

(3) When a person identified in paragraph (1) of this subsection has reasonable cause to believe that child abuse has occurred involving a person who attends to a child pursuant to such person's duties as an employee of or volunteer at a hospital, school, social agency, or similar facility, the person who received such information shall notify the person in charge of such hospital, school, agency, or facility, or the designated delegate thereof, and the person so notified shall report or cause a report to be made in accordance with this Code section. An employee or volunteer who makes a report to the person designated pursuant to this paragraph shall be deemed to have fully complied with this subsection. Under no circumstances shall any person in charge of such hospital, school, agency, or facility, or the designated delegate thereof, to whom such notification has been made exercise any control, restraint, or modification or make any other change to the information provided by the reporter, although each of the aforementioned persons may be consulted prior to the making of a report and may provide any additional, relevant, and necessary information when making the report.

(d) Any other person, other than one specified in subsection (c) of this Code section, who has reasonable cause to believe that suspected child abuse has occurred may report or cause reports to be made as provided in this Code section.

(e) With respect to reporting required by subsection (c) of this Code section, an oral report by telephone or other oral communication or a written report by electronic submission or facsimile shall be made immediately, but in no case later than 24 hours from the time there is reasonable cause to believe that suspected child abuse has occurred. When a report is being made by electronic submission or facsimile to the Division of Family and Children Services of the Department of Human Services, it shall be done in the manner specified by the division. Oral reports shall be followed by a later report in writing, if requested, to a child welfare agency providing protective services, as designated by the Division of Family and Children Services of the Department of Human Services, or, in the absence of such agency, to an appropriate police authority or district attorney. If a report of child abuse is made to the child welfare agency or independently discovered by the agency, and the agency has reasonable cause to believe such report is true or the report contains any allegation or evidence of child abuse, then the agency shall immediately notify the appropriate police authority or district attorney. Such reports shall contain the names and addresses of the child and the child's parents or caretakers, if known, the child's age, the nature and extent of the child's injuries, including any evidence of previous injuries, and any other information that the reporting person believes might be helpful in establishing the cause of the injuries and the identity of the perpetrator. Photographs of the child's injuries to be used as documentation in support of allegations by hospital employees or volunteers, physicians, law enforcement personnel, school officials, or employees or volunteers of legally mandated public or private child protective agencies may be taken without the permission of the child's parent or guardian. Such photographs shall be made available as soon as possible to the chief welfare agency providing protective services and to the appropriate police authority.

(f) Any person or persons, partnership, firm, corporation, association, hospital, or other entity participating in the making of a report or causing a report to be made to a child welfare agency providing protective services or to an appropriate police authority pursuant to this Code section or any other law or participating in any judicial proceeding or any other proceeding resulting therefrom shall in so doing be immune from any civil or criminal liability that might otherwise be incurred or imposed, provided that such participation pursuant to this Code section or any other law is made in good faith. Any person making a report, whether required by this Code section or not, shall be immune from liability as provided in this subsection.

(g) Suspected child abuse which is required to be reported by any person pursuant to this Code section shall be reported notwithstanding that the reasonable cause to believe such abuse has occurred or is occurring is based in whole or in part upon any communication to that person which is otherwise made privileged or confidential by law; provided, however, that a member of the clergy shall not be required to report child abuse reported solely within the context of confession or other similar communication required to be kept confidential under church doctrine or practice. When a clergy member receives information about child abuse from any other source, the clergy member shall comply with the reporting requirements of this Code section, even though the clergy member may have also received a report of child abuse from the confession of the perpetrator.

(h) Any person or official required by subsection (c) of this Code section to report a suspected case of child abuse who knowingly and willfully fails to do so shall be guilty of a misdemeanor.

(i) A report of child abuse or information relating thereto and contained in such report, when provided to a law enforcement agency or district attorney pursuant to subsection (e) of this Code section or pursuant to Code Section 49-5-41, shall not be subject to public inspection under Article 4 of Chapter 18 of Title 50 even though such report or information is contained in or part of closed records compiled for law enforcement or prosecution purposes unless:

(1) There is a criminal or civil court proceeding which has been initiated based in whole or in part upon the facts regarding abuse which are alleged in the child abuse reports and the person or entity seeking to inspect such records provides clear and convincing evidence of such proceeding; or

(2) The superior court in the county in which is located the office of the law enforcement agency or district attorney which compiled the records containing such reports, after application for inspection and a hearing on the issue, shall permit inspection of such records by or release of information from such records to individuals or entities who are engaged in legitimate research for educational, scientific, or public purposes and who comply with the provisions of this paragraph. When those records are located in more than one county, the application may be made to the superior court of any one of such counties. A copy of any application authorized by this paragraph shall be served on the office of the law enforcement agency or district attorney which compiled the records containing such reports. In cases where the location of the records is unknown to the applicant, the application may be made to the Superior Court of Fulton County. The superior court to which an application is made shall not grant the application unless:

(A) The application includes a description of the proposed research project, including a specific statement of the information required, the purpose for which the project requires that information, and a methodology to assure the information is not arbitrarily sought;

(B) The applicant carries the burden of showing the legitimacy of the research project; and

(C) Names and addresses of individuals, other than officials, employees, or agents of agencies receiving or investigating a report of abuse which is the subject of a report, shall be deleted from any information released pursuant to this subsection unless the court determines that having the names and addresses open for review is essential to the research and the child, through his or her representative, gives permission to release the information.

§ 19-7-6. Reporting of juvenile drug use

(a) The purpose of this Code section is to provide for the protection of children whose health and welfare are adversely affected and further threatened by the unlawful use and abuse of controlled substances or marijuana. The General Assembly recognizes the need for early intervention, counseling, and treatment as an effective means of addressing the problem of child controlled substance and marijuana abuse. It is intended that the reporting of the unlawful use of any controlled substance or marijuana will cause the protective services of the state to be brought to bear on this situation in an effort to protect and enhance the welfare of children. This Code section shall be liberally construed so as to carry out the purposes thereof.

(b) Any person exercising in loco parentis control over a child under the age of 18 years who has reasonable cause to believe that the child is habitually using in an unlawful manner any controlled substance or marijuana, as defined in Code Section 16-13-21, is encouraged to report such information to the child's parents and a child welfare agency providing protective services, as designated by the Department of Human Services.

(c) When the attendance of the person exercising in loco parentis control over a child is pursuant to the performance of services as a member of the staff of any school, social agency, or similar facility, the reporting person shall notify the person in charge of the facility or his designated delegate; and such person or his delegate shall report or cause reports to be made in accordance with this Code section.

(d) An oral report shall be made as soon as possible by telephone or otherwise and shall be followed by a report in writing, if requested, to the child welfare agency providing protective services, as designated by the Department of Human Services. Such report shall contain the names and addresses of the child and his parents or caretakers, if known, the child's age, and the nature and extent of the child's controlled substance or marijuana abuse history, if known.

(e) No agency or political subdivision of this state shall enact or enforce any disciplinary rule or penalty against an employee of the state or of any political subdivision of the state for failure to make any report referred to in subsection (b), (c), or (d) of this Code section.

(f) Any person or persons, partnership, firm, corporation, association, hospital, or other entity participating in the making of a report or causing a report to be made to a child welfare agency providing protective services pursuant to this Code section or any other law or participating in any judicial proceeding or any other proceeding resulting therefrom shall, in doing so, be immune from any civil or criminal liability that might otherwise be incurred or imposed if such participation, pursuant to this Code section or any other law, is made in good faith. Any person making a report, whether required by this Code section or not, shall be immune from liability as provided in this subsection.

(g) Any person or official required to report under this Code section shall be exempt from reporting any information received from the child during a counseling or treatment program.

(h) The child welfare agency providing protective services, as designated by the Department of Human Services, shall forward a copy of all reports wherein the reporting person or official has actual knowledge that a child under the age of 18 has unlawfully consumed or otherwise used any controlled substance or marijuana to the juvenile court. As used in this subsection, the term "juvenile court" means the court exercising jurisdiction over juvenile matters, as defined under Code Section 15-11-2, in the county where the report was made.

ARTICLE 2. LEGITIMACY

§ 19-7-20. Circumstances of legitimacy; disproving legitimacy; legitimation by marriage of parents and recognition of child

(a) All children born in wedlock or within the usual period of gestation thereafter are legitimate.
(b) The legitimacy of a child born as described in subsection (a) of this Code section may be disputed. Where possibility of access exists, the strong presumption is in favor of legitimacy and the proof must be clear to establish the contrary. If pregnancy existed at the time of the marriage and a divorce is sought and obtained on that ground, the child, although born in wedlock, will not be legitimate.
(c) The marriage of the mother and reputed father of a child born out of wedlock and the recognition by the father of the child as his shall render the child legitimate; in such case the child shall immediately take the surname of his father.

§ 19-7-21. When children conceived by artificial insemination legitimate

All children born within wedlock or within the usual period of gestation thereafter who have been conceived by means of artificial insemination are irrebuttably presumed legitimate if both spouses have consented in writing to the use and administration of artificial insemination.

§ 19-7-21.1. "Acknowledgment of legitimation" and "legal father" defined; signing acknowledgment of legitimation; when acknowledgment not recognized; making false statement; rescinding acknowledgment

Repealed by Ga. L. 2016, p. 304, § 2/SB 64, effective July 1, 2016.

§ 19-7-22. Petition for legitimation of child; requirement that mother be named as a party; court order; effect; claims for custody or visitation; third-party action for legitimation in response to petition to establish paternity

(a) As used in this Code section, the term:
(1) "Biological father" means the male who impregnated the biological mother resulting in the birth of a child.
(2) "Legal father" means a male who has not surrendered or had terminated his rights to a child and who:
(A) Has legally adopted such child;
(B) Was married to the biological mother of such child at the time such child was born or within the usual period of gestation, unless paternity was disproved by a final order pursuant to Article 3 of this chapter;
(C) Married the legal mother of such child after such child was born and recognized such child as his own, unless paternity was disproved by a final order pursuant to Article 3 of this chapter; or
(D) Has legitimated such child pursuant to this Code section.
(b) The biological father of a child born out of wedlock may render his relationship with the child legitimate by petitioning the superior court of the county of the residence of the child's mother or other party having legal custody or guardianship of the child; provided, however, that if the mother or other party having legal custody or guardianship of the child resides outside this state or cannot, after due diligence, be found within this state, the petition may be filed in the county of the biological father's residence or the county of the child's residence. If a petition for the adoption of the child is pending, the biological father shall file the petition for legitimation in the county in which the adoption petition is filed.
(c) A legitimation petition shall set forth the name, age, and sex of the child, the name of the mother, and, if the biological father desires the name of the child to be changed, the new name. If the mother is alive, she shall be named as a party and shall be served and provided an opportunity to be heard as in other civil actions under Chapter 11 of Title 9, the "Georgia Civil Practice Act." If there is a legal father who is not the biological father, he shall be named as a party by the petitioner and shall be served and provided an opportunity to be heard as in other civil actions under Chapter 11 of Title 9, the "Georgia Civil Practice Act."
(d) (1) Upon the presentation and filing of a legitimation petition, and after a hearing for which notice was provided to all interested parties, the court may issue an order declaring the biological father's relationship with the child to be legitimate, provided that such order is in the best interests of the child. If such order is issued, the biological father and child shall be capable of inheriting from each other in the same manner as if born in lawful wedlock. Such order shall specify the name by which the child shall be known.

(2) (A) If the court determines by clear and convincing evidence that the father caused his child to be conceived as a result of having nonconsensual sexual intercourse with the mother of his child or when the mother is less than ten years of age, or an offense which consists of the same or similar elements under federal law or the laws of another state or territory of the United States, it shall create a presumption against legitimation.

(B) Notwithstanding Code Section 53-2-3, if the court denies a legitimation petition under this paragraph, the child shall be capable of inheriting from or through his or her father. Notwithstanding Code Section 53-2-4, if the court denies a legitimation petition under this paragraph, the father shall not be capable of inheriting from or through his child.

(C) If there is a pending criminal proceeding in connection with an allegation made pursuant to subparagraph (A) of this paragraph, the court shall stay discovery in the legitimation action until the completion of such criminal proceeding.

(e) A legitimation petition may be filed, pursuant to Code Section 15-11-11, in the juvenile court of the county in which a dependency proceeding regarding the child is pending; provided, however, that if either parent has demanded a jury trial as to child support, that issue of the case shall be transferred to superior court for a jury trial. Such petition shall contain the same information and require the same service and opportunity to be heard as set forth in subsection (c) of this Code section. After a hearing, the juvenile court may issue the same orders as set forth in subsection (d) of this Code section.

(f) A superior court shall, after notice and hearing, enter an order establishing the obligation to support a child as provided under Code Section 19-6-15.

(g) A legitimation petition may also include claims for visitation, parenting time, or custody. If such claims are raised in the legitimation action, the court may order, in addition to legitimation, visitation, parenting time, or custody based on the best interests of the child standard. In a case involving allegations of family violence, the provisions of paragraph (4) of subsection (a) of Code Section 19-9-3 shall also apply.

(h) In any petition to establish paternity pursuant to paragraph (4) of subsection (a) of Code Section 19-7-43, the alleged biological father's response may assert a third-party action for the legitimation of the child born out of wedlock if the alleged biological father is, in fact, the biological father. Upon the determination of paternity or if a voluntary acknowledgment of paternity has been made and has not been rescinded pursuant to Code Section 19-7-46.1, the court or trier of fact as a matter of law and pursuant to the provisions of Code Section 19-7-51 may enter an order or decree legitimating a child born out of wedlock, provided that such is in the best interests of the child. In determining the best interests of the child, the court should ensure that the petitioning alleged biological father is, in fact, the biological father and may order the mother, the alleged biological father, and the child to submit to genetic testing in accordance with Code Section 19-7-45. Whenever a petition to establish the paternity of a child is brought by the Department of Human Services, issues of name change, visitation, and custody shall not be determined by the court until such time as a separate petition is filed by one of the parents or by the legal guardian of the child, in accordance with Code Section 19-11-8; if the petition to establish paternity is brought by a party other than the Department of Human Services or if the alleged biological father seeks legitimation, the court may determine issues of name change, visitation, and custody in accordance with subsections (c) and (g) of this Code section. Custody of the child shall remain in the mother unless or until a court order is entered addressing the issue of custody.

§ 19-7-23. "Child born out of wedlock" defined

The term "child born out of wedlock" means:
(1) A child whose parents are not married when that child is born or who do not subsequently intermarry;
(2) A child who is the issue of adulterous intercourse of the wife during wedlock; or
(3) A child who is not legitimate within the meaning of Code Section 19-7-20.

§ 19-7-24. Parents' obligations to child born out of wedlock

It is the joint and several duty of each parent of a child born out of wedlock to provide for the maintenance, protection, and education of the child until the child reaches the age of 18 or becomes emancipated, except to the extent that the duty of one parent is otherwise or further defined by court order.

§ 19-7-25. In whom parental power over child born out of wedlock lies

Only the mother of a child born out of wedlock is entitled to custody of the child, unless the father legitimates the child as provided in Code Section 19-7-22. Otherwise, the mother may exercise all parental power over the child.

§ 19-7-26. Mother of child born out of wedlock not to be discriminated against in action to recover for injury or death of the child

In an action brought by the mother of a child born out of wedlock in her own right or in her capacity as guardian, executor, or administrator for damages for the child's injury or death, the mother shall not be discriminated against because of her child's having been born out of wedlock.

§ 19-7-27. Hospital program for establishment of paternity

(a) Except in the event of a medical emergency, prior to the birth of a child to an unmarried woman in a public or private hospital, the hospital that provides labor and delivery services shall provide to the mother and alleged father:
 (1) Written materials about administratively establishing paternity;
 (2) The forms necessary to voluntarily acknowledge paternity;
 (3) A written description of the rights and responsibilities of voluntarily acknowledging paternity, the differences between paternity and legitimation, and the duty to support a child upon acknowledgment of paternity; and
 (4) The opportunity, prior to discharge from the hospital, to speak with staff, either by telephone or in person, who are trained to clarify information and answer questions about administratively establishing paternity and the availability of judicial determinations of paternity.
(b) Providing the written materials describing rights and responsibilities shall not constitute the unlawful practice of law.
(c) After the birth of a child to an unmarried woman in a public or private hospital, the hospital that provides labor and delivery services shall:
 (1) Provide the child's mother and alleged father if he is present at the hospital the opportunity to execute a voluntary acknowledgment of paternity if a notary public is available at such hospital;
 (2) File the signed voluntary acknowledgment of paternity with the State Office of Vital Records within 30 days of its execution, provided that such acknowledgment is signed at the hospital on or before the mother is discharged; and
 (3) Provide to the child's mother and alleged father copies of the signed voluntary acknowledgment of paternity.

ARTICLE 3. DETERMINATION OF PATERNITY
§ 19-7-40. Jurisdiction; administrative determination of paternity

(a) The superior and state courts of the several counties shall have concurrent jurisdiction in all proceedings for the determination of paternity of children who are residents of this state. The state courts shall have such concurrent jurisdiction notwithstanding any contrary provision of local law. Parties to an action to establish paternity shall not be entitled to a trial by jury.
(b) Whenever the Department of Human Services seeks to establish paternity of a child, the Office of State Administrative Hearings shall have authority to adjudicate the issue of paternity, pursuant to Chapter 13 of Title 50, the "Georgia Administrative Procedure Act"; provided, however, that if the putative father demands a trial in the superior court, it shall be the duty of the judge to cause an issue to be made and tried at the first session of the next term of court succeeding the putative father's demand for trial. The administrative determination shall have the same force and effect as a judicial decree.

§ 19-7-41. Service outside state

In a proceeding under this article, the court, pursuant to Chapter 11 of Title 9, may order service upon a person outside the state upon a finding that there is a constitutionally permissible basis for jurisdiction over the person, including those enumerated in Article 3 of Chapter 11 of this title.

§ 19-7-42. Venue

The action shall be brought in the county in which the alleged father resides, except that, if the alleged father is not a resident of this state, the action shall be brought in the county in which the child resides.

§ 19-7-43. Petition; by whom brought; effect of agreement on right to bring petition; stay pending birth of child; court order for blood tests; genetic tests

(a) A petition to establish the paternity of a child may be brought by:
(1) The child;
(2) The mother of the child;
(3) Any relative in whose care the child has been placed;
(4) The Department of Human Services in the name of and for the benefit of a child for whom public assistance is received or in the name of and for the benefit of a child not the recipient of public services whose custodian has applied for services for the child; or
(5) One who is alleged to be the father.
(b) Regardless of its terms, an agreement, other than an agreement approved by the court in accordance with this article, between an alleged or presumed father and the mother or child does not bar a petition under this Code section.
(c) If a petition under this article is brought before the birth of the child, all proceedings shall be stayed until after the birth except service of process, discovery, and the taking of depositions.
(d) In any case in which the paternity of a child or children has not been established, the court, either on its own motion or on the motion of any party, may order the mother, the alleged father, and the child or children to submit to genetic tests as specified in Code Section 19-7-45. Such motion, if made by a party, shall be supported by a sworn statement alleging paternity and setting forth facts establishing a reasonable possibility of the requisite sexual contact between the parties or denying paternity and setting forth facts establishing a reasonable possibility of the nonexistence of sexual contact between the parties. Appropriate orders shall be issued by the court. The court shall grant a party's motion unless it finds a good excuse for noncooperation.
(e) In any case for the collection of child support involving the Department of Human Services in which the paternity of a child or children has not been established or in which the individual receiving services alleges that paternity rests in a person other than the previously established father, the Department of Human Services shall order genetic testing of the mother, the alleged father, and the child or children as specified in Code Section 19-7-45. No genetic testing shall be undertaken by the Department of Human Services if the child was adopted either by the applicant for services or other alleged parent or if the child was conceived by means of artificial insemination. The need for genetic testing shall be supported by a sworn statement alleging paternity and setting forth facts establishing a reasonable possibility of the requisite sexual contact between the parties. The parties shall be given notice and an opportunity to contest the order before the Department of Human Services prior to the testing or the imposition of any noncooperation sanction.
(f) In any case in which the court or the Department of Human Services orders genetic testing and one or both of the parties to the action is receiving child support services pursuant to Code Section 19-11-6, the Department of Human Services shall pay the costs of such tests subject to recoupment from the alleged father if paternity is established. If the genetic test excludes the possibility of the alleged father being the biological father, then the applicant for services who named the alleged father shall be liable to the Department of Human Services for reimbursement of the paternity testing fee. Upon completion of the first test, but prior to the entry of any order, a second genetic test shall be ordered if the person making the request tenders payment in full of the cost of the initial test as well as the cost of the second test at the time of the request. Any party who, after notice sent by mail to his or her last known address, fails to cooperate with paternity testing or fails to make any child available for paternity testing may be sanctioned by the Department of Human Services. Such sanctions may include but shall not be limited to loss of the opportunity for paternity testing, loss of state benefits, denial of services, and administrative case closure. The Department of Human Services may bring a petition for contempt in the event of such noncooperation in violation of any court order.

§ 19-7-44. Appointment of guardian ad litem; payment of guardian; notice to natural mother

(a) The court may, in its discretion, appoint a guardian ad litem to represent a minor child who is the subject of a paternity petition. Payment of the guardian ad litem shall be as ordered by the court. Neither the child's mother nor the alleged or presumed father may represent the child as guardian ad litem.
(b) The natural mother shall be made a party or, if not subject to the jurisdiction of the court, shall be given notice in a manner prescribed by the court and an opportunity to be heard.

§ 19-7-45. Genetic tests

(a) All orders requiring parties to submit to genetic tests shall be issued in conformance with Code Sections 19-7-43, 19-7-46, and 19-7-54. In all cases such tests shall be conducted by a laboratory certified by the

American Association of Blood Banks and shall be conducted so that the results meet the standards the American Association of Blood Banks requires in order for such results to be admitted as evidence in a court of law.
(b) When an action to determine paternity is initiated prior to the birth of a child, the court shall order that the genetic tests be made as soon as medically feasible after the birth.
(c) Genetic tests shall be performed by a duly qualified licensed practicing physician, duly qualified immunologist, or other qualified person. In all cases, however, the court shall determine the number and qualifications of the experts. In all cases the results shall be made known to all parties at interest as soon as available.
(d) An order issued under this Code section is enforceable by contempt, provided that, if the petitioner refuses to submit to an order for a genetic test, the court may dismiss the action upon motion of the respondent.
(e) (1) The Department of Human Services and any court issuing an order with respect to a determination of paternity shall not, insofar as possible, attach the written results from a genetic test to any pleading or court order.
   (2) The genetic material collected for a genetic test shall be destroyed within a reasonable time, as set forth by rule of the Department of Human Services.
   (3) The genetic material collected for a genetic test shall not be shared with any other person or entity.

§ 19-7-46. Evidence at trial

(a) The results of medical tests and comparisons ordered by the court, including the statistical likelihood of the alleged parent's parentage, if available, unless a party to the paternity genetic test objects in writing at least 30 days prior to a hearing at which the results of the testing may be introduced into evidence, shall be admitted in evidence without the need for foundation testimony or other proof of authenticity or accuracy. When an objection is filed at least 30 days prior to a hearing at which the results may be introduced into evidence, the results of medical tests and comparisons ordered by the court including the statistical likelihood of the alleged parent's parentage, if available, shall be admitted in evidence when offered by a duly qualified, licensed practicing physician, duly qualified immunologist, duly qualified geneticist, or other duly qualified person.
(b) There shall exist a rebuttable presumption of paternity of a child born out of wedlock if there has been performed scientifically credible parentage-determination genetic testing which establishes at least a 97 percent probability of paternity. The rebuttable presumption of paternity can be overcome by the presentation of clear and convincing evidence as determined by the trier of fact. Parentage-determination testing shall include, but not necessarily be limited to, red cell antigen, human leucocyte antigen (HLA), red cell enzyme, and serum protein electrophoresis tests or testing by deoxyribonucleic acid (DNA) probes.
(c) Evidence of a refusal to submit to a genetic test or other ordered medical or anthropological test is admissible to show that the alleged father is not precluded from being the father of the child.
(d) An expert's opinion concerning the time of conception is as admissible as is other expert testimony.
(e) Testimony relating to sexual access to the mother by any person on or about the probable time of conception of the child is admissible in evidence.
(f) Other relevant evidence shall be admitted as is appropriate.

§ 19-7-46.1. Effect of father's name or social security number on records as evidence of paternity; signed voluntary acknowledgment of paternity; certified copy of voluntary acknowledgment of paternity

(a) The appearance of the name or social security account number of the father, entered with his written consent, on the certificate of birth or a certified copy of such certificate or records on which the name of the alleged father was entered with his written consent from the vital records department of another state or the registration of the father, entered with his written consent, in the putative father registry of this state, pursuant to subsection (d) of Code Section 19-11-9, shall constitute a prima-facie case of establishment of paternity and the burden of proof shall shift to the putative father to rebut such in a proceeding for the determination of paternity.
(b) When both the mother and father have signed a voluntary acknowledgment of paternity in the presence of a notary public swearing or affirming the statements contained in the acknowledgment are true and such acknowledgment is filed with the State Office of Vital Records within 30 days of its execution and is recorded in the putative father registry established by subsection (d) of Code Section 19-11-9, the acknowledgment shall constitute a legal determination of paternity, subject to the right of any signatory to rescind the acknowledgment prior to the date of the support order, any other order adjudicating paternity, or 60 days from the signing of the agreement, whichever is earlier. Recording such information in the putative father registry shall constitute a legal determination of paternity for purposes of establishing a future order for support and other matters under Code Section 19-7-51. Acknowledgment of paternity shall establish the

biological father, as such term is defined in Code Section 19-7-22, but shall not constitute a legal determination of legitimation pursuant to Code Section 19-7-22.
(c) After the 60 day rescission period specified in subsection (b) of this Code section, the signed voluntary acknowledgment of paternity may be challenged in court only on the basis of fraud, duress, or material mistake of fact, with the burden of proof on the person challenging the acknowledgment. The legal responsibilities of any signatory, including child support obligations, arising from the acknowledgment may not be suspended during the challenge, except for good cause shown.
(d) A copy of a signed voluntary acknowledgment of paternity shall be provided to any signatory upon request.
(e) (1) As used in this subsection, the term:
    (A) "Child-placing agency" means an agency licensed as such pursuant to Chapter 5 of Title 49.
    (B) "Legal custodian" shall have the same meaning as set forth in Code Section 15-11-2.
    (C) "Local custodian" shall have the same meaning as set forth in Code Section 31-10-1.
    (D) "State registrar" shall have the same meaning as set forth in Code Section 31-10-1.
(2) The state registrar or local custodian, upon receipt of a written application, shall issue a certified copy of voluntary acknowledgment of paternity in the state registrar's or local custodian's custody to:
    (A) The person who signed such acknowledgment and his or her guardian or temporary guardian;
    (B) The person whose paternity was acknowledged, if he or she is at least 18 years of age;
    (C) The guardian, temporary guardian, or legal custodian of the person whose paternity was acknowledged;
    (D) The living legal spouse or next of kin, the legal representative, or the person who in good faith has applied and produced a record of such application to become the legal representative of the person whose paternity is registered;
    (E) A court of competent jurisdiction upon its order or subpoena;
    (F) Any governmental agency, state or federal, provided that such certificate shall be needed for official purposes;
    (G) A member in good standing of the State Bar of Georgia, provided that such certificate shall be needed for purposes of legal investigation on behalf of a client; and
    (H) A child-placing agency, provided that such certificate shall be needed for official purposes.

§ 19-7-46.2. Temporary order of support

(a) Upon motion by a party to a paternity action, a temporary order shall be issued in accordance with the guidelines prescribed in Code Section 19-6-15 if there is clear and convincing evidence of paternity. Such temporary order will be valid pending an administrative or judicial determination of parentage.
(b) All child support payments made pursuant to the temporary order prescribed in subsection (a) of this Code section shall be paid to the court which shall deposit the amount of the payment in a separate account in a bank approved as a federal depository. Such bank shall hold the amount as a special escrow fund and, except as provided in this Code section, shall not distribute any portion of the payment to any party to the action. Each full payment made into the escrow account pursuant to this Code section shall be effective to discharge any duty of the putative father to pay the ordered child support amount.
(c) Upon final judgment in a paternity action that the alleged putative father is the father of the child, the court shall order that the amount retained in the special escrow fund shall be paid to the appropriate person or entity along with any interest that may have accrued.
(d) Upon final judgment in a paternity action that the alleged putative father is not the father of the child, the amount retained in the special escrow fund shall be returned to the putative father along with any interest that may have accrued.

§ 19-7-47. Civil action; testimony of mother and alleged father; default judgments

(a) Any proceeding brought under this article is a civil action governed by the rules of civil procedure. The mother of the child and the alleged father are competent to testify and may be compelled to appear and testify.
(b) If in any paternity action an answer has not been filed within the time required by Chapter 11 of Title 9, the "Georgia Civil Practice Act," the case shall automatically become in default unless the time for filing the answer has been extended as provided by law. The default may be opened as a matter of right by the filing of such defenses within 15 days of the day of default, upon the payment of costs. If the case is still in default after the expiration of the period of 15 days, the plaintiff at any time thereafter shall be entitled to verdict and judgment by default, in open court or in chambers, as if every item and paragraph of the complaint or other original pleading were supported by proper evidence.

§ 19-7-48. Settlement, dismissal, or termination of civil action

The child must be a party to a settlement agreement with the alleged father. The court must approve any settlement agreement, dismissal, or termination of the action which does not adjudicate the merits of the case.

§ 19-7-49. Final order; effect; evidence of costs

(a) On a finding that the alleged father is the father of the child, the court shall issue an order designating the alleged father as the father of the child. The sole effect of the order shall be to establish the duty of the father to support the child.
(b) On a finding that the alleged father is not the father of the child, the court shall issue an order declaring this finding.
(c) The trier of fact shall receive without foundation or the need for third-party testimony evidence of costs of pregnancy, child birth, and genetic testing. The evidence so presented shall constitute prima-facie evidence of amounts incurred for such services or for testing on behalf of the child. The court may award such costs as part of its final decree.

§ 19-7-50. Expenses of litigation

The court may order reasonable fees of counsel, experts, and the child's guardian ad litem and other costs of the action and pretrial proceedings, including blood and other tests, to be paid by the parties in proportions and at times determined by the court.

§ 19-7-51. Order of support and other provisions

The decree or order establishing paternity may contain any other provisions concerning the duty to support the child by periodic or lump sum payments, as provided in Code Section 19-6-15, or any other matter in the best interests of the child.

§ 19-7-52. To whom support payments made; enforcement and modification of orders

(a) The court may order that support payments be made to the mother or other interested party, the child support receiver, the prosecuting attorney, the community supervision officer, or the clerk of court, provided that, in those cases where the action has been brought by the Department of Human Services on behalf of a child, the support payment shall be made to the Department of Human Services for distribution or to the child support receiver if the Department of Human Services so requests.
(b) The same remedies and procedures shall apply for enforcement and modification of visitation and support orders as apply to enforcement and modification of such orders arising from divorce proceedings.

§ 19-7-53. Confidentiality of hearings

Upon motion of any party, any hearing or trial held under this article may be held in closed court without the admittance of any person other than those necessary to the action or proceeding.

§ 19-7-54. Motion to set aside determination of paternity

(a) Unless otherwise specified in this Code section, in any action in which a male is required to pay child support as the father of a child, a motion to set aside a determination of paternity may be made at any time upon the grounds set forth in this Code section. Any such motion shall be filed in the superior or state court that entered the order and shall include:
(1) An affidavit executed by the movant that the newly discovered evidence has come to movant's knowledge since the entry of judgment; and
(2) The results from scientifically credible parentage-
determination genetic testing, as authorized under Code Section 19-7-46 and administered within 90 days prior to the filing of such motion, that finds that there is a 0 percent probability that the male ordered to pay such child support is the father of the child for whom support is required.

(b) The court shall grant relief on a motion filed in accordance with subsection (a) of this Code section upon a finding by the court of all of the following:
  (1) The genetic test required in paragraph (2) of subsection (a) of this Code section was properly conducted;
  (2) The male ordered to pay child support has not adopted the child;
  (3) The child was not conceived by artificial insemination while the male ordered to pay child support and the child's mother were in wedlock;
  (4) The male ordered to pay child support did not act to prevent the biological father of the child from asserting his paternal rights with respect to the child; and
  (5) The male ordered to pay child support with knowledge that he is not the biological father of the child has not:
    (A) Married the mother of the child and voluntarily assumed the parental obligation and duty to pay child support;
    (B) Acknowledged his paternity of the child in a sworn statement;
    (C) Been named as the child's biological father on the child's birth certificate with his consent;
    (D) Been required to support the child because of a written voluntary promise;
    (E) Received written notice from the Department of Human Services, any other state agency, or any court directing him to submit to genetic testing which he disregarded;
    (F) Signed a voluntary acknowledgment of paternity as provided in Code Section 19-7-46.1; or
    (G) Proclaimed himself to be the child's biological father.
(c) In the event movant fails to make the requisite showing provided in subsection (b) of this Code section, the court may grant the motion or enter an order as to paternity, duty to support, custody, and visitation privileges as otherwise provided by law.
(d) (1) In any case when the underlying child support order was issued by a court of this state or by the Department of Human Services and is being enforced by the Department of Human Services, an individual who is involved in the Department of Human Services' enforcement of such order and who intends to file a motion as provided for in subsection (a) of this Code section may request a genetic test from the Department of Human Services, contingent upon advance payment of the genetic test fee. Such request shall be accompanied by a statement setting forth that the requirements to set aside a determination of paternity described in paragraphs (2) through (5) of subsection (b) of this Code section are met. The Department of Human Services may deny such request if:
    (A) Genetic testing was previously completed;
    (B) The child was adopted either by the requester or the other individual involved in the enforcement by the Department of Human Services;
    (C) The child was conceived by means of artificial insemination; or
    (D) The Department of Human Services has previously offered genetic testing and the requester refused the opportunity for such testing at that time.
  (2) In any case when the nonrequesting individual does not consent to genetic testing, the requesting individual may petition the court to ask for such testing of the appropriate individuals.
(e) In the event relief is granted pursuant to subsection (b) of this Code section, relief shall be limited to the issues of prospective child support payments, past due child support payments, termination of parental rights, custody, and visitation rights. In any case when the underlying order was obtained by the Department of Human Services, a court granting the motion to set aside a determination of paternity may relieve the obligor of responsibility for any future or past due amounts, or both, owed to the state. The court may also relieve the obligor of the same that is owed to any other person or entity so long as the obligor adds that person or entity to the underlying motion and provides that person or entity with notice of the action. In all motions brought under this Code section when there is any amount owed to the state, the Department of Human Services shall be made a party. Failure to include the Department of Human Services as a party shall prevent the waiver of any amount owed to the state.
(f) The duty to pay child support and other legal obligations for the child shall not be suspended while the motion is pending except for good cause shown; however, the court may order the child support be held in the registry of the court until final determination of paternity has been made.
(g) (1) In any action brought pursuant to this Code section, if the genetic test results submitted in accordance with paragraph (2) of subsection (a) of this Code section are provided solely by the male ordered to pay child support, the court on its own motion may, and on the motion of any party shall, order the child's mother, the child, and the male ordered to pay child support to submit to genetic tests. The court shall provide that such genetic testing be done no more than 30 days after the court issues its order.
  (2) If the mother of the child or the male ordered to pay child support willfully fails to submit to genetic testing, or if either such party is the custodian of the child and willfully fails to submit the child for testing, the court shall issue an order determining the relief on the motion against the party so failing to submit to genetic testing. If a party shows good cause for failing to submit to genetic testing, such failure shall not be considered willful.
  (3) The party requesting genetic testing shall pay any fees charged for the tests. If the custodian of the child is receiving services from an administrative agency in its role as an agency providing enforcement of child

support orders, such agency shall pay the cost of genetic testing if it requests the test and may seek reimbursement for the fees from the person against whom the court assesses the costs of the action.
(h) If relief on a motion filed in accordance with this Code section is not granted, the court shall assess the costs of the action and attorney's fees against the movant.

CHAPTER 8. ADOPTION

ARTICLE 1. GENERAL PROVISIONS (EFFECTIVE UNTIL SEPTEMBER 1, 2018)
§ 19-8-1. (Effective until September 1, 2018) Definitions

For purposes of this article, the term:
(1) "Biological father" means the male who impregnated the biological mother resulting in the birth of the child.
(2) "Child" means a person who is under 18 years of age and who is sought to be adopted.
(3) "Child-placing agency" means an agency licensed as a child-placing agency pursuant to Chapter 5 of Title 49.
(4) "Department" means the Department of Human Services.
(4.1) "Evaluator" means the person or agency that conducts a home study. An evaluator shall be a licensed child-placing agency, the department, or a licensed professional with at least two years of adoption related professional experience, including a licensed clinical social worker, licensed master social worker, licensed marriage and family therapist, or licensed professional counselor; provided, however, that where none of the foregoing evaluators are available, the court may appoint a guardian ad litem or court appointed special advocate to conduct the home study.
(5) "Guardian" means a legal guardian of the person of a child.
(5.1) "Home study" means an evaluation by an evaluator of the petitioner's home environment for the purpose of determining the suitability of the environment as a prospective adoptive home for a child. Such evaluation shall consider the petitioner's physical health, emotional maturity, financial circumstances, family, and social background and shall conform to the rules and regulations established by the department for child-placing agencies for adoption home studies.
(5.2) "Home study report " means the written report generated as a result of the home study.
(6) "Legal father" means a male who has not surrendered or had terminated his rights to a child and who:
  (A) Has legally adopted such child;
  (B) Was married to the biological mother of such child at the time such child was born or within the usual period of gestation, unless paternity was disproved by a final order pursuant to Article 3 of Chapter 7 of this title;
  (C) Married the legal mother of such child after such child was born and recognized such child as his own, unless paternity was disproved by a final order pursuant to Article 3 of Chapter 7 of this title; or
  (D) Has legitimated such child by a final order pursuant to Code Section 19-7-22.
(7) "Legal mother" means the female who is the biological or adoptive mother of the child and who has not surrendered or had terminated her rights to the child.
(8) "Parent" means either the legal father or the legal mother of the child.
(9) "Petitioner" means a person who petitions to adopt or terminate rights to a child pursuant to this chapter.
(10) "Putative father registry" means the registry established and maintained pursuant to subsections (d) and (e) of Code Section 19-11-9.

§ 19-8-2. (Effective until September 1, 2018) Jurisdiction and venue of adoption proceedings

(a) The superior courts of the several counties shall have exclusive jurisdiction in all matters of adoption, except such jurisdiction as may be granted to the juvenile courts.
(b) All petitions under this chapter shall be filed in the county in which any petitioner resides, except that:
  (1) Upon good cause being shown, the court of the county of the child's domicile or of the county in which is located any child-placing agency having legal custody of the child sought to be adopted may, in its discretion, allow the petition to be filed in that court; and
  (2) Any person who has been a resident of any United States Army post or military reservation within this state for six months next preceding the filing of the petition for adoption may file the petition in any county adjacent to the United States Army post or military reservation.

§ 19-8-3. (Effective until September 1, 2018) Who may adopt a child; when petition must be filed in names of both spouses

(a) Any adult person may petition to adopt a child if the person:
(1) Is at least 25 years of age or is married and living with his spouse;
(2) Is at least ten years older than the child;
(3) Has been a bona fide resident of this state for at least six months immediately preceding the filing of the petition; and
(4) Is financially, physically, and mentally able to have permanent custody of the child.
(b) Any adult person, including but not limited to a foster parent, meeting the requirements of subsection (a) of this Code section shall be eligible to apply to the department or a child-placing agency for consideration as an adoption applicant in accordance with the policies of the department or the agency.
(c) If a person seeking to adopt a child is married, the petition must be filed in the name of both spouses; provided, however, that, when the child is the stepchild of the party seeking to adopt, the petition shall be filed by the stepparent alone.

§ 19-8-4. (Effective until September 1, 2018) When surrender or termination of parental or guardian's rights required; consent of child of 14 or older necessary; acknowledgment of surrender; compliance with Interstate Compact on Placement of Children

(a) Except as otherwise authorized in this chapter, a child who has any living parent or guardian may be adopted through the department or any child-placing agency only if each such parent and each such guardian:
(1) Has voluntarily and in writing surrendered all of his rights to the child to the department or to a child-placing agency as provided in this Code section and the department or agency thereafter consents to the adoption; or
(2) Has had all of his rights to the child terminated by order of a court of competent jurisdiction, the child has been committed by the court to the department or to a child-placing agency for placement for adoption, and the department or agency thereafter consents to the adoption.
(b) In the case of a child 14 years of age or older, the written consent of the child to his adoption must be given and acknowledged in the presence of the court.
(c) The surrender to the department or to a child-placing agency specified in paragraphs (1) and (2) of subsection (e) of this Code section shall be executed following the birth of the child, and the pre-birth surrender to the department or to a child-placing agency specified in paragraph (3) of subsection (e) of this Code section shall be executed prior to the birth of the child. Each surrender shall be executed in the presence of a representative of the department or the agency and a notary. A copy shall be delivered to the individual signing the surrender at the time of the execution thereof.
(d) A person signing a surrender pursuant to this Code section shall have the right to withdraw the surrender as provided in subsection (b) of Code Section 19-8-9.
(e) (1) The surrender by a parent or guardian specified in paragraph (1) of subsection (a) of this Code section shall meet the requirements of subsection (a) of Code Section 19-8-26.
(2) The biological father who is not the legal father of a child may surrender his rights to the child for the purpose of an adoption pursuant to this Code section. That surrender shall meet the requirements of subsection (d) of Code Section 19-8-26.
(3) (A) The biological father who is not the legal father of a child may execute a surrender of his rights to the child prior to the birth of the child for the purpose of an adoption pursuant to this Code section. A pre-birth surrender, when signed under oath by the alleged biological father, shall serve to relinquish the alleged biological father's rights to the child and to waive the alleged biological father's right to notice of any proceeding with respect to the child's adoption, custody, or guardianship. The court in any adoption proceeding shall have jurisdiction to enter a final order of adoption of the child based upon the pre-birth surrender and in other proceedings to determine the child's legal custody or guardianship shall have jurisdiction to enter an order for those purposes.
(B) The responsibilities of an alleged biological father are permanently terminated only upon the entry of a final order of adoption. A person executing a pre-birth surrender pursuant to this Code section shall have the right to withdraw the surrender within ten days from the date of execution thereof, notwithstanding the date of birth of the child.
(C) If a final order of adoption is not entered after the execution of a pre-birth surrender and paternity is established by acknowledgment, by administrative order, or by judicial order, then the alleged biological father shall be responsible for child support or other financial obligations to the child or to the child's mother, or to both.
(D) The pre-birth surrender shall not be valid for use by a legal father as defined under paragraph (6) of Code Section 19-8-1 or for any man who has executed a voluntary acknowledgment of paternity pursuant to the provisions of Code Section 19-7-46.1.
(E) The pre-birth surrender may be executed at any time after the biological mother executes a sworn statement identifying such person as an alleged biological father of the biological mother's unborn child.

(F) The pre-birth surrender shall meet the requirements of subsection (f) of Code Section 19-8-26.
(f) A surrender of rights shall be acknowledged by the person who surrenders those rights by also signing an acknowledgment meeting the requirements of subsection (g) of Code Section 19-8-26.
(g) Whenever the legal mother surrenders her parental rights pursuant to this Code section, she shall execute an affidavit meeting the requirements of subsection (h) of Code Section 19-8-26.
(h) Whenever rights are surrendered to the department or to a child-placing agency, the department or agency representative before whom the surrender is signed shall execute an affidavit meeting the requirements of subsection (j) of Code Section 19-8-26.
(i) A surrender pursuant to this Code section may be given by any parent or biological father who is not the legal father of the child irrespective of whether such parent or biological father has arrived at the age of majority. The surrender given by any such minor shall be binding upon him as if the individual were in all respects sui juris.
(j) In any surrender pursuant to this Code section, the provisions of Chapter 4 of Title 39, relating to the Interstate Compact on the Placement of Children, if applicable, shall be complied with.

§ 19-8-5. (Effective until September 1, 2018) Surrender or termination of parental or guardian's rights where child to be adopted by third party

(a) Except as otherwise authorized in this chapter, a child who has any living parent or guardian may be adopted by a third party who is neither the stepparent nor relative of that child, as described in subsection (a) of Code Sections 19-8-6 and 19-8-7, only if each such living parent and each such guardian has voluntarily and in writing surrendered all of his or her rights to such child to that third party for the purpose of enabling that third party to adopt such child. Except as provided in subsection (m) of this Code section, no child shall be placed with a third party for purposes of adoption unless prior to the date of placement a home study shall have been completed, and the home study report recommends placement of a child in such third party's home.
(b) In the case of a child 14 years of age or older, the written consent of the child to his adoption must be given and acknowledged in the presence of the court.
(c) The surrender specified in paragraphs (1) and (2) of subsection (e) of this Code section shall be executed following the birth of the child, and the pre-birth surrender specified in paragraph (3) of subsection (e) of this Code section shall be executed prior to the birth of the child. Each surrender shall be executed in the presence of a notary. The name and address of each person to whom the child is surrendered may be omitted to protect confidentiality, provided the surrender sets forth the name and address of his agent for purposes of notice of withdrawal as provided for in subsection (d) of this Code section. A copy shall be delivered to the individual signing the surrender at the time of the execution thereof.
(d) A person signing a surrender pursuant to this Code section shall have the right to withdraw the surrender as provided in subsection (b) of Code Section 19-8-9.
(e) (1) The surrender by a parent or guardian specified in subsection (a) of this Code section shall meet the requirements of subsection (c) of Code Section 19-8-26.
(2) The biological father who is not the legal father of a child may surrender all his rights to the child for purposes of an adoption pursuant to this Code section. That surrender shall meet the requirements of subsection (d) of Code Section 19-8-26.
(3) (A) The biological father who is not the legal father of a child may execute a surrender of his rights to the child prior to the birth of the child for the purpose of an adoption pursuant to this Code section. A pre-birth surrender, when signed under oath by the alleged biological father, shall serve to relinquish the alleged biological father's rights to the child and to waive the alleged biological father's right to notice of any proceeding with respect to the child's adoption, custody, or guardianship. The court in any adoption proceeding shall have jurisdiction to enter a final order of adoption of the child based upon the pre-birth surrender and in other proceedings to determine the child's legal custody or guardianship shall have jurisdiction to enter an order for those purposes.
(B) The responsibilities of an alleged biological father are permanently terminated only upon the entry of a final order of adoption. A person executing a pre-birth surrender pursuant to this Code section shall have the right to withdraw the surrender within ten days from the date of execution thereof, notwithstanding the date of birth of the child.
(C) If a final order of adoption is not entered after the execution of a pre-birth surrender and paternity is established by acknowledgment, by administrative order, or by judicial order, then the alleged biological father shall be responsible for child support or other financial obligations to the child or to the child's mother, or to both.
(D) The pre-birth surrender shall not be valid for use by a legal father as defined under paragraph (6) of Code Section 19-8-1 or for any man who has executed a voluntary acknowledgment of paternity pursuant to the provisions of Code Section 19-7-46.1.
(E) The pre-birth surrender may be executed at any time after the biological mother executes a sworn statement identifying such person as an alleged biological father of the biological mother's unborn child.

(F) The pre-birth surrender shall meet the requirements of subsection (f) of Code Section 19-8-26.
(f) A surrender of rights shall be acknowledged by the person who surrenders those rights by also signing an acknowledgment meeting the requirements of subsection (g) of Code Section 19-8-26.
(g) Whenever the legal mother surrenders her parental rights pursuant to this Code section, she shall execute an affidavit meeting the requirements of subsection (h) of Code Section 19-8-26.
(h) Whenever rights are surrendered pursuant to this Code section, the representative of each petitioner shall execute an affidavit meeting the requirements of subsection (k) of Code Section 19-8-26.
(i) A surrender pursuant to this Code section may be given by any parent or biological father who is not the legal father of the child sought to be adopted irrespective of whether such parent or biological father has arrived at the age of majority. The surrender given by any such minor shall be binding upon him as if the individual were in all respects sui juris.
(j) A copy of each surrender specified in subsection (a) of this Code section, together with a copy of the acknowledgment specified in subsection (f) of this Code section and a copy of the affidavits specified in subsections (g) and (h) of this Code section and the name and address of each person to whom the child is surrendered, shall be mailed, by registered or certified mail or statutory overnight delivery, return receipt requested, to the

Office of Adoptions
Georgia Department of Human Services
Atlanta, Georgia

within 15 days from the execution thereof. Upon receipt of the copy the department may commence its investigation as required in Code Section 19-8-16.
(k) A petition for adoption pursuant to subsection (a) of this Code section shall be filed within 60 days from the date of the surrender. If the petition is not filed within the time period specified by this subsection or if the proceedings resulting from the petition are not concluded with an order granting the petition, the surrender shall operate as follows according to the election made therein by the legal parent or guardian of the child:
  (1) In favor of that legal parent or guardian, with the express stipulation that neither this nor any other provision of the surrender shall be deemed to impair the validity, absolute finality, or totality of the surrender under any other circumstance, once the revocation period has elapsed;
  (2) In favor of the licensed child-placing agency designated in the surrender of rights, if any; or
  (3) If the legal parent or guardian is not designated and no child-placing agency is designated in the surrender of rights, or if the designated child-placing agency declines to accept the child for placement for adoption, in favor of the department for placement for adoption pursuant to subsection (a) of Code Section 19-8-4. The court may waive the 60 day time period for filing the petition for excusable neglect.
(l) In any surrender pursuant to this Code section, the provisions of Chapter 4 of Title 39, relating to the Interstate Compact on the Placement of Children, if applicable, shall be complied with.
(m) If the home study for a third-party adoption has not occurred prior to the date of placement, then the third party shall, at the time of the filing of the petition for adoption, file a motion with the court seeking an order authorizing placement of such child prior to the completion of the home study. Such motion shall identify the evaluator that the petitioner has selected to perform the home study. The court may waive the requirement of a preplacement home study in cases when a child to be adopted already resides in the prospective adoptive home pursuant to a court order of guardianship, testamentary guardianship, or custody.
(n) The court may grant the motion for placement prior to the completion of a home study if the court finds that such placement is in the best interest of the child.
(o) If the court grants the motion for placement prior to the completion of a home study and authorizes placement of a child prior to the completion of the home study, then:
  (1) Such child shall be permitted to remain in the home of the third party with whom the parent or guardian placed such child pending further order of the court;
  (2) A copy of the order authorizing placement of such child prior to the completion of the home study shall be delivered to the department and the evaluator selected to perform the home study by the clerk of the court within 15 days of the date of the entry of such order; and
  (3) The home study, if not already in process, shall be initiated by the evaluator selected by the petitioner or appointed by the court within ten days of such evaluator's receipt of the court's order.

§ 19-8-6. (Effective until September 1, 2018) Surrender of parental rights where father and mother not still married; surrender of rights where only one parent still living

  (a) Except as otherwise authorized in this chapter:

(1) A child whose legal father and legal mother are both living but are not still married to each other may be adopted by the spouse of either parent only when the other parent voluntarily and in writing surrenders all of his rights to the child to that spouse for the purpose of enabling that spouse to adopt the child and the other parent consents to the adoption and, where there is any guardian of that child, each such guardian has voluntarily and in writing surrendered to such spouse all of his rights to the child for purposes of such adoption; or

(2) A child who has only one parent still living may be adopted by the spouse of that parent only if that parent consents to the adoption and, where there is any guardian of that child, each such guardian has voluntarily and in writing surrendered to such spouse all of his rights to the child for the purpose of such adoption.

(b) In the case of a child 14 years of age or older, the written consent of the child to his adoption must be given and acknowledged in the presence of the court.

(c) The surrender specified in this Code section shall be executed, following the birth of the child, in the presence of a notary. A copy shall be delivered to the individual signing the surrender at the time of the execution thereof.

(d) A person signing a surrender pursuant to this Code section shall have the right to withdraw the surrender as provided in subsection (b) of Code Section 19-8-9.

(e) (1) The surrender by a parent or guardian specified in subsection (a) of this Code section shall meet the requirements of subsection (e) of Code Section 19-8-26.

(2) The biological father who is not the legal father of a child may surrender all his rights to the child for purposes of an adoption pursuant to this Code section. That surrender shall meet the requirements of subsection (d) of Code Section 19-8-26.

(f) A surrender of rights shall be acknowledged by the person who surrenders those rights by also signing an acknowledgment meeting the requirements of subsection (g) of Code Section 19-8-26.

(g) Whenever the legal mother surrenders her parental rights or consents to the adoption of her child by her spouse pursuant to this Code section, she shall execute an affidavit meeting the requirements of subsection (h) of Code Section 19-8-26.

(h) Whenever rights are surrendered pursuant to this Code section, the representative of each petitioner shall execute an affidavit meeting the requirements of subsection (k) of Code Section 19-8-26.

(i) A surrender or consent pursuant to this Code section may be given by any parent or biological father who is not the legal father of the child sought to be adopted irrespective of whether such parent or biological father has arrived at the age of majority. The surrender given by any such minor shall be binding upon him as if the individual were in all respects sui juris.

(j) The parental consent by the spouse of a stepparent seeking to adopt a child of that spouse and required by subsection (a) of this Code section shall be as provided in subsection (l) of Code Section 19-8-26.

§ 19-8-7. (Effective until September 1, 2018) Surrender or termination of parental or guardian's rights where child adopted by relative

(a) Except as otherwise authorized in this Code section, a child who has any living parent or guardian may be adopted by a relative who is related by blood or marriage to the child as a grandparent, great-grandparent, aunt, uncle, great aunt, great uncle, or sibling only if each such living parent and each such guardian has voluntarily and in writing surrendered to that relative and any spouse of such relative all of his or her rights to the child for the purpose of enabling that relative and any such spouse to adopt the child.

(b) In the case of a child 14 years of age or older, the written consent of the child to his adoption must be given and acknowledged in the presence of the court.

(c) The surrender specified in paragraphs (1) and (2) of subsection (e) of this Code section shall be executed following the birth of the child, and the pre-birth surrender specified in paragraph (3) of subsection (e) of this Code section shall be executed prior to the birth of the child. Each surrender shall be executed in the presence of a notary. A copy shall be delivered to the individual signing the surrender at the time of the execution thereof.

(d) A person signing a surrender pursuant to this Code section shall have the right to withdraw the surrender as provided in subsection (b) of Code Section 19-8-9.

(e) (1) The surrender by a parent or guardian specified in subsection (a) of this Code section shall meet the requirements of subsection (e) of Code Section 19-8-26.

(2) The biological father who is not the legal father of the child may surrender all his rights to the child for purposes of an adoption pursuant to this Code section. That surrender shall meet the requirements of subsection (d) of Code Section 19-8-26.

(3) (A) The biological father who is not the legal father of a child may execute a surrender of his rights to the child prior to the birth of the child for the purpose of an adoption pursuant to this Code section. A pre-birth surrender, when signed under oath by the alleged biological father, shall serve to relinquish the alleged biological father's rights to the child and to waive the alleged biological father's right to notice of any proceeding with respect to the child's adoption, custody, or guardianship. The court in any adoption

proceeding shall have jurisdiction to enter a final order of adoption of the child based upon the pre-birth surrender and in other proceedings to determine the child's legal custody or guardianship shall have jurisdiction to enter an order for those purposes.

(B) The responsibilities of an alleged biological father are permanently terminated only upon the entry of a final order of adoption. A person executing a pre-birth surrender pursuant to this Code section shall have the right to withdraw the surrender within ten days from the date of execution thereof, notwithstanding the date of birth of the child.

(C) If a final order of adoption is not entered after the execution of a pre-birth surrender and paternity is established by acknowledgment, by administrative order, or by judicial order, then the alleged biological father shall be responsible for child support or other financial obligations to the child or to the child's mother, or to both.

(D) The pre-birth surrender shall not be valid for use by a legal father as defined under paragraph (6) of Code Section 19-8-1 or for any man who has executed a voluntary acknowledgment of paternity pursuant to the provisions of Code Section 19-7-46.1.

(E) The pre-birth surrender may be executed at any time after the biological mother executes a sworn statement identifying such person as an alleged biological father of the biological mother's unborn child.

(F) The pre-birth surrender shall meet the requirements of subsection (f) of Code Section 19-8-26.

(f) A surrender of rights shall be acknowledged by the person who surrenders those rights by also signing an acknowledgment meeting the requirements of subsection (g) of Code Section 19-8-26.

(g) Whenever the legal mother surrenders her parental rights pursuant to this Code section, she shall execute an affidavit meeting the requirements of subsection (h) of Code Section 19-8-26.

(h) Whenever rights are surrendered pursuant to this Code section the representative of each petitioner shall execute an affidavit meeting the requirements of subsection (k) of Code Section 19-8-26.

(i) A surrender pursuant to this Code section may be given by any parent or biological father who is not the legal father of the child sought to be adopted irrespective of whether such parent or biological father has arrived at the age of majority. The surrender given by any such minor shall be binding upon him as if the individual were in all respects sui juris.

§ 19-8-8. (Effective until September 1, 2018) Adoption based upon foreign decrees and valid visa

A child may be adopted pursuant to the provisions of this chapter based upon:
(1) A decree which has been entered pursuant to due process of law by a court of competent jurisdiction outside the United States establishing the relationship of parent and child by adoption between each petitioner and a child born in such foreign country; and
(2) The child's having been granted a valid visa by the United States Immigration and Naturalization Service.

§ 19-8-9. (Effective until September 1, 2018) Surrender of parental rights where legal mother puts up for adoption child she previously adopted herself; withdrawal of surrender; expiration of rights

(a) In those cases where the legal mother of the child being placed for adoption has herself previously adopted such child, said adoptive mother shall execute, in lieu of the affidavit specified in subsection (g) of Code Section 19-8-4, 19-8-5, 19-8-6, or 19-8-7, an affidavit meeting the requirements of subsection (i) of Code Section 19-8-26.

(b) A person signing a surrender pursuant to Code Section 19-8-4, 19-8-5, 19-8-6, or 19-8-7 shall have the right to withdraw the surrender by written notice delivered in person or mailed by registered mail or statutory overnight delivery within ten days after signing; and the surrender document shall not be valid unless it so states. The ten days shall be counted consecutively beginning with the day immediately following the date the surrender is executed, however, if the tenth day falls on a Saturday, Sunday, or legal holiday then the last day on which the surrender may be withdrawn shall be the next day that is not a Saturday, Sunday, or legal holiday. After ten days, a surrender may not be withdrawn. The notice of withdrawal of surrender shall be delivered in person or mailed by registered mail or statutory overnight delivery to the address designated in the surrender document.

(c) If a legal mother has voluntarily and in writing surrendered all of her parental rights pursuant to the provisions of subsection (a) of Code Section 19-8-4, 19-8-5, 19-8-6, or 19-8-7 and has not withdrawn her surrender within the ten-day period after signing as permitted by the provisions of subsection (b) of this Code section, she shall have no right or authority to sign a voluntary acknowledgment of paternity pursuant to the provisions of Code Section 19-7-46.1 regarding the same child.

§ 19-8-10. (Effective until September 1, 2018) When surrender or termination of parental rights of living parent not required; service on parents in such cases

(a) Surrender or termination of rights of a parent pursuant to subsection (a) of Code Section 19-8-4, 19-8-5, 19-8-6, or 19-8-7 shall not be required as a prerequisite to the filing of a petition for adoption of a child of that parent pursuant to Code Section 19-8-13 when the court determines by clear and convincing evidence that the:

(1) Child has been abandoned by that parent;
(2) Parent cannot be found after a diligent search has been made;
(3) Parent is insane or otherwise incapacitated from surrendering such rights;
(4) Parent caused his child to be conceived as a result of having nonconsensual sexual intercourse with the mother of his child or when the mother is less than ten years of age; or
(5) Parent has failed to exercise proper parental care or control due to misconduct or inability, as set out in paragraph (3), (4), or (5) of subsection (a) of Code Section 15-11-310,

and the court is of the opinion that the adoption is in the best interests of that child, after considering the physical, mental, emotional, and moral condition and needs of the child who is the subject of the proceeding, including the need for a secure and stable home.

(b) Surrender of rights of a parent pursuant to subsection (a) of Code Section 19-8-6 or 19-8-7 shall not be required as a prerequisite to the filing of a petition for adoption of a child of that parent pursuant to Code Section 19-8-13, if that parent, for a period of one year or longer immediately prior to the filing of the petition for adoption, without justifiable cause, has significantly failed:

(1) To communicate or to make a bona fide attempt to communicate with that child in a meaningful, supportive, parental manner; or
(2) To provide for the care and support of that child as required by law or judicial decree,

and the court is of the opinion that the adoption is for the best interests of that child.

(c) Whenever it is alleged by any petitioner that surrender or termination of rights of a parent is not a prerequisite to the filing of a petition for adoption of a child of that parent in accordance with subsection (a) or (b) of this Code section, that parent shall be personally served with a conformed copy of the adoption petition, together with a copy of the court's order thereon specified in Code Section 19-8-14, or, if personal service cannot be perfected, by registered or certified mail or statutory overnight delivery, return receipt requested, at his last known address. If service cannot be made by either of these methods that parent shall be given notice by publication once a week for three weeks in the official organ of the county where the petition has been filed and of the county of his last known address. A parent who receives notification pursuant to this paragraph may appear in the pending adoption action and show cause why such parent's rights to the child sought to be adopted in that action should not be terminated by that adoption. Notice shall be deemed to have been received the date:

(1) Personal service is perfected;
(2) Of delivery shown on the return receipt of registered or certified mail or statutory overnight delivery; or
(3) Of the last publication.

§ 19-8-11. (Effective until September 1, 2018) Petitioning superior court to terminate parental rights; service of process

(a) (1) In those cases where the department or a child-placing agency has either obtained:

(A) The voluntary written surrender of all parental rights from one of the parents or the guardian of a child; or
(B) An order of a court of competent jurisdiction terminating all of the rights of one of the parents or the guardian of a child,

the department or child-placing agency may in contemplation of the placement of such child for adoption petition the superior court of the county where the child resides to terminate the parental rights of the remaining parent pursuant to this Code section.

(2) In those cases where a person who is the resident of another state has obtained the voluntary written surrender of all parental rights from one of the parents or the guardian of a child, each such person to whom the child has been surrendered may in contemplation of the adoption of such child in such other state petition the superior court of the county where the child resides to terminate the parental rights of the remaining parent pursuant to this Code section.

(3) Parental rights may be terminated pursuant to paragraph (1) or (2) of this subsection when the court determines by clear and convincing evidence that the:

(A) Child has been abandoned by that parent;
(B) Parent of the child cannot be found after a diligent search has been made;
(C) Parent is insane or otherwise incapacitated from surrendering such rights;
(D) Parent caused his child to be conceived as a result of having nonconsensual sexual intercourse with the mother of his child or when the mother is less than ten years of age; or
(E) Parent has failed to exercise proper parental care or control due to misconduct or inability, as set out in paragraph (3), (4), or (5) of subsection (a) of Code Section 15-11-310,

and the court shall set the matter down to be heard in chambers not less than 30 and not more than 60 days following the receipt by such remaining parent of the notice under subsection (b) of this Code section and shall enter an order terminating such parental rights if it so finds and if it is of the opinion that adoption is in the best interests of the child, after considering the physical, mental, emotional, and moral condition and needs of the child who is the subject of the proceeding, including the need for a secure and stable home.
(b) Whenever a petition is filed pursuant to subsection (a) of this Code section, the parent whose rights the petitioner is seeking to terminate shall be personally served with a conformed copy of the petition, and a copy of the court's order setting forth the date upon which the petition shall be considered or, if personal service cannot be perfected, by registered or certified mail or statutory overnight delivery, return receipt requested, at his last known address. If service cannot be made by either of these methods, that parent shall be given notice by publication once a week for three weeks in the official organ of the county where the petition has been filed and of the county of his last known address. A parent who receives notification pursuant to this subsection may appear and show cause why such parent's rights to the child sought to be placed for adoption should not be terminated. Notice shall be deemed to have been received the date:
 (1) Personal service is perfected;
 (2) Of delivery shown on the return receipt of registered or certified mail or statutory overnight delivery; or
 (3) Of the last publication.

§ 19-8-12. (Effective until September 1, 2018) Notice to biological father; procedure when identity or location of father not known; petition, hearing, and order; when rights of biological father terminated; legitimation of child by father; rights of mother

 (a) The General Assembly finds that:
 (1) The state has a compelling interest in promptly providing stable and permanent homes for adoptive children, and in preventing the disruption of adoptive placements;
 (2) Adoptive children have a right to permanence and stability in adoptive placements;
 (3) Adoptive parents have a constitutionally protected liberty and privacy interest in retaining custody of children;
 (4) A biological father who is not the legal father may have an interest in his biological child. This inchoate interest is lost by failure to develop a familial bond with the child and acquires constitutional protection only if the biological father who is not the legal father develops a familial bond with the child;
 (5) The subjective intent of a biological father who is not a legal father, whether expressed or otherwise, unsupported by evidence of acts manifesting such intent, shall not preclude a determination that the biological father who is not a legal father has failed to develop a familial bond with the child; and
 (6) A man who has engaged in a nonmarital sexual relationship with a woman is deemed to be on notice that a pregnancy and adoption proceeding regarding a child may occur and has a duty to protect his own rights and interests in that child. He is therefore entitled to notice of an adoption proceeding only as provided in this Code section.
(b) If there is a biological father who is not the legal father of a child and he has not executed a surrender as specified in paragraph (2) of subsection (e) of Code Section 19-8-4, 19-8-5, 19-8-6, or 19-8-7, he shall be notified of adoption proceedings regarding the child in the following circumstances:
 (1) If his identity is known to the petitioner, department, or licensed child-placing agency or to the attorney for the petitioner, department, or licensed child-placing agency;
 (2) If he is a registrant on the putative father registry who has acknowledged paternity of the child in accordance with subparagraph (d)(2)(A) of Code Section 19-11-9;
 (3) If he is a registrant on the putative father registry who has indicated possible paternity of a child of the child's mother during a period beginning two years immediately prior to the child's date of birth in accordance with subparagraph (d)(2)(B) of Code Section 19-11-9; or
 (4) If the court finds from the evidence, including but not limited to the affidavit of the mother specified in subsection (g) of Code Section 19-8-4, 19-8-5, 19-8-6, or 19-8-7 in the form provided in subsection (h) of Code Section 19-8-26, that such biological father who is not the legal father has performed any of the following acts:
  (A) Lived with the child;
  (B) Contributed to the child's support;
  (C) Made any attempt to legitimate the child; or
  (D) Provided support or medical care for the mother either during her pregnancy or during her hospitalization for the birth of the child.
(c) Notification provided for in subsection (b) of this Code section shall be given to a biological father who is not a legal father by the following methods:
 (1) Registered or certified mail or statutory overnight delivery, return receipt requested, at his last known address, which notice shall be deemed received upon the date of delivery shown on the return receipt;
 (2) Personal service, which notice shall be deemed received when personal service is perfected; or

(3) Publication once a week for three weeks in the official organ of the county where the petition has been filed and of the county of his last known address, which notice shall be deemed received upon the date of the last publication.

If feasible, the methods specified in paragraph (1) or (2) of this subsection shall be used before publication.

(d) (1) Where the rights of a parent or guardian of a child have been surrendered or terminated in accordance with subsection (a) of Code Section 19-8-4, the department or a child-placing agency may file, under the authority of this paragraph, a petition to terminate such biological father's rights to the child with the superior court of the county where the child resides.

(2) Where the rights of a parent or guardian of a child have been surrendered in accordance with subsection (a) of Code Section 19-8-5, 19-8-6, or 19-8-7 or a consent to adopt has been executed pursuant to paragraph (2) of subsection (a) of Code Section 19-8-6, the petitioner shall file, under the authority of this paragraph, with the superior court either a motion, if a petition for adoption of the child has previously been filed with the court, or a petition to terminate such biological father's rights to the child.

(3) Where a petition or motion is filed pursuant to paragraph (1) or (2) of this subsection, the court shall, within 30 days from such filing, conduct a hearing in chambers to determine the facts in the matter. The court shall be authorized to consider the affidavit of the mother specified in subsection (g) of Code Section 19-8-4, 19-8-5, 19-8-6, or 19-8-7, as applicable, in making its determination pursuant to this paragraph. If the court finds from the evidence that such biological father has not performed any of the following acts:

    (A) Lived with the child;
    (B) Contributed to the child's support;
    (C) Made any attempt to legitimate the child; or
    (D) Provided support or medical care for the mother, either during her pregnancy or during her hospitalization for the birth of the child,

and the petitioner provides a certificate as of the date of the petition or the motion, as the case may be, from the putative father registry stating that there is no entry on the putative father registry either acknowledging paternity of the child or indicating possible paternity of a child of the child's mother for a period beginning no later than two years immediately prior to the child's date of birth, then it shall be rebuttably presumed that the biological father who is not the legal father is not entitled to notice of the proceedings. Absent evidence rebutting the presumption, then no further inquiry or notice shall be required by the court and the court shall enter an order terminating the rights of such biological father to the child.

(e) When notice is to be given pursuant to subsection (b) of this Code section, it shall advise such biological father who is not the legal father that he loses all rights to the child and will neither receive notice nor be entitled to object to the adoption of the child unless, within 30 days of receipt of such notice, he files:

(1) A petition to legitimate the child pursuant to Code Section 19-7-22; and
(2) Notice of the filing of the petition to legitimate with the court in which the action under this Code section, if any, is pending and to the person who provided such notice to such biological father.

(f) A biological father who is not the legal father loses all rights to the child and the court shall enter an order terminating all such father's rights to the child and such father may not thereafter object to the adoption and is not entitled to receive further notice of the adoption if within 30 days from his receipt of the notice provided for in subsection (b) of this Code section he:

(1) Does not file a legitimation petition and give notice as required in subsection (e) of this Code section;
(2) Files a legitimation petition which is subsequently dismissed for failure to prosecute; or
(3) Files a legitimation petition and the action is subsequently concluded without a court order declaring a finding that he is the father of the child.

(g) If the child is legitimated by his or her biological father, the adoption shall not be permitted except as provided in Code Sections 19-8-4 through 19-8-7.

(h) If the child is legitimated by his or her biological father and in the subsequent adoption proceeding the petition for adoption is either withdrawn with prejudice or denied by the court, then a surrender of parental rights final release for adoption executed by the legal mother pursuant to the provisions of subsection (a) of Code Section 19-8-4, 19-8-5, or 19-8-7 shall be dissolved by operation of law and her parental rights shall be restored to her. The fact that the legal mother executed a surrender of parental rights final release for adoption, now dissolved, shall not be admissible evidence in any proceedings against the legal mother.

§ 19-8-13. (Effective until September 1, 2018) Petition; filing and contents; financial disclosures; attorney's affidavit

(a) The petition for adoption, duly verified, together with one conformed copy thereof, must be filed with the clerk of the superior court having jurisdiction and shall conform to the following guidelines:

(1) The petition shall set forth:
    (A) The name, age, marital status, and place of residence of each petitioner;
    (B) The name by which the child is to be known should the adoption ultimately be completed;
    (C) The date of birth and the sex of the child;
    (D) The date and circumstances of the placement of the child with each petitioner;

(E) Whether the child is possessed of any property and, if so, a full and complete description thereof;

(F) Whether the child has one or both parents or his biological father who is not the legal father living; and

(G) Whether the child has a guardian.

(2) Where the adoption is pursuant to subsection (a) of Code Section 19-8-4 the following shall be provided or attached or its absence explained when the petition is filed:

(A) An affidavit from the department or a child-placing agency stating that all of the requirements of Code Sections 19-8-4 and 19-8-12 have been complied with;

(B) The written consent of the department or agency to the adoption;

(C) A copy of the appropriate form verifying the allegation of compliance with the requirements of Chapter 4 of Title 39, relating to the Interstate Compact on the Placement of Children; and

(D) A completed form containing background information regarding the child to be adopted, as required by the adoption unit of the department.

(3) Where the adoption is pursuant to subsection (a) of Code Section 19-8-5, the following shall be provided or attached or its absence explained when the petition is filed:

(A) The written voluntary surrender of each parent or guardian specified in subsection (e) of Code Section 19-8-5;

(B) The written acknowledgment of surrender specified in subsection (f) of Code Section 19-8-5;

(C) The affidavits specified in subsections (g) and (h) of Code Section 19-8-5;

(D) Allegations of compliance with Code Section 19-8-12;

(E) Allegations of compliance with Chapter 4 of Title 39, relating to the Interstate Compact on the Placement of Children;

(F) The accounting required by subsection (c) of this Code section;

(G) Copies of appropriate certificates or forms verifying allegations contained in the petition as to guardianship or custody of the child, the marriage of each petitioner, the divorce or death of each parent of the child, and compliance with Chapter 4 of Title 39, relating to the Interstate Compact on the Placement of Children;

(H) A completed form containing background information regarding the child to be adopted, as required by the adoption unit of the department;

(I) A copy of the home study report.

(4) Where the adoption is pursuant to subsection (a) of Code Section 19-8-6, the following shall be provided or attached or its absence explained when the petition is filed:

(A) The written voluntary surrender of the parent or guardian specified in subsection (e) of Code Section 19-8-6;

(B) The written acknowledgment of surrender specified in subsection (f) of Code Section 19-8-6;

(C) The affidavits specified in subsections (g) and (h) of Code Section 19-8-6;

(D) The consent specified in subsection (j) of Code Section 19-8-6;

(E) Allegations of compliance with Code Section 19-8-12;

(F) Copies of appropriate certificates verifying allegations contained in the petition as to guardianship of the child sought to be adopted, the birth of the child sought to be adopted, the marriage of each petitioner, and the divorce or death of each parent of the child sought to be adopted; and

(G) A completed form containing background information regarding the child to be adopted, as required by the adoption unit of the department.

(5) Where the adoption is pursuant to subsection (a) of Code Section 19-8-7, the following shall be provided or attached or its absence explained when the petition is filed:

(A) The written voluntary surrender of each parent specified in subsection (e) of Code Section 19-8-7;

(B) The written acknowledgment of surrender specified in subsection (f) of Code Section 19-8-7;

(C) The affidavits specified in subsections (g) and (h) of Code Section 19-8-7;

(D) Allegations of compliance with Code Section 19-8-12;

(E) Copies of appropriate certificates or forms verifying allegations contained in the petition as to guardianship of the child sought to be adopted, the birth of the child sought to be adopted, the marriage of each petitioner, and the divorce or death of each parent of the child sought to be adopted; and

(F) A completed form containing background information regarding the child to be adopted, as required by the adoption unit of the department.

(6) (A) Where the adoption is pursuant to Code Section 19-8-8, the following shall be provided or attached or its absence explained when the petition is filed:

(i) A certified copy of the final decree of adoption from the foreign country along with a verified English translation. The translator shall provide a statement regarding his qualification to render the translation, his complete name, and his current address. Should the current address be a temporary one, his permanent address shall also be provided;

(ii) A verified copy of the visa granting the child entry to the United States;

(iii) A certified copy along with a verified translation of the child's amended birth certificate or registration showing each petitioner as parent; and

(iv) A copy of the home study which was completed for United States Immigration and Naturalization Service.

(B) It is not necessary to file copies of surrenders or termination on any parent or biological father who is not the legal father when the petition is filed pursuant to paragraph (1) of Code Section 19-8-8.

(7) Where Code Section 19-8-10 is applicable, parental rights need not be surrendered or terminated prior to the filing of the petition; but any petitioner shall allege facts demonstrating the applicability of Code Section 19-8-10 and shall allege compliance with subsection (c) of Code Section 19-8-10.

(8) If the petition is filed in a county other than that of the petitioners' residence, the reason therefor must also be set forth in the petition.

(b) At the time of filing the petition, the petitioner shall deposit with the clerk the deposit required by Code Section 9-15-4; the fees shall be those established by Code Sections 15-6-77 and 15-6-77.1.

(c) Each petitioner in any proceeding for the adoption of a minor pursuant to the provisions of Code Section 19-8-5 shall file with the petition, in a manner acceptable to the court, a report fully accounting for all disbursements of anything of value made or agreed to be made, directly or indirectly, by, on behalf of, or for the benefit of the petitioner in connection with the adoption, including, but not limited to, any expenses incurred in connection with:

(1) The birth of the minor;

(2) Placement of the minor with the petitioner;

(3) Medical or hospital care received by the mother or by the minor during the mother's prenatal care and confinement; and

(4) Services relating to the adoption or to the placement of the minor for adoption which were received by or on behalf of the petitioner, either natural parent of the minor, or any other person.

(d) Every attorney for a petitioner in any proceeding for the adoption of a minor pursuant to the provisions of Code Section 19-8-5 shall file, in a manner acceptable to the court, before the decree of adoption is entered, an affidavit detailing all sums paid or promised to that attorney, directly or indirectly, from whatever source, for all services of any nature rendered or to be rendered in connection with the adoption; provided, however, that if the attorney received or is to receive less than $500.00, the affidavit need only state that fact.

(e) Any report made under this Code section must be signed and verified by the individual making the report.

(f) (1) As used in this subsection, the term "family member" shall have the same meaning as set forth in Code Section 19-7-3.

(2) Whenever a petitioner is a blood relative of the child to be adopted and a family member other than the petitioner has visitation rights to the child granted pursuant to Code Section 19-7-3, the petitioner shall cause a copy of the petition for adoption to be served upon the family member with the visitation rights or upon such person's counsel of record.

(g) Notwithstanding the provisions of Code Sections 19-8-5 and 19-8-7 and this Code section which require obtaining and attaching a written voluntary surrender and acknowledgment thereof and affidavits of the legal mother and a representative of the petitioner, when the adoption is sought under subsection (a) of Code Section 19-8-5 or 19-8-7 following the termination of parental rights and the placement of the child by the juvenile court pursuant to Code Section 15-11-321, obtaining and attaching to the petition a certified copy of the order terminating parental rights of the parent shall take the place of obtaining and attaching those otherwise required surrenders, acknowledgments, and affidavits.

(h) A petition for adoption regarding a child or children who have a living biological father who is not the legal father and who has not surrendered his rights to the child or children shall include a certificate from the putative father registry disclosing the name, address, and social security number of any registrant acknowledging paternity of the child or children pursuant to subparagraph (d)(2)(A) of Code Section 19-11-9 or indicating the possibility of paternity of a child of the child's mother pursuant to subparagraph (d)(2)(B) of Code Section 19-11-9 for a period beginning no later than two years immediately prior to the child's date of birth. Such certificate shall indicate a search of the registry on or after the earliest of the following:

(1) The date of the mother's surrender of parental rights;

(2) The date of entry of the court order terminating the mother's parental rights;

(3) The date of the mother's consent to adoption pursuant to Code Section 19-8-6; or

(4) The date of the filing of the petition for adoption, in which case the certificate may be filed as an amendment to the petition for adoption.

Such certificate shall include a statement that the registry is current as of the earliest date listed in paragraphs (1) through (4) of this subsection, or as of a specified date that is later than the earliest such date.

§ 19-8-14. (Effective until September 1, 2018) Timing of adoption hearing; required records; filing

(a) It is the policy of this state that, in the best interest of the child, uncontested adoption petitions should be heard as soon as possible but not later than 120 days after the date of filing, unless the petitioner has failed to arrange for the court to receive the report required by the provisions of Code Section 19-8-16 or has otherwise failed to provide the court with all exhibits, surrenders, or certificates required by this chapter within that time period. It is the policy of this state that, in contested adoption petitions, the parties shall

make every effort to have the petition considered by the court as soon as practical after the date of filing taking into account the circumstances of the petition and the best interest of the child.
(b) Upon the filing of the petition for adoption, accompanied by the filing fee unless such fee is waived, it shall be the responsibility of the clerk to accept the petition as filed.
(c) Upon the filing of the petition for adoption the court shall fix a date upon which the petition shall be considered, which date shall be not less than 45 days from the date of the filing of the petition.
(d) Notwithstanding the provisions of subsections (a) and (c) of this Code section, it shall be the petitioner's responsibility to request that the court hear the petition on a date that allows sufficient time for fulfillment of notice requirements of Code Section 19-8-10 and Code Section 19-8-12, where applicable.
(e) In the best interest of the child the court may hear the petition less than 45 days from the date of filing upon a showing by the petitioner that either no further notice is required or that any statutory requirement of notice to any person will be fulfilled at an earlier date, and provided that any report required by Code Section 19-8-16 has been completed or will be completed at an earlier date.
(f) The court in the child's best interest may grant such expedited hearings or continuances as may be necessary for completion of applicable notice requirements, investigations, a home study, and reports or for other good cause shown.
(g) Copies of the petition and all documents filed in connection therewith, including, but not limited to, the order fixing the date upon which the petition shall be considered, and all exhibits, surrenders, or certificates required by this chapter, shall be forwarded by the clerk to the department within 15 days after the date of the filing of the petition for adoption.
(h) Copies of the petition, the order fixing the date upon which the petition shall be considered, and all exhibits, surrenders, or certificates required by this chapter shall be forwarded by the clerk to the child-placing agency or other agent appointed by the court pursuant to the provisions of Code Section 19-8-16 within 15 days after the filing of the petition for adoption, together with a request that a report and investigation be made as required by law.
(i) Copies of all motions, amendments, and other pleadings filed and of all orders entered in connection with the petition for adoption shall be forwarded by the clerk to the department within 15 days after such filing or entry.

§ 19-8-15. (Effective until September 1, 2018) When objections may be filed by relatives to petition for adoption

(a) As used in this Code section, the term "family member" shall have the same meaning as set forth in Code Section 19-7-3.
(b) If the child sought to be adopted has no legal father or legal mother living, it shall be the privilege of any person related by blood to the child to file objections to the petition for adoption. A family member with visitation rights to a child granted pursuant to Code Section 19-7-3 shall have the privilege to file objections to the petition of adoption if neither parent has any further rights to the child and if the petition for adoption has been filed by a blood relative of the child. The court, after hearing such objections, shall determine, in its discretion, whether or not the same constitute a good reason for denying the petition and the court shall have the authority to grant or continue such visitation rights of the family member of the child in the adoption order in the event the adoption by the blood relative is approved by the court.

§ 19-8-16. (Effective until September 1, 2018) Investigation by child-placing agency or other agent

(a) Prior to the date set by the court for a hearing on the petition for adoption, it shall be the duty of a child-placing agency appointed by the court or any other independent agent appointed by the court to verify the allegations in the petition for adoption, to make a complete and thorough investigation of the entire matter, including a criminal records check of each petitioner, and to report its findings and recommendations in writing to the court where the petition for adoption was filed. The department, child-placing agency, or other independent agent appointed by the court shall also provide the attorney for petitioner with a copy of the report to the court. If for any reason the child-placing agency or other agent finds itself unable to make or arrange for the proper investigation and report, it shall be the duty of the agency or agent to notify the court immediately, or at least within 20 days after receipt of the request for investigation service, that it is unable to make the report and investigation, so that the court may take such other steps as in its discretion are necessary to have the entire matter investigated.
(b) If the petition has been filed pursuant to subsection (a) of Code Section 19-8-6 or 19-8-7, the court is authorized but not required to appoint a child-placing agency or other independent agent to make an investigation in whatever form the court specifies.
(c) If the petition has been filed pursuant to Code Section 19-8-8, or if the department has conducted an investigation and has consented to the adoption, an investigation shall not be required.

(d) The court shall require the petitioner submit to a criminal history records check. The petitioner shall submit his or her fingerprints to the Georgia Crime Information Center with the appropriate fee. The center shall promptly transmit the fingerprints to the Federal Bureau of Investigation for a search of bureau records and shall obtain an appropriate report. The Georgia Crime Information Center shall also promptly conduct a search of its records and any records to which it has access. The center shall notify the court in writing of the presence or absence of any derogatory finding, including but not limited to any conviction data, regarding the fingerprint records check.

(e) The court may appoint the department to serve as its agent to conduct the investigation required by this Code section if an appropriate child-placing agency or independent agent is not available. If for any reason the department finds itself unable to make or arrange for the proper investigation and report, it shall be the duty of the commissioner of human services to notify the court immediately, or at least within 20 days after receipt of the request for investigation service, that it is unable to make the report and investigation, so that the court may take such other steps as in its discretion are necessary to have the entire matter investigated.

(f) The court shall require the petitioner to reimburse the child-placing agency or other independent agent, including the department, for the full cost of conducting the investigation and preparing the report. Such cost shall not exceed $250.00 unless specifically authorized by the court.

§ 19-8-17. (Effective until September 1, 2018) Report and findings of investigating agency; dismissal of petition; appointment of guardian ad litem

(a) The report and findings of the investigating agency shall include, among other things, the following:
(1) Verification of allegations contained in the petition;
(2) Circumstances under which the child came to be placed for adoption;
(3) Whether each proposed adoptive parent is financially, physically, and mentally able to have the permanent custody of the child; in considering financial ability any adoption supplement approved by the department shall be taken into account;
(4) The physical and mental condition of the child, insofar as this can be determined by the aid of competent medical authority;
(5) Whether or not the adoption is in the best interests of the child, including his general care;
(6) Suitability of the home to the child;
(7) If applicable, whether the identity and location of the biological father who is not the legal father are known or ascertainable and whether the requirements of Code Section 19-8-12 were complied with; and
(8) Any other information that might be disclosed by the investigation that would be of any value or interest to the court in deciding the case.

(b) If the report of the investigating agency or independent agent disapproves of the adoption of the child, motion may be made by the investigating agency or independent agent to the court to dismiss the petition and the court after hearing is authorized to do so. If the court denies the motion to dismiss, the court shall appoint a guardian ad litem who may appeal the ruling to the Georgia Court of Appeals or Supreme Court, as in other cases, as provided by law.

(c) If at any time it appears to the court that the interests of the child may conflict with those of any petitioner, the court may, in its discretion, appoint a guardian ad litem to represent the child and the cost thereof shall be a charge upon the funds of the county.

§ 19-8-18. (Effective until September 1, 2018) Hearing and decree of adoption; district attorney to be directed to review inducement of violations; disposition of child on denial of petition

(a) (1) Upon the date appointed by the court for a hearing of the petition for adoption or as soon thereafter as the matter may be reached for a hearing, the court shall proceed to a full hearing on the petition and the examination of the parties at interest in chambers, under oath, with the right of continuing the hearing and examinations from time to time as the nature of the case may require. The court at such times shall give consideration to the investigation report to the court provided for in Code Section 19-8-16 and the recommendations contained therein.

(2) The court shall examine the petition for adoption and the affidavit specified in subsection (g) of Code Section 19-8-5, 19-8-6, or 19-8-7, as appropriate, to determine whether Code Section 19-8-12 is applicable. If the court determines that Code Section 19-8-12 is applicable to the petition, it shall:
  (A) Determine that an appropriate order has previously been entered;
  (B) Enter an order consistent with Code Section 19-8-12; or
  (C) Continue the hearing until Code Section 19-8-12 is complied with.

(3) If the adoption petition is filed pursuant to subsection (a) of Code Section 19-8-5, the court shall examine the financial disclosures required under subsections (c) and (d) of Code Section 19-8-13 and make such further examination of each petitioner and his attorney as the court deems appropriate in order to make a determination as to whether there is cause to believe that Code Section 19-8-24 has been violated

with regard to the "inducement" of the placement of the child for adoption. Should the court determine that further inquiry is in order, the court shall direct the district attorney for the county to review the matter further and to take such appropriate action as the district attorney in his discretion deems appropriate.

(b) If the court is satisfied that each living parent or guardian of the child has surrendered or had terminated all his rights to the child in the manner provided by law prior to the filing of the petition for adoption or that each petitioner has satisfied his burden of proof under Code Section 19-8-10, that such petitioner is capable of assuming responsibility for the care, supervision, training, and education of the child, that the child is suitable for adoption in a private family home, and that the adoption requested is for the best interest of the child, it shall enter a decree of adoption, terminating all the rights of each parent and guardian to the child, granting the permanent custody of the child to each petitioner, naming the child as prayed for in the petition, and declaring the child to be the adopted child of each petitioner. In all cases wherein Code Section 19-8-10 is relied upon by any petitioner as a basis for the termination of parental rights, the court shall include in the decree of adoption appropriate findings of fact and conclusions of law relating to the applicability of Code Section 19-8-10.

(c) If the court determines that any petitioner has not complied with this chapter, it may dismiss the petition for adoption without prejudice or it may continue the case. Should the court find that any notice required to be given by any petitioner under this chapter has not been given or has not been properly given or that the petition has not been properly filed, the court is authorized to enter an order providing for corrective action and an additional hearing.

(d) If the court is not satisfied that the adoption is in the best interests of the child, it shall deny the petition. If the petition is denied because of such reason or for any other reason under law, the court shall commit the child to the custody of the department or to a child-placing agency, if the petition was filed pursuant to Code Section 19-8-4 or 19-8-5. If the petition was filed pursuant to Code Section 19-8-6, 19-8-7, or 19-8-8, the child shall remain in the custody of each petitioner if that petitioner is fit to have custody or the court may place the child with the department for the purpose of determining whether or not a petition should be initiated under Chapter 11 of Title 15.

(e) A decree of adoption issued pursuant to subsection (b) of this Code section shall not be subject to any judicial challenge filed more than six months after the date of entry of such decree.

(f) Any decree of adoption issued prior to the effective date of this action shall not be subject to any judicial challenge more than six months after July 1, 1995.

§ 19-8-19. (Effective until September 1, 2018) Effect of decree of adoption

(a) A decree of adoption, whether issued by a court of this state or by a court of any other jurisdiction, shall have the following effect as to matters within the jurisdiction of or before a court in this state:

(1) Except with respect to a spouse of the petitioner and relatives of the spouse, a decree of adoption terminates all legal relationships between the adopted individual and his relatives, including his parent, so that the adopted individual thereafter is a stranger to his former relatives for all purposes, including inheritance and the interpretation or construction of documents, statutes, and instruments, whether executed before or after the adoption is decreed, which do not expressly include the individual by name or by some designation not based on a parent and child or blood relationship; and

(2) A decree of adoption creates the relationship of parent and child between each petitioner and the adopted individual, as if the adopted individual were a child of biological issue of that petitioner. The adopted individual shall enjoy every right and privilege of a biological child of that petitioner; shall be deemed a biological child of that petitioner, to inherit under the laws of descent and distribution in the absence of a will, and to take under the provisions of any instrument of testamentary gift, bequest, devise, or legacy, whether executed before or after the adoption is decreed, unless expressly excluded therefrom; shall take by inheritance from relatives of that petitioner; and shall also take as a "child" of that petitioner under a class gift made by the will of a third person.

(b) Notwithstanding the provisions of subsection (a) of this Code section, if a parent of a child dies without the relationship of parent and child having been previously terminated by court order or unrevoked surrender of parental rights to the child, the child's right of inheritance from or through the deceased parent shall not be affected by the adoption.

§ 19-8-20. (Effective until September 1, 2018) Forwarding of decree, report, and subsequent orders to department; issuance of adoption certificate; use as evidence

(a) Upon the entry of the decree of adoption, the clerk of the court granting the same shall forward a copy of the decree, together with the original of the investigation report and background information filed with the court, to the department. If there is any subsequent order or revocation of the adoption a copy of same in like manner shall be forwarded by the clerk to the department.

(b) At any time after the entry of the decree of adoption, upon the request of an adopted person who has reached 18 years of age or upon the request of any adopting parent, the clerk of the court granting the decree shall issue to that requesting adopted person or adopting parent a certificate of adoption, under the seal of the court, upon payment to the clerk of the fee prescribed in paragraph (4) of subsection (g) of Code Section 15-6-77, which adoption certificate shall be received as evidence in any court or proceeding as primary evidence of the facts contained in the certificate.

(c) The adoption certificate shall be in substantially the following form:

This is to certify that   (names of each adopting parent) have obtained a decree of adoption for   (full name of adopted child) in the Superior Court of   County, Georgia, on the   day of   , as shown by the court's records.

Given under the hand and seal of said court, this the   day of   ,

.

Clerk

§ 19-8-21. (Effective until September 1, 2018) Adoption of adult individuals; applicability of Code Sections 19-8-19 and 19-8-20

(a) Adult persons may be adopted on giving written consent to the adoption. In such cases, adoption shall be by a petition duly verified and filed, together with two conformed copies, in the superior court in the county in which either any petitioner or the adult to be adopted resides, setting forth the name, age, and residence of each petitioner and of the adult to be adopted, the name by which the adult is to be known, and his written consent to the adoption. The court may assign the petition for hearing at any time. After examining each petitioner and the adult sought to be adopted, the court, if satisfied that there is no reason why the adoption should not be granted, shall enter a decree of adoption and, if requested, shall change the name of the adopted adult. Thereafter, the relation between each petitioner and the adopted adult shall be, as to their legal rights and liabilities, the relation of parent and child.

(b) Code Section 19-8-19, relating to the effect of a decree of adoption, and Code Section 19-8-20, relating to notice of adoption, shall also apply to the adoption of adults.

§ 19-8-22. (Effective until September 1, 2018) Recognition and effect of foreign decrees

(a) A decree of a court terminating the relationship of parent and child or establishing the relationship of parent and child by adoption, issued pursuant to due process of law by a court of any other jurisdiction within or outside the United States, or the clear and irrevocable release or consent to adoption by the guardian of a child where the appointment of the guardian has been certified by the appropriate and legally authorized court or agency of the government of the foreign country shall be recognized in this state; and the rights and obligations of the parties as to matters within the jurisdiction of this state shall be determined as though any such decree were issued by a court of this state and any such consent or release shall be deemed to satisfy the requirements of Code Sections 19-8-4, 19-8-5, 19-8-6, 19-8-7, and 19-8-12.

(b) Any adoption proceeding in this state in which a final order of adoption was entered by the court prior to April 1, 1986, and to which subsection (a) of this Code section would have been applicable if said subsection, as amended, had been effective at the time such proceeding was filed or concluded shall be governed by the provisions of subsection (a) of this Code section, as amended.

(c) Any adoption proceeding pending in a court of competent jurisdiction in this state in which no final order of adoption has been entered as of April 1, 1986, to which the provisions of subsection (a) of this Code section are applicable shall be governed by the provisions of subsection (a) of this Code section, as amended.

§ 19-8-23. (Effective until September 1, 2018) Where records of adoption kept; examination by parties and attorneys; use of information by agency and department

(a) The original petition, all amendments and exhibits thereto, all motions, documents, affidavits, records, and testimony filed in connection therewith, and all decrees or orders of any kind whatsoever, except the original investigation report and background information referred to in Code Section 19-8-20, shall be recorded in a book kept for that purpose and properly indexed; and the book shall be part of the records of the court in each county which has jurisdiction over matters of adoption in that county. All of the records, including the docket book, of the court granting the adoption, of the department, and of the child-placing agency that relate in any manner to the adoption shall be kept sealed and locked. The records may be examined by the parties at interest in the adoption and their attorneys when, after written petition has been presented to the court having jurisdiction and after the department and the appropriate child-placing agency have received at least 30 days' prior written notice of the filing of such petition, the matter has come on before the court in chambers and, good cause having been shown to the court, the court has entered an order permitting such examination. Notwithstanding the foregoing, if the adoptee who is the subject of the records sought to be examined is less than 18 years of age at the time the petition is filed and the petitioner is someone other than one of the adoptive parents of the adoptee, then the department shall provide written notice of such proceedings to the adoptive parents by certified mail or statutory overnight delivery, return receipt requested, at the last address the department has for such adoptive parents and the court shall continue any hearing on the petition until not less than 60 days after the date the notice was sent. Each such adoptive parent shall have the right to appear in person or through counsel and show cause why such records should not be examined. Adoptive parents may provide the department with their current address for purposes of receiving notice under this subsection by mailing that address to:

Office of Adoptions
Department of Human Services
Atlanta, Georgia

(b) The department or the child-placing agency may, in its sole discretion, make use of any information contained in the records of the respective department or agency relating to the adoptive parents in connection with a subsequent adoption matter involving the same adoptive parents or to provide notice when required by subsection (a) of this Code section.

(b.1) The department may, in its sole discretion, make use of any information contained in the records of the department concerning an adopted child and the adopted child's biological parents in connection with the placement of another child in the home of the adoptive parents of the child or in connection with the investigation of a report of child abuse or neglect made concerning the adopted child's biological parents.

(b.2) (1) As used in this paragraph, the term:
    (A) "Director" means the director of the Division of Family and Children Services of the department.
    (B) "Near fatality" shall have the same meaning as set forth in Code Section 49-5-40.
  (2) Upon the approval of the director, or his or her designee, any information concerning an adopted child, such child's biological parents, and such child's adoptive parents may be used solely by the department when, after the adoption, such child dies, suffers a near fatality, or is an alleged victim of child abuse or neglect; provided, however, that the department may provide such information to the Office of the Child Advocate for the Protection of Children. Such information shall not otherwise be subject to disclosure or release under Article 4 of Chapter 18 of Title 50.

(c) The department or the child-placing agency may, in its sole discretion, make use of any information contained in its records on a child when an adoption disrupts after finalization and when such records are required for the permanent placement of such child, or when the information is required by federal law.

(d) (1) Upon the request of a party at interest in the adoption, a child, legal guardian, or health care agent of an adopted person or a provider of medical services to such a party, child, legal guardian, or health care agent when certain information would assist in the provision of medical care, a medical emergency, or medical diagnosis or treatment, the department or child-placing agency shall access its own records on finalized adoptions for the purpose of adding subsequently obtained medical information or releasing nonidentifying medical and health history information contained in its records pertaining to an adopted person or the biological parents or relatives of the biological parents of the adopted person. For purposes of this paragraph, the term "health care agent" has the meaning provided by Code Section 31-32-2.

  (2) Upon receipt by the State Adoption Unit of the Division of Family and Children Services of the department or by a child-placing agency of documented medical information relevant to an adoptee, the office or child-placing agency shall use reasonable efforts to contact the adoptive parents of the adoptee if the adoptee is under 18 years of age or the adoptee if he or she is 18 years of age or older and provide such documented medical information to the adoptive parents or the adoptee. The office or child-placing agency shall be entitled to reimbursement of reasonable costs for postage and photocopying incurred in the delivery of such documented medical information to the adoptive parents or adoptee.

(e) Records relating in any manner to adoption shall not be open to the general public for inspection.

(f) (1) Notwithstanding Code Section 19-8-1, for purposes of this subsection, the term:
    (A) "Biological parent" means the biological mother or biological father who surrendered that person's rights or had such rights terminated by court order giving rise to the adoption of the child.
    (B) "Commissioner" means the commissioner of human services or that person's designee.
    (C) "Department" means the Department of Human Services or, when the Department of Human Services so designates, the county department of family and children services which placed for adoption the person seeking, or on whose behalf is sought, information under this subsection.
    (D) "Placement agency" means the child-placing agency, as defined in paragraph (3) of Code Section 19-8-1, which placed for adoption the person seeking or on whose behalf is sought information under this subsection.

(2) The department or a placement agency, upon the written request of an adopted person who has reached 18 years of age or upon the written request of an adoptive parent on behalf of that parent's adopted child, shall release to such adopted person or to the adoptive parent on the child's behalf nonidentifying information regarding such adopted person's biological parents and information regarding such adopted person's birth. Such information may include the date and place of birth of the adopted person and the genetic, social, and health history of the biological parents. No information released pursuant to this paragraph shall include the name or address of either biological parent or the name or address of any relative by birth or marriage of either biological parent.

(3) (A) The department or a placement agency upon written request of an adopted person who has reached 21 years of age shall release to such adopted person the name of such person's biological parent if:

(i) The biological parent whose name is to be released has submitted unrevoked written permission to the department or the placement agency for the release of that parent's name to the adopted person;

(ii) The identity of the biological parent submitting permission for the release of that parent's name has been verified by the department or the placement agency; and

(iii) The department or the placement agency has records pertaining to the finalized adoption and to the identity of the biological parent whose name is to be released.

(B) If the adopted person is deceased and leaves a child, such child, upon reaching 21 years of age, may seek the name and other identifying information concerning his or her grandparents in the same manner as the deceased adopted person and subject to the same procedures contained in this Code section.

(4) (A) If a biological parent has not filed written unrevoked permission for the release of that parent's name to the adopted child, the department or the placement agency, within six months of receipt of the written request of the adopted person who has reached 21 years of age, shall make diligent effort to notify each biological parent identified in the original adoption proceedings or in other records of the department or the placement agency relative to the adopted person. For purposes of this subparagraph, "notify" means a personal and confidential contact with each biological parent of the adopted person. The contact shall be by an employee or agent of the placement agency which processed the pertinent adoption or by other agents or employees of the department. The contact shall be evidenced by the person who notified each parent certifying to the department that each parent was given the following information:

(i) The nature of the information requested by the adopted person;

(ii) The date of the request of the adopted person;

(iii) The right of each biological parent to file an affidavit with the placement agency or the department stating that such parent's identity should not be disclosed;

(iv) The right of each biological parent to file a consent to disclosure with the placement agency or the department; and

(v) The effect of a failure of each biological parent to file either a consent to disclosure or an affidavit stating that the information in the sealed adoption file should not be disclosed.

(B) If a biological parent files an unrevoked consent to the disclosure of that parent's identity, such parent's name shall be released to the adopted person who has requested such information as authorized by this paragraph.

(C) If, within 60 days of being notified by the department or the placement agency pursuant to subparagraph (A) of this paragraph, a biological parent has filed with the department or placement agency an affidavit objecting to such release, information regarding that biological parent shall not be released.

(D) (i) If six months after receipt of the adopted person's written request the placement agency or the department has either been unable to notify a biological parent identified in the original adoption record or has been able to notify a biological parent identified in the original adoption record but has not obtained a consent to disclosure from the notified biological parent, then the identity of a biological parent may only be disclosed as provided in division (ii) or (iii) of this subparagraph.

(ii) The adopted person who has reached 21 years of age may petition the Superior Court of Fulton County to seek the release of the identity of each of that person's biological parents from the department or placement agency. The court shall grant the petition if the court finds that the department or placement agency has made diligent efforts to locate each biological parent pursuant to this subparagraph either without success or upon locating a biological parent has not obtained a consent to disclosure from the notified biological parent and that failure to release the identity of each biological parent would have an adverse impact upon the physical, mental, or emotional health of the adopted person.

(iii) If it is verified that a biological parent of the adopted person is deceased, the department or placement agency shall be authorized to disclose the name and place of burial of the deceased biological parent, if known, to the adopted person seeking such information without the necessity of obtaining a court order.

(5) (A) Upon written request of an adopted person who has reached 21 years of age or a person who has reached 21 years of age and who is the sibling of an adopted person, the department or a placement agency shall attempt to identify and notify the siblings of the requesting party, if such siblings are at least 18 years of age. Upon locating the requesting party's sibling, the department or the placement agency shall notify the sibling of the inquiry. Upon the written consent of a sibling so notified, the department or the placement agency shall forward the requesting party's name and address to the sibling and, upon further written

consent of the sibling, shall divulge to the requesting party the present name and address of the sibling. If a sibling cannot be identified or located, the department or placement agency shall notify the requesting party of such circumstances but shall not disclose any names or other information which would tend to identify the sibling. If a sibling is deceased, the department or placement agency shall be authorized to disclose the name and place of burial of the deceased sibling, if known, to the requesting party without the necessity of obtaining a court order.

(B) (i) If six months after receipt of the written request from an adopted individual who has reached 18 years of age or an individual who has reached 18 years of age and who is the sibling of an adopted individual, the department or placement agency has been unable to notify one or more of the siblings of the requesting party or has been able to notify a sibling of the requesting party but has not obtained a consent to disclosure from the notified sibling, then the identity of the siblings may only be disclosed as provided in division (ii) of this subparagraph.

(ii) The adopted person who has reached 21 years of age or a person who has reached 21 years of age and who is the sibling of an adopted person may petition the Superior Court of Fulton County to seek the release of the last known name and address of each of the siblings of the petitioning sibling, that are at least 18 years of age, from the department or placement agency. The court shall grant the petition if the court finds that the department or placement agency has made diligent efforts to locate such siblings pursuant to subparagraph (A) of this paragraph either without success or upon locating one or more of the siblings has not obtained a consent to disclosure from all the notified siblings and that failure to release the identity and last known address of said siblings would have an adverse impact upon the physical, mental, or emotional health of the petitioning sibling.

(C) If the adopted person is deceased and leaves a child, such child, upon reaching 21 years of age, may obtain the name and other identifying information concerning the siblings of his or her deceased parent in the same manner that the deceased adopted person would be entitled to obtain such information pursuant to the procedures contained in this Code section.

(6) (A) Upon written request of a biological parent of an adopted person who has reached 21 years of age, the department or a placement agency shall attempt to identify and notify the adopted person. Upon locating the adopted person, the department or the placement agency shall notify the adopted person of the inquiry. Upon the written consent of the adopted person so notified, the department or the placement agency shall forward the biological parent's name and address to the adopted person and, upon further written consent of the adopted person, shall divulge to the requesting biological parent the present name and address of the adopted person. If the adopted person is deceased, the department or placement agency shall be authorized to disclose the name and place of burial of the deceased adopted person, if known, to the requesting biological parent without the necessity of obtaining a court order.

(B) (i) If six months after receipt of the written request from a biological parent of an adopted person who has reached 21 years of age the placement agency or the department has either been unable to notify the adopted person or has been able to notify the adopted person but has not obtained a consent to disclosure from the notified adopted person, then the identity of the adopted person may only be disclosed as provided in division (ii) of this subparagraph.

(ii) The biological parent of an adopted person who has reached 21 years of age may petition the Superior Court of Fulton County to seek the release of the last known name and address of the adopted person from the department or placement agency. The court shall grant the petition if the court finds that the department or placement agency has made diligent efforts to locate such adopted person pursuant to subparagraph (A) of this paragraph either without success or upon locating the adopted person has not obtained a consent to disclosure from the adopted person and that failure to release the identity and last known address of said adopted person would have an adverse impact upon the physical, mental, or emotional health of the petitioning biological parent.

(C) If the biological parent is deceased, a parent or sibling of the deceased biological parent, or both, may obtain the name and other identifying information concerning the adopted person in the same manner that the deceased biological parent would be entitled to obtain such information pursuant to the procedures contained in this Code section.

(7) If an adoptive parent or the sibling of an adopted person notifies the department or placement agency of the death of an adopted person, the department or placement agency shall add information regarding the date and circumstances of the death to its records so as to enable it to share such information with a biological parent or sibling of the adopted person if they make an inquiry pursuant to the provisions of this Code section.

(8) If a biological parent or parent or sibling of a biological parent notifies the department or placement agency of the death of a biological parent or a sibling of an adopted person, the department or placement agency shall add information regarding the date and circumstances of the death to its records so as to enable it to share such information with an adopted person or sibling of the adopted person if he or she makes an inquiry pursuant to the provisions of this Code section.

(9) The Office of Adoptions within the department shall maintain a registry for the recording of requests by adopted persons for the name of any biological parent, for the recording of the written consent or the written objections of any biological parent to the release of that parent's identity to an adopted person upon

the adopted person's request, and for nonidentifying information regarding any biological parent which may be released pursuant to paragraph (2) of this subsection. The department and any placement agency which receives such requests, consents, or objections shall file a copy thereof with that office.

(10) The department or placement agency may charge a reasonable fee to be determined by the department for the cost of conducting any search pursuant to this subsection.

(11) Nothing in this subsection shall be construed to require the department or placement agency to disclose to any party at interest, including but not limited to an adopted person who has reached 21 years of age, any information which is not kept by the department or the placement agency in its normal course of operations relating to adoption.

(12) Any department employee or employee of any placement agency who releases information or makes authorized contacts in good faith and in compliance with this subsection shall be immune from civil or criminal liability for such release of information or authorized contacts.

(13) Information authorized to be released pursuant to this subsection may be released under the conditions specified in this subsection notwithstanding any other provisions of law to the contrary.

(14) A placement agency which demonstrates to the department by clear and convincing evidence that the requirement that such agency search for or notify any biological parent, sibling, or adopted person under subparagraph (A) of paragraph (4) of this subsection or subparagraph (A) of paragraph (5) of this subsection or subparagraph (A) of paragraph (6) of this subsection will impose an undue hardship upon that agency shall be relieved from that responsibility, and the department shall assume that responsibility upon such finding by the department of undue hardship. The department's determination under this subsection shall be a contested case within the meaning of Chapter 13 of Title 50, the "Georgia Administrative Procedure Act."

(15) Whenever this subsection authorizes both the department and a placement agency to perform any function or requires the placement agency to perform any function which the department is also required to perform, the department or agency may designate an agent to perform that function and in so performing it the agent shall have the same authority, powers, duties, and immunities as an employee of the department or placement agency has with respect to performing that function.

§ 19-8-24. (Effective until September 1, 2018) Unlawful advertisements; unlawful inducements; penalties

(a) It shall be unlawful for any person, organization, corporation, hospital, or association of any kind whatsoever which has not been established as a child-placing agency by the department to:

(1) Advertise, whether in a periodical, by television, by radio, or by any other public medium or by any private means, including letters, circulars, handbills, and oral statements, that the person, organization, corporation, hospital, or association will adopt children or will arrange for or cause children to be adopted or placed for adoption; or

(2) Directly or indirectly hold out inducements to parents to part with their children.

As used in this subsection, "inducements" shall include any financial assistance, either direct or indirect, from whatever source, except payment or reimbursement of the medical expenses directly related to the mother's pregnancy and hospitalization for the birth of the child and medical care for the child.

(b) It shall be unlawful for any person to sell, offer to sell, or conspire with another to sell or offer to sell a child for money or anything of value, except as otherwise provided in this chapter.

(c) Any person who violates subsection (a) or (b) of this Code section shall be guilty of a felony and, upon conviction thereof, shall be punished by a fine not to exceed $10,000.00 or imprisonment for not more than ten years, or both, in the discretion of the court.

(d) (1) Paragraph (1) of subsection (a) of this Code section shall not apply to communication by private means, including only written letters or oral statements, by an individual seeking to:

(A) Adopt a child or children; or
(B) Place that individual's child or children for adoption,
whether the communication occurs before or after the birth of such child or children.

(2) Paragraph (1) of subsection (a) of this Code section shall not apply to any communication described in paragraph (1) of this subsection which contains any attorney's name, address, telephone number, or any combination of such information and which requests any attorney named in such communication to be contacted to facilitate the carrying out of the purpose, as described in subparagraph (A) or (B) of paragraph (1) of this subsection, of the individual making such personal communication.

§ 19-8-25. (Effective until September 1, 2018) Effect of prior consent or surrender of rights

(a) A written consent or surrender, executed on or before June 30, 1990, shall, for purposes of an adoption proceeding commenced on or after July 1, 1990, be deemed to satisfy the surrender requirements of this chapter and it shall not be necessary to have any parent or guardian execute the documents required by Code Section 19-8-4, 19-8-5, 19-8-6, or 19-8-7; however, all other applicable provisions of this chapter must be complied with.

(b) It is the legislative intent of this subsection to clarify and not to change the applicability of certain previously existing provisions of this chapter to adoption proceedings pending on July 1, 1990. Any decree of adoption issued in an adoption proceeding in which the adoption petition was filed in a superior court of this state prior to July 1, 1990, shall be valid if the adoption conformed to the requirements of this chapter either as they existed on June 30, 1990, or on July 1, 1990, and each such adoption decree is hereby ratified and confirmed.

§ 19-8-26. (Effective until September 1, 2018) How surrender of parental rights executed; how and when surrender may be withdrawn; forms

(a) The surrender of rights by a parent or guardian pursuant to paragraph (1) of subsection (e) of Code Section 19-8-4 shall conform substantially to the following form:

SURRENDER OF RIGHTS

FINAL RELEASE FOR ADOPTION

NOTICE TO PARENT OR GUARDIAN:

This is an important legal document and by signing it you are surrendering all of your right, title, and claim to the child identified herein, so as to facilitate the child's placement for adoption. You are to receive a copy of this document and as explained below have the right to withdraw your surrender within ten days from the date you sign it.

I, the undersigned, being solicitous that my (male) (female) child, born (insert name of child) on (insert birthdate of child), should receive the benefits and advantages of a good home, to the end that (she) (he) may be fitted for the requirements of life, consent to this surrender.

I, the undersigned, (insert relationship to child) of the aforesaid child, do hereby surrender the child to (insert name of child-placing agency or Department of Human Services, as applicable) and promise not to interfere in the management of the child in any respect whatever; and, in consideration of the benefits guaranteed by (insert name of child-placing agency or Department of Human Services, as applicable) in thus providing for the child, I do relinquish all right, title, and claim to the child herein named, it being my wish, intent, and purpose to relinquish absolutely all parental control over the child.

Furthermore, I hereby agree that the (insert name of child-placing agency or Department of Human Services, as applicable) may seek for the child a legal adoption by such person or persons as may be chosen by the (insert name of child-placing agency or Department of Human Services, as applicable) or its authorized agents, without further notice to me. I do, furthermore, expressly waive any other notice or service in any of the legal proceedings for the adoption of the child.

Furthermore, I understand that under Georgia law the Department of Human Services or the child-placing agency is required to conduct an investigation and render a report to the court in connection with the legal proceeding for the legal adoption of the child and I hereby agree to cooperate fully with such department or agency in the conduct of its investigation.

Furthermore, I hereby certify that I have received a copy of this document and that I understand I may only withdraw this surrender by giving written notice, delivered in person or mailed by registered mail or statutory overnight delivery, to (insert name and address of child-placing agency or Department of Human Services, as applicable) within ten days from the date hereof; that the ten days shall be counted consecutively beginning with the day immediately following the date hereof; however, if the tenth day falls on a Saturday, Sunday, or legal holiday then the last day on which the surrender may be withdrawn shall be the next day that is not a Saturday, Sunday, or legal holiday; and I understand that it may NOT be withdrawn thereafter.

Furthermore, I hereby certify that I have not been subjected to any duress or undue pressure in the execution of this surrender document and do so freely and voluntarily.

Witness my hand and seal this   day of   , .

(SEAL)
(Parent or guardian)

Unofficial witness

Notary public
(b) Reserved.
(c) The surrender of rights by a parent or guardian pursuant to paragraph (1) of subsection (e) of Code Section 19-8-5 shall conform substantially to the following form:

SURRENDER OF RIGHTS
FINAL RELEASE FOR ADOPTION

NOTICE TO PARENT OR GUARDIAN:

This is an important legal document and by signing it you are surrendering all of your right, title, and claim to the child identified herein so as to facilitate the child's placement for adoption. You are to receive a copy of this document and as explained below have the right to withdraw your surrender within ten days from the date you sign it.

I, the undersigned, being solicitous that my (male) (female) child, born (insert name of child), on (insert birthdate of child), should receive the benefits and advantages of a good home, to the end that (she) (he) may be fitted for the requirements of life, consent to this surrender.

I, the undersigned, (insert relationship to child) of the aforesaid child, do hereby surrender the child to (insert name, surname not required, of each person to whom surrender is made), PROVIDED that each such person is named as petitioner in a petition for adoption of the child filed in accordance with Article 1 of Chapter 8 of Title 19 of the Official Code of Georgia Annotated within 60 days from the date hereof. Furthermore, I promise not to interfere in the management of the child in any respect whatever; and, in consideration of the benefits guaranteed by (insert name, surname not required, of each person to whom surrender is made) in thus providing for the child, I do relinquish all right, title, and claim to the child herein named, it being my wish, intent, and purpose to relinquish absolutely all parental control over the child.

It is also my wish, intent, and purpose that if each such person is not named as petitioner in a petition for adoption as provided for above within the 60 day period, other than for excusable neglect, or, if said petition for adoption is filed within 60 days but the adoption action is dismissed with prejudice or otherwise concluded without an order declaring the child to be the adopted child of each such person, then I do hereby surrender the child as follows:

(Mark one of the following as chosen)

I wish the child returned to me, and I expressly acknowledge that this provision applies only to the limited circumstance that the child is not adopted by the person or persons designated herein and further that this provision does not impair the validity, absolute finality, or totality of this surrender under any circumstance other than the failure of the designated person or persons to adopt the child and that no other provision of this surrender impairs the validity, absolute finality, or totality of this surrender once the revocation period has elapsed; or

I surrender the child to (insert name of designated licensed child-placing agency), a licensed child-placing agency, for placement for adoption; or

I surrender the child to the Department of Human Services, as provided by subsection (k) of Code Section 19-8-5, for placement for adoption; and (insert name of designated licensed child-placing agency) or the Department of Human Services may petition the superior court for custody of the child in accordance with the terms of this surrender.

Furthermore, I hereby agree that the child is to be adopted either by each person named above or by any other such person as may be chosen by the

CHAPTER 8. ADOPTION

ARTICLE 1. GENERAL PROVISIONS (EFFECTIVE UNTIL SEPTEMBER 1, 2018)

§ 19-8-27. (Effective until September 1, 2018) Postadoption contact agreements; definitions; procedure; jurisdiction; warnings; enforcement or termination; modification; costs and expenses of mediation, alternative dispute resolution, and litigation

(a) As used in this Code section, the term "birth relative" means:

(1) A parent, biological father who is not the legal father, grandparent, brother, sister, half-brother, or half-sister who is related by blood or marriage to a child who is being adopted or who has been adopted; or

(2) A grandparent, brother, sister, half-brother, or half-sister who is related by adoption to a child who is being adopted or who has been adopted.

(b) (1) An adopting parent or parents and birth relatives or an adopting parent or parents, birth relatives, and a child who is 14 years of age or older who is being adopted or who has been adopted may voluntarily enter into a written postadoption contact agreement to permit continuing contact between such birth relatives and such child. A child who is 14 years of age or older shall be considered a party to a postadoption contact agreement.

(2) A postadoption contact agreement may provide for privileges regarding a child who is being adopted or who has been adopted, including, but not limited to, visitation with such child, contact with such child, sharing of information about such child, or sharing of information about birth relatives.

(3) In order to be an enforceable postadoption contact agreement, such agreement shall be in writing and signed by all of the parties to such agreement acknowledging their consent to its terms and conditions.

(4) Enforcement, modification, or termination of a postadoption contact agreement shall be under the continuing jurisdiction of the court that granted the petition of adoption; provided, however, that the parties to a postadoption contact agreement may expressly waive the right to enforce, modify, or terminate such agreement under this Code section.

(5) Any party to the postadoption contact agreement may, at any time, file the original postadoption contact agreement with the court that has or had jurisdiction over the adoption if such agreement provides for the court to enforce such agreement or such agreement is silent as to the issue of enforcement.

(c) A postadoption contact agreement shall contain the following warnings in at least 14 point boldface type:

(1) After the entry of a decree for adoption, an adoption cannot be set aside due to the failure of an adopting parent, a birth parent, a birth relative, or the child to follow the terms of this agreement or a later change to this agreement; and

(2) A disagreement between the parties or litigation brought to enforce, terminate, or modify this agreement shall not affect the validity of the adoption and shall not serve as a basis for orders affecting the custody of the child.

(d) (1) As used in this subsection, the term "parties" means the individuals who signed the postadoption contact agreement currently in effect, including the child if he or she is 14 years of age or older at the time of the action regarding such agreement, but such term shall exclude any third party beneficiary to such agreement.

(2) A postadoption contact agreement may always be modified or terminated if the parties have voluntarily signed a written modified postadoption contact agreement or termination of a postadoption contact agreement. A modified postadoption contact agreement may be filed with the court if such agreement provides for the court to enforce such agreement or such agreement is silent as to the issue of enforcement.

(e) With respect to postadoption contact agreements that provide for court enforcement or termination or are silent as to such matters, any party, as defined in paragraph (1) of subsection (d) of this Code section, may file a petition to enforce or terminate such agreement with the court that granted the petition of adoption, and the court shall enforce the terms of such agreement or terminate such agreement if such court finds by a preponderance of the evidence that the enforcement or termination is necessary to serve the best interests of the child.

(f) With respect to postadoption contact agreements that provide for court modification or are silent as to modification, only the adopting parent or parents may file a petition seeking modification. Such petition shall be filed with the court that granted the petition of adoption, and the court shall modify such agreement if such court finds by a preponderance of the evidence that the modification is necessary to serve the best interests of the child and there has been a material change of circumstances since the current postadoption contact agreement was executed.

(g) A court may require the party seeking modification, termination, or enforcement of a postadoption contact agreement to participate in mediation or other appropriate alternative dispute resolution.

(h) All reasonable costs and expenses of mediation, alternative dispute resolution, and litigation shall be borne by the party, other than the child, filing the action to enforce, modify, or terminate a postadoption contact agreement when no party has been found by the court as failing to comply with an existing postadoption contact agreement. Otherwise, a party, other than the child, found by the court as failing to comply without good cause with an existing postadoption contact agreement shall bear all the costs and expenses of mediation, alternative dispute resolution, and litigation of the other party.

(i) A court shall not set aside a decree of adoption, rescind a surrender, or modify an order to terminate parental rights or any other prior court order because of the failure of an adoptive parent, a birth relative, or the child to comply with any or all of the original terms of, or subsequent modifications to, a postadoption contact agreement.

ARTICLE 1. GENERAL PROVISIONS (EFFECTIVE SEPTEMBER 1, 2018)
§ 19-8-1. (Effective September 1, 2018) Definitions

For purposes of this article, the term:

(1) "Alaskan native" means a member of the Alaska Native Regional Corporations formed under the Alaska Native Claims Settlement Act of 1971 (ANCSA).

(2) "Biological father" means a male who impregnated the biological mother resulting in the birth of the child.

(3) "Biological parent" means a biological mother or biological father.

(4) "Child" means an individual who is under 18 years of age and who is sought to be adopted.

(5) "Child-placing agency" means an agency licensed as a child-placing agency pursuant to Chapter 5 of Title 49.

(6) "Department" means the Department of Human Services.

(7) "Evaluator" means a person or agency that conducts a home study. An evaluator shall be a child-placing agency, the department, or a licensed professional with at least two years of adoption related professional experience, including a licensed clinical social worker, licensed master social worker, licensed marriage and family therapist, or licensed professional counselor; provided, however, that when none of the foregoing evaluators are available, the court may appoint a guardian ad litem or court appointed special advocate to conduct a home study.

(8) "'Guardian" means an individual appointed as a:

  (A) Guardian or temporary guardian of a child as provided in Title 29;
  (B) Guardian of a child pursuant to Code Section 15-11-13; or
  (C) Permanent guardian of a child as provided in Part 13 of Article 3 of Chapter 11 of Title 15.

(9) "Home study" means an evaluation by an evaluator of a petitioner's home environment for the purpose of determining the suitability of such environment as a prospective adoptive home for a child. Such evaluation shall consider a petitioner's physical health, emotional maturity, financial circumstances, family, and social background and shall conform to the rules and regulations established by the department for child-placing agencies for adoption home studies.

(10) "Home study report" means the written report generated as a result of the home study.

(11) "Legal father" means a male who has not surrendered or had terminated his rights to a child and who:
   (A) Has legally adopted such child;
   (B) Was married to the biological mother of such child at the time such child was born or within the usual period of gestation, unless paternity was disproved by a final order of a court of competent jurisdiction;
   (C) Married a legal mother of such child after such child was born and recognized such child as his own, unless paternity was disproved by a final order of a court of competent jurisdiction; or
   (D) Has legitimated such child by a final order pursuant to Code Section 19-7-22.
(12) "Legal mother" means a female who is the biological or adoptive mother of the child and who has not surrendered or had terminated her rights to the child.
(13) "Native American heritage" means any individual who is:
   (A) A member of a federally recognized American Indian tribe; or
   (B) An Alaskan native.
(14) "Out-of-state licensed agency" means an agency or entity that is licensed in another state or country to place children for adoption.
(15) "Parent" means a legal father or a legal mother of the child.
(16) "Petitioner" means an individual who petitions to adopt or terminate rights to a child pursuant to this article.
(17) "Putative father registry" means the registry established and maintained pursuant to subsections (d) and (e) of Code Section 19-11-9.

§ 19-8-2. (Effective September 1, 2018) Jurisdiction and venue of adoption proceedings

(a) The superior courts of the several counties shall have exclusive jurisdiction in all matters of adoption.
(b) All petitions for adoption under this article shall be filed in the county in which any petitioner resides, except that:
  (1) Upon good cause being shown, the court may, in its discretion, allow such petition to be filed in the court of the county:
   (A) Of the child's domicile;
   (B) In which is located any child-placing agency having legal custody of the child;
   (C) Where the child was born if such petition is filed within one year of the child's birth; or
   (D) In which is located the office of the department having legal custody of the child;
  (2) Any individual who is a resident of any United States army post or military reservation within this state may file such petition in any county adjacent to the United States army post or military reservation; and
  (3) When a child has been placed for adoption with an individual who is a resident of another state in compliance with Chapter 4 of Title 39, relating to the Interstate Compact on the Placement of Children, such petition shall be filed in:
   (A) The court of the county where the child was born;
   (B) The court of the county in which is located any child-placing agency having legal custody of the child; or
   (C) Superior Court of Fulton County.

§ 19-8-3. (Effective September 1, 2018) Who may adopt a child; when petition must be filed in names of both spouses

(a) Any individual may petition to adopt a child if he or she:
(1) Is at least 25 years of age or is married and living with his or her spouse, or is at least 21 years of age and is a relative of the child;
(2) Is at least ten years older than the child, except such ten-year requirement shall not apply when the petitioner is a stepparent or relative and the petition is filed pursuant to Code Section 19-8-6 or 19-8-7;
(3) Is a bona fide resident of this state at the filing of the petition for adoption or is a bona fide resident of the receiving state when the adoptee was born in this state and was placed in compliance with Chapter 4 of Title 39, relating to the Interstate Compact on the Placement of Children; and
(4) Is financially, physically, and mentally able to have permanent custody of the child.
(b) If an individual seeking to adopt a child is married, the petition for adoption shall be filed in the name of both spouses; provided, however, that, when the child is or was the stepchild of the party seeking to adopt, such petition shall be filed by the stepparent alone.

§ 19-8-4. (Effective September 1, 2018) Adoption through the department, child-placing agency, or out-of-state licensed agency

(a) A child may be adopted through the department, any child-placing agency, or any out-of-state licensed agency only if each living parent and guardian of such child:
  (1) Has voluntarily and in writing surrendered all of his or her rights to the child to the department, a child-placing agency, or an out-of-state licensed agency as provided in this Code section and such department, child-placing agency, or out-of-state licensed agency thereafter consents to the adoption; or
  (2) Has had all of his or her rights to the child terminated by order of a court of competent jurisdiction, the child has been committed by the court to the department, a child-placing agency, or an out-of-state licensed agency for placement for adoption, and such department, child-placing agency, or out-of-state licensed agency thereafter consents to the adoption.
(b) In the case of a child 14 years of age or older, the written consent of the child to his or her adoption shall be given and acknowledged in the presence of the court.
(c) The surrender of rights to the department, a child-placing agency, or an out-of-state licensed agency specified in paragraphs (1) and (2) of subsection (e) of this Code section shall be executed following the birth of the child, and the pre-birth surrender to the department, a child-placing agency, or an out-of-state licensed agency specified in paragraph (3) of subsection (e) of this Code section shall be executed prior to the birth of the child. Each surrender shall be executed under oath and in the presence of a notary public and an adult witness. A copy of the surrender shall be provided to the individual signing the surrender at the time of the execution thereof.
(d) An individual signing a surrender of rights pursuant to this Code section shall have the right to revoke such surrender within four days as provided in subsection (a) of Code Section 19-8-9.
(e) (1) The surrender of rights by a parent or guardian specified in paragraph (1) of subsection (a) of this Code section shall meet the requirements of subsection (a) of Code Section 19-8-26. Such surrender shall be signed under oath and in the presence of a notary public and an adult witness.
  (2) A biological father who is not a legal father of a child may surrender all his rights to the child for the purpose of an adoption pursuant to this Code section. Such surrender shall meet the requirements of subsection (d) of Code Section 19-8-26. Such surrender shall be signed under oath and in the presence of a notary public and an adult witness.
  (3) (A) A biological father who is not a legal father of a child may execute a surrender of his rights to the child prior to the birth of the child for the purpose of an adoption pursuant to this Code section. A pre-birth surrender shall serve to relinquish an alleged biological father's rights to the child and to waive an alleged biological father's right to notice of any proceeding with respect to the child's adoption, custody, or guardianship. The court in any adoption proceeding shall have jurisdiction to enter a final order of adoption of the child based upon the pre-birth surrender and in other proceedings to determine the child's legal custody or guardianship shall have jurisdiction to enter an order for those purposes.
    (B) The rights and responsibilities of an alleged biological father shall be permanently terminated only upon an order from a court of competent jurisdiction terminating such rights or the entry of a final order of adoption. An individual executing a pre-birth surrender pursuant to this Code section shall have the right to revoke such surrender within four days from the date of execution thereof, notwithstanding the date of birth of the child.
    (C) If a final order of adoption is not entered after the execution of a pre-birth surrender and paternity is established by acknowledgment, by administrative order, or by judicial order, then an alleged biological father shall be responsible for child support or other financial obligations to the child or to a legal mother, or to both.
    (D) The pre-birth surrender shall not be valid for use by a legal father.
    (E) The pre-birth surrender may be executed at any time after the biological mother executes a sworn statement identifying such individual as an alleged biological father of the biological mother's unborn child meeting the requirements of subsection (m) of Code Section 19-8-26.
    (F) The pre-birth surrender shall meet the requirements of subsection (f) of Code Section 19-8-26 and shall be signed under oath and in the presence of a notary public and an adult witness.
(f) A surrender of rights shall be acknowledged by the individual who surrenders those rights by also signing an acknowledgment meeting the requirements of subsection (g) of Code Section 19-8-26. Such acknowledgment shall be signed under oath and in the presence of a notary public and an adult witness.
(g) (1) A legal mother who surrenders her parental rights pursuant to this Code section shall execute an affidavit meeting the requirements of subsection (h) of Code Section 19-8-26. Such affidavit shall be signed under oath and in the presence of a notary public.
  (2) A legal mother who is the adoptive mother of the child and who surrenders her parental rights pursuant to this Code section shall execute an affidavit meeting the requirements of subsection (i) of Code Section 19-8-26. Such affidavit shall be signed under oath and in the presence of a notary public.
(h) Whenever rights are surrendered to the department, a child-placing agency, or an out-of-state licensed agency, the department or agency representative before whom the surrender of rights is signed shall execute an affidavit meeting the requirements of subsection (j) of Code Section 19-8-26. Such affidavit shall be signed under oath and in the presence of a notary public.
(i) A surrender of rights pursuant to this Code section may be given by any parent or biological father who is not a legal father of the child regardless of whether such individual is a citizen of the United States, a resident

of this state, or has reached the age of 18 years. Such surrender given by such individual shall be binding upon him or her as if the individual were in all respects sui juris and shall include a consent to the jurisdiction of the courts of this state for any action filed under this article. Such surrender shall state that such individual agrees to be bound by a decree of adoption.
(j) In any surrender of rights pursuant to this Code section, Chapter 4 of Title 39, relating to the Interstate Compact on the Placement of Children, if applicable, shall be complied with.
(k) A biological father or a legal father who signs a surrender of rights may execute an affidavit regarding his Native American heritage and military service meeting the requirements of subsection (n) of Code Section 19-8-26. Such affidavit shall be signed under oath and in the presence of a notary public.

§ 19-8-5. (Effective September 1, 2018) Third party adoption by party who is not stepparent or relative of child

   (a) A child may be adopted by a third party who is neither the stepparent nor relative of that child, as such individuals are described in subsection (a) of Code Sections 19-8-6 and 19-8-7, only if each living parent and guardian of such child has voluntarily and in writing surrendered all of his or her rights to such child to that third party for the purpose of enabling that third party to adopt such child. A third party to whom such child is voluntarily surrendered shall be financially responsible for such child as of the date of surrender by the parent. Except as provided in subsection (l) of this Code section, no child shall be placed with a third party for purposes of adoption unless prior to the date of placement a home study shall have been completed, and the home study report recommends placement of a child in such third party's home.
(b) In the case of a child 14 years of age or older, the written consent of the child to his or her adoption shall be given and acknowledged in the presence of the court.
(c) The surrender of rights specified in paragraphs (1) and (2) of subsection (e) of this Code section shall be executed following the birth of the child, and the pre-birth surrender specified in paragraph (3) of subsection (e) of this Code section shall be executed prior to the birth of the child. Each surrender shall be executed under oath and in the presence of a notary public and an adult witness. The name and address of each individual to whom the child is surrendered may be omitted to protect confidentiality, provided the surrender of rights sets forth the name and address of his or her agent for purposes of notice of revocation as provided for in subsection (d) of this Code section. A copy of the surrender shall be provided to the individual signing the surrender at the time of the execution thereof.
(d) An individual signing a surrender of rights pursuant to this Code section shall have the right to revoke such surrender within four days as provided in subsection (a) of Code Section 19-8-9.
(e) (1) The surrender of rights by a parent or guardian specified in subsection (a) of this Code section shall meet the requirements of subsection (c) of Code Section 19-8-26. Such surrender shall be signed under oath and in the presence of a notary public and an adult witness.
   (2) A biological father who is not a legal father of a child may surrender all his rights to the child for purposes of an adoption pursuant to this Code section. Such surrender shall meet the requirements of subsection (d) of Code Section 19-8-26. Such surrender shall be signed under oath and in the presence of a notary public and an adult witness.
   (3) (A) A biological father who is not a legal father of a child may execute a surrender of his rights to the child prior to the birth of the child for the purpose of an adoption pursuant to this Code section. A pre-birth surrender shall serve to relinquish an alleged biological father's rights to the child and to waive an alleged biological father's right to notice of any proceeding with respect to the child's adoption, custody, or guardianship. The court in any adoption proceeding shall have jurisdiction to enter a final order of adoption of the child based upon the pre-birth surrender and in other proceedings to determine the child's legal custody or guardianship shall have jurisdiction to enter an order for those purposes.
   (B) The rights and responsibilities of an alleged biological father shall be permanently terminated only upon an order from a court of competent jurisdiction terminating such rights or the entry of a final order of adoption. An individual executing a pre-birth surrender pursuant to this Code section shall have the right to revoke such surrender within four days from the date of execution thereof, notwithstanding the date of birth of the child.
   (C) If a final order of adoption is not entered after the execution of a pre-birth surrender and paternity is established by acknowledgment, by administrative order, or by judicial order, then an alleged biological father shall be responsible for child support or other financial obligations to the child or to a legal mother, or to both.
   (D) The pre-birth surrender shall not be valid for use by a legal father.
   (E) The pre-birth surrender may be executed at any time after the biological mother executes a sworn statement identifying such individual as an alleged biological father of the biological mother's unborn child meeting the requirements of subsection (m) of Code Section 19-8-26.
   (F) The pre-birth surrender shall meet the requirements of subsection (f) of Code Section 19-8-26 and shall be signed under oath and in the presence of a notary public and an adult witness.

(f) A surrender of rights shall be acknowledged by the individual who surrenders those rights by also signing an acknowledgment meeting the requirements of subsection (g) of Code Section 19-8-26. Such acknowledgment shall be signed under oath and in the presence of a notary public and an adult witness.

(g) (1) A legal mother who surrenders her parental rights pursuant to this Code section shall execute an affidavit meeting the requirements of subsection (h) of Code Section 19-8-26. Such affidavit shall be signed under oath and in the presence of a notary public.

(2) A legal mother who is the adoptive mother of the child and who surrenders her parental rights pursuant to this Code section shall execute an affidavit meeting the requirements of subsection (i) of Code Section 19-8-26. Such affidavit shall be signed under oath and in the presence of a notary public.

(h) Whenever rights are surrendered pursuant to this Code section, the representative of each petitioner or the representative of the individual signing such surrender shall execute an affidavit meeting the requirements of subsection (k) of Code Section 19-8-26. Such affidavit shall be signed under oath and in the presence of a notary public.

(i) A surrender of rights pursuant to this Code section may be given by any parent or biological father who is not a legal father of the child regardless of whether such individual is a citizen of the United States, a resident of this state, or has reached the age of 18 years. Such surrender given by such individual shall be binding upon him or her as if the individual were in all respects sui juris and shall include a consent to the jurisdiction of the courts of this state for any action filed under this article. Such surrender shall state that such individual agrees to be bound by a decree of adoption.

(j) A petition for adoption pursuant to subsection (a) of this Code section shall be filed within 60 days from the date the surrender of rights is executed; provided, however, that for good cause shown the court may waive the 60 day requirement. If the petition for adoption is not filed within the time period specified by this subsection and the court does not waive the 60 day requirement or if the proceedings resulting from such petition are not concluded with an order granting such petition, then the surrender of rights shall operate as follows according to the election made in such surrender by the parent or guardian of the child:

(1) In favor of such parent or guardian, with the express stipulation that neither this nor any other provision of the surrender of rights shall be deemed to impair the validity, absolute finality, or totality of such surrender under any other circumstance, once the revocation period has elapsed;

(2) In favor of the child-placing agency or out-of-state licensed agency designated in the surrender of rights, if any; or

(3) If the parent or guardian is not designated and no child-placing agency or out-of-state licensed agency is designated in the surrender of rights, or if the designated child-placing agency or out-of-state licensed agency declines to accept the child for placement for adoption, in favor of the department for placement for adoption pursuant to subsection (a) of Code Section 19-8-4.

(k) In any surrender of rights pursuant to this Code section, Chapter 4 of Title 39, relating to the Interstate Compact on the Placement of Children, if applicable, shall be complied with.

(l) If the home study for a third-party adoption has not occurred prior to the date of placement, then the third party shall, within the petition for adoption or in a separate motion, seek an order authorizing placement of such child prior to the completion of the home study. Such petition or such motion shall identify the evaluator that the petitioner has selected to perform the home study. The court may waive the requirement of a preplacement home study in cases when a child already resides in the prospective adoptive home either as a child of one of the residents of such home or pursuant to a court order of guardianship, testamentary guardianship, or custody.

(m) The court may authorize the placement prior to the completion of a home study if the court finds that such placement is in the best interests of the child.

(n) If the court authorizes the placement prior to the completion of a home study, then:

(1) Such child shall be permitted to remain in the home of the third party with whom the parent or guardian placed such child pending further order of the court;

(2) A copy of the order authorizing placement of such child prior to the completion of the home study shall be delivered to the department and the evaluator selected to perform the home study by the clerk of the court within 15 days of the date of the entry of such order; and

(3) The home study, if not already in process, shall be initiated by the evaluator selected by the petitioner or appointed by the court within ten days of such evaluator's receipt of the court's order.

(o) A biological father or a legal father who signs a surrender of rights may execute an affidavit regarding his Native American heritage and military service meeting the requirements of subsection (n) of Code Section 19-8-26. Such affidavit shall be signed under oath and in the presence of a notary public.

§ 19-8-6. (Effective September 1, 2018) Stepparent adoption

(a) (1) A child whose legal father and legal mother are both living but are not still married to each other may be adopted by the spouse of either parent only when the other parent voluntarily and in writing surrenders all of his or her rights to the child to that spouse for the purpose of enabling that spouse to adopt the child and the other parent consents to the adoption and, when there is any guardian of that child, each such guardian has voluntarily and in writing surrendered to such spouse all of his or her rights to the child for the purpose of such adoption.

(2) A child who has only one parent still living may be adopted by the spouse of that parent only if that parent consents to the adoption and, when there is any guardian of that child, each such guardian has voluntarily and in writing surrendered to such spouse all of his or her rights to the child for the purpose of such adoption.

(b) In the case of a child 14 years of age or older, the written consent of the child to his or her adoption shall be given and acknowledged in the presence of the court.

(c) The surrender of rights specified in this Code section shall be executed following the birth of the child under oath and in the presence of a notary public and an adult witness. A copy of the surrender shall be provided to the individual signing the surrender at the time of the execution thereof.

(d) An individual signing a surrender of rights pursuant to this Code section shall have the right to revoke such surrender within four days as provided in subsection (a) of Code Section 19-8-9.

(e) (1) The surrender of rights by a parent or guardian specified in subsection (a) of this Code section shall meet the requirements of subsection (e) of Code Section 19-8-26. Such surrender shall be signed under oath and in the presence of a notary public and an adult witness.

(2) A biological father who is not a legal father of a child may surrender all his rights to the child for purposes of an adoption pursuant to this Code section. Such surrender shall meet the requirements of subsection (d) of Code Section 19-8-26. Such surrender shall be signed under oath and in the presence of a notary public and an adult witness.

(f) A surrender of rights shall be acknowledged by the individual who surrenders those rights by also signing an acknowledgment meeting the requirements of subsection (g) of Code Section 19-8-26. Such acknowledgment shall be signed under oath and in the presence of a notary public and an adult witness.

(g) (1) A legal mother who surrenders her parental rights or consents to the adoption of her child by her spouse pursuant to this Code section shall execute an affidavit meeting the requirements of subsection (h) of Code Section 19-8-26. Such affidavit shall be signed under oath and in the presence of a notary public.

(2) A legal mother who is the adoptive mother of the child and who surrenders her parental rights pursuant to this Code section shall execute an affidavit meeting the requirements of subsection (i) of Code Section 19-8-26. Such affidavit shall be signed under oath and in the presence of a notary public.

(h) Whenever rights are surrendered pursuant to this Code section, the representative of each petitioner or the representative of the individual signing such surrender shall execute an affidavit meeting the requirements of subsection (k) of Code Section 19-8-26. Such affidavit shall be signed under oath and in the presence of a notary public.

(i) A surrender of rights or consent pursuant to this Code section may be given by any parent or biological father who is not a legal father of the child regardless of whether such individual is a citizen of the United States, a resident of this state, or has reached the age of 18 years. Such surrender or consent given by such individual shall be binding upon him or her as if the individual were in all respects sui juris and shall include a consent to the jurisdiction of the courts of this state for any action filed under this article. Such surrender shall state that such individual agrees to be bound by a decree of adoption.

(j) The parental consent by the spouse of a stepparent seeking to adopt a child of that spouse and required by subsection (a) of this Code section shall meet the requirements of subsection (l) of Code Section 19-8-26. Such consent shall be signed under oath and in the presence of a notary public.

(k) A biological father or a legal father who signs a surrender of rights may execute an affidavit regarding his Native American heritage and military service meeting the requirements of subsection (n) of Code Section 19-8-26. Such affidavit shall be signed under oath and in the presence of a notary public.

§ 19-8-7. (Effective September 1, 2018) Adoption by certain relatives related to child by blood or marriage

(a) A child may be adopted by a relative who is related by blood or marriage to the child as a grandparent, great-grandparent, aunt, uncle, great aunt, great uncle, or sibling only if each living parent and guardian of such child has voluntarily and in writing surrendered to that relative and any spouse of such relative all of his or her rights to the child for the purpose of enabling that relative and any such spouse to adopt the child.

(b) In the case of a child 14 years of age or older, the written consent of the child to his or her adoption shall be given and acknowledged in the presence of the court.

(c) The surrender of rights specified in paragraphs (1) and (2) of subsection (e) of this Code section shall be executed following the birth of the child, and the pre-birth surrender specified in paragraph (3) of subsection (e) of this Code section shall be executed prior to the birth of the child. Each surrender shall be executed under oath and in the presence of a notary public and an adult witness. A copy of the surrender shall be provided to the individual signing the surrender at the time of the execution thereof.

(d) An individual signing a surrender of rights pursuant to this Code section shall have the right to revoke such surrender within four days as provided in subsection (a) of Code Section 19-8-9.

(e) (1) The surrender of rights by a parent or guardian specified in subsection (a) of this Code section shall meet the requirements of subsection (e) of Code Section 19-8-26. Such surrender shall be signed under oath and in the presence of a notary public and an adult witness.

(2) A biological father who is not a legal father of the child may surrender all his rights to the child for purposes of an adoption pursuant to this Code section. Such surrender shall meet the requirements of subsection (d) of Code Section 19-8-26. Such surrender shall be signed under oath and in the presence of a notary public and an adult witness.

(3) (A) A biological father who is not a legal father of a child may execute a surrender of his rights to the child prior to the birth of the child for the purpose of an adoption pursuant to this Code section. A pre-birth surrender shall serve to relinquish an alleged biological father's rights to the child and to waive an alleged biological father's right to notice of any proceeding with respect to the child's adoption, custody, or guardianship. The court in any adoption proceeding shall have jurisdiction to enter a final order of adoption of the child based upon the pre-birth surrender and in other proceedings to determine the child's legal custody or guardianship shall have jurisdiction to enter an order for those purposes.

(B) The rights and responsibilities of an alleged biological father shall be permanently terminated only upon an order from a court of competent jurisdiction terminating such rights or the entry of a final order of adoption. An individual executing a pre-birth surrender pursuant to this Code section shall have the right to revoke such surrender within four days from the date of execution thereof, notwithstanding the date of birth of the child.

(C) If a final order of adoption is not entered after the execution of a pre-birth surrender and paternity is established by acknowledgment, by administrative order, or by judicial order, then an alleged biological father shall be responsible for child support or other financial obligations to the child or to a legal mother, or to both.

(D) The pre-birth surrender shall not be valid for use by a legal father.

(E) The pre-birth surrender may be executed at any time after the biological mother executes a sworn statement identifying such individual as an alleged biological father of the biological mother's unborn child meeting the requirements of subsection (m) of Code Section 19-8-26.

(F) The pre-birth surrender shall meet the requirements of subsection (f) of Code Section 19-8-26 and shall be signed under oath and in the presence of a notary public and an adult witness.

(f) A surrender of rights shall be acknowledged by the individual who surrenders those rights by also signing an acknowledgment meeting the requirements of subsection (g) of Code Section 19-8-26. Such acknowledgment shall be signed under oath and in the presence of a notary public and an adult witness.

(g) (1) A legal mother who surrenders her parental rights pursuant to this Code section shall execute an affidavit meeting the requirements of subsection (h) of Code Section 19-8-26. Such affidavit shall be signed under oath and in the presence of a notary public.

(2) A legal mother who is the adoptive mother of the child and who surrenders her parental rights pursuant to this Code section shall execute an affidavit meeting the requirements of subsection (i) of Code Section 19-8-26. Such affidavit shall be signed under oath and in the presence of a notary public.

(h) Whenever rights are surrendered pursuant to this Code section, the representative of each petitioner or the representative of the individual signing such surrender shall execute an affidavit meeting the requirements of subsection (k) of Code Section 19-8-26. Such affidavit shall be signed under oath and in the presence of a notary public.

(i) A surrender of rights pursuant to this Code section may be given by any parent or biological father who is not a legal father of the child regardless of whether such individual is a citizen of the United States, a resident of this state, or has reached the age of 18 years. Such surrender given by such individual shall be binding upon him or her as if the individual were in all respects sui juris and shall include a consent to the jurisdiction of the courts of this state for any action filed under this article. Such surrender shall state that such individual agrees to be bound by a decree of adoption.

(j) In any surrender of rights pursuant to this Code section, Chapter 4 of Title 39, relating to the Interstate Compact on the Placement of Children, if applicable, shall be complied with.

(k) A biological father or a legal father who signs a surrender of rights may execute an affidavit regarding his Native American heritage and military service meeting the requirements of subsection (n) of Code Section 19-8-26. Such affidavit shall be signed under oath and in the presence of a notary public.

§ 19-8-8. (Effective September 1, 2018) Domestication of adoption of child born in foreign country; Certificate of Foreign Birth; authority of court to change date of birth

(a) (1) A child, who was born in a country other than the United States and for whom a decree or order of adoption has been entered pursuant to due process of law by a court of competent jurisdiction or an administrative proceeding in the country of the child's birth or the country in which the child habitually resided immediately prior to coming to the United States establishing the relationship of parent and child by adoption between each petitioner named in the foreign decree or order of adoption and the child according to the law of such foreign country, shall be eligible to have his or her adoption domesticated under this subsection if a consular officer of the United States Department of State has issued and affixed in the child's passport an immediate relative immigrant visa or Hague Convention immigrant visa.

(2) Evidence of the issuance of an immediate relative immigrant visa or Hague Convention immigrant visa by the United States Department of State in the child's passport shall be prima-facie evidence that all parental rights have been terminated, that the child was legally available for adoption by each petitioner named in the foreign decree or order of adoption, that the adoption of the child by each petitioner named in the foreign decree or order of adoption was in the child's best interests, and that the child's adoption by each petitioner named in the foreign decree or order of adoption was finalized in full compliance with the laws of the foreign country and the court need not make any inquiry into those proceedings but shall domesticate the foreign decree or order of adoption hereunder and issue a final decree of adoption pursuant to subsection (c) of Code Section 19-8-18.

(3) A child who qualifies for domestication of his or her foreign adoption under this subsection and whose adoption was full and final prior to entering the United States shall, upon entry of a final decree of domestication of adoption by the court, be entitled to have a Certificate of Foreign Birth issued to him or her by the State Office of Vital Records of the Georgia Department of Public Health pursuant to paragraph (2) of subsection (f) of Code Section 31-10-13.

(b) (1) A child, who was born in a country other than the United States and for whom a decree or order of guardianship has been entered pursuant to due process of law by a court of competent jurisdiction or an administrative proceeding in the country of the child's birth or the country in which the child habitually resided immediately prior to coming to the United States terminating the parental rights of both of his or her parents and establishing a guardian-ward relationship between each petitioner named in the foreign decree or order of guardianship and the child according to the law of such foreign country, shall be eligible to be adopted pursuant to this subsection if a consular officer of the United States Department of State has issued and affixed in the child's passport an immediate relative immigrant visa or Hague Convention immigrant visa.

(2) (A) Evidence of the issuance of an immediate relative immigrant visa or Hague Convention immigrant visa by the United States Department of State in the child's passport shall be prima-facie evidence that all parental rights have been terminated, that the child is legally available for adoption by each petitioner named in the foreign decree or order of guardianship, and that the guardian-ward relationship between each petitioner named in the foreign decree or order of guardianship and the child was granted in full compliance with the laws of the foreign country and the court need not make any inquiry into those proceedings but shall be authorized to finalize the child's adoption as provided in this subsection.

(B) Notwithstanding subparagraph (A) of this paragraph, when the foreign decree or order of guardianship requires specific postplacement supervision, the court shall not be authorized to finalize such child's adoption as provided in this subsection until the petitioner provides documentation of formal evidence that the conditions of the foreign decree or order of guardianship have been satisfied.

(3) Once a child's adoption is granted pursuant to this subsection, he or she shall be entitled to have a Certificate of Foreign Birth issued to him or her by the State Office of Vital Records of the Georgia Department of Public Health pursuant to paragraph (2) of subsection (f) of Code Section 31-10-13.

(c) The court shall have authority to change a child's date of birth from that shown on the child's original birth certificate and as reflected in the child's passport upon presentation by a preponderance of evidence of a more accurate date of birth.

§ 19-8-9. (Effective September 1, 2018) Revocation of surrender of rights; time limit; effect of voluntary surrender of rights by legal mother

(a) Notwithstanding subsection (a) of Code Section 9-10-12 which authorizes the use of certified mail, an individual signing a surrender of rights pursuant to Code Section 19-8-4, 19-8-5, 19-8-6, or 19-8-7 shall have the right to revoke such surrender by written notice delivered in person or mailed by registered mail or statutory overnight delivery within four days after signing such surrender; and such surrender document shall not be valid unless it so states. The four-day revocation period shall be counted consecutively beginning with the day immediately following the date the surrender of rights is executed; provided, however, that, if the fourth day falls on a Saturday, Sunday, or legal holiday, then the last day on which such surrender may be revoked shall be the next day that is not a Saturday, Sunday, or legal holiday. After the four-day period, a surrender of rights cannot be revoked. Notwithstanding subsection (a) of Code Section 9-10-12 which authorizes the use of certified mail, the notice of revocation of a surrender of rights shall be delivered in person or mailed by registered mail or statutory overnight delivery to the address designated in the surrender document. If delivered in person, it shall be delivered to the address shown in the surrender document not later than 5:00 P.M. eastern standard time or eastern daylight time, whichever is applicable, on the fourth day.

(b) If a legal mother has voluntarily and in writing surrendered all of her parental rights pursuant to Code Section 19-8-4, 19-8-5, 19-8-6, or 19-8-7 and has not revoked her surrender within the four-day period after signing as permitted by subsection (a) of this Code section, she shall have no right or authority to sign a voluntary acknowledgment of paternity pursuant to Code Section 19-7-46.1 or consent to the granting of a petition for legitimation filed pursuant to Code Section 19-7-22 regarding the same child.

§ 19-8-10. (Effective September 1, 2018) When surrender or termination of parental rights of living parent not required; service on parents in such cases; involuntary termination of rights

(a) Surrender or termination of rights of a living parent pursuant to Code Section 19-8-4, 19-8-5, 19-8-6, or 19-8-7 shall not be required as a prerequisite to the granting of a petition for adoption of a child of such living parent pursuant to Code Section 19-8-13 when the court determines by clear and convincing evidence that the:
   (1) Child has been abandoned by that parent;
   (2) Parent cannot be found after a diligent search has been made;
   (3) Parent is insane or otherwise incapacitated from surrendering such rights;
   (4) Parent caused his child to be conceived as a result of having nonconsensual sexual intercourse with the biological mother of his child or when the biological mother is less than ten years of age; or
   (5) Parent, without justifiable cause, has failed to exercise proper parental care or control due to misconduct or inability, as set out in paragraph (3), (4), or (5) of subsection (a) of Code Section 15-11-310, and the court is of the opinion that the adoption is in the best interests of that child, after considering the physical, mental, emotional, and moral condition and needs of the child who is the subject of the proceeding, including the need for a secure and stable home.
(b) A surrender of rights of a living parent pursuant to Code Section 19-8-6 or 19-8-7 shall not be required as a prerequisite to the granting of a petition for adoption of a child of such living parent pursuant to Code Section 19-8-13, when the court determines by clear and convincing evidence that the parent, for a period of one year or longer immediately prior to the filing of the petition for adoption, without justifiable cause, has significantly failed:
   (1) To communicate or to make a bona fide attempt to communicate with that child in a meaningful, supportive, parental manner; or
   (2) To provide for the care and support of that child as required by law or judicial decree,
and the court is of the opinion that the adoption is in the best interests of that child, after considering the physical, mental, emotional, and moral condition and needs of the child who is the subject of the proceeding, including the need for a secure and stable home.
(c) (1) Whenever it is alleged by any petitioner that surrender or termination of rights of a living parent is not a prerequisite to the granting of a petition for adoption of a child of such parent in accordance with subsection (a) or (b) of this Code section, such parent shall be personally served with a conformed copy of the adoption petition, together with a copy of the court's order thereon specified in Code Section 19-8-14, or, if personal service cannot be perfected, notwithstanding subsection (a) of Code Section 9-10-12 which authorizes the use of certified mail, by registered mail, return receipt requested, or statutory overnight delivery, one-day service not required, at his or her last known address. If service cannot be made by these methods, such parent shall be given notice by publication once a week for three weeks in the official organ of the county where such petition has been filed and of the county of his or her last known address. In the interest of time, publication may be initiated simultaneously with efforts to perfect service personally, by registered mail, or by statutory overnight delivery. The court shall continue to have the inherent authority to determine the sufficiency of service. A parent who receives notification pursuant to this paragraph shall not be a party to the adoption and shall have no obligation to file an answer, but shall have the right to appear in the pending adoption proceeding and show cause why such parent's rights to the child who is the subject of the proceeding should not be terminated by that adoption. Notice shall be deemed to have been received on the earliest date:
   (A) Personal service is perfected;
   (B) Of delivery shown on the return receipt of registered mail or proof of delivery by statutory overnight delivery; or
   (C) Of the last publication.
   (2) No prior order of court shall be required to publish notice pursuant to this Code section; provided, however, that before publication may be relied upon as a means of service, it shall be averred that, after diligent efforts, service could not be perfected personally, by registered mail, or by statutory overnight delivery.
(d) Consistent with the requirement of paragraph (7) of subsection (a) of Code Section 19-8-13, when the petitioner is seeking to involuntarily terminate the rights of a parent as a prerequisite to the granting of the petition for adoption, the petitioner shall, in lieu of obtaining and attaching those otherwise required surrenders of rights, acknowledgments, and affidavits, allege facts in the petition seeking to involuntarily terminate parental rights that demonstrate the applicability of the grounds set forth in subsection (a) or (b), or both, of this Code section and shall also allege compliance with subsection (c) of this Code section.

§ 19-8-11. (Effective September 1, 2018) Petitioning superior court to terminate rights of one parent or guardian of child; service of process

(a) (1) In those cases when the department, a child-placing agency, or an out-of-state licensed agency has obtained the voluntary written surrender of all parental rights from one of the parents or the guardian of a child or has obtained an order from a court of competent jurisdiction terminating all of the rights of one of the parents or the guardian of a child, such department, child-placing agency, or out-of-state licensed agency may in contemplation of the placement of such child for adoption petition the superior court of the county of the child's domicile, of the county where the child was born, of the county in which is located the principal office of the child-placing agency having legal custody of the child, or of the county in which is located the office of the department having legal custody of the child to terminate the parental rights of the remaining parent pursuant to this Code section.

(2) In those cases when a child has been placed in compliance with Chapter 4 of Title 39, and the individual who is the resident of another state has obtained the voluntary written surrender of all parental rights from one of the parents or the guardian of a child, each such individual to whom the child has been surrendered may in contemplation of the adoption of such child in such other state petition the superior court of the county where the child was born or of Fulton County to terminate the parental rights of the remaining parent pursuant to this Code section.

(3) (A) Parental rights may be terminated pursuant to paragraph (1) or (2) of this subsection when the court determines by clear and convincing evidence that the:

(i) Child has been abandoned by that parent;
(ii) Parent of the child cannot be found after a diligent search has been made;
(iii) Parent is insane or otherwise incapacitated from surrendering such rights;
(iv) Parent caused his child to be conceived as a result of having nonconsensual sexual intercourse with the biological mother of his child or when the biological mother is less than ten years of age; or
(v) Parent, without justifiable cause, has failed to exercise proper parental care or control due to misconduct or inability, as set out in paragraph (3), (4), or (5) of subsection (a) of Code Section 15-11-310.

(B) If the court determines that a circumstance described in subparagraph (A) of this paragraph has been met, it shall set the matter down to be heard in chambers not less than 30 and not more than 60 days following the receipt by such remaining parent of the notice under subsection (b) of this Code section and shall enter an order terminating such parental rights if it so finds and if it is of the opinion that adoption is in the best interests of the child, after considering the physical, mental, emotional, and moral condition and needs of the child who is the subject of the proceeding, including the need for a secure and stable home.

(b) (1) Whenever a petition to terminate parental rights is filed pursuant to subsection (a) of this Code section, the parent whose rights the petitioner is seeking to terminate shall be personally served with a conformed copy of the petition to terminate parental rights and a copy of the court's order setting forth the date upon which such petition shall be considered or, if personal service cannot be perfected, notwithstanding subsection (a) of Code Section 9-10-12 which authorizes the use of certified mail, by registered mail, return receipt requested, or statutory overnight delivery, one-day service not required, at his or her last known address. If service cannot be made by these methods, such parent shall be given notice by publication once a week for three weeks in the official organ of the county where such petition has been filed and of the county of his or her last known address. In the interest of time, publication may be initiated simultaneously with efforts to perfect service personally, by registered mail, or by statutory overnight delivery. The court shall continue to have the inherent authority to determine the sufficiency of service. A parent who receives notification pursuant to this paragraph shall not be a party to the adoption and shall have no obligation to file an answer, but shall have the right to appear in the pending termination of parental rights proceeding and show cause why such parent's rights to the child who is the subject of the proceeding should not be terminated. Notice shall be deemed to have been received on the earliest date:

(A) Personal service is perfected;
(B) Of delivery shown on the return receipt of registered mail or proof of delivery by statutory overnight delivery; or
(C) Of the last publication.

(2) No prior order of court shall be required to publish notice pursuant to this Code section; provided, however, that before publication may be relied upon as a means of service, it shall be averred that, after diligent efforts, service could not be perfected personally, by registered mail, or by statutory overnight delivery.

§ 19-8-12. (Effective September 1, 2018) Notice to biological father; procedure when identity or location of father not known; effect of order terminating biological father's rights; legitimation of child by father; rights of mother

(a) The General Assembly finds that:

(1) The state has a compelling interest in promptly providing stable and permanent homes for adoptive children, and in preventing the disruption of adoptive placements;

(2) Adoptive children have a right to permanence and stability in adoptive placements;

(3) Adoptive parents have a constitutionally protected liberty and privacy interest in retaining custody of children placed with them for adoption;

(4) A biological father who is not a legal father may have an interest in his biological child. This inchoate interest is lost by failure to develop a familial bond with the child and acquires constitutional protection only if a biological father who is not a legal father develops a familial bond with the child;

(5) The subjective intent of a biological father who is not a legal father, whether expressed or otherwise, unsupported by evidence of acts manifesting such intent, shall not preclude a determination that a biological father who is not a legal father has failed to develop a familial bond with the child; and

(6) A man who has engaged in a nonmarital sexual relationship with a woman is deemed to be on notice that a pregnancy and adoption proceeding regarding a child may occur and has a duty to protect his own rights and interests in that child. He is therefore entitled to notice of an adoption proceeding only as provided in this Code section.

(b) If there is a biological father who is not a legal father of a child and he has not executed a surrender of rights as specified in paragraph (2) of subsection (e) of Code Section 19-8-4, 19-8-5, 19-8-6, or 19-8-7 or paragraph (3) of subsection (e) of Code Section 19-8-4, 19-8-5, or 19-8-7, he shall be notified of adoption proceedings regarding the child in the following circumstances:

(1) If his identity is known to the petitioner, department, child-placing agency, or out-of-state licensed agency or to the attorney for such individual or entity;

(2) If he is a registrant on the putative father registry who has acknowledged paternity of the child in accordance with subparagraph (d)(2)(A) of Code Section 19-11-9; or

(3) If he is a registrant on the putative father registry who has indicated possible paternity of the child during a period beginning two years immediately prior to the child's date of birth in accordance with subparagraph (d)(2)(B) of Code Section 19-11-9.

(c) (1) Notification provided for in subsection (b) of this Code section shall be given to a biological father who is not a legal father by the following methods:

(A) Notwithstanding subsection (a) of Code Section 9-10-12 which authorizes the use of certified mail, registered mail, return receipt requested, or statutory overnight delivery, one-day service not required, at his last known address, which notice shall be deemed received upon the date of delivery shown on the return or delivery receipt;

(B) Personal service, which notice shall be deemed received when personal service is perfected; or

(C) Publication once a week for three weeks in the official organ of the county where the adoption petition has been filed and of the county of his last known address, which notice shall be deemed received upon the date of the last publication.

(2) If feasible, the methods specified in subparagraph (A) or (B) of paragraph (1) of this subsection shall be used before publication; provided, however, that in the interest of time, publication may be initiated simultaneously with efforts to perfect service personally, by registered mail, or by statutory overnight delivery.

(3) No prior order of court shall be required to publish notice pursuant to this Code section; provided, however, that before publication may be relied upon as a means of service, it shall be averred that, after diligent efforts, service could not be perfected personally, by registered mail, or by statutory overnight delivery.

(d) (1) When the rights of a parent or guardian of a child have been surrendered or terminated in accordance with subsection (a) of Code Section 19-8-4 or the child does not have a living parent or guardian, the department, child-placing agency, or out-of-state licensed agency may file, under the authority of this paragraph, a petition to terminate a biological father's rights to the child with the superior court of the county of the child's domicile, of the county where the child was born, of the county in which is located the principal office of the child-placing agency having legal custody of the child, or of the county in which is located the office of the department having legal custody of the child.

(2) When the rights of a parent or guardian of a child have been surrendered in accordance with subsection (a) of Code Section 19-8-5, 19-8-6, or 19-8-7, the child does not have a living parent or guardian, a consent to adopt has been executed pursuant to paragraph (2) of subsection (a) of Code Section 19-8-6, or the petitioner is seeking to involuntarily terminate parental rights pursuant to Code Section 19-8-10, the petitioner shall file, under the authority of this paragraph, with the superior court of the county of the child's domicile or of the county where the child was born a motion, if a petition for adoption of the child has previously been filed with the court, or a petition to terminate a biological father's rights to the child.

(3) When a petition or motion is filed pursuant to paragraph (1) or (2) of this subsection, the court shall, within 30 days from the date of receipt of the notice required by subsection (b) of this Code section or, when no notice is required to be given, from the date of such filing, conduct a hearing in chambers to determine the facts in the matter.

(4) Unless the identity of a biological father is known to the petitioner, department, child-placing agency, or out-of-state licensed agency or to the attorney for such individual or entity such that he is entitled to notice

of the proceedings as provided in this Code section, when the petitioner provides a certificate from the putative father registry stating that there is no registrant identified on the putative father registry acknowledging paternity of the child or indicating possible paternity of the child for a period beginning no later than two years immediately prior to the child's date of birth, then it shall be rebuttably presumed that an unnamed biological father who is not a legal father is not entitled to notice of the proceedings. Absent evidence rebutting the presumption, then no further inquiry or notice shall be required by the court and the court shall enter an order terminating the rights of such unnamed biological father to the child.

(e) When notice is to be given pursuant to subsection (b) of this Code section, it shall advise such biological father who is not a legal father that he loses all rights to the child and will neither receive notice nor be entitled to object to the adoption of the child unless, within 30 days of receipt of such notice, he files:

(1) A petition to legitimate the child pursuant to Code Section 19-7-22 as a separate civil action;

(2) Notice of the filing of the petition to legitimate with the court in which the action under this Code section, if any, is pending; and

(3) Notice of the filing of the petition to legitimate to the person or agency who provided such notice to such biological father.

(f) A biological father who is not a legal father shall lose all rights to the child and the court shall enter an order terminating all of his rights to the child and he shall not thereafter be allowed to object to the adoption and shall not be entitled to receive further notice of the adoption if, within 30 days from his receipt of the notice provided for in subsection (b) of this Code section, he:

(1) Does not file a legitimation petition and give notice as required in subsection (e) of this Code section;

(2) Files a legitimation petition which is subsequently dismissed for failure to prosecute; or

(3) Files a legitimation petition and the action is subsequently concluded without a court order granting such petition and declaring that he is a legal father of the child.

(g) If an alleged biological father who is not a legal father files a legitimation petition after the mother of such child has surrendered her parental rights, the court shall be authorized to consider the affidavit of the mother specified in subsection (g) of Code Section 19-8-4, 19-8-5, 19-8-6, or 19-8-7, as applicable. If the court finds from the evidence that such biological father has not lived with the child, contributed to the child's support, or provided support or medical care during the mother's pregnancy or hospitalization for the birth of such child, there shall be a rebuttable presumption that the biological father abandoned his opportunity interest to legitimate such child and may deny his petition for legitimation. Such biological father shall not thereafter be allowed to object to the adoption nor be entitled to receive further notice of the adoption proceedings.

(h) If the child is legitimated by his or her biological father, the adoption shall not be permitted except as provided in Code Sections 19-8-4 through 19-8-7.

(i) If the child is legitimated by his or her biological father and in the adoption proceeding the petition for adoption is revoked with prejudice or denied by the court, then a SURRENDER OF RIGHTS/FINAL RELEASE FOR ADOPTION executed by a legal mother pursuant to subsection (a) of Code Section 19-8-4, 19-8-5, or 19-8-7 shall be dissolved by operation of law and her parental rights shall be restored to her. The fact that a legal mother executed a SURRENDER OF RIGHTS/FINAL RELEASE FOR ADOPTION, now dissolved, shall not be admissible as evidence against a legal mother in any proceeding against her.

§ 19-8-13. (Effective September 1, 2018) Petition; filing and contents; financial disclosures; attorney's affidavit; redaction of certain information unnecessary

(a) The petition for adoption, duly verified, together with one conformed copy thereof, shall be filed with the clerk of the superior court having jurisdiction and shall conform to the following guidelines:

(1) The petition for adoption shall set forth:

(A) The name, age, date and place of birth, marital status, and place of residence of each petitioner;

(B) The name by which the child is to be known should the adoption ultimately be completed;

(C) The sex, date and place of birth, and citizenship or immigration status of the child, and if the child is neither a United States citizen nor a lawful permanent resident of the United States on the date such petition is filed, the petitioner shall explain how such child will be able to obtain lawful permanent resident status;

(D) The date and circumstances of the placement of the child with each petitioner;

(E) Whether the child is possessed of any property and, if so, a full and complete description thereof;

(F) Whether the child has one or both parents or his or her biological father who is not a legal father living;

(G) Whether the child has a guardian and, if so, the name of the guardian and the name of the court that appointed such guardian;

(H) Whether the child has a legal custodian and, if so, the name of the legal custodian and the name of the court that appointed such custodian; and

(I) Whether each petitioner or his or her attorney is aware of any other adoption proceeding pending to date, in this or any other state or country, regarding the child who is the subject of the proceeding that is not fully disclosed in such petition and whether each petitioner or his or her attorney is aware of any individual who has or claims to have physical custody of or visitation rights with the child who is the subject of the proceeding whose name and address and whose custody or visitation rights are not fully disclosed in such petition. Each petitioner and his or her attorney shall have a continuing duty to inform the court of any proceeding in this or any other state or country that could affect the adoption proceeding or the legal custody of or visitation with the child who is the subject of the proceeding;

(2) When the adoption is pursuant to subsection (a) of Code Section 19-8-4, the following shall be provided or attached to the petition for adoption or its absence explained when the petition for adoption is filed:

(A) If the adoption is pursuant to:

(i) Paragraph (1) of such Code section, a copy of the written voluntary surrender of rights of each parent or guardian specified in subsection (e) of Code Section 19-8-4 and a copy of the written acknowledgment of surrender of rights specified in subsection (f) of Code Section 19-8-4; or

(ii) Paragraph (2) of such Code section, a certified copy of the order entered by a court of competent jurisdiction terminating parental rights of the parent and committing the child to the department, child-placing agency, or out-of-state licensed agency;

(B) A copy of the affidavits specified in subsections (g) and (h) of Code Section 19-8-4;

(C) An original affidavit from the department or a child-placing agency stating that all of the requirements of Code Sections 19-8-4 and 19-8-12 have been complied with and that the child is legally available for adoption or, in the case of a placement by an out-of-state licensed agency, that the comparable provisions dealing with the termination of parental rights of the parents and of a biological father who is not a legal father of the child have been complied with under the laws of the state or country in which the out-of-state licensed agency is licensed and that the child is legally available for adoption thereunder;

(D) The original written consent of the department, child-placing agency, or out-of-state licensed agency to the adoption;

(E) Uncertified copies of appropriate certificates or forms verifying the allegations contained in such petition as to guardianship of the child, including, but not limited to, the marriage of each petitioner, the death of each parent in lieu of a surrender of his or her parental rights, and compliance with 4 of Title 39, relating to the Interstate Compact on the Placement of Children; and

(F) A completed form containing background information regarding the child, as required by the adoption unit of the department, or an equivalent medical and social history background form;

(3) When the adoption is pursuant to subsection (a) of Code Section 19-8-5, the following shall be provided or attached to the petition for adoption or its absence explained when the petition for adoption is filed:

(A) The original written voluntary surrender of rights of each parent, biological father who is not a legal father, or guardian specified in subsection (e) of Code Section 19-8-5;

(B) The original written acknowledgment of surrender of rights specified in subsection (f) of Code Section 19-8-5;

(C) The original affidavits specified in subsections (g) and (h) of Code Section 19-8-5;

(D) A copy of the appropriate form verifying the allegation of compliance with Code Section 19-8-12 and the original certification evidencing the search of the putative father registry;

(E) The original accounting required by subsection (c) of this Code section;

(F) Uncertified copies of appropriate certificates or forms verifying the allegations contained in such petition as to guardianship of the child, including, but not limited to, the marriage of each petitioner, the death of each parent in lieu of a surrender of his or her parental rights, and compliance with 4 of Title 39, relating to the Interstate Compact on the Placement of Children;

(G) A completed form containing background information regarding the child, as required by the adoption unit of the department, or an equivalent medical and social history background form; and

(H) A copy of the home study report;

(4) When the adoption is pursuant to subsection (a) of Code Section 19-8-6, the following shall be provided or attached to the petition for adoption or its absence explained when the petition for adoption is filed:

(A) The original written voluntary surrender of rights of each parent, biological father who is not a legal father, or guardian specified in subsection (e) of Code Section 19-8-6;

(B) The original written acknowledgment of surrender of rights specified in subsection (f) of Code Section 19-8-6;

(C) The original affidavits specified in subsections (g) and (h) of Code Section 19-8-6;

(D) The original consent specified in subsection (j) of Code Section 19-8-6;

(E) A copy of the appropriate form verifying the allegation of compliance with Code Section 19-8-12 and the original certification evidencing the search of the putative father registry;

(F) Uncertified copies of appropriate certificates or forms verifying the allegations contained in such petition as to guardianship of the child, including, but not limited to, the birth of the child, the marriage of each petitioner, and the death of each parent in lieu of a surrender of his or her parental rights; and

(G) A completed form containing background information regarding the child, as required by the adoption unit of the department, or an equivalent medical and social history background form;

(5) When the adoption is pursuant to subsection (a) of Code Section 19-8-7, the following shall be provided or attached to the petition for adoption or its absence explained when the petition for adoption is filed:

(A) The original written voluntary surrender of rights of each parent or biological father who is not a legal father specified in subsection (e) of Code Section 19-8-7;

(B) The original written acknowledgment of surrender of rights specified in subsection (f) of Code Section 19-8-7;

(C) The original affidavits specified in subsections (g) and (h) of Code Section 19-8-7;

(D) A copy of the appropriate form verifying the allegation of compliance with Code Section 19-8-12 and the original certification evidencing the search of the putative father registry;

(E) Uncertified copies of appropriate certificates or forms verifying allegations contained in the petition as to guardianship or custody of the child and the birth of the child, including but not limited to, the marriage of each petitioner, the death of each parent in lieu of a surrender of his or her parental rights, and compliance with 4 of Title 39, relating to the Interstate Compact on the Placement of Children;

(F) A completed form containing background information regarding the child, as required by the adoption unit of the department, or an equivalent medical and social history background form;

(6) (A) When the adoption is pursuant to subsection (a) of Code Section 19-8-8, the following shall be provided or attached to the petition for adoption when the petition for adoption is filed:

(i) A copy of the child's passport page showing an immediate relative immigrant visa or Hague Convention immigrant visa obtained to grant the child entry into the United States as a result of a full and final adoption in the foreign country; and

(ii) A copy along with an English translation of the child's birth certificate or registration.

(B) Because the issuance of an immediate relative immigrant visa or Hague Convention immigrant visa by the United States Department of State in the child's passport is prima-facie evidence that all parental rights have been terminated and that the child is legally available for adoption, it shall not be necessary to file any documents related to the surrender or termination of the parental rights of the child's parents or comply with Code Section 19-8-12 regarding the rights of a biological father who is not a legal father when the petition for adoption is filed pursuant to subsection (a) of Code Section 19-8-8.

(C) When the adoption is pursuant to subsection (b) of Code Section 19-8-8, the following shall be provided or attached to the petition for adoption when the petition for adoption is filed:

(i) A copy along with an English translation of the final decree or order of guardianship from the foreign country;

(ii) Copies of all postplacement reports, if required by the foreign country that entered the guardianship decree or order;

(iii) Authorization to proceed with adoption if specifically required by the decree or order entered by the court or administrative agency in the foreign country;

(iv) A copy of the child's passport page showing an immediate relative immigrant visa or Hague Convention immigrant visa obtained to grant the child entry into the United States in order to finalize his or her adoption; and

(v) A copy along with an English translation of the child's birth certificate or registration;

(7) When Code Section 19-8-10 is applicable, parental rights need not be surrendered or terminated prior to the filing of the petition for adoption; but the petitioner shall, in lieu of obtaining and attaching those otherwise required surrenders of rights, acknowledgments, and affidavits, allege facts in the petition for adoption demonstrating the applicability of subsection (a) or (b), or both, of Code Section 19-8-10 and shall also allege compliance with subsection (c) of Code Section 19-8-10; and

(8) If the petition for adoption is filed in a county other than that of the petitioner's residence, the reason therefor shall be set forth in such petition.

(b) At the time of filing the petition for adoption, the petitioner shall deposit with the clerk the deposit required by Code Section 9-15-4; the fees shall be those established by Code Sections 15-6-77, 15-6-77.1, and 15-6-77.2.

(c) Each petitioner for adoption in any proceeding for the adoption of a child pursuant to Code Section 19-8-5 shall file with the petition for adoption, in a manner acceptable to the court, a report fully accounting for all disbursements of anything of value made or agreed to be made, directly or indirectly, by, on behalf of, or for the benefit of the petitioner in connection with the adoption, including, but not limited to, any expenses incurred in connection with:

(1) The birth of the child;

(2) Placement of the child with the petitioner;

(3) Counseling services or legal services for a legal mother;

(4) Reasonable expenses for the biological mother as set forth in subparagraph (c)(1)(C) or (c)(1)(D) of Code Section 19-8-24;

(5) Medical or hospital care received by the biological mother or by the child during such mother's prenatal care and confinement; and

(6) Services relating to the adoption or to the placement of the child for adoption which were received by or on behalf of the petitioner, either biological parent of the child, or any other individual.

(d) Every attorney for a petitioner in any proceeding for the adoption of a child pursuant to Code Section 19-8-5 shall file, in a manner acceptable to the court, before the decree of adoption is entered, an affidavit detailing all sums paid or promised to that attorney, directly or indirectly, from whatever source, for all services of any nature rendered or to be rendered in connection with the adoption; provided, however, that, if the attorney received or is to receive less than $500.00, the affidavit need only state that fact.

(e) Any report made under this Code section shall be signed under oath and in the presence of a notary public by the individual making the report.

(f) (1) As used in this subsection, the term "family member" shall have the same meaning as set forth in Code Section 19-7-3.

(2) Whenever a family member other than the petitioner has visitation rights to such child granted pursuant to Code Section 19-7-3, the petitioner shall cause a copy of the petition for adoption to be served upon the family member with the visitation rights or upon such family member's counsel of record at least 30 days prior to the date upon which the petition for adoption will be considered as such time frames are set forth in Code Section 19-8-14.

(g) Notwithstanding Code Sections 19-8-5 and 19-8-7 and this Code section which require obtaining and attaching a written voluntary surrender of rights and acknowledgment thereof and affidavits of a legal mother and a representative of the petitioner or of the individual signing such surrender, when the adoption is sought under subsection (a) of Code Section 19-8-5 or 19-8-7 following the termination of parental rights and the placement of the child by the juvenile court pursuant to Code Section 15-11-321, obtaining and attaching to the petition for adoption a certified copy of the order terminating parental rights of the parent shall take the place of obtaining and attaching those otherwise required surrenders of rights, acknowledgments, and affidavits.

(h) (1) A petition for adoption regarding a child who has a living biological father who is not a legal father and who has not surrendered his rights to the child shall include a certificate from the putative father registry disclosing the name, address, and social security number of any registrant acknowledging paternity of the child pursuant to subparagraph (d)(2)(A) of Code Section 19-11-9 or indicating the possibility of paternity of such child pursuant to subparagraph (d)(2)(B) of Code Section 19-11-9 for a period beginning no later than two years immediately prior to the child's date of birth. Such certificate shall indicate the results of a search of the registry on or after the earliest of the following:

(A) The date of a legal mother's surrender of parental rights;
(B) The date of entry of the court order terminating a legal mother's parental rights; or
(C) The date of a legal mother's consent to adoption pursuant to Code Section 19-8-6.

(2) Such certificate shall include a statement that the registry is current as of the earliest date listed in subparagraphs (A) through (D) of paragraph (1) of this subsection, or as of a specified date that is later than the earliest such date.

(3) When a legal mother of the child who is the subject of the proceeding identifies her husband as the biological father of the child and he has executed a surrender of his parental rights in favor of the petitioner, the petitioner shall obtain a certificate from the putative father registry and submit it with the petition for adoption to confirm that no male other than the legal mother's husband has expressed an interest in the child or to identify a registrant other than the legal mother's husband who shall be notified pursuant to Code Section 19-8-12.

(i) Because adoption records are sealed pursuant to subsection (a) of Code Section 19-8-23, it shall not be necessary to redact social security numbers, taxpayer identification numbers, financial account numbers, or dates of birth from pleadings and all documents filed therewith that are filed pursuant to this article as they are deemed to be a filing under seal under subsection (d) of Code Section 9-11-7.1.

§ 19-8-14. (Effective September 1, 2018) Timing of adoption hearing; record retention; clerk's duties

(a) It is the policy of this state that, in the best interests of the child, uncontested adoption petitions shall be heard as soon as possible but not later than 120 days after the date of filing, unless the petitioner has failed to arrange for the court to receive the report required by Code Section 19-8-16 or has otherwise failed to provide the court with all exhibits, surrenders of rights, or certificates required by this article within that time period. It is the policy of this state that, in contested adoption petitions, the parties shall make every effort to have the petition considered by the court as soon as practical after the date of filing, taking into account the circumstances of the petition and the best interests of the child.

(b) Upon the filing of the petition for adoption, accompanied by the filing fee unless such fee is waived, it shall be the responsibility of the clerk to accept such petition as filed. Such petition shall not be subject to court approval before it is filed.

(c) Upon the filing of the petition for adoption, the court shall fix a date upon which such petition shall be considered, which date shall be not less than 45 days from the date of the filing of such petition and shall not be less than 30 days following the last date a parent or biological father is deemed to have received service of notice as required in those cases when Code Section 19-8-10 or 19-8-12, or both, is applicable.

(d) Notwithstanding subsections (a) and (c) of this Code section, it shall be the petitioner's responsibility to request that the court hear the petition for adoption on a date that allows sufficient time for fulfillment of the notice requirements of Code Sections 19-8-10 and 19-8-12, when applicable.

(e) In the best interests of the child, the court may hear the petition for adoption less than 45 days from the date of its filing upon a showing by the petitioner that no further notice is required or any statutory requirement of notice to any individual will be fulfilled at an earlier date, and provided that any report required by Code Section 19-8-16 has been completed or will be completed at an earlier date.

(f) The court in the child's best interests may grant such expedited hearings or continuances as may be necessary for completion of applicable notice requirements, investigations, a home study, and reports or for other good cause shown.

(g) Copies of the petition for adoption and all documents filed in connection therewith, including, but not limited to, the order fixing the date upon which such petition shall be considered, motions, other pleadings filed, all orders entered in connection with such petition, and all exhibits, surrenders of rights, or certificates required by this article, shall be forwarded by the clerk to the department within 15 days after the date of such filing for retention by the State Adoption Unit of the department.

(h) Copies of the petition for adoption, the order fixing the date upon which such petition shall be considered, and all exhibits, surrenders of rights, or certificates required by this article shall be forwarded by the clerk to the agent appointed by the court pursuant to Code Section 19-8-16 within 15 days after the filing of the petition for adoption, together with a request that a report and investigation be made as required by Code Section 19-8-16.

(i) The clerk of court shall provide the petitioner or his or her attorney with a copy of the petition for adoption and of each amendment, motion, and other pleading filed with a stamp confirming the date each pleading was filed with the court and shall also provide the petitioner or his or her attorney with a copy of each order entered by the court in the adoption proceeding, confirming the date the order was filed of record by the court.

§ 19-8-15. (Effective September 1, 2018) Objections to petition for adoption

(a) As used in this Code section, the term "family member" shall have the same meaning as set forth in Code Section 19-7-3.

(b) If a legal mother and biological father, whether he was a legal father or not, of the child who is the subject of the proceeding are both deceased, regardless of whether either individual had surrendered his or her parental rights or had his or her rights terminated, it shall be the privilege of any individual related by blood to such child to file objections to the petition for adoption.

(c) A family member with visitation rights to a child granted pursuant to Code Section 19-7-3 shall have the privilege to file objections to the petition for adoption if neither parent has any further rights to the child and if the petition for adoption has been filed by a blood relative of the child. The court, after hearing such objections, shall determine, in its discretion, whether or not such objections constitute a good reason for denying the petition for adoption and the court shall have the authority to grant or continue such visitation rights of the family member of the child in the adoption order in the event the adoption by the blood relative is approved by the court.

§ 19-8-16. (Effective September 1, 2018) Investigation by court-appointed agent; criminal history records check for adoption petitioners

(a) Prior to the date set by the court for a hearing on the petition for adoption, it shall be the duty of the agent appointed by the court to verify the allegations in the petition for adoption, to make a complete and thorough investigation of the entire matter, including any specific issue the court requests to be investigated, and to report its findings and recommendations in writing to the court where the petition for adoption was filed. The agent may be the department, a child-placing agency, an evaluator, or an individual who the court determines is qualified to conduct the required investigation. The agent appointed by the court shall also provide the petitioner or his or her attorney with a copy of its report. If for any reason the agent appointed by the court finds itself unable to make or arrange for the proper investigation and report, it shall be the duty of the agent to notify the court immediately, or at least within 20 days after receipt of the request for investigation service, that it is unable to make the report and investigation, so that the court may take such other steps as in its discretion are necessary to have the investigation and report prepared. The investigation required by this Code section shall be in addition to the requirement of a home study in the case of a petition for adoption filed pursuant to subsection (a) of Code Section 19-8-5.

(b) If the petition for adoption has been filed pursuant to subsection (a) of Code Section 19-8-6 or 19-8-7, the court shall be authorized but shall not be required to appoint an agent to make an investigation pursuant to subsection (a) of this Code section; provided, however, that a home study shall not be required.

(c) (1) If the petition for adoption has been filed pursuant to Code Section 19-8-8, the appointment of an agent to make an investigation and render a report pursuant to subsection (a) of this Code section shall not be required.

(2) If the petition for adoption has been filed pursuant to Code Section 19-8-4 and the department or child-placing agency has consented to the adoption, the appointment of an agent to make an investigation and render a report pursuant to subsection (a) of this Code section shall not be required.

(d) The court shall require the petitioner to submit to a criminal history records check. The petitioner shall submit his or her fingerprints to the Georgia Crime Information Center with the appropriate fee. The center shall promptly transmit the fingerprints to the Federal Bureau of Investigation for a search of bureau records and shall obtain an appropriate report. The Georgia Crime Information Center shall also promptly conduct a search of its records and any records to which it has access. The center shall notify the court in writing of the presence or absence of any criminal record from the state fingerprint records check. In those cases when the petitioner has submitted a fingerprint based criminal history report that includes the results of a records search of both the Georgia Crime Information Center and the Federal Bureau of Investigation to the department, child-placing agency, or evaluator as part of the home study and such results are dated within 12 months of filing of the petition for adoption and are included in the home study report filed with or otherwise made available to the court, such results shall satisfy the requirements of this subsection. Because the court shall not be authorized to share the results of the fingerprint records check with the agent appointed by the court pursuant to subsection (a) or (e) of this Code section, the court shall determine the acceptability of the petitioner's criminal history, inform the petitioner or his or her attorney at least five days prior to the final hearing on the petition for adoption if the court will require additional evidence with respect to the petitioner's criminal history or if the court is inclined to deny such petition because of such criminal history, and afford the petitioner or his or her attorney an opportunity to present evidence as to why the petitioner's criminal history should not be grounds for denial of such petition.

(e) The court shall require the petitioner to reimburse the agent appointed by the court, including the department, for the full cost of conducting the investigation and preparing its report. Such cost shall not exceed $250.00 unless specifically authorized by the court, provided that the court shall furnish the petitioner or his or her attorney with written notice of the name of the agent that the court intends to appoint and the amount of any increased costs, together with a request to agree to pay such increased costs. If the petitioner does not agree to pay the increased costs, then the petitioner shall have an opportunity to present to the court information regarding other persons that are qualified to conduct the investigation and render the report to the court and the cost of their services, and the court shall appoint the person that is qualified to conduct the investigation and render the report to the court at the lowest cost to the petitioner.

§ 19-8-17. (Effective September 1, 2018) Report and findings of investigating agent; dismissal of petition; appointment of guardian ad litem

(a) The report and findings of the investigating agent appointed by the court pursuant to Code Section 19-8-16 shall include, among other things, the following:
 (1) Verification of allegations contained in the petition for adoption;
 (2) Circumstances under which the child came to be placed for adoption;
 (3) Whether each prospective adoptive parent is financially, physically, and mentally able to have the permanent custody of the child; in considering financial ability any adoption supplement approved by the department shall be taken into account;
 (4) The physical and mental condition of the child, insofar as this can be determined by the aid of competent medical authority;
 (5) Whether or not the adoption is in the best interests of the child, including his or her general care;
 (6) Suitability of the home to the child;
 (7) If applicable, whether the identity and location of a biological father who is not a legal father are known or ascertainable and whether the requirements of Code Section 19-8-12 were complied with;
 (8) Any other information that might be disclosed by the investigation that in the agent's opinion would be of value or interest to the court in deciding the case; and
 (9) Any other information that might be disclosed by the investigation in response to any specific issue that the court requested be investigated in its order appointing such agent.

(b) If the report of the investigating agent disapproves of the adoption of the child, motion may be made by the investigating agent to the court to dismiss the petition for adoption and the court after hearing such motion shall be authorized to dismiss such petition. If the court denies the motion to dismiss, the court shall appoint a guardian ad litem who may appeal the ruling to the Court of Appeals or Supreme Court, as in other cases, as provided by law.

(c) If at any time it appears to the court that the interests of the child may conflict with those of any petitioner, the court may, in its discretion, appoint a guardian ad litem to represent the child and the cost thereof shall be a charge upon the funds of the county.

§ 19-8-18. (Effective until September 1, 2018) Hearing; district attorney to be directed to review inducement violations; decree of adoption; factors considered in determining best interests of child; disposition of child on denial of petition

(a) (1) Upon the date appointed by the court for a hearing of the petition for adoption or as soon thereafter as the matter may be reached for a hearing, the court shall proceed to a full hearing on such petition and the examination of the parties at interest in chambers, under oath, with the right of continuing the hearing and examinations from time to time as the nature of the case may require. The court at such times shall give consideration to the investigation report to the court provided for in Code Section 19-8-16 and the recommendations contained in such report. The court may in its discretion allow the petitioner or any witness to appear via electronic means in lieu of requiring his or her physical presence before the court.

(2) The court shall examine the petition for adoption and the affidavit specified in subsection (g) of Code Section 19-8-4, 19-8-5, 19-8-6, or 19-8-7, as appropriate, to determine whether Code Section 19-8-12 is applicable. If the court determines that Code Section 19-8-12 is applicable to the petition for adoption, it shall:

  (A) Determine that an appropriate order has previously been entered;
  (B) Enter an order consistent with Code Section 19-8-12; or
  (C) Continue the hearing until Code Section 19-8-12 is complied with.

(3) If the adoption petition is filed pursuant to subsection (a) of Code Section 19-8-5, the court shall examine the financial disclosures required under subsections (c) and (d) of Code Section 19-8-13 and make such further examination of each petitioner and his or her attorney as the court deems appropriate in order to make a determination as to whether there is cause to believe that Code Section 19-8-24 has been violated with regard to the inducement, as such term is defined in Code Section 19-8-24, of the placement of the child for adoption. Should the court determine that further inquiry is in order, the court shall direct the district attorney for the county to review the matter further and to take such appropriate action as the district attorney in his or her discretion deems appropriate.

(b) (1) If the petition for adoption was filed pursuant to Code Section 19-8-4, 19-8-5, 19-8-6, or 19-8-7, the court shall enter a decree of adoption naming the child as prayed for in such petition; terminating all of the rights of each living parent, guardian, and legal custodian of the child, other than the spouse of the petitioner in the case of a stepparent adoption pursuant to Code Section 19-8-6; granting the permanent custody of the child to each petitioner; and declaring the child to be the adopted child of each petitioner if the court is satisfied that:

  (A) Each living parent or guardian of the child has surrendered or had terminated all of his or her rights to the child in the manner provided by law or that each petitioner has complied with the notice requirements of subsection (c) of Code Section 19-8-10 and satisfied his or her burden of proof under Code Section 19-8-10 or that the spouse has consented to the petitioner's adoption of the child as required by Code Section 19-8-6;
  (B) Each petitioner is capable of assuming responsibility for the care, supervision, training, and education of the child;
  (C) The child is suitable for adoption in a private family home; and
  (D) The adoption requested is in the best interests of the child.

(2) When Code Section 19-8-10 has been relied upon by any petitioner for the termination of rights of a living parent, the court shall include in the decree of adoption appropriate findings of fact and conclusions of law relating to the termination of rights of such living parent and the court's determination that the adoption is in the child's best interests.

(3) When the child was born in a country other than the United States, the court shall examine the evidence submitted and determine that sufficient evidence has been proffered to show that the child will be able to obtain lawful permanent resident status, if not already obtained, before the court shall have authority to determine if it is in the best interests of the child to grant the petition for adoption.

(4) If there is an existing visitation order pursuant to Code Section 19-7-3 in favor of a family member, the court shall have the authority to continue or discontinue such visitation rights in the adoption order as it deems is in the best interests of the child.

(c) If the petition for adoption was filed pursuant to subsection (a) of Code Section 19-8-8 and if the court is satisfied that the petitioner has fully complied with the requirements of Code Section 19-8-13 and has established that he or she finalized his or her adoption of the child in the foreign country, then the court shall enter a decree of adoption naming the child as prayed for in such petition; domesticating the foreign decree of adoption; granting the permanent custody of the child to each petitioner; changing the date of birth of the child if so requested, provided that evidence was presented justifying such change; and declaring the child to be the adopted child of each petitioner. Notwithstanding the requirements of subsection (a) of this Code section, the court may domesticate the foreign decree of adoption upon the pleadings without a hearing.

(d) If the petition for adoption was filed pursuant to subsection (b) of Code Section 19-8-8, the court shall enter a decree of adoption naming the child as prayed for in such petition; terminating the guardianship; granting the permanent custody of the child to each petitioner; changing the date of birth of the child if so requested, provided that evidence was presented justifying such change; and declaring the child to be the adopted child of each petitioner if the court is satisfied that the petitioner has fully complied with the requirements of Code Section 19-8-13 and that:

(1) Each petitioner in his or her capacity as guardian of the child has surrendered all of his or her rights to the child in the manner provided by law;
(2) Each petitioner is capable of assuming responsibility for the care, supervision, training, and education of the child;
(3) The child is suitable for adoption in a private family home; and
(4) The adoption requested is in the best interests of the child.
(e) In exercising its discretion to determine whether the adoption requested is in the best interests of the child, the court shall consider the following factors:
(1) The ability of each petitioner and, if applicable, each respondent to provide for the physical safety and welfare of the child, including food, shelter, health, and clothing;
(2) The love, affection, bonding, and emotional ties existing between the child and each petitioner and, if applicable, each respondent;
(3) The child's need for permanence, including the child's need for stability and continuity of relationships with his or her siblings;
(4) The capacity and disposition of each petitioner and, if applicable, each respondent to give the child his or her love, affection, and guidance and to continue the education and rearing of the child;
(5) The home environment of each petitioner and, if applicable, each respondent, considering the promotion of the child's nurturance and safety rather than superficial or material factors;
(6) The stability of the family unit and the presence or absence of support systems within the community to benefit the child;
(7) The mental and physical health of all individuals involved;
(8) The home, school, and community record and history of the child, as well as any health or educational special needs of the child;
(9) The child's background and ties, including familial, cultural, and religious;
(10) The uniqueness of every family and child;
(11) The child's wishes and long-term goals;
(12) Any evidence of family violence, substance abuse, criminal history, or sexual, mental, or physical child abuse in the petitioner's home and, if applicable, each respondent's home;
(13) Any recommendation by a court appointed agent or guardian ad litem; and
(14) Any other factors considered by the court to be relevant and proper to its determination.
(f) If the court determines that any petitioner has not complied with this article, it may dismiss the petition for adoption without prejudice or it may continue the case. Should the court find that any notice required to be given by any petitioner under this article has not been given or has not been properly given or that the petition for adoption has not been properly filed, the court shall be authorized to enter an order providing for corrective action and an additional hearing.
(g) If the court is not satisfied that the adoption is in the best interests of the child, it shall deny the petition for adoption. If such petition is denied because the court determines that the adoption requested is not in the best interests of the child or for any other reason under law, the court shall set forth specific findings of fact explaining its decision in its order denying the adoption and shall commit the child to the custody of the department, a child-placing agency, or an out-of-state licensed agency if such petition was filed pursuant to Code Section 19-8-4. If such petition was filed pursuant to Code Section 19-8-5, the court shall commit the child to the third party named by the parent in the written surrender of rights pursuant to subsection (a) of Code Section 19-8-5; and if there is no surrender of rights, the court shall place the child with the department for the purpose of determining whether or not a petition should be initiated under Chapter 11 of Title 15. If such petition was filed pursuant to Code Section 19-8-6, 19-8-7, or 19-8-8, the child shall remain in the custody of each petitioner if each petitioner is fit to have custody or the court may place the child with the department for the purpose of determining whether or not a petition should be initiated under Chapter 11 of Title 15. If the petition for adoption is denied, each surrender of rights executed in support of the adoption, whether by a parent, biological father who is not a legal father, or guardian, shall be dissolved by operation of law and the individual's rights shall be restored. The fact that the individual executed a surrender of his or her rights in support of the adoption shall not be admissible as evidence against him or her in any subsequent proceeding.
(h) A decree of adoption issued pursuant to subsection (b) of this Code section shall not be subject to any judicial challenge filed more than six months after the date of entry of such decree. Notwithstanding Code Section 9-3-31, any action for damages against an adoptee or the adoptive parents for fraud in obtaining a consent or surrender of rights shall be brought within six months of the time the fraud is or ought to reasonably have been discovered.
(i) Notwithstanding subsection (a) of Code Section 19-8-23, the decree of adoption issued pursuant to subsection (b) of this Code section shall authorize the clerk of the court to issue one or more certified copies of the decree of adoption to the petitioner or his or her attorney at the time of entry of the final decree without further order of the court and without cost.

§ 19-8-19. (Effective September 1, 2018) Effect of decree of adoption

(a) A decree of adoption, whether issued by a court of this state or by a court of any other jurisdiction, shall have the following effect as to matters within the jurisdiction of or before a court in this state:

(1) Except with respect to a spouse of the petitioner and relatives of the spouse, a decree of adoption shall terminate all legal relationships between the adopted individual and his or her relatives, including his or her parent, so that the adopted individual thereafter shall be a stranger to his or her former relatives for all purposes, including inheritance and the interpretation or construction of documents, statutes, and instruments, whether executed before or after the adoption is decreed, which do not expressly include the individual by name or by some designation not based on a parent and child or blood relationship; and

(2) A decree of adoption shall create the relationship of parent and child between each petitioner and the adopted individual, as if the adopted individual were a child of biological issue of that petitioner. The adopted individual shall enjoy every right and privilege of a biological child of that petitioner; shall be deemed a biological child of that petitioner, to inherit under the laws of descent and distribution in the absence of a will, and to take under any instrument of testamentary gift, bequest, devise, or legacy, whether executed before or after the adoption is decreed, unless expressly excluded therefrom; shall take by inheritance from relatives of that petitioner; and shall also take as a child of that petitioner under a class gift made by the will of a third person.

(b) Notwithstanding subsection (a) of this Code section, if a parent of a child dies without the relationship of parent and child having been previously terminated by court order, the child's right of inheritance from or through the deceased parent shall not be affected by the adoption.

§ 19-8-20. (Effective September 1, 2018) Forwarding of decree, report, and subsequent orders to department; issuance of adoption certificate; use as evidence

(a) Upon the entry of the decree of adoption, the clerk of the court granting the same shall forward a copy of the decree, together with the original of the investigation report and background information filed with the court, to the department. If there is any subsequent order or revocation of the adoption, a copy of same in like manner shall be forwarded by the clerk to the department.

(b) At any time after the entry of the decree of adoption, upon the request of an adopted individual who has reached 18 years of age or upon the request of any adopting parent, the clerk of the court granting the decree shall issue to that requesting adopted individual or adopting parent a certificate of adoption, under the seal of the court, upon payment to the clerk of the fee prescribed in paragraph (4) of subsection (g) of Code Section 15-6-77, which adoption certificate shall be received as evidence in any court or proceeding as primary evidence of the facts contained in the certificate.

(c) The adoption certificate shall conform substantially to the following form:

This is to certify that   (names of each adopting parent) have obtained a decree of adoption for   (full name of adoptee and date of birth of adoptee) in the Superior Court of   County, Georgia, on the   day of   , as shown by the court's records   (adoption file number).

Given under the hand and seal of said court, this the   day of   ,   .

Clerk

§ 19-8-21. (Effective September 1, 2018) Adoption of adult individuals; applicability of Code Sections 19-8-19 and 19-8-20

(a) Adult individuals may be adopted on giving written consent to the adoption. In such cases, adoption shall be by a petition duly verified and filed, together with one conformed copy, in the superior court in the county in which any petitioner or the adult to be adopted resides, setting forth the name, age, and residence of each petitioner and of the adult to be adopted, the name by which the adult is to be known, and his or her written consent to the adoption. The court may assign the petition for adoption for hearing at any time. The petition for adoption shall state whether one or both parents of the adult to be adopted will be replaced by the grant of such petition, and if only one parent is to be replaced, then the decree of adoption shall make clear which parent is to be replaced by adoption. After examining each petitioner and the adult to be adopted, the court, if satisfied that there is no reason why the adoption should not be granted, shall enter a decree of adoption and, if requested, shall change the name of the adopted adult. Thereafter, the relation between each petitioner and the adopted adult shall be, as to their legal rights and liabilities, the same as the relation of a parent and adult child.

(b) Code Sections 19-8-19 and 19-8-20 shall also apply to the adoption of adults.

§ 19-8-22. (Effective September 1, 2018) Recognition and effect of order by court or administrative body within or outside United States

(a) A decree of a court or an administrative proceeding terminating the relationship of parent and child, establishing the relationship of guardian and ward, or establishing the relationship of parent and child by adoption, issued pursuant to due process of law by a court or administrative body of any other jurisdiction within or outside the United States, or the clear and irrevocable release or consent to adoption by the guardian of a child when the appointment of the guardian has been certified by the appropriate and legally authorized court or agency of the government of the foreign country, shall be recognized in this state; and the rights and obligations of the parties as to matters within the jurisdiction of this state shall be determined as though any such decree were issued by a court of this state and any such consent or release shall be deemed to satisfy the requirements of Code Sections 19-8-4, 19-8-5, 19-8-6, 19-8-7, 19-8-8, and 19-8-12.
(b) Any adoption proceeding in this state in which a final order of adoption was entered by the court prior to April 1, 1986, and to which subsection (a) of this Code section would have been applicable if said subsection had been effective at the time such proceeding was filed or concluded shall be governed by subsection (a) of this Code section.

§ 19-8-23. (Effective September 1, 2018) Where records of adoption kept; examination by parties and attorneys; use of information by agency and department

(a) (1) The original petition for adoption, all amendments, attachments, and exhibits thereto, all motions, documents, affidavits, records, and testimony filed in connection therewith, and all decrees or orders of any kind whatsoever, except the original investigation report and background information referred to in Code Section 19-8-20, shall be recorded in a book kept for such purpose and properly indexed; and such book shall be part of the records of the court in each county which has jurisdiction over matters of adoption in that county. All of such court records, including the docket book, that relate in any manner to the adoption shall be kept sealed and locked. The department shall keep its records that relate in any manner to an adoption sealed and locked.
(2) The court records and department records may be examined by the parties at interest in the adoption and their attorneys when, after written petition, which shall be filed under seal, has been presented to the court having jurisdiction and after the department and the appropriate child-placing agency or out-of-state licensed agency, if any, have received at least 30 days' prior written notice of the filing of such petition, the matter has come on before the court in chambers and the court has entered an order permitting such examination.
(3) Notwithstanding paragraph (2) of this subsection, if the adoptee who is the subject of the records sought to be examined is less than 18 years of age at the time the petition for examination is filed and such petitioner is someone other than one of the adoptive parents of the adoptee, then the department shall provide written notice of such proceedings to the adoptive parents by certified mail, return receipt requested, or statutory overnight delivery at the last address the department has for such adoptive parents, and the court shall continue any hearing on such petition until not less than 60 days after the date the notice to the adoptive parents was sent. Each such adoptive parent shall have the right to appear in person or through counsel and show cause why such records should not be examined. Adoptive parents may provide the department with their current address for purposes of receiving notice under this subsection by mailing that address to:

State Adoption Unit
Department of Human Services
Atlanta, Georgia 30303

(b) The department or child-placing agency may, in its sole discretion, make use of any information contained in the records of the respective department or child-placing agency relating to the adoptive parents in connection with a subsequent adoption matter involving the same adoptive parents or to provide notice when required by subsection (a) of this Code section.
(b.1) The department may, in its sole discretion, make use of any information contained in the records of the department concerning an adopted child and the adopted child's biological parents in connection with the placement of another child in the home of the adoptive parents of the child or in connection with the investigation of a report of child abuse or neglect made concerning the adopted child's biological parents.
(b.2) (1) As used in this paragraph, the term:
(A) "Director" means the director of the Division of Family and Children Services of the department.
(B) "Near fatality" shall have the same meaning as set forth in Code Section 49-5-40.

(2) Upon the approval of the director, or his or her designee, any information concerning an adopted child, such child's biological parents, and such child's adoptive parents may be used solely by the department when, after the adoption, such child dies, suffers a near fatality, or is an alleged victim of child abuse or neglect; provided, however, that the department may provide such information to the Office of the Child Advocate for the Protection of Children. Such information shall not otherwise be subject to disclosure or release under Article 4 of Chapter 18 of Title 50.

(c) The department or child-placing agency may, in its sole discretion, make use of any information contained in its records on a child when an adoption disrupts after finalization and when such records are required for the permanent placement of such child, or when the information is required by federal law.

(d) (1) Upon the request of a party at interest in the adoption, a child, legal guardian, or health care agent of an adopted individual or a provider of medical services to such a party, child, legal guardian, or health care agent when certain information would assist in the provision of medical care, a medical emergency, or medical diagnosis or treatment, the department or child-placing agency shall access its own records on finalized adoptions for the purpose of adding subsequently obtained medical information or releasing nonidentifying medical and health history information contained in its records pertaining to an adopted individual or the biological parents or relatives of the biological parents of the adopted individual. For purposes of this paragraph, the term "health care agent" shall have the meaning provided by Code Section 31-32-2.

(2) Upon receipt by the State Adoption Unit of the department or by a child-placing agency of documented medical information relevant to an adoptee, the department or child-placing agency shall use reasonable efforts to contact the adoptive parents of the adoptee if the adoptee is under 18 years of age or the adoptee if he or she is 18 years of age or older and provide such documented medical information to the adoptive parents or the adult adoptee. The department or child-placing agency shall be entitled to reimbursement of reasonable costs for postage and photocopying incurred in the delivery of such documented medical information to the adoptive parents or adult adoptee.

(e) Records relating in any manner to adoption shall not be open to the general public for inspection.

(f) (1) Notwithstanding Code Section 19-8-1, for purposes of this subsection, the term:

(A) "Biological parent" means the biological mother or biological father who surrendered such individual's rights or had such rights terminated by court order giving rise to the adoption of the child.

(B) "Commissioner" means the commissioner of human services or his or her designee.

(C) "Department" means the Department of Human Services or, when the Department of Human Services so designates, the county division of family and children services which placed for adoption the individual seeking, or on whose behalf is sought, information under this subsection.

(D) "Placement agency" means the child-placing agency, as defined in paragraph (5) of Code Section 19-8-1, which placed for adoption the individual seeking, or on whose behalf is sought, information under this subsection.

(2) The department or a placement agency, upon the written request of an adopted individual who has reached 18 years of age or upon the written request of an adoptive parent on behalf of that parent's adopted child, shall release to such adopted individual or to the adoptive parent on the child's behalf nonidentifying information regarding such adopted individual's biological parents and information regarding such adopted individual's birth. Such information may include the date and place of birth of the adopted individual and the genetic, social, and health history of the biological parents. No information released pursuant to this paragraph shall include the name or address of either biological parent or the name or address of any relative by birth or marriage of either biological parent.

(3) (A) The department or a placement agency, upon the written request of an adopted individual who has reached 18 years of age, shall release to such adopted individual the name of such individual's biological parent, together with a detailed summary of all information the department or placement agency has concerning the adoptee's birth, foster care, placement for adoption, and finalization of his or her adoption, if:

(i) A biological parent whose name is to be released has submitted unrevoked written permission to the department or placement agency for the release of that parent's name to the adopted individual;

(ii) The identity of a biological parent submitting permission for the release of that parent's name has been verified by the department or placement agency; and

(iii) The department or placement agency has records pertaining to the finalized adoption and to the identity of a biological parent whose name is to be released.

(B) If the adopted individual is deceased and leaves a child, such child, upon reaching 18 years of age, may seek the name and other identifying information concerning his or her grandparents in the same manner as the deceased adopted individual and subject to the same procedures contained in this Code section.

(4) (A) If a biological parent has not filed written unrevoked permission for the release of that parent's name to the adopted child, the department or placement agency, within six months of receipt of the written request of the adopted individual who has reached 18 years of age, shall make diligent effort to notify each living biological parent identified in the original adoption proceedings or in other records of the department or placement agency relative to the adopted individual. For purposes of this subparagraph, the term "notify" means a personal and confidential contact with each biological parent of the adopted individual. The contact shall be by an employee or agent of the placement agency which processed the pertinent adoption or by

other agents or employees of the department. The contact shall be evidenced by the individual who notified each biological parent, certifying to the department or placement agency that each biological parent was given the following information:

(i) The nature of the information requested by the adopted individual;

(ii) The date of the request of the adopted individual;

(iii) The right of each biological parent to file an affidavit with the placement agency or the department stating that such parent's identity should not be disclosed;

(iv) The right of each biological parent to file a consent to disclosure with the placement agency or the department; and

(v) The effect of a failure of each biological parent to file a consent to disclosure or an affidavit stating that the information in the sealed adoption file should not be disclosed.

(B) If a biological parent files an unrevoked consent to the disclosure of that parent's identity, such parent's name, together with a detailed summary of all information the department or placement agency has concerning the adoptee's birth, foster care, placement for adoption, and finalization of his or her adoption, shall be released to the adopted individual who has requested such information as authorized by this paragraph.

(C) If, within 60 days of being notified by the department or placement agency pursuant to subparagraph (A) of this paragraph, a biological parent has filed with the department or placement agency an affidavit objecting to such release, information regarding the identity of that biological parent shall not be released.

(D) (i) If six months after receipt of the adopted individual's written request the placement agency or the department has been unable to notify a biological parent identified in the original adoption record or has been able to notify a biological parent identified in the original adoption record but has not obtained a consent to disclosure from the notified biological parent, then the identity of a biological parent may only be disclosed as provided in division (ii) or (iii) of this subparagraph.

(ii) The adopted individual who has reached 18 years of age may petition the Superior Court of Fulton County to seek the release of the identity of each of his or her biological parents from the department or placement agency. The court shall grant the petition if the court finds that the department or placement agency has made diligent efforts to locate each biological parent pursuant to this subparagraph without success or upon locating a biological parent has not obtained a consent to disclosure from the notified biological parent and that failure to release the identity of each biological parent would have an adverse impact upon the physical, mental, or emotional health of the adopted individual.

(iii) If it is verified that a biological parent of the adopted individual is deceased, the department or placement agency shall be authorized to disclose the name and place of burial of the deceased biological parent, if known, together with a detailed summary of all information the department or placement agency has concerning the adoptee's birth, foster care, placement for adoption, and finalization of his or her adoption, to the adopted individual seeking such information without the necessity of obtaining a court order.

(5) (A) Upon written request of an adopted individual who has reached 18 years of age or an individual who has reached 18 years of age and who is the sibling of an adopted individual, the department or placement agency shall attempt to identify and notify the siblings of the requesting party, if such siblings are at least 18 years of age. Upon locating the requesting party's sibling, the department or placement agency shall notify the sibling of the inquiry. Upon the written consent of a sibling so notified, the department or placement agency shall forward the requesting party's name and address to the sibling and, upon further written consent of the sibling, shall divulge to the requesting party the present name and address of the sibling. If a sibling cannot be identified or located, the department or placement agency shall notify the requesting party of such circumstances but shall not disclose any names or other information which would tend to identify the sibling. If a sibling is deceased, the department or placement agency shall be authorized to disclose the name and place of burial of the deceased sibling, if known, to the requesting party without the necessity of obtaining a court order.

(B) (i) If six months after receipt of the written request from an adopted individual who has reached 18 years of age or an individual who has reached 18 years of age and who is the sibling of an adopted individual, the department or placement agency has been unable to notify one or more of the siblings of the requesting party or has been able to notify a sibling of the requesting party but has not obtained a consent to disclosure from the notified sibling, then the identity of the siblings may only be disclosed as provided in division (ii) of this subparagraph.

(ii) The adopted individual who has reached 18 years of age or an individual who has reached 18 years of age and who is the sibling of an adopted individual may petition the Superior Court of Fulton County to seek the release of the last known name and address of each of the siblings of the petitioning sibling, who are at least 18 years of age, from the department or placement agency. The court shall grant the petition if the court finds that the department or placement agency has made diligent efforts to locate such siblings pursuant to subparagraph (A) of this paragraph without success or upon locating one or more of the siblings has not obtained a consent to disclosure from all the notified siblings and that failure to release the identity and last known address of said siblings would have an adverse impact upon the physical, mental, or emotional health of the petitioning sibling.

(C) If the adopted individual is deceased and leaves a child, such child, upon reaching 18 years of age, may obtain the name and other identifying information concerning the siblings of his or her deceased parent in the same manner that the deceased adopted individual would be entitled to obtain such information pursuant to the procedures contained in this Code section.

(6) (A) Upon written request of a biological parent of an adopted individual who has reached 18 years of age, the department or placement agency shall attempt to identify and notify the adopted individual. Upon locating the adopted individual, the department or placement agency shall notify the adopted individual of the inquiry. Upon the written consent of the adopted individual so notified, the department or placement agency shall forward such biological parent's name and address to the adopted individual, together with a detailed summary of all information the department or placement agency has concerning the adoptee's birth, foster care, placement for adoption, and finalization of his or her adoption, and, upon further written consent of the adopted individual, shall divulge to such requesting biological parent the present name and address of the adopted individual. If the adopted individual is deceased, the department or placement agency shall be authorized to disclose the name and place of burial of the deceased adopted individual, if known, to such requesting biological parent without the necessity of obtaining a court order.

(B) (i) If six months after receipt of the written request from a biological parent of an adopted individual who has reached 18 years of age, the department or placement agency has been unable to notify the adopted individual or has been able to notify the adopted individual but has not obtained a consent to disclosure from the notified adopted individual, then the identity of the adopted individual may only be disclosed as provided in division (ii) of this subparagraph.

(ii) A biological parent of an adopted individual who has reached 18 years of age may petition the Superior Court of Fulton County to seek the release of the last known name and address of the adopted individual from the department or placement agency. The court shall grant the petition if the court finds that the department or placement agency has made diligent efforts to locate such adopted individual pursuant to subparagraph (A) of this paragraph without success or upon locating the adopted individual has not obtained a consent to disclosure from the adopted individual and that failure to release the identity and last known address of said adopted individual would have an adverse impact upon the physical, mental, or emotional health of the petitioning biological parent.

(C) If a biological parent is deceased, a parent or sibling of the deceased biological parent, or both, may obtain the name and other identifying information concerning the adopted individual in the same manner that the deceased biological parent would be entitled to obtain such information pursuant to the procedures contained in this Code section.

(7) If an adoptive parent or the sibling of an adopted individual notifies the department or placement agency of the death of an adopted individual, the department or placement agency shall add information regarding the date and circumstances of the death to its records so as to enable it to share such information with a biological parent or sibling of the adopted individual if they make an inquiry pursuant to this Code section.

(8) If a biological parent or his or her parent or sibling notifies the department or placement agency of the death of a biological parent or a sibling of an adopted individual, the department or placement agency shall add information regarding the date and circumstances of the death to its records so as to enable it to share such information with an adopted individual or sibling of the adopted individual if they make an inquiry pursuant to this Code section.

(9) The State Adoption Unit within the department shall maintain a registry for the recording of requests by adopted individuals for the name of any biological parent, for the recording of the written consent or the written objections of any biological parent to the release of that parent's identity to an adopted individual upon the adopted individual's request, and for nonidentifying information regarding any biological parent which may be released pursuant to paragraph (2) of this subsection. The department and any placement agency which receives such requests, consents, or objections shall file a copy thereof with the State Adoption Unit.

(10) The department or placement agency may charge a reasonable fee to be determined by the department for the cost of conducting any search pursuant to this subsection.

(11) Nothing in this subsection shall be construed to require the department or placement agency to disclose to any party at interest, including but not limited to an adopted individual who has reached 18 years of age, any information which is not kept by the department or placement agency in its normal course of operations relating to adoption.

(12) Any department employee or employee of any placement agency who releases information or makes authorized contacts in good faith and in compliance with this subsection shall be immune from civil liability or criminal responsibility for such release of information or authorized contacts.

(13) Information authorized to be released pursuant to this subsection may be released under the conditions specified in this subsection, notwithstanding any other provisions of law to the contrary.

(14) A placement agency which demonstrates to the department by clear and convincing evidence that the requirement that such agency search for or notify any biological parent, sibling, or adopted individual under subparagraph (A) of paragraph (4), (5), or (6) of this subsection will impose an undue hardship upon that agency shall be relieved from that responsibility, and the department shall assume that responsibility upon

such finding by the department of undue hardship. The department's determination under this subsection shall be a contested case within the meaning of Chapter 13 of Title 50, the "Georgia Administrative Procedure Act."

(15) Whenever this subsection authorizes both the department and a placement agency to perform any function or requires the placement agency to perform any function which the department is also required to perform, the department or agency may designate an agent to perform that function and in so performing it the agent shall have the same authority, powers, duties, and immunities as an employee of the department or placement agency has with respect to performing that function.

§ 19-8-24. (Effective September 1, 2018) Advertising restrictions and requirements; "inducements" defined; unlawful inducements; penalties; exemption for personal communications; civil actions

(a) (1) It shall be unlawful for any person, organization, corporation, hospital, facilitator, or association of any kind whatsoever which is not a child-placing agency, a prospective adoptive parent who has a valid, approved preplacement home study report, or an attorney who is a member of the State Bar of Georgia representing a prospective adoptive parent who has a valid, approved preplacement home study report to advertise, whether in a periodical, by television, by radio, or by any other public medium or by any private means, including, but not limited to, letters, circulars, handbills, Internet postings including social media, and oral statements, that the person, organization, corporation, hospital, facilitator, or association will adopt children or will arrange for or cause children to be adopted or placed for adoption.

(2) (A) Any person, organization, corporation, hospital, facilitator, or association of any kind which is not a child-placing agency that places an advertisement concerning adoption or prospective adoption shall include in such advertisement its license number issued by the department;

(B) Any attorney representing a prospective adoptive parent who has a valid, approved preplacement home study report who places an advertisement concerning adoption or prospective adoption shall include in such advertisement his or her State Bar of Georgia license number; and

(C) Any individual who places an advertisement concerning being an adoptive parent shall include in such advertisement that he or she has a valid, approved preplacement home study report.

(b) It shall be unlawful for any person, organization, corporation, hospital, facilitator, or association of any kind whatsoever to sell, offer to sell, or conspire with another to sell or offer to sell a child for money or anything of value, except as otherwise provided in this article.

(c) (1) As used in this subsection, the term "inducements" means any financial assistance, either direct or indirect, from whatever source, but shall expressly not include:

(A) The payment or reimbursement of the medical expenses directly related to the biological mother's pregnancy and hospitalization for the birth of the child and medical care for such child if paid by a licensed child-placing agency or an attorney;

(B) The payment or reimbursement of expenses for counseling services or legal services for a biological parent that are directly related to the placement by such parent of her or his child for adoption if paid by a licensed child-placing agency or an attorney;

(C) The payment or reimbursement of reasonable living expenses for the biological mother if paid by a licensed child-placing agency; or

(D) The payment or reimbursement of reasonable expenses for rent, utilities, food, maternity garments, and maternity accessories for the biological mother if paid from the trust account of an attorney who is a member of the State Bar of Georgia in good standing.

(2) It shall be unlawful for any person, organization, corporation, hospital, facilitator, or association of any kind whatsoever to directly or indirectly hold out inducements to any biological parent to part with his or her child.

(3) It shall be unlawful for any person, organization, corporation, hospital, facilitator, or association of any kind whatsoever to conspire with another to offer or provide inducements to a biological parent to part with his or her child.

(4) It shall be unlawful for an individual to knowingly make false representations in order to obtain inducements.

(5) The report and affidavit filed pursuant to subsections (c) and (d) of Code Section 19-8-13 shall include an itemized accounting of all expenses paid or reimbursed pursuant to this subsection.

(d) (1) It shall be unlawful for an individual to knowingly accept expenses as set forth in subparagraph (c)(1)(C) or (c)(1)(D) of this Code section for the adoption of her child or unborn child if she knows or should have known that she is not pregnant or is not a legal mother.

(2) It shall be unlawful for an individual to knowingly accept expenses as set forth in subparagraph (c)(1)(C) or (c)(1)(D) of this Code section from an adoption agency or an attorney without disclosing that he or she is receiving such expenses from another adoption agency or attorney in an effort to allow for the adoption of the same child or unborn child.

(3) It shall be unlawful for an individual to knowingly make false representations in order to obtain expenses as set forth in subparagraph (c)(1)(C) or (c)(1)(D) of this Code section.

(e) Any person who violates this Code section shall be guilty of a felony and, upon conviction thereof, shall be punished by a fine not to exceed $10,000.00, imprisonment for not less than one nor more than ten years, or both.

(f) (1) Subsection (a) of this Code section shall not apply to communication by private means, including written or oral statements, by an individual seeking to:

   (A) Adopt a child or children; or

   (B) Place that individual's child or children for adoption,

whether the communication occurs before or after the birth of such child or children.

  (2) Subsection (a) of this Code section shall not apply to any communication described in paragraph (1) of this subsection which contains the name of an attorney who is a member of the State Bar of Georgia, his or her address, his or her telephone number, or any combination of such information and which requests that the attorney named in such communication be contacted to facilitate the carrying out of the purpose, as described in subparagraph (A) or (B) of paragraph (1) of this subsection, of the individual making such personal communication.

(g) Any child-placing agency or individual who is seeking to adopt or seeking to place a child for adoption who is damaged by a violation of this Code section may file a civil action to recover damages, treble damages, reasonable attorney's fees, and expenses of litigation.

§ 19-8-25. (Effective September 1, 2018) Effect of prior consent or surrender of rights

  (a) A written consent or surrender of rights, executed on or before August 31, 2018, shall, for purposes of an adoption proceeding commenced on or after September 1, 2018, be deemed to satisfy the surrender requirements of this article and it shall not be necessary to have any parent or guardian execute the documents required by Code Section 19-8-4, 19-8-5, 19-8-6, or 19-8-7; however, all other applicable provisions of this article shall be complied with.

(b) It is the legislative intent of this subsection to clarify and not to change the applicability of certain previously existing provisions of this article to adoption proceedings pending on August 31, 2018. Any decree of adoption issued in an adoption proceeding in which the adoption petition was filed in a superior court of this state prior to September 1, 2018, shall be valid if the adoption conformed to the requirements of this article either as they existed on August 31, 2018, or on September 1, 2018, and each such adoption decree is hereby ratified and confirmed.

§ 19-8-26. (Effective September 1, 2018) Forms

  (a) The surrender of rights by a parent or guardian pursuant to paragraph (1) of subsection (e) of Code Section 19-8-4 shall conform substantially to the following form:

      "SURRENDER OF RIGHTS
      FINAL RELEASE FOR ADOPTION

     NOTICE TO PARENT OR GUARDIAN:

  This is an important legal document and by signing it, you are surrendering all of your rights to the child identified in this document, so as to place the child for adoption. Understand that you are signing this document under oath and that if you knowingly and willfully make a false statement in this document you will be guilty of the crime of false swearing. As explained below in paragraph 5, you have the right to revoke this surrender within four days from the date you sign it.

STATE OF GEORGIA

COUNTY OF

Personally appeared before me, the undersigned officer duly authorized to administer oaths, _____ (name of parent or guardian) who, after having been sworn, deposes and says as follows:

1.

I, the undersigned, being mindful that my (male) (female) [circle one] child, born _____ (name of child) on _____ (birthdate of child) at _:_ (A.M.) (P.M.) [circle one], should receive the benefits and advantages of a good home, to the end that (she) (he) [circle one] may be fitted for the requirements of life, consent to this surrender of my parental rights.

2.

I, the undersigned, _____ (relationship to child) of the aforesaid child, do hereby surrender my rights to the child to _____ (name of child-placing agency, out-of-state licensed agency, or Department of Human Services, as applicable) and promise not to interfere in the management of the child in any respect whatever; and, in consideration of the benefits guaranteed by _____ (name of child-placing agency, out-of-state licensed agency, or Department of Human Services, as applicable) in providing for the child, I do relinquish all rights to the child named in this document, it being my wish, intent, and purpose to relinquish absolutely all parental control over the child. Furthermore, I hereby agree that the _____ (name of child-placing agency, out-of-state licensed agency, or Department of Human Services, as applicable) may seek for the child a legal adoption by such individual or individuals as may be chosen by the _____ (name of child-placing agency, out-of-state licensed agency, or Department of Human Services, as applicable) or its authorized agents, without further notice to me. I do, furthermore, expressly waive any other notice or service in any of the legal proceedings for the adoption of the child.

3.

I understand that under Georgia law an agent appointed by the court is required to conduct an investigation and render a report to the court in connection with the legal proceeding for the legal adoption of the child, and I hereby agree to cooperate fully with such agent in the conduct of its investigation.

4.

I understand that I will receive a copy of this document after the witness and I have signed it and it has been notarized.

5.

I understand that under Georgia law I have the unconditional right to a four-day revocation period. I understand I may only revoke this surrender by giving written notice, delivered in person or mailed by registered mail or statutory overnight delivery, to _____ (name and address of child-placing agency, out-of-state licensed agency, or Department of Human Services, as applicable) within four days from the date of signing this document. I understand that certified mail cannot be used for mail delivery of the notice to revoke this surrender. I understand that the four days will be counted consecutively beginning with the day immediately following the date I sign this document; provided, however, that, if the fourth day falls on a Saturday, Sunday, or legal holiday, then the last day on which this surrender may be revoked will be the next day that is not a Saturday, Sunday, or legal holiday. I understand that, if I deliver the notice to revoke this surrender in person, it must be delivered to   (name and address) not later than 5:00 P.M. eastern standard time or eastern daylight time, whichever is applicable, on the fourth day. I understand that I CANNOT revoke this surrender after that time.

                              6.

  I understand that if I am not a resident of this state that I am agreeing to be subject to the jurisdiction of the courts of Georgia for any action filed in connection with the adoption of the child. I agree to be bound by a decree of adoption rendered as a result of this surrender of my parental rights.

                              7.

  Furthermore, I hereby certify that I have not been subjected to any duress or undue pressure in the execution of this document and I am signing it freely and voluntarily.

This   day of   ,   .

                          (Parent or guardian)

Adult witness

Sworn to and subscribed

before me this

day of   , .

Notary Public (SEAL)

My commission expires: ."
(b) The notice to revoke a surrender of rights pursuant to subsection (a) of Code Section 19-8-9 shall conform substantially to the following form:

              "NOTICE TO REVOKE SURRENDER OF RIGHTS/
                   FINAL RELEASE FOR ADOPTION

  I, the undersigned, executed a (SURRENDER OF RIGHTSINAL RELEASE FOR ADOPTION) (PRE-BIRTH SURRENDER OF RIGHTSINAL RELEASE FOR ADOPTION) [circle one] as to the child identified in the surrender of rights document on   (date). My relationship to the (child) (unborn child) [circle one] is that I am the (mother) (father) (alleged biological father) (guardian) [circle one].
  (Complete this paragraph if the child has been born.) This notice to revoke my surrender of rights applies to the (female) (male) [circle one] child born   (name of child) on   (birthdate of child).

I now wish to exercise my right to revoke my surrender of rights.
I understand that for my revocation of surrender to be effective I must:
   A. Deliver the original of this document in person to the address designated in the surrender of rights document no later than 5:00 P.M. eastern standard time or eastern daylight time, whichever is applicable, on the fourth day of the revocation period specified in the surrender of rights document;
OR
   B. Mail the original of this document by registered mail or by statutory overnight delivery to the address designated in the surrender of rights document no later than the fourth day of the revocation period specified in the surrender of rights document.

This   day of   ,   .

_____
(Parent, guardian, or alleged biological father)

_____
(Printed name)

Adult witness"

(c) The surrender of rights by a parent or guardian pursuant to paragraph (1) of subsection (e) of Code Section 19-8-5 shall conform substantially to the following form:

"SURRENDER OF RIGHTS
FINAL RELEASE FOR ADOPTION

NOTICE TO PARENT OR GUARDIAN:

This is an important legal document and by signing it, you are surrendering all of your rights to the child identified in this document, so as to place the child for adoption. Understand that you are signing this document under oath and that if you knowingly and willfully make a false statement in this document you will be guilty of the crime of false swearing. As explained below in paragraph 8, you have the right to revoke this surrender within four days from the date you sign it.

STATE OF GEORGIA

COUNTY OF
   Personally appeared before me, the undersigned officer duly authorized to administer oaths,   (name of parent or guardian) who, after having been sworn, deposes and says as follows:

1.

I, the undersigned, being mindful that my (male) (female) [circle one] child, born   (name of child) on   (birthdate of child) at   :   (A.M.) (P.M.) [circle one], should receive the benefits and advantages of a good home, to the end that (she) (he) [circle one] may be fitted for the requirements of life, consent to this surrender of my parental rights.

2.

I, the undersigned, _____ (relationship to child) of the aforesaid child, do hereby surrender my rights to the child to _____ (name, surname not required, of each individual to whom surrender is made), PROVIDED that each such individual is named as petitioner in a petition for adoption of the child filed in accordance with Article 1 of Chapter 8 of Title 19 of the Official Code of Georgia Annotated within 60 days from the date that I sign this document. Furthermore, I promise not to interfere in the management of the child in any respect whatever; and, in consideration of the benefits guaranteed by _____ (name, surname not required, of each individual to whom surrender is made) in providing for the child, I do relinquish all rights to the child named in this document, it being my wish, intent, and purpose to relinquish absolutely all parental control over the child.

3.

It is also my wish, intent, and purpose that if each such individual identified in paragraph 2 is not named as petitioner in a petition for adoption within the 60 day period, other than for justifiable good cause, or, if said petition for adoption is filed within 60 days but the adoption proceeding is dismissed with prejudice or otherwise concluded without an order declaring the child to be the adopted child of each such individual, then I do hereby surrender my rights to the child as follows:

Indicate your choice by signing ONE of the following statements (you may choose statement A, B, or C):

A. _____ (Signature) I wish the child returned to me, as provided by subsection (j) of Code Section 19-8-5, and I expressly acknowledge that this provision applies only to the limited circumstance that the child is not adopted by the individual or individuals designated in this document and further that this provision does not impair the validity, absolute finality, or totality of this surrender under any circumstance other than the failure of the designated individual or individuals to adopt the child and that no other provision of this surrender impairs the validity, absolute finality, or totality of this surrender once the four-day revocation period has elapsed;

OR

B. _____ (Signature) I surrender the child to _____ (name of child-placing agency or out-of-state licensed agency), as provided in subsection (j) of Code Section 19-8-5, for placement for adoption. I understand that if the child-placing agency or out-of-state licensed agency declines to accept the child for placement for adoption, this surrender will be in favor of the Department of Human Services for placement for adoption and _____ (name of child-placing agency or out-of-state licensed agency) or the Department of Human Services may petition the superior court for custody of the child in accordance with the terms of this surrender;

OR

C. _____ (Signature) I surrender the child to the Department of Human Services, as provided by subsection (j) of Code Section 19-8-5, for placement for adoption; and the Department of Human Services may petition the superior court for custody of the child in accordance with the terms of this surrender.

4.

I hereby agree that the child is to be adopted by each individual named in paragraph 2 or by any other individual as may be chosen by

_____ (name of child-placing agency or out-of-state licensed agency) or the Department of Human Services and I do expressly waive any other notice or service in any of the legal proceedings for the adoption of the child.

5.

I understand that under Georgia law an evaluator is required to conduct and provide to the court a home study and make recommendations to the court regarding the qualification of each individual named in paragraph 2 to adopt the child concerning the circumstances of placement of the child for adoption.

6.

I understand that under Georgia law an agent appointed by the court is required to conduct an investigation and render a report to the court in connection with the legal proceeding for the legal adoption of the child, and I hereby agree to cooperate fully with such agent in the conduct of its investigation.

7.

I understand that I will receive a copy of this document after the witness and I have signed it and it has been notarized.

8.

I understand that under Georgia law I have the unconditional right to a four-day revocation period. I understand I may only revoke this surrender by giving written notice, delivered in person or mailed by registered mail or statutory overnight delivery, to _____ (name and address of each individual to whom surrender is made or his or her agent) within four days from the date of signing this document. I understand that certified mail cannot be used for mail delivery of the notice to revoke this surrender. I understand that the four days will be counted consecutively beginning with the day immediately following the date I sign this document; provided, however, that, if the fourth day falls on a Saturday, Sunday, or legal holiday, then the last day on which this surrender may be revoked will be the next day that is not a Saturday, Sunday, or legal holiday. I understand that, if I deliver the notice to revoke this surrender in person, it must be delivered to _____ (name and address) not later than 5:00 P.M. eastern standard time or eastern daylight time, whichever is applicable, on the fourth day. I understand that I CANNOT revoke this surrender after that time.

9.

I understand that if I am not a resident of this state that I am agreeing to be subject to the jurisdiction of the courts of Georgia for any action filed in connection with the adoption of the child. I agree to be bound by a decree of adoption rendered as a result of this surrender of my parental rights.

10.

Furthermore, I hereby certify that I have not been subjected to any duress or undue pressure in the execution of this document and I am signing it freely and voluntarily.

This   day of   ,   .

(Parent or guardian)

Adult witness

Sworn to and subscribed

before me this

day of   ,   .

Notary Public (SEAL)

My commission expires: ."

(d) The surrender of rights by a biological father who is not a legal father of the child pursuant to paragraph (2) of subsection (e) of Code Section 19-8-4, 19-8-5, 19-8-6, or 19-8-7 shall conform substantially to the following form:

"SURRENDER OF RIGHTS
FINAL RELEASE FOR ADOPTION

NOTICE TO ALLEGED BIOLOGICAL FATHER:

This is an important legal document and by signing it you are surrendering all of your rights to the child identified in this document. Understand that you are signing this document under oath and that if you knowingly and willfully make a false statement in this document you will be guilty of the crime of false swearing. As explained below in paragraph 4, you have the right to revoke this surrender within four days from the date you sign it.

STATE OF GEORGIA

COUNTY OF

Personally appeared before me, the undersigned officer duly authorized to administer oaths,   (name of alleged biological father) who, after having been sworn, deposes and says as follows:

1.

I, the undersigned, alleged biological father of a (male) (female) [circle one] child, born   (name of child) to

(name of legal mother) on   (birthdate of child) at
  :   (A.M.) (P.M.) [circle one], being mindful that the child should receive the benefits and advantages of a good home, to the end that (she) (he) [circle one] may be fitted for the requirements of life, consent to this surrender of my rights. I, the undersigned, do hereby surrender my rights to the child. I promise not to interfere in the management of the child in any respect whatever; and, in consideration of the benefits provided to the child through adoption, I do relinquish all rights to the child named in this document, it being my wish, intent, and purpose to relinquish absolutely all control over the child.

2.

I hereby agree that the child is to be adopted and I do expressly waive any other notice or service in any of the legal proceedings for the adoption of the child. I understand that under Georgia law an agent appointed by the court is required to conduct an investigation and render a report to the court in connection with the legal proceeding for the legal adoption of the child, and I hereby agree to cooperate fully with such agent in the conduct of its investigation.

3.

I understand that I will receive a copy of this document after the witness and I have signed it and it has been notarized.

4.

I understand that under Georgia law I have the unconditional right to a four-day revocation period. I understand I may only revoke this surrender by giving written notice, delivered in person or mailed by registered mail or statutory overnight delivery, to   (name and address of child-placing agency representative, out-of-state licensed agency representative, Department of Human Services representative, individual to whom surrender is made or his or her agent, or petitioner's representative, as applicable) within four days from the date of signing this document. I understand that certified mail cannot be used for mail delivery of the notice to revoke this surrender. I understand that the four days will be counted consecutively beginning with the day immediately following the date I sign this document; provided, however, that, if the fourth day falls on a Saturday, Sunday, or legal holiday, then the last day on which this surrender may be revoked will be the next day that is not a Saturday, Sunday, or legal holiday. I understand that, if I deliver the notice to revoke this surrender in person, it must be delivered to
(name and address) not later than 5:00 P.M. eastern standard time or eastern daylight time, whichever is applicable, on the fourth day. I understand that I CANNOT revoke this surrender after that time.

5.

I understand that if I am not a resident of this state that I am agreeing to be subject to the jurisdiction of the courts of Georgia for any action filed in connection with the adoption of the child. I agree to be bound by a decree of adoption rendered as a result of this surrender of my parental rights.

6.

Furthermore, I hereby certify that I have not been subjected to any duress or undue pressure in the execution of this document and I am signing it freely and voluntarily.

This   day of   ,   .

(Alleged biological father)

Adult witness
Sworn to and subscribed
before me this
day of   ,   .

Notary public (SEAL)
My commission expires: ."

(e) The surrender of rights by a parent or guardian pursuant to paragraph (1) of subsection (e) of Code Section 19-8-6 or 19-8-7 shall conform substantially to the following form:

"SURRENDER OF RIGHTS
FINAL RELEASE FOR ADOPTION

NOTICE TO PARENT OR GUARDIAN:

This is an important legal document and by signing it, you are surrendering all of your rights to the child identified in this document, so as to place the child for adoption. Understand that you are signing this document under oath and that if you knowingly and willfully make a false statement in this document you will be guilty of the crime of false swearing. As explained below in paragraph 6, you have the right to revoke this surrender within four days from the date you sign it.

STATE OF GEORGIA

COUNTY OF
Personally appeared before me, the undersigned officer duly authorized to administer oaths,   (name of parent or guardian) who, after having been sworn, deposes and says as follows:

1.

I, the undersigned, being mindful that my (male) (female) [circle one] child, born   (name of child) on   (birthdate of child) at   :   (A.M.) (P.M.) [circle one], should receive the benefits and advantages of a good home, to the end that (she) (he) [circle one] may be fitted for the requirements of life, consent to this surrender of my parental rights.

2.

I, the undersigned,   (relationship to child) of the aforesaid child, do hereby surrender my rights to the child to   (name of each individual to whom surrender is made) and promise not to interfere in the management of the child in any respect whatever; and, in consideration of the benefits guaranteed by _____ (name of each individual to whom surrender is made) in providing for the child, I do relinquish all rights to the child named in this document, it being my wish, intent, and purpose to relinquish absolutely all parental control over the child.

3.

I hereby agree that _____ (name of each individual to whom surrender is made) may initiate legal proceedings for the legal adoption of the child without further notice to me. I do, furthermore, expressly waive any other notice or service in any of the legal proceedings for the adoption of the child.

4.

I understand that under Georgia law an agent may be appointed by the court to conduct an investigation and render a report to the court in connection with the legal proceeding for the legal adoption of the child, and I hereby agree to cooperate fully with such agent in the conduct of its investigation.

5.

I understand that I will receive a copy of this document after the witness and I have signed it and it has been notarized.

6.

I understand that under Georgia law I have the unconditional right to a four-day revocation period. I understand I may only revoke this surrender by giving written notice, delivered in person or mailed by registered mail or statutory overnight delivery, to _____ (name and address of each individual to whom surrender is made or petitioner's representative, as applicable) within four days from the date of signing this document. I understand that certified mail cannot be used for mail delivery of the notice to revoke this surrender. I understand that the four days will be counted consecutively beginning with the day immediately following the date I sign this document; provided, however, that, if the fourth day falls on a Saturday, Sunday, or legal holiday, then the last day on which this surrender may be revoked will be the next day that is not a Saturday, Sunday, or legal holiday. I understand that, if I deliver the notice to revoke my surrender in person, it must be delivered to _____ (name and address) not later than 5:00 P.M. eastern standard time or eastern daylight time, whichever is applicable, on the fourth day. I understand that I CANNOT revoke this surrender after that time.

7.

I understand that if I am not a resident of this state that I am agreeing to be subject to the jurisdiction of the courts of Georgia for any action filed in connection with the adoption of the child. I agree to be bound by a decree of adoption rendered as a result of this surrender of my parental rights.

8.

Furthermore, I hereby certify that I have not been subjected to any duress or undue pressure in the execution of this document and I am signing it freely and voluntarily.

This   day of   ,   .

(Parent or guardian)

Adult witness

Sworn to and subscribed

before me this

day of   ,   .

Notary public (SEAL)
My commission expires: ."

(f) The pre-birth surrender of rights by a biological father who is not a legal father of the child pursuant to paragraph (3) of subsection (e) of Code Section 19-8-4, 19-8-5, or 19-8-7 shall conform substantially to the following form:

"PRE-BIRTH SURRENDER OF RIGHTS
FINAL RELEASE FOR ADOPTION

NOTICE TO ALLEGED BIOLOGICAL FATHER:

This is an important legal document and by signing it, you are surrendering any and all of your rights to the child identified in this document, so as to place the child for adoption. You have the right to wait to execute a PRE-BIRTH SURRENDER OF RIGHTS/FINAL RELEASE FOR ADOPTION after the child is born, but by signing this document, you are electing to surrender your rights prior to the birth of this child. Understand that you are signing this document under oath and that if you knowingly and willfully make a false statement in this document you will be guilty of the crime of false swearing. As explained below in paragraph 6, you have the right to revoke this pre-birth surrender within four days from the date you sign it.

STATE OF GEORGIA

COUNTY OF
Personally appeared before me, the undersigned officer duly authorized to administer oaths,   (name of alleged biological father) who, after having been sworn, deposes and says as follows:

1.

I, the undersigned, understand that I have been named by _____, the biological mother of the child expected to be born in _____ (city) _____ (county) _____ (state) on or about the _____ day of _____ (month), _____ (year), as the biological father or possible biological father of her child. I further understand that the biological mother wishes to place this child for adoption.

2.

To the best of my knowledge and belief, the child has not been born as of the date I am signing this pre-birth surrender; however, if in fact the child has been born, this surrender shall have the same effect as if it were a surrender executed following the birth of the child.

3.

I understand that by signing this document I am not admitting that I am the biological father of this child, but if I am, I hereby agree that adoption is in this child's best interest. I consent to adoption of this child by any individual chosen by the child's legal mother or by any public or private agency that places children without further notice to me. I expressly waive any other notice or service in any of the legal proceedings for the adoption of the child. I understand that I have the option to wait until after the child is born to execute a surrender of my rights (with a corresponding four-day right of revocation) and, further, that by executing this document I am electing instead to surrender my rights before the child's birth.

4.

I understand that signing this document does not fully and finally terminate my rights and responsibilities until an order from a court of competent jurisdiction terminating my rights or a final order of adoption is entered. I understand that if the child is not adopted after I sign this document, legal proceedings can be brought to establish paternity, and I may become liable for financial obligations related to the birth and support of this child.

5.

I understand that I will receive a copy of this document after the witness and I have signed it and it has been notarized.

6.

I understand that under Georgia law I have the unconditional right to a four-day revocation period. I understand that I may only revoke this pre-birth surrender by giving written notice, delivered in person or mailed by registered mail or statutory overnight delivery, to _____ (name and address of child-placing agency representative, out-of-state licensed agency representative, Department of Human Services representative, individual to whom surrender is made or his or her agent, or petitioner's representative, as applicable) within four days from the date of signing this document. I understand that certified mail cannot be used for mail delivery of the notice to revoke this pre-birth surrender. I understand that the four days will be counted consecutively beginning with the day immediately following the date I sign this document; provided, however, that, if the fourth day falls on a Saturday, Sunday, or legal holiday, then the last day on which this surrender may be revoked will be the next day that is not a Saturday, Sunday, or legal holiday. I understand that, if I deliver the notice to revoke this surrender in person, it must be delivered to   (name and address) not later than 5:00 P.M. eastern standard time or eastern daylight time, whichever is applicable, on the fourth day. I understand that I CANNOT revoke this surrender after that time.

7.

If prior to my signing this pre-birth surrender I have registered on Georgia's putative father registry then, if I do not revoke this surrender within the time permitted, I waive the notice I would be entitled to receive pursuant to Code Section 19-8-12 of the Official Code of Georgia Annotated because of my registration on the putative father registry.

8.

I understand that if I am not a resident of this state that I am agreeing to be subject to the jurisdiction of the courts of Georgia for any action filed in connection with the adoption of the child. I agree to be bound by a decree of adoption rendered as a result of this surrender of my parental rights.

9.

Furthermore, I hereby certify that I have not been subjected to any duress or undue pressure in the execution of this document and I am signing it freely and voluntarily.

This   day of   ,   .

(Alleged biological father)

Adult witness

Sworn to and subscribed

before me this   day of

    ,   .

Notary public (SEAL)

My commission expires: ."

(g) The acknowledgment of surrender of rights pursuant to subsection (f) of Code Section 19-8-4, 19-8-5, 19-8-6, or 19-8-7 shall conform substantially to the following form:

"ACKNOWLEDGMENT OF SURRENDER
OF RIGHTS

STATE OF GEORGIA

COUNTY OF

Personally appeared before me, the undersigned officer duly authorized to administer oaths, _____ (name of parent, guardian, or alleged biological father) who, after having been sworn, deposes and says as follows:

(A) That I have read the accompanying (PRE-BIRTH SURRENDER OF RIGHTS/FINAL RELEASE FOR ADOPTION) (SURRENDER OF RIGHTS/FINAL RELEASE FOR ADOPTION) [circle one] relating to the child born _____ (name of child), a (male) (female) [circle one] on _____ (birthdate of child);

(B) That I understand that this is a full, final, and complete surrender, release, and termination of all of my rights to the child;

(C) That I have chosen to retain the unconditional right to revoke the surrender by giving written notice, delivered in person or mailed by registered mail or statutory overnight delivery, to _____ (name and address of child-placing agency or its representative, out-of-state licensed agency or its representative, Department of Human Services or its representative, individual to whom surrender is made or his or her agent, or petitioner's representative, as applicable) within four days from the date of signing the surrender and that after such four-day revocation period I shall have no right to revoke the surrender. I understand that certified mail cannot be used for mail delivery of the notice to revoke the surrender of my rights. I understand that, if I deliver the notice to revoke my surrender in person, it must be delivered to _____ (name and address) not later than 5:00 P.M. eastern standard time or eastern daylight time, whichever is applicable, on the fourth day. I understand that the four days will be counted consecutively beginning with the day immediately following the date I signed the surrender; provided, however, that, if the fourth day falls on a Saturday, Sunday, or legal holiday, then the last day on which the surrender may be revoked will be the next day that is not a Saturday, Sunday, or legal holiday;

(D) That I have read the accompanying surrender of rights and received a copy thereof;

(E) That any and all questions regarding the effect of such surrender and its provisions have been satisfactorily explained to me;

(F) That I have been given an opportunity to consult with an attorney of my choice before signing of the surrender of my rights; and

(G) That the surrender of my rights has been knowingly, intentionally, freely, and voluntarily made by me.

This _____ day of _____, _____.

_____
(Parent, guardian, or alleged biological father)

_____
Adult witness

Sworn to and subscribed

before me this   day of

    ,   .

Notary public (SEAL)

My commission expires: ."

(h) The affidavit of a legal mother required by paragraph (1) of subsection (g) of Code Section 19-8-4, 19-8-5, 19-8-6, or 19-8-7 for the surrender of her rights shall meet the following requirements:
  (1) The affidavit shall set forth:
    (A) Her name;
    (B) Her relationship to the child;
    (C) Her age;
    (D) Her marital status at the time of conception and of the birth of the child;
    (E) The identity and last known address of her spouse or former spouse and whether any such spouse is the biological father of the child;
    (F) The identity, last known address, and relationship to the legal mother of the biological father of the child, provided that she shall have the right not to disclose the name and address of the biological father of the child should she so desire;
    (G) Whether or not she has consented to the appointment of a temporary guardian for the child and, if so, provide the name and address of the temporary guardian and the probate court in which the petition for temporary guardianship was filed;
    (H) Whether custody of the child has been awarded to another individual and, if so, provide the name of the child's custodian and the court in which custody was awarded;
    (I) Whether or not the biological father of the child is or was in a branch of the United States armed forces and, if so, provide details as to his military service;
    (J) Whether or not the biological mother or any member of her family is or was an enrolled member of a federally recognized American Indian tribe, is or was a resident of an American Indian reservation, or is or was an Alaskan native;
    (K) Whether or not the biological father of the child or any member of his family is or was an enrolled member of a federally recognized American Indian tribe, is or was a resident of an American Indian reservation, or is or was an Alaskan native; and
    (L) All financial assistance received by or promised her either directly or indirectly, from whatever source, in connection with her pregnancy, the birth of the child, or the placement or arranging for the placement of the child for adoption (including the date, amount or value, description, payor, and payee), provided that financial assistance provided directly by her husband, mother, father, sister, brother, aunt, uncle, grandfather, or grandmother need not be detailed and instead she need only state the nature of the assistance received; and
  (2) The affidavit shall conform substantially to the following form:

"LEGAL MOTHER'S AFFIDAVIT

NOTICE TO LEGAL MOTHER:

This is an important legal document which deals with the child's right to have his or her biological father's rights properly determined. You have the right not to disclose the name and address of the biological father of the child. Understand that you are providing this affidavit under oath and that if you knowingly and willfully make a false statement in this affidavit you will be guilty of the crime of false swearing. The information you provide will be held in strict confidence and will be used only in connection with the adoption of the child.
STATE OF GEORGIA
COUNTY OF

Personally appeared before me, the undersigned officer duly authorized to administer oaths,   , who, after having been sworn, deposes and says as follows:

That my name is   .

That I am the legal mother of a (male) (female) [circle one] child born   (name of child) in the State of   , County of   on   (birthdate of child) at   :   (A.M.) (P.M.) [circle one].

That I am   years of age, having been born in the State of   , County of   on   .

That my social security number is   .

That my marital status at the time of the conception of the child was (check the status and complete the appropriate information):

( ) Single, never having been married.

( ) Separated but not legally divorced; the name of my spouse (was) (is) [circle one]   ; my spouse's last known address is   ; we were married in the State of   , County of   on   ; we have been separated since   ; we last had sexual relations on   (date); my spouse (is) (is not) [circle one] the biological father of said child.

( ) Divorced; the name of my former spouse is   ; we were married in the State of   , County of   on   ; we last had sexual relations on   (date); my former spouse's last known address is   ; divorce granted in the State of   , County of   on   ; my former spouse (is) (is not) [circle one] the biological father of said child.

( ) Legally married; the name of my spouse (was) (is) [circle one]   ; we were married in the State of   , County of   on   ; and my spouse's last known address is   ; my spouse (is) (is not) [circle one] the biological father of said child.

( ) Married through common-law marriage relationship prior to January 1, 1997; the name of my spouse (was) (is) [circle one]   ; my spouse's last known address is   ; our relationship began in the State of   , County of   on   ; my spouse (is) (is not) [circle one] the biological father of said child.

( ) Widowed; the name of my deceased spouse was   ; we were married in the State of   , County of   on   ; my spouse died on   in the County of   , State of   .

That my name and marital status at the time of the birth of the child was (check the status and complete the appropriate information):

Name

( ) Single, never having been married.

( ) Separated, but not legally divorced; the name of my spouse (was) (is) [circle one]   ; my spouse's last known address is   ; we were married in the State of   , County of   on   ; we have been separated since   ; we last had sexual relations on   (date); my spouse (is) (is not) [circle one] the biological father of said child.

( ) Divorced; the name of my former spouse is   ; we were married in the State of   , County of   on   ; we last had sexual relations on   (date); my spouse's last known address is   ; divorce granted in the State of   , County of   ; my former spouse (is) (is not) [circle one] the biological father of said child.

( ) Legally married; the name of my spouse (was) (is) [circle one]   ; we were married in the State of   , County of   on   ; my spouse's last known address is   ; my spouse (is) (is not) [circle one] the biological father of said child.

( ) Married through common-law relationship prior to January 1, 1997; the name of my spouse (was) (is) [circle one]   ; my spouse's last known address is   ; our relationship began in the State of   , County of   on   ; my spouse (is) (is not) [circle one] the biological father of said child.

( ) Widowed; the name of my deceased spouse was   ; we were married in the State of   , County of   on   ; my spouse died on   in the County of   , State of   ; he (was) (was not) [circle one] the biological father of said child.

That the name of the biological father of the child is (complete appropriate response):

   Known to me and is (   );

   Known to me but I expressly decline to identify him because   ; or

   Unknown to me because   .

That the last known address of the biological father of the child is (complete appropriate response):

   Known to me and is   ;

   Known to me but I expressly decline to provide his address because   ; or

   Unknown to me because   .

That, to the best of my knowledge, I (am) (am not) [circle one] an enrolled member of a federally recognized American Indian tribe, (am) (am not) [circle one] a resident of an American Indian reservation, or (am) (am not) [circle one] an Alaskan native. If so:

   (A) The name of my American Indian tribe is   .
   (B) The percentage of my American Indian blood is   percent.

That, to the best of my knowledge, a member of my family (is or was) (is not or was not) [circle one] an enrolled member of a federally recognized American Indian tribe, (is or was) (is not or was not) [circle one] a resident of an American Indian reservation, or (is or was) (is not or was not) [circle one] an Alaskan native. If so:

   (A) The name of the American Indian tribe is   .
   (B) The percentage of my American Indian blood is   percent.
   (C) My relatives with American Indian or Alaskan native blood are   .

   (D) The name of the American Indian tribe is   .
   (E) The name of each enrolled member is   , and his or her corresponding registration or identification number is   .

That, to the best of my knowledge, the biological father or a member of his family (is or was) (is not or was not) [circle one] an enrolled member of a federally recognized American Indian tribe, (is or was) (is not or was not) [circle one] a resident of an American Indian reservation, or (is or was) (is not or was not) [circle one] an Alaskan native. If so:

   (A) The name of his American Indian tribe is   .
   (B) The percentage of his American Indian blood is   percent.
   (C) His relatives with American Indian or Alaskan native blood are   .

   (D) The name of each enrolled member is   , and his or her corresponding registration or identification number is   .

That the date of birth of the biological father (is   ,   ) (is not known to me) [circle one].

That the biological father (is) (is not) [circle one] on active duty in a branch of the United States armed forces. If so:

   (A) The branch of his service is (Army) (Navy) (Marine) (Air Force) (Coast Guard) [circle one].
   (B) His rank is   .
   (C) His duty station is   .

   If applicable, please provide any additional available information regarding his military service.

That the biological father of the child, whether or not identified in this document (circle the appropriate phrase):

(Was) (Was not) married to me at the time this child was conceived;

(Was) (Was not) married to me at any time during my pregnancy with this child;

(Was) (Was not) married to me at the time that this child was born;

(Did) (Did not) marry me after the child was born and recognize the child as his own;

(Has) (Has not) been determined to be the child's father by a final paternity order of a court;

(Has) (Has not) legitimated the child by a final court order;

(Has) (Has not) lived with the child;

(Has) (Has not) contributed to its support;

(Has) (Has not) provided for my support during my pregnancy or hospitalization for the birth of the child; and

(Has) (Has not) provided for my medical care during my pregnancy or hospitalization for the birth of the child.

That I (have) (have not) [circle one] consented to the appointment of a temporary guardian for the child. If so, the name of the temporary guardian is   , and the probate court in which the petition for temporary guardianship was filed is   .

That custody of the child has been awarded to   (name and address of custodian) by order of the   Court of   County, State of   , entered on   (date).

That I have received or been promised the following financial assistance, either directly or indirectly, from whatever source, in connection with my pregnancy, the birth of the child, and the child's placement for adoption: .

That I recognize that if I knowingly and willfully make a false statement in this affidavit I will be guilty of the crime of false swearing.

(Legal mother)

Sworn to and subscribed

before me this

day of   ,   .

Notary public (SEAL)

My commission expires   ."

(i) The affidavit of an adoptive mother required by paragraph (2) of subsection (g) of Code Section 19-8-4, 19-8-5, 19-8-6, or 19-8-7 for the surrender of her rights shall meet the following requirements:

(1) The affidavit shall set forth:

(A) Her name;

(B) Her relationship to the child;

(C) Her age;

(D) Her marital status;

(E) The name and last known address of any spouse or former spouse at the time the child was adopted and whether any such spouse also adopted the child or is the biological father of the child;

(F) The circumstances surrounding her adoption of the child, including the date the adoption was finalized, the state and county where finalized, and the name and address of the adoption agency, if any;

(G) Whether or not she has consented to the appointment of a temporary guardian for the child and, if so, provide the name of the temporary guardian and the probate court in which the petition for temporary guardianship was filed;

(H) Whether custody of the child has been awarded to another individual and, if so, provide the name of the child's custodian and the court in which custody was awarded; and

(I) All financial assistance received by or promised her either directly or indirectly, from whatever source, in connection with the placement or arranging for the placement of the child for adoption (including the date, amount or value, description, payor, and payee), provided that financial assistance provided directly by her husband, mother, father, sister, brother, aunt, uncle, grandfather, or grandmother need not be detailed and instead she need only state the nature of the assistance received.

(2) The affidavit shall be in substantially the following form:

"ADOPTIVE MOTHER'S AFFIDAVIT

NOTICE TO ADOPTIVE MOTHER:

This is an important legal document which deals with the adopted child's right to have his or her legal father's rights properly determined. Understand that you are providing this affidavit under oath and that if you knowingly and willfully make a false statement in this affidavit you will be guilty of the crime of false swearing. The information you provide will be held in strict confidence and will be used only in connection with the adoption of the child.

STATE OF GEORGIA
COUNTY OF

Personally appeared before me, the undersigned officer duly authorized to administer oaths,   , who, after having been sworn, deposes and says as follows:

That my name is   .

That I am the adoptive mother of a (male) (female) [circle one] child born   (name of child) in the State of   , County of   on   (birthdate of child) at   :   (A.M.) (P.M.) [circle one].

That I am   years of age, having been born in the State of   , County of   on   .

That my social security number is   .

That my marital status is (check the status and complete the appropriate information):

( ) Single, never having been married.

( ) Separated but not legally divorced; the name of my spouse (was) (is) [circle one]   ; my spouse's last known address is   ; we were married in the State of   , County of   on   ; we have been separated since   ; we last had sexual relations on   (date); my spouse (did) (did not) [circle one] also adopt said child; my spouse (is) (is not) [circle one] the biological father of said child.

( ) Divorced; the name of my former spouse is   ; we were married in the State of   , County of   on   ; we last had sexual relations on   (date); my former spouse's last known address is   ; divorce granted in the State of   , County of   on   ; my former spouse (did) (did not) [circle one] also adopt said child; my former spouse (is) (is not) [circle one] the biological father of said child.

( ) Legally married; the name of my spouse (was) (is) [circle one]   ; we were married in the State of   , County of   on   ; my spouse's last known address is   ; my spouse (did) (did not) [circle one] also adopt said child; my spouse (is) (is not) [circle one] the biological father of said child.

( ) Married through common-law marriage relationship prior to January 1, 1997; the name of my spouse (was) (is) [circle one]   ; my spouse's last known address is   ; our relationship began in the State of   , County of   on   ; my spouse (did) (did not) [circle one] also adopt said child; my spouse (is) (is not) [circle one] the biological father of said child.

( ) Widowed; the name of my deceased spouse was   ; we were married in the State of   , County of   on   ; my spouse died on   in the County of   , State of   ; he (did) (did not) [circle one] also adopt said child; he (was) (was not) [circle one] the biological father of said child.

That I adopted the child in the State of   , County of   .

That the final order of adoption was entered on   .

That there (was) (was not) [circle one] an adoption agency involved in the placement of the child with me for adoption; and if so its name was   , and its address is   .

That I (have) (have not) [circle one] consented to the appointment of a temporary guardian for the child. If so, the name of the temporary guardian is: , and the probate court in which the petition for temporary guardianship was filed is   .

That custody of the child has been awarded to   (name and address of custodian) by order of the   Court of   County, State of   , entered on   (date).

That I have received or been promised the following financial assistance, either directly or indirectly, from whatever source, in connection with the child's placement for adoption: .

That I recognize that if I knowingly and willfully make a false statement in this affidavit I will be guilty of the crime of false swearing.

(Adoptive mother)

Sworn to and subscribed before me this day of   ,   .

Notary public (SEAL)
My commission expires: ."

(j) The affidavit of a child-placing agency, out-of-state licensed agency, or department representative required by subsection (h) of Code Section 19-8-4 shall conform substantially to the following form:

"AFFIDAVIT OF CHILD-PLACING AGENCY,
OUT-OF-STATE LICENSED AGENCY, OR
DEPARTMENT REPRESENTATIVE

STATE OF GEORGIA

COUNTY OF

Personally appeared before me, the undersigned officer duly authorized to administer oaths,   , who, after having been sworn, deposes and says as follows:

That I am   (position) of   (name of department, child-placing agency, or out-of-state licensed agency).

That prior to the execution of the accompanying SURRENDER OF RIGHTS/FINAL RELEASE FOR ADOPTION by   , releasing and surrendering all of (his) (her) [circle one] rights in a (male) (female) [circle one] child born   (name of child) on   (birthdate of child) at   :   (A.M.) (P.M.) [circle one], I reviewed with and explained to such individual all of the provisions of the surrender of rights, and particularly the provisions which provide that the surrender is a full surrender of all rights to the child.

That based on my review and explanation to such individual, it is my opinion that such individual knowingly, intentionally, freely, and voluntarily executed the SURRENDER OF RIGHTS/FINAL RELEASE FOR ADOPTION.

(Representative)

(Department or agency name)

Sworn to and subscribed
before me this
day of   ,   .

Notary public (SEAL)
My commission expires: ."

(k) The affidavit of a petitioner's representative or of the representative of the individual signing the surrender of rights required by subsection (h) of Code Section 19-8-5, 19-8-6, or 19-8-7 shall conform substantially to the following form:

"AFFIDAVIT OF REPRESENTATIVE

STATE OF GEORGIA

COUNTY OF
Personally appeared before me, the undersigned officer duly authorized to administer oaths,   , who, after having been sworn, deposes and says as follows:
   That my name is   .
   That my address is   .
   That prior to the execution of the accompanying SURRENDER OF RIGHTS/FINAL RELEASE FOR ADOPTION by   , releasing and surrendering all of (his) (her) [circle one] rights in a (male) (female) [circle one] child born   (name of child) on   (birthdate of child) at   :   (A.M.) (P.M.) [circle one], I reviewed with and explained to such individual all of the provisions of the surrender of rights, and particularly the provisions which provide that the surrender is a full surrender of all rights to the child.
   That based on my review and explanation to such individual, it is my opinion that such individual knowingly, intentionally, freely, and voluntarily executed the SURRENDER OF RIGHTS/FINAL RELEASE FOR ADOPTION.

(Petitioner's representative or the

representative of the individual

signing the surrender)

Sworn to and subscribed

before me this

day of   ,   .

Notary public (SEAL)

My commission expires: ."

(l) The parental consent to a stepparent adoption required by subsection (j) of Code Section 19-8-6 shall conform substantially to the following form:

"PARENTAL CONSENT TO STEPPARENT ADOPTION

STATE OF GEORGIA

COUNTY OF

   Personally appeared before me, the undersigned officer duly authorized to administer oaths,   (name of parent) who, after having been sworn, deposes and says as follows:
   I, the undersigned, hereby consent that my spouse   (name of spouse) adopt my (son) (daughter) [circle one],   (name of child), whose date of birth is   , and in so doing I in no way relinquish or surrender my parental rights to the child. I further acknowledge service of a copy of the petition for adoption of the child as filed on behalf of my spouse, and I hereby consent to the granting of the prayers of the petition for adoption. I also waive all other and further service and notice of any kind and nature in connection with the proceedings.

   This   day of   ,   .

                                             (Parent)

Sworn to and subscribed

before me this

day of   ,   .

Notary public (SEAL)

My commission expires: ."

(m) The sworn statement executed by the biological mother identifying an alleged biological father of her unborn child authorized and required by subparagraph (e)(3)(E) of Code Section 19-8-4, 19-8-5, or 19-8-7 shall conform substantially to the following form:

"NOTICE TO BIOLOGICAL MOTHER:

   This is an important legal document which will enable the individual you identify as the biological father of your unborn child to sign a pre-birth surrender of his rights so as to place your child for adoption. Understand that you are signing this affidavit under oath and that the information you provide will be held in strict confidence and will be used only in connection with the adoption of your unborn child.

STATE OF GEORGIA

COUNTY OF

BIOLOGICAL MOTHER'S AFFIDAVIT IDENTIFYING
BIOLOGICAL FATHER OF HER UNBORN CHILD

Personally appeared before me, the undersigned officer duly authorized to administer oaths,   , who, after having been sworn, deposes and says as follows:

That my name is   .

That I am   years of age, having been born in the State of   , County of   on   .

That my social security number is   .

That I am currently pregnant with a (male) (female) (sex unknown) [circle one] child who is expected to be born on   (due date of child).

That the name of any alleged biological father is   , and his last known address is   .

That I execute this affidavit so that any alleged biological father I have identified above can be asked to sign a pre-birth surrender of his rights to assist me in placing the child for adoption once the child is born.

That I recognize that if I knowingly and willfully make a false statement in this affidavit I will be guilty of the crime of false swearing.

(Biological mother)

Sworn to and subscribed

before me this

day of   ,   .

Notary public (SEAL)

My commission expires: ."

(n) The affidavit regarding Native American heritage and military service authorized and required by subsection (k) of Code Sections 19-8-4, 19-8-6, and 19-8-7 and subsection (o) of Code Section 19-8-5 shall conform substantially to the following form:

"NOTICE TO BIOLOGICAL OR LEGAL FATHER:

This is an important legal document. Understand that you are providing this affidavit under oath and that if you knowingly and willfully make a false statement in this affidavit you will be guilty of the crime of false swearing.

AFFIDAVIT REGARDING NATIVE AMERICAN HERITAGE
AND MILITARY SERVICE

STATE OF GEORGIA

COUNTY OF

Personally appeared before me, the undersigned officer duly authorized to administer oaths,   (name of affiant) who, after having been sworn, deposes and says as follows:

1. That my name is   .
2. That I am the (biological) (legal) [circle one] father of a (male) (female) (sex unknown) [circle one] child (born) (yet to be born) [circle one] in the State of   , County of   on   .
3. That I am   years of age, having been born in the State of   , County of   on   .
4. That my social security number is   .
5. That, to the best of my knowledge, I (am) (am not) [circle one] an enrolled member of a federally recognized American Indian tribe, (am) (am not) [circle one] a resident of an American Indian reservation, or (am) (am not) [circle one] an Alaskan native. If so:
   A. The name of my American Indian tribe is   .
   B. My registration or identification number is   .
   C. The percentage of my American Indian blood is   percent.
6. That, to the best of my knowledge, a member of my family (is or was) (is not or was not) [circle one] an enrolled member of a federally recognized American Indian tribe, (is or was) (is not or was not) [circle one] a resident of an American Indian reservation, or (is or was) (is not or was not) [circle one] an Alaskan native. If so:
   A. The name of the American Indian tribe is   .
   B. The percentage of my American Indian blood is   percent.
   C. My relatives with American Indian or Alaskan native blood are   .
   D. The name of the American Indian tribe is   .
   E. The name of each enrolled member is   , and his or her corresponding registration or identification number is   .
7. That I (am) (am not) [circle one] on active duty in a branch of the United States armed forces. If so:
   A. The branch of my service is (Army) (Navy) (Marine) (Air Force) (Coast Guard) [circle one].
   B. My rank is   .
   C. My duty station is   .
   D. Additional information regarding my military service is   .

8. That I have received or been promised the following financial assistance, either directly or indirectly, from whatever source, in connection with the birth of the child and the child's placement for adoption: .
9. That I recognize that if I knowingly and willfully make a false statement in this affidavit I will be guilty of the crime of false swearing.

(Biological or legal father)

Sworn to and subscribed

before me this

day of   ,   .

Notary public (SEAL)

My commission expires: _____ ."

§ 19-8-27. (Effective September 1, 2018) Postadoption contact agreements; definitions; procedure; jurisdiction; warnings; enforcement, termination, or modification; expenses of litigation

(a) As used in this Code section, the term "birth relative" means:
(1) A parent, biological father who is not a legal father, grandparent, brother, sister, half-brother, or half-sister who is related by blood or marriage to a child who is being adopted or who has been adopted; or
(2) A grandparent, brother, sister, half-brother, or half-sister who is related by adoption to a child who is being adopted or who has been adopted.
(b) (1) An adopting parent or parents and birth relatives or an adopting parent or parents, birth relatives, and a child who is 14 years of age or older who is being adopted or who has been adopted may voluntarily enter into a written postadoption contact agreement to permit continuing contact between such birth relatives and such child. A child who is 14 years of age or older shall be considered a party to a postadoption contact agreement.
(2) A postadoption contact agreement may provide for privileges regarding a child who is being adopted or who has been adopted, including, but not limited to, visitation with such child, contact with such child, sharing of information about such child, or sharing of information about birth relatives.
(3) In order to be an enforceable postadoption contact agreement, such agreement shall be in writing and signed by all of the parties to such agreement acknowledging their consent to its terms and conditions.
(4) Enforcement, modification, or termination of a postadoption contact agreement shall be under the continuing jurisdiction of the court that granted the petition for adoption; provided, however, that the parties to a postadoption contact agreement may expressly waive the right to enforce, modify, or terminate such agreement under this Code section.
(5) Any party to the postadoption contact agreement may, at any time, file the original postadoption contact agreement with the court that has or had jurisdiction over the adoption if such agreement provides for the court to enforce such agreement or such agreement is silent as to the issue of enforcement.
(c) A postadoption contact agreement shall contain the following warnings in at least 14 point boldface type:
(1) After the entry of a decree for adoption, an adoption cannot be set aside due to the failure of an adopting parent, a biological parent, a birth relative, or the child to follow the terms of this agreement or a later change to this agreement; and
(2) A disagreement between the parties or litigation brought to enforce, terminate, or modify this agreement shall not affect the validity of the adoption and shall not serve as a basis for orders affecting the custody of the child.
(d) (1) As used in this subsection, the term "parties" means the individuals who signed the postadoption contact agreement currently in effect, including the child if he or she is 14 years of age or older at the time of the action regarding such agreement, but such term shall exclude any third-party beneficiary to such agreement.
(2) A postadoption contact agreement may always be modified or terminated if the parties have voluntarily signed a written modified postadoption contact agreement or termination of a postadoption contact agreement. A modified postadoption contact agreement may be filed with the court if such agreement provides for the court to enforce such agreement or such agreement is silent as to the issue of enforcement.
(e) With respect to postadoption contact agreements that provide for court enforcement or termination or are silent as to such matters, any party, as defined in paragraph (1) of subsection (d) of this Code section, may file a petition to enforce or terminate such agreement with the court that granted the petition for adoption, and the court shall enforce the terms of such agreement or terminate such agreement if such court finds by a preponderance of the evidence that the enforcement or termination is necessary to serve the best interests of the child.
(f) With respect to postadoption contact agreements that provide for court modification or are silent as to modification, only the adopting parent or parents may file a petition seeking modification. Such petition shall be filed with the court that granted the petition for adoption, and the court shall modify such agreement if such court finds by a preponderance of the evidence that the modification is necessary to serve the best interests of the child and there has been a material change of circumstances since the current postadoption contact agreement was executed.
(g) A court may require the party seeking modification, termination, or enforcement of a postadoption contact agreement to participate in mediation or other appropriate alternative dispute resolution.
(h) All reasonable costs and expenses of mediation, alternative dispute resolution, and litigation shall be borne by the party, other than the child, filing the action to enforce, modify, or terminate a postadoption contact agreement when no party has been found by the court as failing to comply with an existing

postadoption contact agreement. Otherwise, a party, other than the child, found by the court as failing to comply without good cause with an existing postadoption contact agreement shall bear all the costs and expenses of mediation, alternative dispute resolution, and litigation of the other party.
(i) A court shall not set aside a decree of adoption, rescind a surrender of rights, or modify an order to terminate parental rights or any other prior court order because of the failure of an adoptive parent, a birth relative, or the child to comply with any or all of the original terms of, or subsequent modifications to, a postadoption contact agreement.

§ 19-8-28. (Effective September 1, 2018) Adoption of an orphan

When a child is an orphan, the petitioner shall not be required to have a guardian appointed for such child in order for a guardian to execute a surrender of rights. Such child shall be adoptable without a surrender of rights.

ARTICLE 2. EMBRYO TRANSFERS
§ 19-8-40. Definitions

As used in this article, the term:
(1) "Embryo" or "human embryo" means an individual fertilized ovum of the human species from the single-cell stage to eight-week development.
(2) "Embryo relinquishment" or "legal transfer of rights to an embryo" means the relinquishment of rights and responsibilities by the person or persons who hold the legal rights and responsibilities for an embryo and the acceptance of such rights and responsibilities by a recipient intended parent.
(3) "Embryo transfer" means the medical procedure of physically placing an embryo into the uterus of a female.
(4) "Legal embryo custodian" means the person or persons who hold the legal rights and responsibilities for a human embryo and who relinquishes said embryo to another person or persons.
(5) "Recipient intended parent" means a person or persons who receive a relinquished embryo and who accepts full legal rights and responsibilities for such embryo and any child that may be born as a result of embryo transfer.

§ 19-8-41. Release of responsibility by legal embryo custodian; procedures; presumption of parentage

(a) A legal embryo custodian may relinquish all rights and responsibilities for an embryo to a recipient intended parent prior to embryo transfer. A written contract shall be entered into between each legal embryo custodian and each recipient intended parent prior to embryo transfer for the legal transfer of rights to an embryo and to any child that may result from the embryo transfer. The contract shall be signed by each legal embryo custodian for such embryo and by each recipient intended parent in the presence of a notary public and a witness. Initials or other designations may be used if the parties desire anonymity. The contract may include a written waiver by the legal embryo custodian of notice and service in any legal adoption or other parentage proceeding which may follow.
(b) If the embryo was created using donor gametes, the sperm or oocyte donors who irrevocably relinquished their rights in connection with in vitro fertilization shall not be entitled to any notice of the embryo relinquishment, nor shall their consent to the embryo relinquishment be required.
(c) Upon embryo relinquishment by each legal embryo custodian pursuant to subsection (a) of this Code section, the legal transfer of rights to an embryo shall be considered complete, and the embryo transfer shall be authorized.
(d) A child born to a recipient intended parent as the result of embryo relinquishment pursuant to subsection (a) of this Code section shall be presumed to be the legal child of the recipient intended parent; provided that each legal embryo custodian and each recipient intended parent has entered into a written contract.

§ 19-8-42. Petition for expedited order of adoption or parentage; notice; waiver of technical requirements

(a) Prior to the birth of a child or following the birth of a child, a recipient intended parent may petition the superior court for an expedited order of adoption or parentage. In such cases, the written contract between each legal embryo custodian and each recipient intended parent shall be acceptable in lieu of a surrender of rights.
(b) All petitions under this article shall be filed in the county in which any petitioner or any respondent resides.

(c) The court shall give effect to any written waiver of notice and service in the legal proceeding for adoption or parentage.
(d) In the interest of justice, to promote the stability of embryo transfers, and to promote the interests of children who may be born following such embryo transfers, the court in its discretion may waive such technical requirements as the court deems just and proper.

§ 19-8-43. Finality of orders of adoption or parentage

Upon a filing of a petition for adoption or parentage and the court finding that such petition meets the criteria required by this article, an expedited order of adoption or parentage shall be issued and shall be a final order. Such order shall terminate any future parental rights and responsibilities of any past or present legal embryo custodian or gamete donor in a child which results from the embryo transfer and shall vest such rights and responsibilities in the recipient intended parent.

CHAPTER 9. CHILD CUSTODY PROCEEDINGS

ARTICLE 1. GENERAL PROVISIONS
§ 19-9-1. Parenting plans; requirements for plan

(a) Except when a parent seeks emergency relief for family violence pursuant to Code Section 19-13-3 or 19-13-4, in all cases in which the custody of any child is at issue between the parents, each parent shall prepare a parenting plan or the parties may jointly submit a parenting plan. It shall be in the court's discretion as to when a party shall be required to submit a parenting plan to the court. A parenting plan shall be required for permanent custody and modification actions and in the court's discretion may be required for temporary hearings. The final order in any legal action involving the custody of a child, including modification actions, shall incorporate a permanent parenting plan as further set forth in this Code section; provided, however, that unless otherwise ordered by the court, a separate court order exclusively devoted to a parenting plan shall not be required.
(b) (1) Unless otherwise ordered by the court, a parenting plan shall include the following:
   (A) A recognition that a close and continuing parent-child relationship and continuity in the child's life will be in the child's best interest;
   (B) A recognition that the child's needs will change and grow as the child matures and demonstrate that the parents will make an effort to parent that takes this issue into account so that future modifications to the parenting plan are minimized;
   (C) A recognition that a parent with physical custody will make day-to-day decisions and emergency decisions while the child is residing with such parent; and
   (D) That both parents will have access to all of the child's records and information, including, but not limited to, education, health, health insurance, extracurricular activities, and religious communications.
  (2) Unless otherwise ordered by the court, or agreed upon by the parties, a parenting plan shall include, but not be limited to:
   (A) Where and when a child will be in each parent's physical care, designating where the child will spend each day of the year;
   (B) How holidays, birthdays, vacations, school breaks, and other special occasions will be spent with each parent including the time of day that each event will begin and end;
   (C) Transportation arrangements including how the child will be exchanged between the parents, the location of the exchange, how the transportation costs will be paid, and any other matter relating to the child spending time with each parent;
   (D) Whether supervision will be needed for any parenting time and, if so, the particulars of the supervision;
   (E) An allocation of decision-making authority to one or both of the parents with regard to the child's education, health, extracurricular activities, and religious upbringing, and if the parents agree the matters should be jointly decided, how to resolve a situation in which the parents disagree on resolution;
   (F) What, if any, limitations will exist while one parent has physical custody of the child in terms of the other parent contacting the child and the other parent's right to access education, health, extracurricular activity, and religious information regarding the child; and
   (G) If a military parent is a party in the case:
      (i) How to manage the child's transition into temporary physical custody to a nondeploying parent if a military parent is deployed;
      (ii) The manner in which the child will maintain continuing contact with a deployed parent;
      (iii) How a deployed parent's parenting time may be delegated to his or her extended family;

(iv) How the parenting plan will be resumed once the deployed parent returns from deployment; and
(v) How divisions (i) through (iv) of this subparagraph serve the best interest of the child.
(c) If the parties cannot reach agreement on a permanent parenting plan, each party shall file and serve a proposed parenting plan on or before the date set by the court. Failure to comply with filing a parenting plan may result in the court adopting the plan of the opposing party if the judge finds such plan to be in the best interests of the child.

§ 19-9-1.1. Binding arbitration on issue of child custody and related matters

In all proceedings under this article, it shall be expressly permissible for the parents of a child to agree to binding arbitration on the issue of child custody and matters relative to visitation, parenting time, and a parenting plan. The parents may select their arbiter and decide which issues will be resolved in binding arbitration. The arbiter's decisions shall be incorporated into a final decree awarding child custody unless the judge makes specific written factual findings that under the circumstances of the parents and the child the arbiter's award would not be in the best interests of the child. In its judgment, the judge may supplement the arbiter's decision on issues not covered by the binding arbitration.

§ 19-9-1.2. Required domestic relations case filing information form

Pursuant to Code Section 9-11-3, and in addition to the filing requirements contained in Code Section 19-6-15, in all proceedings under this article the plaintiff shall file a domestic relations case filing information form as prescribed by the Judicial Council of Georgia.

§ 19-9-2. Right of surviving parent to custody of child; discretion of judge

Upon the death of either parent, the survivor is entitled to custody of the child; provided, however, that the judge, upon petition, may exercise discretion as to the custody of the child, looking solely to the child's best interest and welfare.

§ 19-9-3. Establishment and review of child custody and visitation

(a) (1) In all cases in which the custody of any child is at issue between the parents, there shall be no prima-facie right to the custody of the child in the father or mother. There shall be no presumption in favor of any particular form of custody, legal or physical, nor in favor of either parent. Joint custody may be considered as an alternative form of custody by the judge and the judge at any temporary or permanent hearing may grant sole custody, joint custody, joint legal custody, or joint physical custody as appropriate.
(2) The judge hearing the issue of custody shall make a determination of custody of a child and such matter shall not be decided by a jury. The judge may take into consideration all the circumstances of the case, including the improvement of the health of the party seeking a change in custody provisions, in determining to whom custody of the child should be awarded. The duty of the judge in all such cases shall be to exercise discretion to look to and determine solely what is for the best interest of the child and what will best promote the child's welfare and happiness and to make his or her award accordingly.
(3) In determining the best interests of the child, the judge may consider any relevant factor including, but not limited to:
(A) The love, affection, bonding, and emotional ties existing between each parent and the child;
(B) The love, affection, bonding, and emotional ties existing between the child and his or her siblings, half siblings, and stepsiblings and the residence of such other children;
(C) The capacity and disposition of each parent to give the child love, affection, and guidance and to continue the education and rearing of the child;
(D) Each parent's knowledge and familiarity of the child and the child's needs;
(E) The capacity and disposition of each parent to provide the child with food, clothing, medical care, day-to-day needs, and other necessary basic care, with consideration made for the potential payment of child support by the other parent;
(F) The home environment of each parent considering the promotion of nurturance and safety of the child rather than superficial or material factors;
(G) The importance of continuity in the child's life and the length of time the child has lived in a stable, satisfactory environment and the desirability of maintaining continuity;
(H) The stability of the family unit of each of the parents and the presence or absence of each parent's support systems within the community to benefit the child;
(I) The mental and physical health of each parent;

(J) Each parent's involvement, or lack thereof, in the child's educational, social, and extracurricular activities;

(K) Each parent's employment schedule and the related flexibility or limitations, if any, of a parent to care for the child;

(L) The home, school, and community record and history of the child, as well as any health or educational special needs of the child;

(M) Each parent's past performance and relative abilities for future performance of parenting responsibilities;

(N) The willingness and ability of each of the parents to facilitate and encourage a close and continuing parent-child relationship between the child and the other parent, consistent with the best interest of the child;

(O) Any recommendation by a court appointed custody evaluator or guardian ad litem;

(P) Any evidence of family violence or sexual, mental, or physical child abuse or criminal history of either parent; and

(Q) Any evidence of substance abuse by either parent.

(4) In addition to other factors that a judge may consider in a proceeding in which the custody of a child or visitation or parenting time by a parent is at issue and in which the judge has made a finding of family violence:

(A) The judge shall consider as primary the safety and well-being of the child and of the parent who is the victim of family violence;

(B) The judge shall consider the perpetrator's history of causing physical harm, bodily injury, assault, or causing reasonable fear of physical harm, bodily injury, or assault to another person;

(C) If a parent is absent or relocates because of an act of domestic violence by the other parent, such absence or relocation for a reasonable period of time in the circumstances shall not be deemed an abandonment of the child for the purposes of custody determination; and

(D) The judge shall not refuse to consider relevant or otherwise admissible evidence of acts of family violence merely because there has been no previous finding of family violence. The judge may, in addition to other appropriate actions, order supervised visitation or parenting time pursuant to Code Section 19-9-7.

(5) In all custody cases in which the child has reached the age of 14 years, the child shall have the right to select the parent with whom he or she desires to live. The child's selection for purposes of custody shall be presumptive unless the parent so selected is determined not to be in the best interests of the child. The parental selection by a child who has reached the age of 14 may, in and of itself, constitute a material change of condition or circumstance in any action seeking a modification or change in the custody of that child; provided, however, that such selection may only be made once within a period of two years from the date of the previous selection and the best interests of the child standard shall apply.

(6) In all custody cases in which the child has reached the age of 11 but not 14 years, the judge shall consider the desires and educational needs of the child in determining which parent shall have custody. The judge shall have complete discretion in making this determination, and the child's desires shall not be controlling. The judge shall further have broad discretion as to how the child's desires are to be considered, including through the report of a guardian ad litem. The best interests of the child standard shall be controlling. The parental selection of a child who has reached the age of 11 but not 14 years shall not, in and of itself, constitute a material change of condition or circumstance in any action seeking a modification or change in the custody of that child. The judge may issue an order granting temporary custody to the selected parent for a trial period not to exceed six months regarding the custody of a child who has reached the age of 11 but not 14 years where the judge hearing the case determines such a temporary order is appropriate.

(7) The judge is authorized to order a psychological custody evaluation of the family or an independent medical evaluation. In addition to the privilege afforded a witness, neither a court appointed custody evaluator nor a court appointed guardian ad litem shall be subject to civil liability resulting from any act or failure to act in the performance of his or her duties unless such act or failure to act was in bad faith.

(8) If requested by any party on or before the close of evidence in a contested hearing, the permanent court order awarding child custody shall set forth specific findings of fact as to the basis for the judge's decision in making an award of custody including any relevant factor relied upon by the judge as set forth in paragraph (3) of this subsection. Such order shall set forth in detail why the court awarded custody in the manner set forth in the order and, if joint legal custody is awarded, a manner in which final decision making on matters affecting the child's education, health, extracurricular activities, religion, and any other important matter shall be decided. Such order shall be filed within 30 days of the final hearing in the custody case, unless extended by order of the judge with the agreement of the parties.

(b) In any case in which a judgment awarding the custody of a child has been entered, on the motion of any party or on the motion of the judge, that portion of the judgment effecting visitation rights between the parties and their child or parenting time may be subject to review and modification or alteration without the necessity of any showing of a change in any material conditions and circumstances of either party or the child, provided that the review and modification or alteration shall not be had more often than once in each two-year period following the date of entry of the judgment. However, this subsection shall not limit or restrict the power of the judge to enter a judgment relating to the custody of a child in any new proceeding based upon a showing of a change in any material conditions or circumstances of a party or the child. A military parent's absences caused by the performance of his or her deployments, or the potential for future deployments, shall not be the sole factor considered in supporting a claim of any change in material conditions or circumstances of either party or the child; provided, however, that the court may consider evidence of the effect of a deployment in assessing a claim of any change in material conditions or circumstances of either party or the child.

(c) In the event of any conflict between this Code section and any provision of Article 3 of this chapter, Article 3 shall apply.

(d) It is the express policy of this state to encourage that a child has continuing contact with parents and grandparents who have shown the ability to act in the best interest of the child and to encourage parents to share in the rights and responsibilities of raising their child after such parents have separated or dissolved their marriage or relationship.

(e) Upon the filing of an action for a change of child custody, the judge may in his or her discretion change the terms of custody on a temporary basis pending final judgment on such issue. Any such award of temporary custody shall not constitute an adjudication of the rights of the parties.

(f) (1) In any case in which a judgment awarding the custody of a child has been entered, the court entering such judgment shall retain jurisdiction of the case for the purpose of ordering the custodial parent to notify the court of any changes in the residence of the child.

(2) In any case in which visitation rights or parenting time has been provided to the noncustodial parent and the court orders that the custodial parent provide notice of a change in address of the place for pickup and delivery of the child for visitation or parenting time, the custodial parent shall notify the noncustodial parent, in writing, of any change in such address. Such written notification shall provide a street address or other description of the new location for pickup and delivery so that the noncustodial parent may exercise such parent's visitation rights or parenting time.

(3) Except where otherwise provided by court order, in any case under this subsection in which a parent changes his or her residence, he or she must give notification of such change to the other parent and, if the parent changing residence is the custodial parent, to any other person granted visitation rights or parenting time under this title or a court order. Such notification shall be given at least 30 days prior to the anticipated change of residence and shall include the full address of the new residence.

(g) Except as provided in Code Section 19-6-2, and in addition to the attorney's fee provisions contained in Code Section 19-6-15, the judge may order reasonable attorney's fees and expenses of litigation, experts, and the child's guardian ad litem and other costs of the child custody action and pretrial proceedings to be paid by the parties in proportions and at times determined by the judge. Attorney's fees may be awarded at both the temporary hearing and the final hearing. A final judgment shall include the amount granted, whether the grant is in full or on account, which may be enforced by attachment for contempt of court or by writ of fieri facias, whether the parties subsequently reconcile or not. An attorney may bring an action in his or her own name to enforce a grant of attorney's fees made pursuant to this subsection.

(h) In addition to filing requirements contained in Code Section 19-6-15, upon the conclusion of any proceeding under this article, the domestic relations final disposition form as prescribed by the Judicial Council of Georgia shall be filed.

(i) Notwithstanding other provisions of this article, whenever a military parent is deployed, the following shall apply:

(1) A court shall not enter a final order modifying parental rights and responsibilities under an existing parenting plan earlier than 90 days after the deployment ends, unless such modification is agreed to by the deployed parent;

(2) Upon a petition to establish or modify an existing parenting plan being filed by a deploying parent or nondeploying parent, the court shall enter a temporary modification order for the parenting plan to ensure contact with the child during the period of deployment when:

(A) A military parent receives formal notice from military leadership that he or she will deploy in the near future, and such parent has primary physical custody, joint physical custody, or sole physical custody of a child, or otherwise has parenting time with a child under an existing parenting plan; and

(B) The deployment will have a material effect upon a deploying parent's ability to exercise parental rights and responsibilities toward his or her child either in the existing relationship with the other parent or under an existing parenting plan;

(3) Petitions for temporary modification of an existing parenting plan because of a deployment shall be heard by the court as expeditiously as possible and shall be a priority on the court's calendar;

(4) (A) All temporary modification orders for parenting plans shall include a reasonable and specific transition schedule to facilitate a return to the predeployment parenting plan over the shortest reasonable time period after the deployment ends, based upon the child's best interest.

(B) Unless the court determines that it would not be in the child's best interest, a temporary modification order for a parenting plan shall set a date certain for the anticipated end of the deployment and the start of the transition period back to the predeployment parenting plan. If a deployment is extended, the temporary modification order for a parenting plan shall remain in effect, and the transition schedule shall take effect at the end of the extension of the deployment. Failure of the nondeploying parent to notify the court in accordance with this paragraph shall not prejudice the deploying parent's right to return to the predeployment parenting plan once the temporary modification order for a parenting plan expires as provided in subparagraph (C) of this paragraph.

(C) A temporary modification order for a parenting plan shall expire upon the completion of the transition period and the predeployment parenting plan shall establish the rights and responsibilities between parents for the child;

(5) Upon a petition to modify an existing parenting plan being filed by a deploying parent and upon a finding that it serves the best interest of the child, the court may delegate for the duration of the deployment any portion of such deploying parent's parenting time with the child to anyone in his or her extended family, including but not limited to an immediate family member, a person with whom the deploying parent cohabits, or another person having a close and substantial relationship to the child. Such delegated parenting time shall not create any separate rights to such person once the period of deployment has ended;

(6) If the court finds it to be in the child's best interest, a temporary modification order for a parenting plan issued under this subsection may require any of the following:

(A) The nondeploying parent make the child reasonably available to the deploying parent to exercise his or her parenting time immediately before and after the deploying parent departs for deployment and whenever the deploying parent returns to or from leave or furlough from his or her deployment;

(B) The nondeploying parent facilitate opportunities for the deployed parent to have regular and continuing contact with his or her child by telephone, e-mail exchanges, virtual video parenting time through the Internet, or any other similar means;

(C) The nondeploying parent not interfere with the delivery of correspondence or packages between the deployed parent and child of such parent; and

(D) The deploying parent provide timely information regarding his or her leave and departure schedule to the nondeploying parent;

(7) Because actual leave from a deployment and departure dates for a deployment are subject to change with little notice due to military necessity, such changes shall not be used by the nondeploying parent to prevent contact between the deployed parent and his or her child;

(8) A court order temporarily modifying an existing parenting plan or other order governing parent-child rights and responsibilities shall specify when a deployment is the basis for such order and it shall be entered by the court only as a temporary modification order or interlocutory order;

(9) A relocation by a nondeploying parent during a period of a deployed parent's absence and occurring during the period of a temporary modification order for a parenting plan shall not act to terminate the exclusive and continuing jurisdiction of the court for purposes of later determining custody or parenting time under this chapter;

(10) A court order temporarily modifying an existing parenting plan or other order shall require the nondeploying parent to provide the court and the deploying parent with not less than 30 days' advance written notice of any intended change of residence address, telephone numbers, or e-mail address;

(11) Upon a deployed parent's final return from deployment, either parent may file a petition to modify the temporary modification order for a parenting plan on the grounds that compliance with such order will result in immediate danger or substantial harm to the child, and may further request that the court issue an ex parte order. The deployed parent may file such a petition prior to his or her return. Such petition shall be accompanied by an affidavit in support of the requested order. Upon a finding of immediate danger or substantial harm to the child based on the facts set forth in the affidavit, the court may issue an ex parte order modifying the temporary parenting plan or other parent-child contact in order to prevent immediate danger or substantial harm to the child. If the court issues an ex parte order, the court shall set the matter for hearing within ten days from the issuance of the ex parte order;

(12) Nothing in this subsection shall preclude either party from filing a petition for permanent modification of an existing parenting plan under subsection (b) of this Code section; provided, however, that the court shall not conduct a final hearing on such petition until at least 90 days after the final return of the deploying parent. There shall exist a presumption favoring the predeployment parenting plan or custody order as one that still serves the best interest of the child, and the party seeking to permanently modify such plan or order shall have the burden to prove that it no longer serves the best interest of the child;

(13) When the deployment of a military parent has a material effect upon his or her ability to appear in person at a scheduled hearing, then upon request by the deploying parent and provided reasonable advance notice is given to other interested parties, the court may allow a deployed parent to present testimony and other evidence by electronic means for any matter considered by the court under this subsection. For purposes of this paragraph, the term "electronic means" shall include, but not be limited to, communications by telephone, video teleconference, Internet connection, or electronically stored affidavits or documents sent from the deployment location or elsewhere;

(14) (A) When deployment of a military parent appears imminent and there is no existing parenting plan or other order setting forth the parent's rights and responsibilities, then upon a petition filed by either parent the court shall:

(i) Expedite a hearing to establish a temporary parenting plan;

(ii) Require that the deploying parent shall have continued access to the child, provided that such contact is in the child's best interest;

(iii) Ensure the disclosure of financial information pertaining to both parties;

(iv) Determine the child support responsibilities under Code Section 19-6-15 of both parents during the deployment; and

(v) Determine the child's best interest and consider delegating to any third parties with close contacts to the child any reasonable parenting time during the deployment. In deciding such request the court shall consider the reasonable requests of the deployed parent.

(B) Any pleading filed to establish a parenting plan or child support order under this paragraph shall be identified at the time of filing by stating in the text of the pleading the specific facts related to the deployment and by referencing this paragraph and subsection of this Code section;

(15) When an impending deployment precludes court expedited adjudication before deployment, the court may agree to allow the parties to arbitrate any issues as allowed under Code Section 19-9-1.1, or order the parties to mediation under any court established alternative dispute resolution program. For purposes of arbitration or mediation, each party shall be under a duty to provide to the other party information relevant to any parenting plan or support issues pertaining to the children or the parties;

(16) Each military parent shall be under a continuing duty to provide written notice to the nondeploying parent within 14 days of the military parent's receipt of oral or written orders requiring deployment or any other absences due to military service that will impact the military parent's ability to exercise his or her parenting time with a child. If deployment orders do not allow for 14 days' advance notice, then the military parent shall provide written notice to the other parent immediately upon receiving such notice; and

(17) A military parent shall ensure that any military family care plan that he or she has filed with his or her commander is consistent with any existing court orders for his or her child. In all instances any court order will be the first course of action for the care of a child during the absence of a military parent, and the military family care plan will be the alternative plan if the nondeploying parent either refuses to provide care for the child or acknowledges an inability to provide reasonable care for the child. A military parent shall not be considered in contempt of any court order or parenting plan when he or she in good faith implements his or her military family care plan based upon the refusal or claimed inability of a nondeploying parent to provide reasonable care for a child during a deployment.

§ 19-9-4. Investigation of abuse, neglect, or other acts which adversely affect health of child in custody disputes; cost

(a) On motion of either party in any action or proceeding involving determination of the award of child custody between parents of the child, when such motion contains a specific recitation of actual abuse, neglect, or other overt acts which have adversely affected the health and welfare of the child, the judge may direct the appropriate family and children services agency or any other appropriate entity to investigate the home life and home environment of each of the parents. In any action or proceeding involving determination of the award of child custody between parents of the child when during such proceedings a specific recitation of actual abuse, neglect, or other overt acts which have adversely affected the health and welfare of the child has been made the judge shall also have authority on his or her own motion to order such an investigation if in the judge's opinion the investigation would be useful in determining placement or custody of the child. The judge may also direct either party to pay to the agency the reasonable cost, or any portion thereof, of the investigation. The report of the investigation will be made to the judge directing the investigation. Any report made at the direction of the judge shall be made available to either or both parties for a reasonable period of time prior to the proceedings at which any temporary or permanent custody is to be determined. Both parties shall have the right to confront and cross-examine the person or persons who conducted the investigation or compiled the report if adequate and legal notice is given.

(b) This Code section shall apply only with respect to actions or proceedings in which the issue of child custody is contested; and this Code section is not intended to alter or repeal Code Sections 49-5-40 through 49-5-44.

§ 19-9-5. Custody agreements; ratification; supplementation

(a) In all proceedings under this article between parents, it shall be expressly permissible for the parents of a child to present to the judge an agreement respecting any and all issues concerning custody of the child. As used in this Code section, the term "custody" shall include, without limitation, joint custody as such term is defined in Code Section 19-9-6. As used in this Code section, the term "custody" shall not include payment of child support.

(b) The judge shall ratify the agreement and make such agreement a part of the judge's final judgment in the proceedings unless the judge makes specific written factual findings as a part of the final judgment that under the circumstances of the parents and the child in such agreement that the agreement would not be in

the best interests of the child. The judge shall not refuse to ratify such agreement and to make such agreement a part of the final judgment based solely upon the parents' choice to use joint custody as a part of such agreement.
(c) In his or her judgment, the judge may supplement the agreement on issues not covered by such agreement.

§ 19-9-6. Definitions

As used in this article, the term:
(1) "Armed forces" means the national guard and the reserve components of the armed forces, the United States army, navy, marine corps, coast guard, and air force.
(2) "Deploy" or "deployment" means military service in compliance with the military orders received by a member of the armed forces to report for combat operations, contingency operations, peacekeeping operations, a remote tour of duty, temporary duty, or other such military service for which a parent is required to report unaccompanied by family members. Deployment shall include the period during which a military parent remains subject to deployment orders and remains deployed on account of sickness, wounds, leave, or other lawful cause. Such term shall include mobilization.
(3) "Deploying parent" or "deployed parent" means a military parent who has been formally notified by military leadership that he or she will deploy or mobilize or who is currently deployed or mobilized.
(4) "Joint custody" means joint legal custody, joint physical custody, or both joint legal custody and joint physical custody. In making an order for joint custody, the judge may order joint legal custody without ordering joint physical custody.
(5) "Joint legal custody" means both parents have equal rights and responsibilities for major decisions concerning the child, including the child's education, health care, extracurricular activities, and religious training; provided, however, that the judge may designate one parent to have sole power to make certain decisions while both parents retain equal rights and responsibilities for other decisions.
(6) "Joint physical custody" means that physical custody is shared by the parents in such a way as to assure the child of substantially equal time and contact with both parents.
(7) "Military family care plan" means a plan that is periodically reviewed by a military parent's commander that provides for care of a military parent's child whenever his or her military duties prevent such parent from providing care to his or her child and ensures that a military parent has made adequate and reasonable arrangements to provide for the needs and supervision of his or her child whenever a nondeploying parent is unable or unavailable to provide care in the military parent's absence.
(8) "Military parent" means a member of the armed forces who is a legal parent, adoptive parent, or guardian of a child under the age of 18, whose parental rights are established either by operation of law or the process of legitimation, and who has not had his or her parental rights terminated by a court of competent jurisdiction.
(9) "Mobilization" or "mobilize" means the call-up of the national guard and the reserve components of the armed forces to extended active duty service. Such term shall not include National Guard or Reserves component annual training, inactive duty days, drill weekends, or state active duty performed within the boundaries of this state.
(10) "Nondeploying parent" means:
  (A) A parent who is not a member of the armed forces; or
  (B) A military parent who is currently not also a deploying parent.
(11) "Sole custody" means a person, including, but not limited to, a parent, has been awarded permanent custody of a child by a court order. Unless otherwise provided by court order, the person awarded sole custody of a child shall have the rights and responsibilities for major decisions concerning the child, including the child's education, health care, extracurricular activities, and religious training, and the noncustodial parent shall have the right to visitation or parenting time. A person who has not been awarded custody of a child by court order shall not be considered as the sole legal custodian while exercising visitation rights or parenting time.
(12) "State active duty" means the call-up by a governor for the performance of any military duty while serving within the boundaries of that state.
(13) "Temporary duty" means the assignment of a military parent to a geographic location outside of this state for a limited period of time to accomplish training or to assist in the performance of a military mission.

§ 19-9-7. Visitation by parent who has committed acts of family violence; conditional orders; confidentiality; joint counseling; conditions for supervised visitation

(a) A judge may award visitation or parenting time to a parent who committed one or more acts involving family violence only if the judge finds that adequate provision for the safety of the child and the parent who is a victim of family violence can be made. In a visitation or parenting time order, a judge may:

(1) Order an exchange of a child to occur in a protected setting;
(2) Order visitation or parenting time supervised by another person or agency;
(3) Order the perpetrator of family violence to attend and complete, to the satisfaction of the judge, a certified family violence intervention program for perpetrators as defined in Article 1A of Chapter 13 of this title as a condition of the visitation or parenting time;
(4) Order the perpetrator of family violence to abstain from possession or consumption of alcohol, marijuana, or any Schedule I controlled substance listed in Code Section 16-13-25 during the visitation or parenting time and for 24 hours preceding the visitation or parenting time;
(5) Order the perpetrator of family violence to pay a fee to defray the costs of supervised visitation or parenting time;
(6) Prohibit overnight visitation or parenting time;
(7) Require a bond from the perpetrator of family violence for the return and safety of the child; and
(8) Impose any other condition that is deemed necessary to provide for the safety of the child, the victim of family violence, or another family or household member.
(b) Whether or not visitation or parenting time is allowed, the judge may order the address of the child and the victim of family violence to be kept confidential.
(c) The judge shall not order an adult who is a victim of family violence to attend joint counseling with the perpetrator of family violence as a condition of receiving custody of a child or as a condition of visitation or parenting time.
(d) If a judge allows a family or household member to supervise visitation or parenting time, the judge shall establish conditions to be followed during visitation or parenting time.

ARTICLE 2. CHILD CUSTODY INTRASTATE JURISDICTION ACT

§ 19-9-20. Short title

This article shall be known and may be cited as the "Georgia Child Custody Intrastate Jurisdiction Act of 1978."

§ 19-9-21. Purpose; construction

(a) The general purposes of this article are to:
(1) Avoid jurisdictional competition and conflict by courts within this state in matters of child custody, which have in the past resulted in the shifting of children from county to county with harmful effects on their well-being;
(2) Promote cooperation by the courts of this state, to the end that a custody decree is rendered by the court which can best decide the case in the interest of the child;
(3) Assure that litigation concerning the custody of a child ordinarily takes place in the court with which the child and his family have the closest connection and where significant evidence concerning the care, protection, training, and personal relationships of the child is most readily available and that courts of this state decline the exercise of jurisdiction when the child and his family have a closer connection with another court of this state;
(4) Discourage continuing controversies over child custody, in the interest of greatest stability of home environment and of secure family relationships for the child;
(5) Deter abductions and other unilateral removals of children undertaken to obtain custody awards;
(6) Avoid relitigation of custody decisions of other courts in this state insofar as is feasible;
(7) Facilitate the enforcement of custody decrees;
(8) Make uniform the practice and procedure of the courts of this state in child custody matters.
(b) This article shall be construed to promote the general purposes stated in subsection (a) of this Code section.

§ 19-9-22. Definitions

As used in this article, the term:
(1) "Custody" includes visitation rights.
(2) "Legal custodian" means a person, including, but not limited to, a parent, who has been awarded permanent custody of a child by a court order. A person who has not been awarded custody of a child by court order shall not be considered as the legal custodian while exercising visitation rights. Where custody of a child is shared by two or more persons or where the time of visitation exceeds the time of custody, that person who has the majority of time of custody or visitation shall be the legal custodian.

(3) "Physical custodian" means a person, including, but not limited to, a parent, who is not the "legal custodian" of a child but who has physical custody of the child.

§ 19-9-23. Actions to obtain change of legal custody; how and where brought; use of certain complaints prohibited

(a) Except as otherwise provided in this Code section, after a court has determined who is to be the legal custodian of a child, any complaint seeking to obtain a change of legal custody of the child shall be brought as a separate action in the county of residence of the legal custodian of the child.
(b) A complaint by the legal custodian seeking a change of legal custody or visitation rights shall be brought as a separate action in compliance with Article VI, Section II, Paragraph VI of the Constitution of this state.
(c) No complaint specified in subsection (a) or (b) of this Code section shall be made:
   (1) As a counterclaim or in any other manner in response to a petition for a writ of habeas corpus seeking to enforce a child custody order; or
   (2) In response to any other action or motion seeking to enforce a child custody order.
(d) The use of a complaint in the nature of habeas corpus seeking a change of child custody is prohibited.

§ 19-9-24. Actions by physical or legal custodian not permitted in certain instances

(a) A physical custodian shall not be allowed to maintain against the legal custodian any action for divorce, alimony, child custody, change of alimony, change of child custody, or change of visitation rights or any application for contempt of court so long as custody of the child is withheld from the legal custodian in violation of the custody order.
(b) A legal custodian shall not be allowed to maintain any action for divorce, alimony, child custody, change of alimony, change of child custody, or change of visitation rights or any application for contempt of court so long as visitation rights are withheld in violation of the custody order.

ARTICLE 3. UNIFORM CHILD CUSTODY JURISDICTION AND ENFORCEMENT ACT

§ 19-9-40. Short title

This article may be cited as the "Uniform Child Custody Jurisdiction and Enforcement Act."

ARTICLE TO BE CONSIDERED IN PARI MATERIA WITH APPLICABLE LEGISLATION. --Former Uniform Child Custody Jurisdiction Act does not expressly repeal any particular provisions of the Civil Practice Act, nor existing statutory provisions covering divorce, custody, alimony, and child support procedures, and must be considered in pari materia with other applicable provisions of law. Gambrell v. Gambrell, 246 Ga. 516, 272 S.E.2d 70 (1980) (decided under former Code 1933, § 74-510).

§ 19-9-41. Definitions

In this article:
(1) "Abandoned" means left without provision for reasonable and necessary care or supervision.
(2) "Child" means an individual who has not attained 18 years of age.
(3) "Child custody determination" means a judgment, decree, or other order of a court providing for the legal custody, physical custody, or visitation with respect to a child. The term includes a permanent, temporary, initial, and modification order. The term does not include an order relating to child support or other monetary obligations of an individual.
(4) "Child custody proceeding" means a proceeding in which legal custody, physical custody, or visitation with respect to a child is an issue. The term includes a proceeding for divorce, separation, neglect, abuse, dependency, guardianship, paternity, termination of parental rights, and protection from family violence, in which the issue may appear. The term does not include a proceeding involving juvenile delinquency, contractual emancipation, or enforcement under Part 3 of this article.
(5) "Commencement" means the filing of the first pleading in a proceeding.
(6) "Court" means an entity authorized under the law of a state to establish, enforce, or modify a child custody determination.
(7) "Home state" means the state in which a child lived with a parent or a person acting as a parent for at least six consecutive months immediately before the commencement of a child custody proceeding. In the case of a child less than six months of age, the term means the state in which the child lived from birth with

any of the persons mentioned. A period of temporary absence of any of the mentioned persons is part of the period.

(8) "Initial determination" means the first child custody determination concerning a particular child.

(9) "Issuing court" means the court that makes a child custody determination for which enforcement is sought under this article.

(10) "Issuing state" means the state in which a child custody determination is made.

(11) "Modification" means a child custody determination that changes, replaces, supersedes, or is otherwise made after a previous determination concerning the same child, whether or not it is made by the court that made the previous determination.

(12) "Person" means an individual, corporation, business trust, estate, trust, partnership, limited liability company, association, joint venture, government; governmental subdivision, agency, or instrumentality; public corporation; or any other legal or commercial entity.

(13) "Person acting as a parent" means a person, other than a parent, who:

(A) Has physical custody of the child or has had physical custody for a period of six consecutive months, including any temporary absence, within one year immediately before the commencement of a child custody proceeding; and

(B) Has been awarded legal custody by a court or claims a right to legal custody under the law of this state.

(14) "Physical custody" means the physical care and supervision of a child.

(15) "State" means a state of the United States, the District of Columbia, Puerto Rico, the United States Virgin Islands, or any territory or insular possession subject to the jurisdiction of the United States.

(16) "Tribe" means an Indian tribe or band or Alaskan Native village which is recognized by federal law or formally acknowledged by a state.

(17) "Warrant" means an order issued by a court authorizing law enforcement officers to take physical custody of a child.

§ 19-9-42. Article inapplicable to adoptions or authorizations for emergency care

This article does not govern an adoption proceeding or a proceeding pertaining to the authorization of emergency medical care for a child.

§ 19-9-43. Proceeding pertaining to Indian child exempted from article

(a) A child custody proceeding that pertains to an Indian child as defined in the Indian Child Welfare Act, 25 U.S.C. Section 1901 et seq., is not subject to this article to the extent that it is governed by the Indian Child Welfare Act.
(b) A court of this state shall treat a tribe as if it were a state of the United States for the purpose of applying this part and Part 2 of this article.
(c) A child custody determination made by a tribe under factual circumstances in substantial conformity with the jurisdictional standards of this article must be recognized and enforced under Part 3 of this article.

§ 19-9-44. Child custody determinations of foreign country

(a) A court of this state shall treat a foreign country as if it were a state of the United States for the purpose of applying this part and Part 2 of this article.
(b) Except as otherwise provided in subsection (c) of this Code section, a child custody determination made in a foreign country under factual circumstances in substantial conformity with the jurisdictional standards of this article must be recognized and enforced under Part 3 of this article.
(c) A court of this state need not apply this article if the child custody law of a foreign country violates fundamental principles of human rights.

§ 19-9-45. Binding authority of child custody determination

A child custody determination made by a court of this state that had jurisdiction under this article binds all persons who have been served in accordance with the laws of this state or notified in accordance with Code Section 19-9-47 or who have submitted to the jurisdiction of the court, and who have been given an opportunity to be heard. As to those persons, the determination is conclusive as to all decided issues of law and fact except to the extent the determination is modified.

§ 19-9-46. Priority of question of jurisdiction

If a question of existence or exercise of jurisdiction under this article is raised in a child custody proceeding, the question, upon request of a party, must be given priority on the calendar and handled expeditiously.

§ 19-9-47. Notice and proof of service on persons outside the state

(a) Notice required for the exercise of jurisdiction when a person is outside this state may be given in a manner prescribed by the law of this state for service of process or by the law of the state in which the service is made. Notice must be given in a manner reasonably calculated to give actual notice but may be by publication if other means are not effective.
(b) Proof of service may be made in the manner prescribed by the law of this state or by the law of the state in which the service is made.
(c) Notice is not required for the exercise of jurisdiction with respect to a person who submits to the jurisdiction of the court.

§ 19-9-48. Personal jurisdiction not obtained in other matters; service of process

(a) A party to a child custody proceeding, including a modification proceeding, or a petitioner or respondent in a proceeding to enforce or register a child custody determination is not subject to personal jurisdiction in this state for another proceeding or purpose solely by reason of having participated, or of having been physically present for the purpose of participating, in the proceeding.
(b) A person who is subject to personal jurisdiction in this state on a basis other than physical presence is not immune from service of process in this state. A party present in this state who is subject to the jurisdiction of another state is not immune from service of process allowable under the laws of that state.
(c) The immunity granted by subsection (a) of this Code section does not extend to civil litigation based on acts unrelated to the participation in a proceeding under this article committed by an individual while present in this state.

§ 19-9-49. Communication between court of this state and other states

(a) A court of this state may communicate with a court in another state concerning a proceeding arising under this article and concerning any proceeding or court order in another state relating to family violence. A court of this state may consult any state or national registry of court orders relating to family violence with regard to any party.
(b) The court may allow the parties to participate in the communication. If the parties are not able to participate in the communication, they must be given the opportunity to present facts and legal arguments before a decision on jurisdiction is made.
(c) Communication between courts on schedules, calendars, court records, and similar matters may occur without informing the parties. A record need not be made of the communication.
(d) Except as otherwise provided in subsection (c) of this Code section, a record must be made of any communication under this Code section. The parties must be informed promptly of the communication and granted access to the record.
(e) For the purposes of this Code section, "record" means information that is inscribed on a tangible medium or that is stored in an electronic or other medium and is retrievable in perceivable form.

§ 19-9-50. Testimony by deposition; electronic deposition; evidence transmitted by technological means not to be excluded

(a) In addition to other procedures available to a party, a party to a child custody proceeding may offer testimony of witnesses who are located in another state, including testimony of the parties and the child, by deposition or other means allowable in this state for testimony taken in another state. The court on its own motion may order that the testimony of a person be taken in another state and may prescribe the manner in which and the terms upon which the testimony is taken.
(b) A court of this state may permit an individual residing in another state to be deposed or to testify by telephone, audiovisual means, or other electronic means before a designated court or at another location in that state. A court of this state shall cooperate with courts of other states in designating an appropriate location for the deposition or testimony.

(c) Documentary evidence transmitted from another state to a court of this state by technological means that do not produce an original writing may not be excluded from evidence on an objection based on the means of transmission.

§ 19-9-51. Hearings and studies in another state; costs

(a) A court of this state may request the appropriate court of another state to:
(1) Hold an evidentiary hearing;
(2) Order a person to produce or give evidence pursuant to procedures of that state;
(3) Order that an evaluation be made with respect to the custody of a child involved in a pending proceeding;
(4) Forward to the court of this state a certified copy of the transcript of the record of the hearing, the evidence otherwise presented, and any evaluation prepared in compliance with the request; and
(5) Order a party to a child custody proceeding or any person having physical custody of the child to appear in the proceeding with or without the child.
(b) Upon request of a court of another state, a court of this state may hold a hearing or enter an order described in subsection (a) of this Code section.
(c) Travel and other necessary and reasonable expenses incurred under subsections (a) and (b) of this Code section may be assessed against the parties according to the law of this state.
(d) A court of this state shall preserve the pleadings, orders, decrees, records of hearings, evaluations, and other pertinent records with respect to a child custody proceeding until the child attains 18 years of age. Upon appropriate request by a court or law enforcement official of another state, the court shall forward a certified copy of those records.

§§ 19-9-52 through 19-9-60.

Repealed by Ga. L. 2001, p. 129, § 1, effective April 7, 2001.

§ 19-9-61. Jurisdiction requirements for initial child custody determinations; physical presence alone insufficient

(a) Except as otherwise provided in Code Section 19-9-64, a court of this state has jurisdiction to make an initial child custody determination only if:
(1) This state is the home state of the child on the date of the commencement of the proceeding, or was the home state of the child within six months before the commencement of the proceeding and the child is absent from this state but a parent or person acting as a parent continues to live in this state;
(2) A court of another state does not have jurisdiction under paragraph (1) of this subsection, or a court of the home state of the child has declined to exercise jurisdiction on the ground that this state is the more appropriate forum under Code Section 19-9-67 or 19-9-68 and:
  (A) The child and the child's parents, or the child and at least one parent or a person acting as a parent, have a significant connection with this state other than mere physical presence; and
  (B) Substantial evidence is available in this state concerning the child's care, protection, training, and personal relationships;
(3) All courts having jurisdiction under paragraph (1) or (2) of this subsection have declined to exercise jurisdiction on the ground that a court of this state is the more appropriate forum to determine the custody of the child under Code Section 19-9-67 or 19-9-68; or
(4) No court of any other state would have jurisdiction under the criteria specified in paragraph (1), (2), or (3) of this subsection.
(b) Subsection (a) of this Code section is the exclusive jurisdictional basis for making a child custody determination by a court of this state.
(c) Physical presence of, or personal jurisdiction over, a party or a child is not necessary or sufficient to make a child custody determination.

§ 19-9-62. Prerequisites for termination of exclusive, continuing jurisdiction

(a) Except as otherwise provided in Code Section 19-9-64, a court of this state which has made a child custody determination consistent with Code Section 19-9-61 or 19-9-63 has exclusive, continuing jurisdiction over the determination until:

(1) A court of this state determines that neither the child nor the child's parents or any person acting as a parent has a significant connection with this state and that substantial evidence is no longer available in this state concerning the child's care, protection, training, and personal relationships; or

(2) A court of this state or a court of another state determines that neither the child nor the child's parents or any person acting as a parent presently resides in this state.

(b) A court of this state which has made a child custody determination and does not have exclusive, continuing jurisdiction under this Code section may modify that determination only if it has jurisdiction to make an initial determination under Code Section 19-9-61.

§ 19-9-63. Prerequisites for modifying custody determination from foreign court

Except as otherwise provided in Code Section 19-9-64, a court of this state may not modify a child custody determination made by a court of another state unless a court of this state has jurisdiction to make an initial determination under paragraph (1) or (2) of subsection (a) of Code Section 19-9-61 and:

(1) The court of the other state determines it no longer has exclusive, continuing jurisdiction under Code Section 19-9-62 or that a court of this state would be a more convenient forum under Code Section 19-9-67; or

(2) A court of this state or a court of the other state determines that neither the child nor the child's parents or any person acting as a parent presently resides in the other state.

§ 19-9-64. Temporary emergency jurisdiction; continuing effect; communicating with other courts

(a) A court of this state has temporary emergency jurisdiction if the child is present in this state and the child has been abandoned or it is necessary in an emergency to protect the child because the child or a sibling or parent of the child is subjected to or threatened with mistreatment or abuse.

(b) If there is no previous child custody determination that is entitled to be enforced under this article and a child custody proceeding has not been commenced in a court of a state having jurisdiction under Code Sections 19-9-61 through 19-9-63, a child custody determination made under this Code section remains in effect until an order is obtained from a court of a state having jurisdiction under Code Sections 19-9-61 through 19-9-63. If a child custody proceeding has not been or is not commenced in a court of a state having jurisdiction under Code Sections 19-9-61 through 19-9-63, a child custody determination made under this Code section becomes a final determination, if it so provides and this state becomes the home state of the child.

(c) If there is a previous child custody determination that is entitled to be enforced under this article, or a child custody proceeding has been commenced in a court of a state having jurisdiction under Code Sections 19-9-61 and 19-9-63, any order issued by a court of this state under this Code section must specify in the order a period that the court considers adequate to allow the person seeking an order to obtain an order from the state having jurisdiction under Code Sections 19-9-61 through 19-9-63. The order issued in this state remains in effect until an order is obtained from the other state within the period specified or the period expires.

(d) A court of this state which has been asked to make a child custody determination under this Code section, upon being informed that a child custody proceeding has been commenced in, or a child custody determination has been made by, a court of a state having jurisdiction under Code Sections 19-9-61 through 19-9-63, shall immediately communicate with the other court. A court of this state which is exercising jurisdiction pursuant to Code Sections 19-9-61 through 19-9-63, upon being informed that a child custody proceeding has been commenced in, or a child custody determination has been made by, a court of another state under a statute similar to this Code section, shall immediately communicate with the court of that state to resolve the emergency, protect the safety of the parties and the child, and determine a period for the duration of the temporary order.

§ 19-9-65. Notice required; intervention

(a) Before a child custody determination is made under this article, notice and an opportunity to be heard in accordance with the standards of Code Section 19-9-47 must be given to all persons entitled to notice under the law of this state as in a child custody proceeding between residents of this state, any parent whose parental rights have not been previously terminated, and any person having physical custody of the child.

(b) This article does not govern the enforceability of a child custody determination made without notice or an opportunity to be heard.

(c) The obligation to join a party and the right to intervene as a party in a child custody proceeding under this article are governed by the law of this state as in child custody proceedings between residents of this state.

§ 19-9-66. Procedure when proceedings pending in another state

(a) Except as otherwise provided in Code Section 19-9-64, a court of this state may not exercise its jurisdiction under this part if, at the time of the commencement of the proceeding, a proceeding concerning the custody of the child has been commenced in a court of another state having jurisdiction substantially in conformity with this article; unless the proceeding has been terminated or is stayed by the court of the other state because a court of this state is a more convenient forum under Code Section 19-9-67.

(b) Except as otherwise provided in Code Section 19-9-64, a court of this state, before hearing a child custody proceeding, shall examine the court documents and other information supplied by the parties pursuant to Code Section 19-9-69. If the court determines that a child custody proceeding has been commenced in a court in another state having jurisdiction substantially in accordance with this article, the court of this state shall stay its proceeding and communicate with the court of the other state. If the court of the state having jurisdiction substantially in accordance with this article does not determine that the court of this state is a more appropriate forum, the court of this state shall dismiss the proceeding.

(c) In a proceeding to modify a child custody determination, a court of this state shall determine whether a proceeding to enforce the determination has been commenced in another state. If a proceeding to enforce a child custody determination has been commenced in another state, the court may:

  (1) Stay the proceeding for modification pending the entry of an order of a court of the other state enforcing, staying, denying, or dismissing the proceeding for enforcement;

  (2) Enjoin the parties from continuing with the proceeding for enforcement; or

  (3) Proceed with the modification under conditions it considers appropriate.

§ 19-9-67. Finding of inconvenient forum; conditions

(a) A court of this state which has jurisdiction under this article to make a child custody determination may decline to exercise its jurisdiction at any time if it determines that it is an inconvenient forum under the circumstances and that a court of another state is a more appropriate forum. The issue of inconvenient forum may be raised upon motion of a party, the court's own motion, or request of another court.

(b) Before determining whether it is an inconvenient forum, a court of this state shall consider whether it is appropriate for a court of another state to exercise jurisdiction. For this purpose, the court shall allow the parties to submit information and shall consider all relevant factors, including:

  (1) Whether family violence has occurred and is likely to continue in the future and which state could best protect the parties and the child;

  (2) The length of time the child has resided outside this state;

  (3) The distance between the court in this state and the court in the state that would assume jurisdiction;

  (4) The relative financial circumstances of the parties;

  (5) Any agreement of the parties as to which state should assume jurisdiction;

  (6) The nature and location of the evidence required to resolve the pending litigation, including testimony of the child;

  (7) The ability of the court of each state to decide the issue expeditiously and the procedures necessary to present the evidence; and

  (8) The familiarity of the court of each state with the facts and issues in the pending litigation.

(c) If a court of this state determines that it is an inconvenient forum and that a court of another state is a more appropriate forum, it shall stay the proceedings upon condition that a child custody proceeding be promptly commenced in another designated state and may impose any other condition the court considers just and proper.

(d) A court of this state may decline to exercise its jurisdiction under this article if a child custody determination is incidental to an action for divorce or another proceeding while still retaining jurisdiction over the divorce or other proceeding.

§ 19-9-68. Wrongfully obtained jurisdiction; actions to prevent repetition of unjustifiable conduct; expenses

(a) Except as otherwise provided in Code Section 19-9-64 or by any other law of this state, if a court of this state has jurisdiction under this article because a person seeking to invoke its jurisdiction has engaged in unjustifiable conduct, the court shall decline to exercise its jurisdiction unless:

  (1) The parents and all persons acting as parents have acquiesced in the exercise of jurisdiction;

  (2) A court of the state otherwise having jurisdiction under Code Sections 19-9-61 through 19-9-63 determines that this state is a more appropriate forum under Code Section 19-9-67; or

  (3) No court of any other state would have jurisdiction under the criteria specified in Code Sections 19-9-61 through 19-9-63.

(b) If a court of this state declines to exercise its jurisdiction pursuant to subsection (a) of this Code section, it may fashion an appropriate remedy to ensure the safety of the child and prevent a repetition of the unjustifiable conduct, including staying the proceeding until a child custody proceeding is commenced in a court having jurisdiction under Code Sections 19-9-61 through 19-9-63.

(c) If a court dismisses a petition or stays a proceeding because it declines to exercise its jurisdiction pursuant to subsection (a) of this Code section, it shall assess against the party seeking to invoke its jurisdiction necessary and reasonable expenses including costs, communication expenses, attorney's fees, investigative fees, expenses for witnesses, travel expenses, and child care during the course of the proceedings, unless the party from whom fees are sought establishes that the assessment would be clearly inappropriate. The court may not assess fees, costs, or expenses against this state unless authorized by law other than this article.

§ 19-9-69. Information required as part of pleading or affidavit; continuing duty; sealing of information; children residing in family violence shelters

(a) In a child custody proceeding, each party, in its first pleading or in an attached affidavit, shall give information, if reasonably ascertainable, under oath as to the child's present address or whereabouts, the places where the child has lived during the last five years, and the names and present addresses of the persons with whom the child has lived during that period. The pleading or affidavit must state whether the party:

(1) Has participated, as a party or witness or in any other capacity, in any other proceeding concerning the custody of or visitation with the child and, if so, identify the court, the case number, and the date of the child custody determination, if any;

(2) Knows of any proceeding that could affect the current proceeding, including proceedings for enforcement and proceedings relating to family violence, protective orders, termination of parental rights, and adoptions and, if so, identify the court, the case number, and the nature of the proceeding; and

(3) Knows the names and addresses of any person not a party to the proceeding who has physical custody of the child or claims rights of legal custody or physical custody of, or visitation with, the child and, if so, the names and addresses of those persons.

(b) If the information required by subsection (a) of this Code section is not furnished, the court, upon motion of a party or its own motion, may stay the proceeding until the information is furnished.

(c) If the declaration as to any of the items described in paragraphs (1) through (3) of subsection (a) of this Code section is in the affirmative, the declarant shall give additional information under oath as required by the court. The court may examine the parties under oath as to details of the information furnished and other matters pertinent to the court's jurisdiction and the disposition of the case.

(d) Each party has a continuing duty to inform the court of any proceeding in this or any other state that could affect the current proceeding.

(e) If a party alleges in an affidavit or a pleading under oath that the health, safety, or liberty of a party or child would be jeopardized by disclosure of identifying information, the information must be sealed and may not be disclosed to the other party or the public unless the court orders the disclosure to be made after a hearing in which the court takes into consideration the health, safety, or liberty of the party or child and determines that the disclosure is in the interest of justice.

(f) In providing the information required by subsection (a) of this Code section, a party who is disclosing that the child is or has been a resident of a family violence shelter shall provide only the name of the shelter and the state in which the shelter is located to avoid a violation of Code Section 19-13-23. A disclosure of the name of the shelter and the state in which the shelter is located shall be sufficient for the purposes of subsection (a) of this Code section.

§ 19-9-70. Requiring appearance for in state and out of state residents; other court orders

(a) In a child custody proceeding in this state, the court may order a party to the proceeding who is in this state to appear before the court in person with or without the child. The court may order any person who is in this state and who has physical custody or control of the child to appear in person with the child.

(b) If a party to a child custody proceeding whose presence is desired by the court is outside this state, the court may order that a notice given pursuant to Code Section 19-9-47 include a statement directing the party to appear in person with or without the child and informing the party that failure to appear may result in a decision adverse to the party.

(c) The court may enter any orders necessary to ensure the safety of the child and of any person ordered to appear under this Code section.

(d) If a party to a child custody proceeding who is outside this state is directed to appear under subsection (b) of this Code section or desires to appear personally before the court with or without the child, the court may require another party to pay reasonable and necessary travel and other expenses of the party so appearing and of the child.

§ 19-9-81. Definitions

As used in this part, the term:
(1) "Petitioner" means a person who seeks enforcement of an order for return of a child under the Hague Convention on the Civil Aspects of International Child Abduction or enforcement of a child custody determination.
(2) "Respondent" means a person against whom a proceeding has been commenced for enforcement of an order for return of a child under the Hague Convention on the Civil Aspects of International Child Abduction or enforcement of a child custody determination.

§ 19-9-82. Orders made under the Hague Convention

Under this part a court of this state may enforce an order for the return of the child made under the Hague Convention on the Civil Aspects of International Child Abduction as if it were a child custody determination.

§ 19-9-83. Recognition of foreign custody decrees; remedies

(a) A court of this state shall recognize and enforce a child custody determination of a court of another state if the latter court exercised jurisdiction in substantial conformity with this article or the determination was made under factual circumstances meeting the jurisdictional standards of this article and the determination has not been modified in accordance with this article.
(b) A court of this state may utilize any remedy available under other laws of this state to enforce a child custody determination made by a court of another state. The remedies provided in this part are cumulative and do not affect the availability of other remedies to enforce a child custody determination.

§ 19-9-84. Authority to enter temporary orders if lacking jurisdiction; remedy from court with jurisdiction; victims of family violence

(a) A court of this state which does not have jurisdiction to modify a child custody determination may issue a temporary order enforcing:
(1) A visitation schedule made by a court of another state; or
(2) The visitation provisions of a child custody determination of another state that does not provide for a specific visitation schedule.
(b) If a court of this state makes an order under paragraph (2) of subsection (a) of this Code section, it shall specify in the order a period that it considers adequate to allow the petitioner to obtain an order from a court having jurisdiction under the criteria specified in Part 2 of this article. The order remains in effect until an order is obtained from the other court or the period expires.
(c) If a court of another state or a court of this state has made a finding of family violence on the part of either parent of the child, in issuing a temporary order enforcing a visitation schedule or the visitation provisions of a child custody determination of another state in accordance with subsection (a) of this Code section, a court of this state may enter any orders necessary to ensure the safety of the child and of any person who has been the victim of family violence, including but not limited to an order for supervised visitation pursuant to Code Section 19-9-7.

§ 19-9-85. Registering foreign custody determinations; requirements of registering court; contesting registration; confirmation of registered order

(a) A child custody determination issued by a court of another state may be registered in this state, with or without a simultaneous request for enforcement, by sending to the superior court in the appropriate venue in this state:
(1) A letter or other document requesting registration;
(2) Two copies, including one certified copy, of the determination sought to be registered, and a statement under penalty of perjury that to the best of the knowledge and belief of the person seeking registration the order has not been modified; and
(3) Except as otherwise provided in Code Section 19-9-69, the name and address of the person seeking registration and any parent or person acting as a parent who has been awarded custody or visitation in the child custody determination sought to be registered.
(b) On receipt of the documents required by subsection (a) of this Code section, the registering court shall:

(1) Cause the determination to be filed as a foreign judgment, together with one copy of any accompanying documents and information, regardless of their form; and

(2) Serve notice upon the persons named pursuant to paragraph (3) of subsection (a) of this Code section and provide them with an opportunity to contest the registration in accordance with this Code section.

(c) The notice required by paragraph (2) of subsection (b) of this Code section must state that:

(1) A registered determination is enforceable as of the date of the registration in the same manner as a determination issued by a court of this state;

(2) A hearing to contest the validity of the registered determination must be requested within 20 days after service of notice; and

(3) Failure to contest the registration will result in confirmation of the child custody determination and preclude further contest of that determination with respect to any matter that could have been asserted.

(d) A person seeking to contest the validity of a registered order must request a hearing within 20 days after service of the notice. At that hearing, the court shall confirm the registered order unless the person contesting registration establishes that:

(1) The issuing court did not have jurisdiction under Part 2 of this article;

(2) The child custody determination sought to be registered has been vacated, stayed, or modified by a court having jurisdiction to do so under Part 2 of this article; or

(3) The person contesting registration was entitled to notice, but notice was not given in accordance with the standards of Code Section 19-9-47 in the proceedings before the court that issued the order for which registration is sought.

(e) If a timely request for a hearing to contest the validity of the registration is not made, the registration is confirmed as a matter of law, and the person requesting registration and all persons served must be notified of the confirmation.

(f) Confirmation of a registered order, whether by operation of law or after notice and hearing, precludes further contest of the order with respect to any matter that could have been asserted at the time of registration.

§ 19-9-86. Granting relief and enforcing registered custody determinations

(a) A court of this state may grant any relief normally available under the laws of this state to enforce a registered child custody determination made by a court of another state.

(b) A court of this state shall recognize and enforce, but may not modify, except in accordance with Part 2 of this article, a registered child custody determination of a court of another state.

§ 19-9-87. Communication between enforcing court and modifying court

If a proceeding for enforcement under this part is commenced in a court of this state and the court determines that a proceeding to modify the determination is pending in a court of another state having jurisdiction to modify the determination under Part 2 of this article, the enforcing court shall immediately communicate with the modifying court. The proceeding for enforcement continues unless the enforcing court, after consultation with the modifying court, stays or dismisses the proceeding.

§ 19-9-88. Verification and petition for enforcement requirements; sealing; appearance; expenses

(a) A petition under this part must be verified. Certified copies of all orders sought to be enforced and of any order confirming registration must be attached to the petition. A copy of a certified copy of an order may be attached instead of the original.

(b) A petition for enforcement of a child custody determination must state:

(1) Whether the court that issued the determination identified the jurisdictional basis it relied upon in exercising jurisdiction and, if so, what the basis was;

(2) Whether the determination for which enforcement is sought has been vacated, stayed, or modified by a court whose decision must be enforced under this article and, if so, identify the court, the case number, and the nature of the proceeding;

(3) Whether any proceeding has been commenced that could affect the current proceeding, including proceedings relating to family violence, protective orders, termination of parental rights, and adoptions and, if so, identify the court, the case number, and the nature of the proceeding;

(4) The present physical address of the child and the respondent, if known, except in cases involving a parent who has been the subject of a finding of family violence by a court of this state or another state;

(5) Whether relief in addition to the immediate physical custody of the child and attorney's fees is sought, including a request for assistance from law enforcement officials and, if so, the relief sought; and

(6) If the child custody determination has been registered and confirmed under Code Section 19-9-85, the date and place of registration.

(c) If a party alleges in an affidavit or pleading under oath that the health, safety, or liberty of a party or child would be jeopardized by disclosure of information required by this Code section, the information must be sealed and may not be disclosed to the other party or the public unless the court orders the disclosure to be made after a hearing in which the court takes into consideration the health, safety, or liberty of the party or child and determines that the disclosure is in the interest of justice.

(d) Upon the filing of a petition, the court shall issue an order directing the respondent to appear in person with or without the child at a hearing and may enter any order necessary to ensure the safety of the parties and the child. The hearing must be held on the next judicial day after service of the order unless that date is impossible. In that event, the court shall hold the hearing on the first judicial day possible. The court may extend the date of hearing at the request of the petitioner.

(e) An order issued under subsection (d) of this Code section must state the time and place of the hearing and advise the respondent that at the hearing the court will order that the petitioner may take immediate physical custody of the child and the payment of fees, costs, and expenses under Code Section 19-9-92, and may schedule a hearing to determine whether further relief is appropriate, unless the respondent appears and establishes that:

(1) The child custody determination has not been registered and confirmed under Code Section 19-9-85 and that:

(A) The issuing court did not have jurisdiction under Part 2 of this article;

(B) The child custody determination for which enforcement is sought has been vacated, stayed, or modified by a court having jurisdiction to do so under Part 2 of this article;

(C) The respondent was entitled to notice, but notice was not given in accordance with the standards of Code Section 19-9-47, in the proceedings before the court that issued the order for which enforcement is sought; or

(2) The child custody determination for which enforcement is sought was registered and confirmed under Code Section 19-9-85, but has been vacated, stayed, or modified by a court of a state having jurisdiction to do so under Part 2 of this article.

§ 19-9-89. Service of petitions and orders

Except as otherwise provided in Code Section 19-9-91, the petition and order must be served, by any method authorized by the laws of this state, upon respondent and any person who has physical custody of the child.

§ 19-9-90. Finding of immediate physical custody; awarding of fees, costs, and expenses; drawing adverse inference from refusal to testify; spousal relationship irrelevant

(a) Unless the court issues a temporary emergency order pursuant to Code Section 19-9-64, upon a finding that a petitioner is entitled to immediate physical custody of the child, the court shall order that the petitioner may take immediate physical custody of the child unless the respondent establishes that:

(1) The child custody determination has not been registered and confirmed under Code Section 19-9-85 and that:

(A) The issuing court did not have jurisdiction under Part 2 of this article;

(B) The child custody determination for which enforcement is sought has been vacated, stayed, or modified by a court of a state having jurisdiction to do so under Part 2 of this article; or

(C) The respondent was entitled to notice, but notice was not given in accordance with the standards of Code Section 19-9-47, in the proceedings before the court that issued the order for which enforcement is sought; or

(2) The child custody determination for which enforcement is sought was registered and confirmed under Code Section 19-9-85 but has been vacated, stayed, or modified by a court of a state having jurisdiction to do so under Part 2 of this article.

(b) The court shall award the fees, costs, and expenses authorized under Code Section 19-9-92 and may grant additional relief, including a request for the assistance of law enforcement officials, and set a further hearing to determine whether additional relief is appropriate.

(c) If a party called to testify refuses to answer on the ground that the testimony may be self-incriminating, the court may draw an adverse inference from the refusal.

(d) A privilege against disclosure of communications between spouses and a defense of immunity based on the relationship of husband and wife or parent and child may not be invoked in a proceeding under this part.

§ 19-9-91. Verified application for warrant seeking physical custody; requirement for serious physical harm; warrant requirements; enforceability; conditions

(a) Upon the filing of a petition seeking enforcement of a child custody determination, the petitioner may file a verified application for the issuance of a warrant to take physical custody of the child if the child is immediately likely to suffer serious physical harm or be removed from this state.
(b) If the court, upon the testimony of the petitioner or other witness, finds that the child is imminently likely to suffer serious physical harm or be removed from this state, it may issue a warrant to take physical custody of the child. The petition must be heard on the next judicial day after the warrant is executed unless that date is impossible. In that event, the court shall hold the hearing on the first judicial day possible. The application for the warrant must include the statements required by subsection (b) of Code Section 19-9-88.
(c) A warrant to take physical custody of a child must:
   (1) Recite the facts upon which a conclusion of imminent serious physical harm or removal from the jurisdiction is based;
   (2) Direct law enforcement officers to take physical custody of the child immediately; and
   (3) Provide for the placement of the child pending final relief.
(d) The respondent must be served with the petition, warrant, and order immediately after the child is taken into physical custody.
(e) A warrant to take physical custody of a child is enforceable throughout this state. If the court finds on the basis of the testimony of the petitioner or other witness that a less intrusive remedy is not effective, it may authorize law enforcement officers to enter private property to take physical custody of the child. If required by exigent circumstances of the case, the court may authorize law enforcement officers to make a forcible entry at any hour.
(f) The court may impose conditions upon placement of a child to ensure the appearance of the child and the child's custodian.

§ 19-9-92. Awarding of necessary and reasonable expenses

(a) The court shall award the prevailing party, including a state, necessary and reasonable expenses incurred by or on behalf of the party, including costs, communication expenses, attorney's fees, investigative fees, expenses for witnesses, travel expenses, and child care during the course of the proceedings, unless the party from whom fees or expenses are sought establishes that the award would be clearly inappropriate.
(b) The court may not assess fees, costs, or expenses against a state unless authorized by law other than this article.

§ 19-9-93. Full faith and credit to orders of other states

A court of this state shall accord full faith and credit to an order issued by another state and consistent with this article which enforces a child custody determination by a court of another state unless the order has been vacated, stayed, or modified by a court having jurisdiction to do so under Part 2 of this article.

§ 19-9-94. Appeals

An appeal may be taken from a final order in a proceeding under this article in accordance with expedited appellate procedures in other civil cases. Unless the court enters a temporary emergency order under Code Section 19-9-64, the enforcing court may not stay an order enforcing a child custody determination pending appeal.

§ 19-9-95. Actions by district attorney

(a) In a case arising under this article or involving the Hague Convention on the Civil Aspects of International Child Abduction, the district attorney may take any lawful action, including resort to a proceeding under this part or any other available civil proceeding to locate a child, obtain the return of a child, or enforce a child custody determination if there is:
   (1) An existing child custody determination;
   (2) A request to do so from a court in a pending child custody proceeding;
   (3) A reasonable belief that a criminal statute has been violated; or
   (4) A reasonable belief that the child has been wrongfully removed or retained in violation of the Hague Convention on the Civil Aspects of International Child Abduction.
(b) A district attorney acting under this Code section acts on behalf of the court and may not represent any party.

§ 19-9-96. Assistance by law enforcement

At the request of a district attorney acting under Code Section 19-9-95, a law enforcement officer may take any lawful action reasonably necessary to locate a child or a party and assist a district attorney with responsibilities under Code Section 19-9-95.

§ 19-9-97. Recovering expenses of district attorney and law enforcement

If the respondent is not the prevailing party, the court may assess against the respondent all direct expenses and costs incurred by the district attorney and law enforcement officers under Code Section 19-9-95 or 19-9-96.

§ 19-9-101. Promotion of uniformity between states

In applying and construing this uniform Act, consideration must be given to the need to promote uniformity of the law with respect to its subject matter among states that enact it.

§ 19-9-102. Application

A motion or other request for relief made in a child custody proceeding or to enforce a child custody determination which was commenced before July 1, 2001, is governed by the law in effect at the time the motion or other request was made.

§ 19-9-103. Construction

This article shall not be construed to repeal, amend, or impair the provisions of Code Section 19-13-23.

§ 19-9-104. Conflicts with Child Custody Intrastate Jurisdiction Act

In the event of any conflict between this article and Article 2 of this chapter, the "Georgia Child Custody Intrastate Jurisdiction Act of 1978," this article shall apply.

ARTICLE 4. POWER OF ATTORNEY FOR THE CARE OF A MINOR CHILD

§ 19-9-120. (Effective until September 1, 2018) Short title

This article shall be known and may be cited as the "Power of Attorney for the Care of a Minor Child Act."

§ 19-9-121. (Effective until September 1, 2018) Definitions

As used in this article, the term:
(1) "Grandchild" means the minor child of a grandparent.
(2) "Grandparent" shall have the same meaning as provided in subsection (a) of Code Section 19-7-3 and shall include the biological great-grandparent or stepgreat-grandparent who is the parent or stepparent of a grandparent of a minor child.
(3) "Parent" shall have the same meaning as provided in Code Section 19-3-37. Such term used in the singular shall mean both parents if both parents share joint legal custody of the child, unless otherwise clearly indicated.
(4) "Reasonable evidence" means evidence that a reasonable person would find sufficient to determine whether one conclusion is more likely than another.
(5) "School" means:
  (A) Any county or independent school system as defined in Code Section 20-1-9;
  (B) Any private school as such term is defined in Code Section 20-2-690;
  (C) A home study program meeting the requirements set forth in subsection (c) of Code Section 20-2-690;
  (D) Pre-kindergarten programs; or

(E) Early care and education programs as such term is defined in paragraph (6) of Code Section 20-1A-2.
(6) "School term" means the part of the year in which school is in session.
(7) "Serious illness" means a physical or mental illness as determined by a licensed health care professional, including a psychiatrist or psychologist, that causes the parent to be unable to care for the minor child due to the physical or mental condition or health of the parent, including a condition created by medical treatment.
(8) "Terminal illness" has the same meaning as the term "terminal condition" as provided in paragraph (14) of Code Section 31-32-2.

§ 19-9-122. (Effective until September 1, 2018) Delegation of authority; hardships; exception

(a) A parent of a minor child may delegate to any grandparent residing in this state caregiving authority regarding the minor child when hardship prevents the parent from caring for the child. This authority may be delegated without the approval of a court by executing in writing a power of attorney for the care of a minor child in a form substantially complying with the provisions of this article.
(b) Hardships may include, but are not limited to:
  (1) A parent being unable to provide care due to the death of the other parent;
  (2) A serious illness or terminal illness of a parent;
  (3) The physical or mental condition of the parent or the child such that proper care and supervision of the child cannot be provided by the parent;
  (4) The incarceration of a parent;
  (5) The loss or uninhabitability of the child's home as the result of a natural disaster; or
  (6) A period of active military duty of a parent exceeding 24 months.
(c) Hardship shall not include the granting of a power of attorney for the care of a minor child for the purpose of subverting an investigation of the child's welfare initiated by the Department of Human Services or other agency responsible for such investigations.

§ 19-9-123. (Effective until September 1, 2018) Powers granted by power of attorney

Through the power of attorney for the care of a minor child, the parent may authorize the agent grandparent to perform the following functions:
  (1) Enroll the child in school and in extracurricular activities;
  (2) Enroll the child in any health insurance program offered to the grandparent;
  (3) Provide access to school records and may disclose the contents to others;
  (4) Arrange for and consent to medical, dental, and mental health treatment for the child;
  (5) Provide access to medical, dental, and mental health records and may disclose the contents thereof to others;
  (6) Provide for the child's food, lodging, housing, recreation, and travel; and
  (7) Any additional powers as specified by the parent.

§ 19-9-124. (Effective until September 1, 2018) Liability; education; compliance with court orders

(a) An agent grandparent under a power of attorney for the care of a minor child shall act in the best interests of the minor child. Such agent grandparent shall not be liable for consenting or refusing to consent to medical, dental, or mental health care for a minor child when such decision is made in good faith and is exercised in the best interests of the minor child.
(b) (1) The agent grandparent shall have the right to enroll the minor child in a public school serving the area where the agent grandparent resides and may enroll the minor child in a private school, pre-kindergarten program, or home study program.
  (2) The public school shall allow such agent grandparent with a properly executed power of attorney for the care of a minor child to enroll the minor child.
  (3) At the time of enrollment the grandparent shall provide to the school such residency documentation as is customary in that school district.
  (4) The school may request reasonable evidence of the stated hardship.
  (5) If a public school denies enrollment of a minor child under this Code section, such denial may be appealed and shall be treated as any other denial of enrollment of a child in that school district, including all of the remedies otherwise available when enrollment is denied to a child.
  (6) Except where limited by federal law, the agent grandparent shall have the same rights, duties, and responsibilities that would otherwise be exercised by the parent pursuant to the laws of this state.
  (7) An agent grandparent shall be obligated to comply with any existing court order relative to the child, including, but not limited to, any visitation order.

§ 19-9-125. (Effective until September 1, 2018) Protection from criminal or civil liability

No person, school official, or health care provider who acts in good faith reliance on a power of attorney for the care of a minor child shall be subject to criminal or civil liability or professional disciplinary action for such reliance.

§ 19-9-126. (Effective until September 1, 2018) Grant of temporary written permission for emergency services

Nothing in this article shall preclude a parent or agent grandparent from granting temporary written permission to seek emergency medical treatment or other services for a minor child while in the custody of an adult who is not the parent or agent grandparent and who is temporarily supervising the child at the parent's or agent grandparent's request.

§ 19-9-127. (Effective until September 1, 2018) Violations; execution of power of attorney; power of attorney to be signed and acknowledged

(a) Except as may be permitted by the federal No Child Left Behind Act, 20 U.S.C.A. Section 6301, et seq., and Section 7801, et seq., a parent executing the power of attorney for the care of a minor child shall certify that such action is not for the primary purpose of enrolling the child in a school for the sole purpose of participating in the academic or interscholastic athletic programs provided by that school or for any other unlawful purpose. Violation of this subsection shall be punishable in accordance with Georgia law and may require, in addition to any other remedies, repayment by such parent or grandparent of all costs incurred by the school as a result of the violation.
(b) (1) The instrument providing for the power of attorney for the care of a minor child shall be executed by both parents, if both parents are living and have joint legal custody of the minor child, and shall specify which hardship prevents the parent or parents from caring for the child. If the parents do not have joint legal custody, the parent having sole permanent legal custody shall have authority to grant the power of attorney.
(2) The power of attorney for the care of a minor child shall be signed and acknowledged before a notary public by the parent executing the power of attorney. Any noncustodial parent shall be notified in writing of the name and address of the grandparent who has been appointed the agent grandparent under the power of attorney. The executing parent shall send the notification by certified mail or statutory overnight delivery, return receipt requested, to the noncustodial parent at the noncustodial parent's last known address within five days of the execution of the power of attorney. A noncustodial parent who has joint legal custody shall have the same authority to execute a revocation of the power of attorney as granted to the custodial parent.
(c) If only one parent has sole permanent legal custody of the minor child, then that parent shall have authority to execute the power of attorney for the care of a minor child and to revoke the power of attorney.

§ 19-9-128. (Effective until September 1, 2018) Revocation of power of attorney; termination of power of attorney; resignation of agent grandparent

(a) (1) The agent grandparent shall have the authority to act on behalf of the minor child until each parent who executed the power of attorney for the care of a minor child revokes the power of attorney in writing and provides notice of the revocation to the agent grandparent as provided in this Code section.
(2) The agent grandparent shall have the authority to act on behalf of the child until a copy of the revocation of the power of attorney is received by certified mail or statutory overnight delivery, return receipt requested, and upon receipt of the revocation the agent grandparent shall cease to act as agent.
(3) The parent shall send a copy of the revocation of the power of attorney to the agent grandparent within five days of the execution of the revocation by certified mail or statutory overnight delivery, return receipt requested.
(4) The revoking parent shall notify the school, health care providers, and others known to the parent to have relied upon such power of attorney.
(b) The power of attorney for the care of a minor child may also be terminated by any order of a court of competent jurisdiction.
(c) (1) The agent grandparent shall notify the school in which the agent grandparent had enrolled the child whenever a change in circumstances results in a change in residence for such child that is expected to last more than six weeks during a school term and such change in residence is not due to hospitalization, vacation, study abroad, or some reason otherwise acceptable to the school.
(2) The agent grandparent may resign by notifying the parent in writing by certified mail or statutory overnight delivery, return receipt requested, and, if the agent grandparent is aware that the parent's

hardship still exists, such agent grandparent shall also notify child protective services or such government authority that is charged with assuring proper care of such minor child.

(3) Upon the death of the authorizing parent, the agent grandparent shall notify the surviving parent as soon as practicable. With consent of the surviving parent or if the whereabouts of the surviving parent are unknown, the power of attorney for the care of a minor child may continue for up to six months so that the child may receive consistent care until more permanent custody arrangements are made.

(d) The authority to designate an agent to act on behalf of a minor child is in addition to any other lawful action a parent may take for the benefit of such minor child, and the parent shall continue to have the right to medical, dental, mental health, and school records pertaining to the minor child.

§ 19-9-129. (Effective until September 1, 2018) Power of attorney form

(a) The statutory power of attorney for the care of a minor child form contained in this Code section may be used to grant an agent grandparent powers over the minor child's enrollment in school, medical, dental, and mental health care, food, lodging, recreation, travel, and any additional powers as specified by the parent. This power of attorney is not intended to be exclusive. No provision of this article shall be construed to bar use by the parent of any other or different form of power of attorney for the care of a minor child which complies with this article. A power of attorney for the care of a minor child in substantially the form set forth in this Code section shall have the same meaning and effect as prescribed in this article. Substantially similar forms may include forms from other states.

(b) The power of attorney for the care of a minor child shall be in substantially the following form:

"GEORGIA POWER OF ATTORNEY FOR THE CARE OF A MINOR CHILD

NOTICE:

(1) THE PURPOSE OF THIS POWER OF ATTORNEY IS TO GIVE THE GRANDPARENT THAT YOU DESIGNATE (THE AGENT GRANDPARENT) POWERS TO CARE FOR YOUR MINOR CHILD, INCLUDING THE POWER TO: ENROLL THE CHILD IN SCHOOL AND IN EXTRACURRICULAR SCHOOL ACTIVITIES; HAVE ACCESS TO SCHOOL RECORDS AND DISCLOSE THE CONTENTS TO OTHERS; ARRANGE FOR AND CONSENT TO MEDICAL, DENTAL, AND MENTAL HEALTH TREATMENT FOR THE CHILD; HAVE ACCESS TO SUCH RECORDS RELATED TO TREATMENT OF THE CHILD AND DISCLOSE THE CONTENTS OF THOSE RECORDS TO OTHERS; PROVIDE FOR THE CHILD'S FOOD, LODGING, RECREATION, AND TRAVEL; AND HAVE ANY ADDITIONAL POWERS AS SPECIFIED BY THE PARENT.
(2) THE AGENT GRANDPARENT IS REQUIRED TO EXERCISE DUE CARE TO ACT IN THE CHILD'S BEST INTEREST AND IN ACCORDANCE WITH THE GRANT OF AUTHORITY SPECIFIED IN THIS FORM.
(3) A COURT OF COMPETENT JURISDICTION MAY REVOKE THE POWERS OF THE AGENT GRANDPARENT IF IT FINDS THAT THE AGENT GRANDPARENT IS NOT ACTING PROPERLY.
(4) THE AGENT GRANDPARENT MAY EXERCISE THE POWERS GIVEN IN THIS POWER OF ATTORNEY FOR THE CARE OF A MINOR CHILD THROUGHOUT THE CHILD'S MINORITY UNLESS THE PARENT REVOKES THIS POWER OF ATTORNEY AND PROVIDES NOTICE OF THE REVOCATION TO THE AGENT GRANDPARENT OR UNTIL A COURT OF COMPETENT JURISDICTION TERMINATES THIS POWER.
(5) THE AGENT GRANDPARENT MAY RESIGN AS AGENT AND MUST IMMEDIATELY COMMUNICATE SUCH RESIGNATION TO THE PARENT, AND IF COMMUNICATION WITH SUCH PARENT IS NOT POSSIBLE, THE AGENT GRANDPARENT SHALL NOTIFY CHILD PROTECTIVE SERVICES OR SUCH GOVERNMENT AUTHORITY THAT IS CHARGED WITH ASSURING PROPER CARE OF SUCH MINOR CHILD.
(6) THIS POWER OF ATTORNEY MAY BE REVOKED IN WRITING BY ANY AUTHORIZING PARENT. IF THE POWER OF ATTORNEY IS REVOKED, THE REVOKING PARENT SHALL

NOTIFY THE AGENT GRANDPARENT, SCHOOL, HEALTH CARE PROVIDERS, AND OTHERS KNOWN TO THE PARENT TO HAVE RELIED UPON SUCH POWER OF ATTORNEY.

(7) IF THERE IS ANYTHING ABOUT THIS FORM THAT YOU DO NOT UNDERSTAND, YOU SHOULD ASK A LAWYER TO EXPLAIN IT TO YOU.

POWER OF ATTORNEY FOR THE CARE OF A MINOR CHILD

made this   day of   ,   .

(1) (A) I,   (insert name and address of parent or parents), hereby appoint   (insert name and address of grandparent to be named as agent) as attorney in fact (the agent grandparent) for my child   (insert name of child) to act for me and in my name in any way that I could act in person.

(B) I hereby certify that the agent grandparent named herein is the (place a check mark beside the appropriate description):

Biological grandparent;

Stepgrandparent;

Biological great-grandparent; or

Stepgreat-grandparent.

(2) The agent grandparent may:

(A) Enroll the child in school and in extracurricular activities, have access to school records, and may disclose the contents to others;

(B) Arrange for and consent to medical, dental, and mental health treatment of the child, have access to such records related to treatment of the child, and disclose the contents of such records to others;

(C) Provide for the child's food, lodging, recreation, and travel; and

(D) Carry out any additional powers specified by the parent as follows:

(3) The powers granted above shall not include the following powers or shall be subject to the following rules or limitations (here you may include any specific limitations that you deem appropriate):

(4) This power of attorney for the care of a minor child is being executed because of the following hardship (initial all that apply):

(A) The death, serious illness, or terminal illness of a parent;

(B) The physical or mental condition of the parent or the child such that proper care and supervision of the child cannot be provided by the parent;

(C) The loss or uninhabitability of the child's home as the result of a natural disaster;

    (D) The incarceration of a parent; or

    (E) A period of active military duty of a parent.

  (5) (Optional) If a guardian of my minor child is to be appointed, I nominate the following person to serve as such guardian: (insert name and address of person nominated to be guardian of the minor child).

  (6) I am fully informed as to all of the contents of this form and I understand the full import of this grant of powers to the agent grandparent.

  (7) I certify that the minor child is not emancipated, and, if the minor child becomes emancipated, this power of attorney shall no longer be valid.

  (8) Except as may be permitted by the federal No Child Left Behind Act, 20 U.S.C.A. Section 6301, et seq., and Section 7801, et seq., I hereby certify that this power of attorney is not executed for the primary purpose of unlawfully enrolling the child in a school so that the child may participate in the academic or interscholastic athletic programs provided by that school.

  (9) I certify that, to my knowledge, the minor child's welfare is not the subject of an investigation by the Department of Human Services.

  (10) I declare under penalty of perjury under the laws of the State of Georgia that the foregoing is true and correct.

Parent Signature:

Printed name:

Parent Signature:

Printed name:

Signed and sealed in the presence of:
    Notary public

        My commission expires
"
(c) The following notice shall be attached to the power of attorney:

"ADDITIONAL INFORMATION:

To the grandparent designated as attorney in fact:

(1) If a change in circumstances results in the child not living with you for more than six weeks during a school term and such change is not due to hospitalization, vacation, study abroad, or some reason otherwise acceptable to the school, you should notify in writing the school in which you have enrolled the child and to which you have given this power of attorney form.

(2) You have the authority to act on behalf of the minor child until each parent who executed the power of attorney for the care of the minor child revokes the power of attorney in writing and provides notice of revocation to you as provided in O.C.G.A. Section 19-9-128.

(3) If you are made aware of the death of the parent who executed the power of attorney, you must notify the surviving parent as soon as practicable. With the consent of the surviving parent, or if the whereabouts of the surviving parent are unknown, the power of attorney may continue for up to six months so that the child may receive consistent care until more permanent custody arrangements are made.

(4) You may resign as agent by notifying each parent in writing by certified mail or statutory overnight delivery, return receipt requested, and if you become unable to care for the child, you shall cause such resignation to be communicated to the parent. If communication with such parent is not possible, you must notify child protective services or such government authority that is charged with assuring proper care of such minor child.

To school officials:

(1) Except as provided in the policies and regulations of the county school board and the federal No Child Left Behind Act, 20 U.S.C.A. Section 6301, et seq., and Section 7801, et seq., this power of attorney, properly completed and notarized, authorizes the agent grandparent named herein to enroll the child named herein in school in the district in which the agent grandparent resides. That agent grandparent is authorized to provide consent in all school related matters and to obtain from the school district educational and behavioral information about the child. Furthermore, this power of attorney shall not prohibit the parent of the child from having access to all school records pertinent to the child.

(2) The school district may require such residency documentation as is customary in that school district.

(3) No school official who acts in good faith reliance on a power of attorney for the care of a minor child shall be subject to criminal or civil liability or professional disciplinary action for such reliance.

To health care providers:

(1) No health care provider who acts in good faith reliance on a power of attorney for the care of a minor child shall be subject to criminal or civil liability or professional disciplinary action for such reliance.

(2) The parent continues to have the right to all medical, dental, and mental health records pertaining to the minor child."

ARTICLE NOTES
ARTICLE 4. POWER OF ATTORNEY FOR THE CARE OF A CHILD
§ 19-9-120. (Effective September 1, 2018) Short title

This article shall be known and may be cited as the "Supporting and Strengthening Families Act."

§ 19-9-121. (Effective September 1, 2018) Definitions

As used in this article, the term:
(1) "Child" means an unemancipated individual who is under 18 years of age.
(2) "Child-placing agency" means an agency licensed as such pursuant to Chapter 5 of Title 49.
(3) "Criminal background check" means the results of an unrestricted search of the criminal records maintained by the Georgia Crime Information Center and the Federal Bureau of Investigation pursuant to Code Section 35-3-34.
(4) "Department" means the Department of Human Services.
(5) "Nonprofit entity or faith based organization" means a business that provides child or family services and that is in good standing with the Internal Revenue Service, if applicable.
(6) "Parent" shall have the same meaning as provided in Code Section 19-3-37.

§ 19-9-122. (Effective September 1, 2018) Delegation of child caregiving authority

A parent of a child may delegate caregiving authority regarding such child to an individual who is an adult, who resides in this state, and who is the grandparent, great-grandparent, stepparent, former stepparent, step-grandparent, aunt, uncle, great aunt, great uncle, cousin, or sibling of such child or is a nonrelative who is approved as an agent by a child-placing agency or a nonprofit entity or faith based organization for a period not to exceed one year, except as provided in Code Section 19-9-132, by executing a power of attorney that substantially complies with this article.

§ 19-9-123. (Effective September 1, 2018) Reporting requirement from nonprofit entities or faith based organizations; departmental responsibilities and liabilities; regulation

(a) A nonprofit entity or faith based organization that is not licensed by the department but is providing services under this article shall annually provide the department with the following information:
(1) Its legal name, address, telephone number, e-mail address, and any other contact information;
(2) The name of its director;
(3) The names and addresses of the officers and members of its governing body;
(4) The total number of approved volunteer families with which it works; and
(5) The total number of children served in the previous calendar year.
(b) The department shall maintain a list of nonprofit entities or faith based organizations for which it has been provided the information required by subsection (a) of this Code section.
(c) The department may refer an individual who is seeking to execute a power of attorney under this article to a nonprofit entity or faith based organization if the information required by subsection (a) of this Code section has been provided. The department shall not be liable for civil damages or be subject to any claim, demand, cause of action, or proceeding of any nature as a result of referring such individual to a nonprofit entity or faith based organization.
(d) The department shall promulgate rules and regulations in order to implement this Code section.

§ 19-9-124. (Effective September 1, 2018) Parental limitation on delegation of power of attorney; rights, duties, and responsibilities of agents; acknowledgment of acceptance of responsibilities; approval of agents; organizational and entity record keeping

(a)(1) A parent of a child may delegate to an agent in a power of attorney any power and authority regarding the care and custody of such child, except the power to consent to the marriage or adoption of such child, the performance or inducement of an abortion on or for such child, or the termination of parental rights to such child. Such power and authority may be delegated without the approval of a court, provided that such delegation of power and authority shall not operate to change or modify any parental or legal rights, obligations, or authority established by an existing court order, including a standing order, or deprive a parent of a child of any parental or legal rights, obligations, or authority regarding the custody, parenting time, visitation, or support of such child. Such delegation of power and authority shall not deprive or limit any support for a child that should be received by such child pursuant to a court order or for any other reason. When support is being collected for the child by the Child Support Enforcement Agency of the department, such agency shall be authorized to redirect support payments to the agent for the duration of the power of attorney or until the power of attorney is revoked or superseded by a court order.

(2) A power of attorney executed under this article during the pendency of a divorce or custody action shall be void ab initio unless executed or agreed upon by both parties to such action, if both parties have custodial rights to the child or the court presiding over such divorce or custody action enters an order allowing the execution of the power of attorney as being in the best interests of such child.

(b) Except as limited by federal law, this article, or the direction of a parent of a child as expressed in the power of attorney, an agent shall have the same rights, duties, and responsibilities that would otherwise be exercised by such parent of a child pursuant to the laws of this state.

(c) An agent shall acknowledge in writing his or her acceptance of the responsibility for caring for a child for the duration of the power of attorney and, if applicable, shall identify his or her association with a child-placing agency or nonprofit entity or faith based organization.

(d) An agent shall certify that he or she is not currently on the state sexual offender registry or child abuse registry of this state or the sexual offender registry or child abuse registry for any other state, a United States territory, the District of Columbia, or any American Indian tribe nor has he or she ever been required to register for any such registry.

(e) The individual executing a power of attorney shall require a prospective agent to provide him or her with a criminal background check if such agent is a nonrelative. At the time of executing such power of attorney, the individual executing it shall acknowledge having read and reviewed the prospective agent's criminal background check or shall waive such requirement if the prospective agent is the grandparent, great-grandparent, stepparent, former stepparent, step-grandparent, aunt, uncle, great aunt, great uncle, cousin, or sibling of such child.

(f) The agent under a power of attorney shall act in the best interests of the child. Such agent shall not be liable to the individual executing the power of attorney for consenting or refusing to consent to medical, dental, or mental health care for a child when such decision is made in good faith and is exercised in the best interests of the child.

(g) Each child-placing agency and nonprofit entity or faith based organization that assists with the execution of a power of attorney under this article shall maintain a record of all powers of attorney executed by agents approved by such agency, entity, or organization for at least five years after the expiration of such powers of attorney.

§ 19-9-125. (Effective September 1, 2018) Notice to noncustodial parent of execution of power of attorney; objection by noncustodial parent; compliance with relocation notice requirements

(a) An individual with sole custody of a child who executes a power of attorney authorized under this article shall provide written notice of such execution to the noncustodial parent by certified mail, return receipt requested, or statutory overnight delivery within 15 days after the date upon which such power of attorney was executed.

(b) A noncustodial parent receiving the notice as set forth in subsection (a) of this Code section may object to the execution of such power of attorney within 21 days of the delivery of such notice and shall serve his or her objection on the individual who executed such power of attorney by certified mail, return receipt requested, or statutory overnight delivery. An objection shall prohibit the action of a power of attorney under this article and the child shall be returned to the individual with sole custody.

(c) In addition to the notice provided for in subsection (a) of this Code section, an individual with sole custody of a child who executes a power of attorney under this article shall comply with any applicable relocation notice requirements under subsection (f) of Code Section 19-9-3.

§ 19-9-126. (Effective September 1, 2018) Impact of execution on parental rights

(a) The execution of a power of attorney under this article shall, in the absence of other evidence, not constitute abandonment, abuse, neglect, or any indication of unfitness as a parent.

(b) An individual shall not execute a power of attorney under this article with the intention of divesting or negating another individual's legal responsibility for the care of a child.

(c) The parental obligations set forth in Chapter 7 of this title to his or her child shall not be extinguished or serve as a defense when a parent executes a power of attorney. Any individual giving a power of attorney to a nonrelative shall carefully consider such agent's criminal background check, and such consideration shall not absolve the signer from liability.

(d) Nothing in this article shall prevent the Division of Family and Children Services of the department or law enforcement from investigating and taking appropriate action regarding allegations of abuse, neglect, abandonment, desertion, or other mistreatment of a child.

§ 19-9-127. (Effective September 1, 2018) Temporary written permission to seek emergency medical treatment or other services for children

Nothing in this article shall preclude a parent or agent from granting temporary written permission to seek emergency medical treatment or other services for a child while such child is in the custody of an adult who is not the parent or agent and who is temporarily supervising the child at the request of such parent or agent.

§ 19-9-128. (Effective September 1, 2018) No limitation on role of Division of Family and Children Services

An individual shall not execute a power of attorney under this article for the purpose of subverting an investigation of the child's welfare initiated by the Division of Family and Children Services of the department and shall not execute such power of attorney so long as the Division of Family and Children Services has an open child welfare and youth services case with regard to the child, his or her parent, or another child of the parent. Nothing in this article shall be construed to diminish or limit any rights, power, or authority of or by the Division of Family and Children Services for the protection of any child.

§ 19-9-129. (Effective September 1, 2018) Execution of power of attorney; probate court responsibilities; revocation or execution of subsequent power of attorney

(a) A power of attorney executed under this article shall be:
(1) Signed under oath and acknowledged before a notary public by the individual executing such power of attorney and by the agent accepting such delegation; and
(2) A copy of it shall be filed by the individual executing the power of attorney, or his or her designee, within ten days of the power of attorney being executed, in the probate court of the county in which the child resides. If the residence of the child changes to a different county during the term of the power of attorney, the agent shall file the power of attorney in the probate court of the county of the new residence and notify the original court in writing of such change.
(b) Each probate court shall maintain a docket in which a power of attorney will be registered. The docket shall include the name of the agent, the name of the child, the date the power of attorney was deposited with the court, and the date the power of attorney expires, if applicable. The power of attorney shall be confidential; provided, however, that the individual who executed the power of attorney or his or her legal representative shall have access to such power of attorney and the department and any local, state, or federal authority that is conducting an investigation involving the agent or the individual who executed such power of attorney may be granted access upon good cause shown to the court. The docket shall be publicly accessible as are other dockets for the probate court. Notwithstanding Article 3 of Chapter 9 of Title 15, the probate court shall not impose any filing fee for the depositing of a power of attorney under this Code section.
(c) Nothing in this Code section shall be construed so as to prohibit an individual from revoking a power of attorney or executing a subsequent power of attorney.

§ 19-9-130. (Effective September 1, 2018) Authority of agent; revocation, termination, or resignation of agent exercising power of attorney; right of parent to access records while power of attorney in effect

(a) (1) An agent shall have the authority to act on behalf of the child on a continuous basis, without compensation:
 (A) For the duration of the power of attorney so long as the duration does not exceed one year or the time period authorized in Code Section 19-9-132; or
 (B) Until the individual who executed the power of attorney revokes the power of attorney in writing and provides notice of the revocation to the agent by certified mail, return receipt requested, or statutory overnight delivery. Upon receipt of such revocation, the agent shall cease to act as agent.
 (2) The individual revoking the power of attorney shall send a copy of the revocation of the power of attorney to the agent within five days of executing such revocation. If an individual revokes a power of attorney, the child shall be returned to the custody of such individual who executed the power of attorney within 48 hours of receiving such revocation.

(3) The revoking individual shall notify schools, health care providers, the probate court where the power of attorney is filed, and others known to the revoking individual to have relied upon such power of attorney within 48 hours of submitting such resignation to the agent.

(b) A power of attorney executed under this article may be terminated by an order of a court of competent jurisdiction.

(c) Upon receipt of a revocation of a power of attorney, an agent shall notify schools, health care providers, and others known to the agent to have relied upon such power of attorney within 48 hours of receiving such revocation.

(d) An agent may resign by notifying the individual who appointed the agent in writing by certified mail, return receipt requested, or statutory overnight delivery and he or she shall notify schools, health care providers, the probate court where the power of attorney is filed, and others known to the agent to have relied upon such power of attorney within 48 hours of submitting such notification.

(e) Upon the death of an individual who executed a power of attorney, the agent shall notify the surviving parent of the child, if known, as soon as practicable.

(f) The authority to designate an agent to act on behalf of a child shall be in addition to any other lawful action a parent may take for the benefit of such child.

(g) A parent shall continue to have the right to receive medical, dental, mental health, and educational records pertaining to his or her child, even when a power of attorney has been executed under this article.

§ 19-9-131. (Effective September 1, 2018) Child's status upon execution of power of attorney; delegation of authority must specify applicability

(a) A child subject to a power of attorney executed under this article shall not be considered placed in foster care under Chapter 5 of Title 49, and the parties to the power of attorney shall not be subject to any of the requirements or licensing regulations for foster care or other regulations relating to community care for children.

(b) Caregiving authority delegated under this article shall not constitute an out-of-home child placement.

(c) The execution of a power of attorney under this article shall not delegate caregiving authority for more than one child unless such power of attorney delegates caregiving authority for children who are siblings or stepsiblings.

§ 19-9-132. (Effective September 1, 2018) Delegation to grandparent; delegation by deployed parents

(a) When a power of attorney delegates caregiving authority to a grandparent of a child, it may have an unlimited duration.

(b) Except as limited by or in conflict with federal law regarding the armed forces of the United States, a parent who is a member of the armed forces of the United States, including any reserve component thereof, or the commissioned corps of the National Oceanic and Atmospheric Administration or the Public Health Service of the United States Department of Health and Human Services detailed by proper authority for duty with the armed forces of the United States, or who is required to enter or serve in the active military service of the United States under a call or order of the President of the United States or to serve on state active duty, may delegate caregiving authority for a period longer than one year if such parent is deployed as defined in Code Section 19-9-6. Such term of delegation, however, shall not exceed the term of deployment plus 30 days.

§ 19-9-133. (Effective September 1, 2018) Continuing application of former provisions as applicable to grandparents

This article shall not affect a power of attorney given to a grandparent prior to September 1, 2018, to which the provisions of former Code Sections 19-9-120 through 19-9-129, as such existed on August 30, 2018, shall continue to apply.

§ 19-9-134. (Effective September 1, 2018) Power of attorney form

(a) The power of attorney contained in this Code section may be used for the temporary delegation of caregiving authority to an agent. The form contained in this Code section shall be sufficient for the purpose of creating a power of attorney under this article, provided that nothing in this Code section shall be construed to require the use of this particular form.

(b) A power of attorney shall be legally sufficient if the form is properly completed and the signatures of the parties are notarized.

(c) The power of attorney delegating caregiving authority of a child shall be in substantially the following form:

"FORM FOR POWER OF ATTORNEY TO DELEGATE
THE POWER AND AUTHORITY FOR THE CARE OF A CHILD

NOTICE:

(1) THE PURPOSE OF THIS POWER OF ATTORNEY IS TO GIVE THE INDIVIDUAL WHOM YOU DESIGNATE (THE AGENT) POWERS TO CARE FOR YOUR CHILD, INCLUDING THE POWER TO: HAVE ACCESS TO EDUCATIONAL RECORDS AND DISCLOSE THE CONTENTS TO OTHERS; ARRANGE FOR AND CONSENT TO MEDICAL, DENTAL, AND MENTAL HEALTH TREATMENT FOR THE CHILD; HAVE ACCESS TO RECORDS RELATED TO SUCH TREATMENT OF THE CHILD AND DISCLOSE THE CONTENTS OF THOSE RECORDS TO OTHERS; PROVIDE FOR THE CHILD'S FOOD, LODGING, RECREATION, AND TRAVEL; AND HAVE ANY ADDITIONAL POWERS AS SPECIFIED BY THE INDIVIDUAL EXECUTING THIS POWER OF ATTORNEY.

(2) THE AGENT IS REQUIRED TO EXERCISE DUE CARE TO ACT IN THE CHILD'S BEST INTERESTS AND IN ACCORDANCE WITH THE GRANT OF AUTHORITY SPECIFIED IN THIS FORM.

(3) A COURT OF COMPETENT JURISDICTION MAY REVOKE THE POWERS OF THE AGENT.

(4) THE AGENT MAY EXERCISE THE POWERS GIVEN IN THIS POWER OF ATTORNEY FOR THE CARE OF A CHILD FOR THE PERIOD SET FORTH IN THIS FORM UNLESS THE INDIVIDUAL EXECUTING THIS POWER OF ATTORNEY REVOKES THIS POWER OF ATTORNEY AND PROVIDES NOTICE OF THE REVOCATION TO THE AGENT OR A COURT OF COMPETENT JURISDICTION TERMINATES THIS POWER OF ATTORNEY.

(5) THE AGENT MAY RESIGN AS AGENT AND MUST IMMEDIATELY COMMUNICATE SUCH RESIGNATION TO THE INDIVIDUAL EXECUTING THIS POWER OF ATTORNEY AND TO SCHOOLS, HEALTH CARE PROVIDERS, AND OTHERS KNOWN TO THE AGENT TO HAVE RELIED UPON SUCH POWER OF ATTORNEY.

(6) THIS POWER OF ATTORNEY MAY BE REVOKED IN WRITING. IF THIS POWER OF ATTORNEY IS REVOKED, THE REVOKING INDIVIDUAL SHALL NOTIFY THE AGENT, SCHOOLS, HEALTH CARE PROVIDERS, AND OTHERS KNOWN TO THE INDIVIDUAL EXECUTING THIS POWER OF ATTORNEY TO HAVE RELIED UPON SUCH POWER OF ATTORNEY.

(7) IF THERE IS ANYTHING ABOUT THIS FORM THAT YOU DO NOT UNDERSTAND, YOU SHOULD ASK AN ATTORNEY TO EXPLAIN IT TO YOU.

STATE OF GEORGIA
COUNTY OF
Personally appeared before me, the undersigned officer duly authorized to administer oaths, _____ (name of parent) who, after having been sworn, deposes and says as follows:

1. I certify that I am the parent of:

   (Full name of child)   (Date of birth)

2. I designate:

   (Full name of agent)

   (Street address, city, state, and ZIP Code of agent)

   (Personal and work telephone numbers of agent)

as the agent of the child named above.

3. The agent named above is related or known to me as follows (write in your relationship to the agent; for example, aunt of the child, maternal grandparent of the child, sibling of the child, godparent of the child, associated with a nonprofit or faith based organization):

4. Sign by the statement you wish to choose (you may only choose one):

    (A) _____ (Signature) The agent named above is related to me by blood or marriage and I have elected not to have him or her obtain a criminal background check.

OR

    (B) _____ (Signature) The agent named above is not related to me and I have reviewed his or her criminal background check. (If the agent has a criminal conviction, complete the rest of this paragraph.) I know that the agent has a conviction but I want him or her to be the agent because (write in):

5. Sign by the statement you wish to choose (you may only choose one):

    (A) _____ (Signature) I delegate to the agent all my power and authority regarding the care and custody of the child named above, including but not limited to the right to inspect and obtain copies of educational records and other records concerning the child, attend school activities and other functions concerning the child, and give or withhold any consent or waiver with respect to school activities, medical and dental treatment, and any other activity, function, or treatment that may concern the child. This delegation shall not include the power or authority to consent to the marriage or adoption of the child, the performance or inducement of an abortion on or for the child, or the termination of parental rights to the child.

OR

    (B) _____ (Signature) I delegate to the agent the following specific powers and responsibilities (write in):

This delegation shall not include the power or authority to consent to the marriage or adoption of the child, the performance or inducement of an abortion on or for the child, or the termination of parental rights to the child.

6. Initial by the statement you wish to choose (you may only choose one of the three options) and complete the information in the paragraph:

    (A) _____ (Initials) This power of attorney is effective for a period not to exceed one year, beginning _____, 2___, and ending _____, 2___. I reserve the right to revoke this power and authority at any time.

OR

    (B) _____ (Initials) This power of attorney is being given to a grandparent of my child and is effective until I revoke this power of attorney.

OR

    (C) _____ (Initials) I am a parent as described in O.C.G.A. § 19-9-130(b). My deployment is scheduled to begin on _____, 2___, and is estimated to end on _____, 2___. I acknowledge that in no event shall this delegation of power and authority last more than one year or the term of my deployment plus 30 days, whichever is longer. I reserve the right to revoke this power and authority at any time.

7. I hereby swear or affirm under penalty of law that I provided the notice required by O.C.G.A. § 19-9-125 and received no objection in the required time period.

By: _____
    (Parent signature)

    _____
    (Printed name)

(Street address, city, state, and ZIP Code of parent)

(Personal and work telephone numbers of parent)
Sworn to and subscribed
before me this
day of   ,   .

Notary public (SEAL)
My commission expires: .

STATE OF GEORGIA
COUNTY OF
Personally appeared before me, the undersigned officer duly authorized to administer oaths,   (name of agent) who, after having been sworn, deposes and says as follows:

8. I hereby accept my designation as agent for the child specified in this power of attorney and by doing so acknowledge my acceptance of the responsibility for caring for such child for the duration of this power of attorney. Furthermore, I hereby certify that:

   (A)(i) I am related to the individual giving me this power of attorney by blood or marriage as follows (write in your relationship to the individual designating you as agent; for example, sister, mother, father, etc.):

OR

   (ii) I am not related to the individual giving me this power of attorney but was referred to him or her by: (write in the name of the child-placing agency, nonprofit entity, or faith based organization).

   (B) I am not currently on the state sexual offender registry or child abuse registry of this state or the sexual offender registry or child abuse registry for any other state, a United States territory, the District of Columbia, or any American Indian tribe nor have I ever been required to register for any such registry;

   (C) I have provided a criminal background check to the individual designating me as an agent, if it was required;

   (D) I understand that I have the authority to act on behalf of the child:
     --For the period of time set forth in this form;
     --Until the power of attorney is revoked in writing and notice is provided to me as required by O.C.G.A. § 19-9-130; or
     --Until the power of attorney is terminated by order of a court;

   (E) I understand that if I am made aware of the death of the individual who executed the power of attorney, I must notify the surviving parent of the child, if known, as soon as practicable; and

   (F) I understand that I may resign as agent by notifying the individual who executed the power of attorney in writing by certified mail, return receipt requested, or statutory overnight delivery and I must also notify any schools, health care providers, and others to whom I give a copy of this power of attorney.

(Agent signature)

(Printed name)
Sworn to and subscribed
before me this
day of   ,   .

Notary public (SEAL)

My commission expires: _____.

(Organization signature, if applicable)

(Printed name and title)"

CHAPTER 10. ABANDONMENT OF CHILD OR SPOUSE

§ 19-10-1. Abandonment of dependent child; criminal penalties; continuing offense; venue; evidence; expenses of birth of child born out of wedlock; support of child born out of wedlock

(a) A child abandoned by its father or mother shall be considered to be in a dependent condition when the father or mother does not furnish sufficient food, clothing, or shelter for the needs of the child.

(b) If any father or mother willfully and voluntarily abandons his or her child, either legitimate or born out of wedlock, leaving it in a dependent condition, he or she shall be guilty of a misdemeanor. Moreover, if any father or mother willfully and voluntarily abandons his or her child, either legitimate or born out of wedlock, leaving it in a dependent condition, and leaves this state or if any father or mother willfully and voluntarily abandons his or her child, either legitimate or born out of wedlock, leaving it in a dependent condition, after leaving this state, he or she shall be guilty of a felony punishable by imprisonment for not less than one nor more than three years. The felony shall be reducible to a misdemeanor. Any person, upon conviction of the third offense for violating this Code section, shall be guilty of a felony and shall be imprisoned for not less than one nor more than three years, which felony shall not be reducible to a misdemeanor. The husband and wife shall be competent witnesses in such cases to testify for or against the other.

(c) The offense of abandonment is a continuing offense. Except as provided in subsection (i) of this Code section, former acquittal or conviction of the offense shall not be a bar to further prosecution therefor under this Code section, if it is made to appear that the child in question was in a dependent condition, as defined in this Code section, for a period of 30 days prior to the commencement of prosecution.

(d) In prosecutions under this Code section when the child is born out of wedlock, the venue of the offense shall be in the county in which the child and the mother are domiciled at the time of the swearing out of the arrest warrant; but, if the child and the mother are domiciled in different counties, venue shall be in the county in which the child is domiciled.

(e) Upon the trial of an accused father or mother under this Code section, it shall be no defense that the accused father or mother has never supported the child.

(f) In the trial of any abandonment proceeding in which the question of parentage arises, regardless of any presumptions with respect to parentage, the accused father may request a paternity blood test and agree and arrange to pay for same; and in such cases the court before which the matter is brought, upon pretrial motion of the defendant, shall order that the alleged parent, the known natural parent, and the child submit to any blood tests and comparisons which have been developed and adapted for purposes of establishing or disproving parentage and which are reasonably accessible to the alleged parent, the known natural parent, and the child. The results of those blood tests and comparisons, including the statistical likelihood of the alleged parent's parentage, if available, shall be admitted in evidence when offered by a duly qualified, licensed practicing physician, duly qualified immunologist, duly qualified geneticist, or other duly qualified person. Upon receipt of a motion and the entry of an order under this subsection, the court shall proceed as follows:

(1) Where the issue of parentage is to be decided by a jury, where the results of those blood tests and comparisons are not shown to be inconsistent with the results of any other blood tests and comparisons, and where the results of those blood tests and comparisons indicate that the alleged parent cannot be the natural parent of the child, the jury shall be instructed that if they believe that the witness presenting the results testified truthfully as to those results and if they believe that the tests and comparisons were conducted properly, then it will be their duty to decide that the alleged parent is not the natural parent;

(2) The court shall require the defendant requesting the blood tests and comparisons pursuant to this subsection to be initially responsible for any of the expenses thereof. Upon the entry of a verdict incorporating a finding of parentage or nonparentage, the court shall tax the expenses for blood tests and comparisons, in addition to any fees for expert witnesses whose testimonies supported the admissibility thereof, as costs.

(g) In prosecutions under this Code section, when the child is born out of wedlock and the accused father is convicted, the father may be required by the court to pay the reasonable medical expenses paid by or incurred on behalf of the mother due to the birth of the child.

(h) The accused father and the mother of a child born out of wedlock may enter into a written agreement providing for future support of the child by regular periodic payments to the mother until the child reaches the age of 18 years, marries, or becomes self-supporting; provided, however, that the agreement shall not be binding on either party until it has been approved by the court having jurisdiction to try the pending case.

(i) If, during the trial of any person charged with the offense of abandonment as defined in this Code section, the person contends that he or she is not the father or mother of the child alleged to have been abandoned, in a jury trial the trial judge shall charge the jury that if its verdict is for the acquittal of the person and its reason for so finding is that the person is not the father or mother of the child alleged to have been abandoned, then its verdict shall so state. In a trial before the court without the intervention of the jury, if the court renders a verdict of acquittal based on the contention of the person that he or she is not the father or mother of the child alleged to have been abandoned, the trial judge shall so state this fact in his verdict of acquittal. Where the verdict of the jury or the court is for acquittal of a person on the grounds that the person is not the father or mother of the child alleged to have been abandoned, the person cannot thereafter again be tried for the offense of abandoning the child, and the verdict of acquittal shall be a bar to all civil and criminal proceedings attempting to compel the person to support the child.

(j) (1) In a prosecution for and conviction of the offense of abandonment, the trial court may suspend the service of the sentence imposed in the case, upon such terms and conditions as it may prescribe for the support, by the defendant, of the child or children abandoned during the minority of the child or children. Service of the sentence, when so suspended, shall not begin unless and until ordered by the court having jurisdiction thereof, after a hearing as in cases of revocation or probated sentences, because of the failure or refusal of the defendant to comply with the terms and conditions upon which service of a sentence was suspended.

(2) Service of any sentence suspended in abandonment cases may be ordered by the court having jurisdiction thereof at any time before the child or children reach the age of 18 or become emancipated, after a hearing as provided in paragraph (1) of this subsection and a finding by the court that the defendant has failed or refused to comply with the terms and conditions upon which service of the sentence was suspended by the court having jurisdiction thereof.

(3) Notwithstanding any other provisions of law, in abandonment cases where the suspension of sentence has been revoked and the defendant is serving the sentence, the court may thereafter again suspend the service of sentence under the same terms and conditions as the original suspension. The sentence shall not be considered probated and the defendant shall not be on probation, but the defendant shall again be under a suspended sentence. However, the combined time of incarceration of the defendant during the periods of revocation of suspended sentences shall not exceed the maximum period of punishment for the offense.

(4) Notwithstanding any other provision of law to the contrary, the terms and conditions prescribed by the court as to support by the defendant shall be subject to review and modification by the court, upon notice and hearing to the defendant, as to the ability of the defendant to furnish support and as to the adequacy of the present support payments to the child's or children's needs. The review provided for in this paragraph as to the ability of the defendant to furnish support and as to the adequacy of the present support payments to the child's or children's needs shall not be had in less than two-year intervals and shall authorize the court to increase as well as to decrease the amount of child support to be paid as a term and condition of the suspended sentence. The review as to ability to support and adequacy of support shall not be equivalent to a hearing held in cases of revocation of probated sentences for purposes of service of the suspended sentence; nor shall a modification, if any, be deemed a change in sentence; nor shall a modification, if any, be deemed to change the suspended sentence to a probated sentence.

§ 19-10-2. Abandonment of dependent pregnant wife; criminal penalties; continuing offense

(a) A wife who is pregnant with her husband's child shall be deemed to be in a dependent condition when her husband does not furnish her sufficient food, clothing, or medical treatment to meet her needs, both before and immediately upon the birth of the child.

(b) Any husband who willfully and voluntarily abandons his wife, while she is pregnant with his child, leaving her in a dependent condition, shall be guilty of a misdemeanor.

(c) Any husband who willfully and voluntarily abandons his wife while she is pregnant with his child and leaves the jurisdiction of this state shall be guilty of a felony punishable by imprisonment for not less than one year nor more than three years. The felony shall be reducible to a misdemeanor.

(d) For purposes of this Code section, a husband shall not be deemed to have abandoned his wife willfully and voluntarily unless he has actual knowledge of her pregnant condition.

(e) The offense of abandonment as set forth in this Code section is a continuing offense.

(f) The wife shall be competent to be a witness against her husband in any proceedings or cases brought against the husband for abandonment as set forth in this Code section.

Made in the USA
Columbia, SC
20 September 2021